Country Plus

Discover, Design and Run Your Own Country!

Explore Your Land

Meet your People

Create your Government

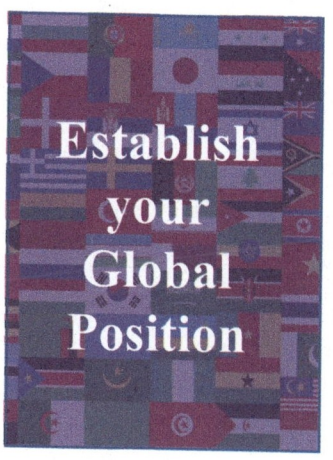
Establish your Global Position

A Cross-Curricular, Full Year, Project-Based Curriculum

Science ✦ Social Studies ✦ Language Arts ✦ Electives

By Brandy Champeau, Samantha Champeau and Nancy Holt

Copyright © 2022 Exploring Expression LLC
All rights reserved.

No part of this publication may be reproduced, distributed, or transmitted in any form by any means, including photocopying, recording or other electronic or mechanical methods, without the prior written permission of the publisher, except in the case of brief quotations embodied in reviews and certain other non-commercial used permitted by copyright law.

ISBN-13: 978-1-954057-22-7

TABLE OF CONTENTS

Introduction: What Makes a Country?	5
Unit 1: Your Land	21
Chapter 1: Introduction to Your Land	33
Chapter 2: Getting the Lay of the Land	47
Chapter 3: Checking out the Ecosystem	87
Chapter 4: Your Previous People	105
Chapter 5: Announcing Your Country	125
Unit 2: Your People	141
Chapter 6: Growing Your Population	151
Chapter 7: Establishing Your Unique Culture	181
Chapter 8: Meeting Your People	195
Unit 3: Your Government	209
Chapter 9: Creating Your Government	219
Chapter 10: Creating Your Economic System	251
Chapter 11: Fleshing Out Your Governmental Infrastructures	279
Chapter 12: Making Hard Choices with your Priorities	307
Unit 4: Your Global Position	325
Chapter 13: Establishing Your Global Focus	337
Chapter 14: Forging Your Global Alliances	355
Chapter 15: Bringing Everything Together	373

TABLE OF CONTENTS

Appendices -- **389**

   Appendix I: Resources for Unit 1: Your Land   **389**

   Appendix II: Resources for Unit 2: Your People   **419**

   Appendix III: Resources for Unit 3: Your Government   **439**

   Appendix IV: Resources for Unit 4: Your Global Position   **467**

   Appendix V: Data Sets   **493**

   Appendix VI: Science Project Report Sections and Display Board   **539**

   Appendix VII: Glossary   **545**

   Appendix VIII: About Exploring Expression   **567**

INTRODUCTION

What Makes a Country?

Introduction

Have you ever wanted to create and run your own country? **Well, here is your chance!**

As you navigate this course you will learn all about the many pieces that come together to form a successful country. By the end you will have developed and run a functional, fictional country complete with a working government, international relations, and a cultural identity all of its own.

Let the adventure begin...

This course is intended for Middle and High School level students. However, this can be adapted for younger students or to accommodate teaching multiple levels at once.

Considerations to Help You

This course will be what you make it. The quality of the product that comes **This course assumes an amount of knowledge and research on your part.** However, to help you out I have included some foundation and useful information pages to give specific and useful tips, hints, and knowledge along the way.

In unit 1 you will make an initial political boundaries map. **Do not take this task lightly.** NEARLY EVERY MAP (and there will be a lot of maps) you do from then on will begin with a copy of this map. In fact, it may be a good idea to make several copies of this map and hang on to them for when you need them.

Speaking of Maps… Your **Compass Rose and your Scale** should be the same on every map that you do that starts with the political boundaries map

Choose your own Adventure: Cause and Effect

This is more than just a cookie-cutter course. This is a personalized adventure based on the decisions YOU make. You see, the making and running of a country involves many variables. Your land, your people, your ideals and ideas all come together to form a unique creation. This creation, once established, will behave in unique ways.

In the same manner, this course is filled with decisions and choices. What you decide early on will make a difference later in the course, so make your choices carefully.

The decisions you make in life often have no right or wrong answer, only consequences. Those consequences can be good or bad depending on your choices and what you do next. The same is true for this course. There is no one correct solution to most of the activities you will find, only consequences. This course is the ultimate test of cause and effect.

What are the elements that go into your decisions (the causes)? What are the consequences that come out of them (the effects)? YOU get to decide…

Subjects and Questions

A good project (like this one) will consist of three key factors

1. *It will require the use of multiple knowledge areas.*

2. *It will force you to think critically about complex issues.*

3. *It will answer questions about the world around you.*

This course will force you to use your whole brain and skills from all of the major subject areas. You will study science, math, civics, government, language arts and more. In doing so, you will discover answers to some basic questions:

1. *What role does your physical environment play in the success of a country?*

2. *What is culture and how does culture help shape a government?*

3. *What are the most important factors to consider when making social policy and how does the type of government that you have affect the decision-making process?*

4. *How does a country's environment, culture, and government work together to respond to global events?*

> Keep these questions in mind as you proceed through this course.

5. How can mathematics and statistics help us to understand and make better decisions about our world?

Objectives

Upon completion of this course the you should:

- Understand the characteristics of what makes a country
    - Identify the Montevideo formula and the 4 qualifications to become a state

Government

- Understand the role of government in society and how government makes decisions
    - Understand the Principles and Philosophies of Government
    - Identify the different types of government
        - Identify the structure and use of basic governmental documents such as a constitution, bills and treaties
        - Identify the difference between justice and defense and the role of the government in each
- Understand the role of a country in a global system
    - Define foreign policy and identify the elements that make up a foreign policy
    - Identify the methods a country must resolve global dispute
    - Identify the major global institutions and the roles of each

- Interpret maps and spatial data to analyze the organization of people and places

Geography

- Examine the effect of changing political, economic, cultural, and physical systems on the relationships among places

- Understand the flow of energy and cycling of matter within an ecosystem.
    - Evaluate types, availability, allocation, and sustainability of energy resources.
    - Investigate ways the environment has influenced human inhabitance.
    - Analyze human impact on natural resources.
    - Understand the effects of human population growth on global ecosystems.
- Understand the role of the environment in human interaction and a country's responsibility in worldwide environmental issues
    - Identify the different types of biomes

Science

- Understand how sociology views society and develop a broader and more comprehensive understanding of the complex society in which we live.
    - Identify the different types of maps and their uses
    - Identify the different methods of demographics collection and their uses
- Define culture and understand the elements that make up culture
    - Identify the different types of cultural narratives
    - Identify the difference between norms and values and how cultures communicate these across the generations

Sociology

- Understand the role of the citizen and the interaction between a citizen and the government
    - Identify the differences between rights and responsibilities of citizenship

Civics

Economics

- Understand basic economic principles and how they influence decision making
    - Identify the different types of economic systems
- Understand the role of industry as part of a culture and a government
    - Identify the 3 types of industry and the activities that make up each

English Composition

- Produce writing for specific purposes and audiences as required by various writing situations
    - Employ conventions of format, structure, voice, tone, and level of formality appropriate to the writing situation
    - Demonstrate flexible strategies for prewriting, developing, drafting, revising, editing, and proofreading
    - Control syntax, grammar, punctuation, and spelling

Critical Thinking

- Be able to apply critical thinking and problem-solving techniques to make decisions in scenarios
    - Identify the steps for effective problem solving
    - Identify the steps to critical thinking

*Complete the Science exploration projects to expand this course into a Scientific Exploration of Applied Agriculture course as well.

*Check out some of the literature book suggestions for each unit to add an English Literature component to this course.

Course Structure

This course is broken down into four units, each highlighting a crucial component of the makeup of a country: your land, your people, your government, and your global presence. The units are further broken down into chapters which focus on specific aspects of that component. In each chapter you will find the following elements:

Overview

Each chapter will have an overview. This is your continuing storyline. This will tell you how the passage of time is proceeding and what you will be focusing on in that unit/chapter.

Foundational information and Text

We will give you some basic information that we consider critical to performing each task. However, it is not our intention to spoon feed you a bunch of information. As an explorer it is your job to go find the information that you need to help you in your tasks. We are here to guide you in your own exploration of discovery. With that said, we will not simply let you drift.

Throughout the course we will be providing lists of the following to help you on your journey.

Tasks

The tasks are the backbone of this course. These are a series of projects for you to complete as you develop and run your country.

Extension Activities

These are optional hands on activities to extend the learning and enjoyment of the tasks. These may include building a model or diorama or similar activities.

Composition Activities –

These are optional writing activities to extend the learning and enjoyment of the tasks. These may include research and a variety of writing types both fiction and nonfiction.

Chapter and Unit Reviews

Each chapter concludes with a chapter review section and at the end of each unit there is a full review. These sections give you some questions and activities designed to make sure you grasp the information you have learned as well as help you think about how you can apply the ideas and information in your daily life and in the real world.

Science Exploration Projects

For each unit we have included a science exploration project. These projects are optional however, you will need to either complete these or a similar project or read/view some of the items from the book list or movie list to count for a full credit of science. Without these this course only gives one semester worth of credit.

Symbols to Watch For

Along the way, you will find some symbols that will point you to specific information.

Booklist

At the beginning of each unit we will give you a list of books that may pertain to the information in the unit. These may include nonfiction books, fiction books, biographies and picture books. This list is not meant to be exhaustive nor are you meant to read EVERY book on the list (although you can, they are all fantastic). This list is a starting point. In the appendix for each unit we have provided a description of all of the books that we reference throughout that section. In the back of the workbook we have provided a couple book review sheets that you can copy and use as you read each book.

Movie List

Like the book list, we have given you a list of movies for each unit to help you explore the topics you will be addressing. Again, the intention is not for you to view them all, but to choose the ones that you feel will enhance your journey in creating your country. In the appendix for each unit we have provided a description of all of the movies that we reference throughout that section. In the back of the workbook we have provided a couple movie review sheets that you can copy and use as you watch each movie.

Gameschooling

We love games. We feel that games, like projects, can often lead us to a deeper understanding of many topics. In that light we have included a list of games ideas as well at the beginning of each unit. . In the appendix for each unit we have provided a description of all of the games that we reference throughout that section.

Websites

Periodically throughout the text we have provided a list of websites and articles to help you expand upon the foundational information and learn additional things you may want to know as you read each section and complete each task. The URLs to those websites and articles are provided in the appendix for each unit.

Videos

As with the websites we have provided a list of videos to help you expand upon the foundational information and learn additional things you may want to know as you complete each task. The URLs for all videos will be in the appendix for each unit.

Considerations

These are questions or items we want you to think about before you begin specific tasks. As mentioned earlier the decisions you make in one task will often affect your choices in future tasks. At times we will highlight some aspects of this for you to consider.

Interesting Facts

Several fun and interesting tidbits are thrown into each chapter. These include special facts and statistics that pertain to the topic

Career Spotlight

Throughout the course we have highlighted several careers that pertain to the different topics we will cover over the course of the year

Helpful Information

In several places throughout your journey through this course you will have to know some mathematical techniques and formulas. Information on how to use the data given will be identified with:

Words Worth Knowing Review

As with any course, you'll come upon many terms that you need to be familiar with. This little gent with the dictionary is here to help you with these terms. Most of those words will be defined within the text and

highlighted in orange. At the end of each chapter and unit there will be activities to help reinforce these terms.

For Discussion

These are questions for you to either ponder on your own or to discuss with your classmates, teachers, friends or family (depending on the setting in which you are taking this course).

You as a Citizen

The you as a citizen questions will take you from a position of the leader of a country to a citizen of a country. Sometimes this will be a citizen of your fictional country and sometimes this will be your real life country. These questions will get you thinking about the role that each of us plays in the success or failure of a nation.

National Library

As you proceed through the course you will be building a National Library for your country. At the end of each chapter will also find a list of items from the work you've done that need to be archived into the national library

Check Your Knowledge Questions

At the end of each unit you are going to find several review sections. These will act like a unit test and check your understanding of all of the concepts that you have worked through during the course of the unit.

Current Events in Your World

At the end of each unit you will have an opportunity to apply some of the information that you have learned to a current event that is happening in your world. This may take the form of research, analysis, forming an opinion or exploration.

Contents of Unit 1: Your Land

Chapter 1: Introduction to Your Land

Chapter 2: Getting the Lay of the Land

Chapter 3: Checking out the Ecosystem

Chapter 4: Your Previous People

Chapter 5: Announcing Your Country

Unit Overview

It's hard to say this land is my land, without land. To build a country, the first thing that you need is... well, country.

But today is your lucky day!

You have discovered some unclaimed land just waiting for you. The first thing you should do is take a look around. Let's see what you have to work with. Let's hope this is the perfect place on which to build your future country.

In Unit 1 you will focus on the land itself. Look around your new land and discover the home that you plan to build your country upon. You will be preparing all of the documents that you will need to convince potential investors and residents that this is the perfect place to establish your new country.

Books Worth Reading with this Unit

Below are some suggested books that you can use to compliment the "Your Land" unit. For descriptions these books please refer to **Appendix I: Resources for Your Land Unit.**

- **Informational**
  - *On The Map: A Mind-expanding Exploration Of The Way The World Looks* by Simon Garfield
  - *The Big Ones: How Natural Disasters Have Shaped Us* by Dr. Lucy Jones
  - *Nature Anatomy: The Curious Parts And Pieces Of The Natural World* by Julia Rothman
  - *The Weather Book: An Easy To Understand Guide To USA's Weather* by Jack Williams
  - *The Road To There: Mapmakers And Their Stories* by Val Ross
  - *Prisoners Of Geography* by Tim Marshall
  - *Cannibals And Kings: Origins Of Cultures* by Marvin Harris
  - *Tribe: On Homecoming And Belonging* by Sebastian Junger

- **Literature**
  - *Journey To The Center Of The Earth* by Jules Verne
  - *The Clan of The Cave Bear* by Jean M Auel
  - *Salvage the Bones* by Jesmyn Ward
  - *In The Beginning: Creation Stories From Around The World* by Virginia Hamilton
  - *The Story Of World Mythologies* by Terri-ann White

Movie Selections for this Unit

Below are some suggested movies that you can use to compliment the "Your Land" unit. For descriptions of each of these movies as well as parental guidance ratings please refer to **Appendix I: Resources for Your Land Unit.**

- Planet Earth (2016)
- Our Planet (2019)
- Oceans (2009)
- Wings of Life (2011)
- Seasons (2015)
- The Day after Tomorrow (2004)
- The Wave (2015)
- Twister (1996)
- The Clan of the Cave Bear (1986)

- Planet Ocean (2012)
- Into the Storm (2014)
- A Beautiful Planet (2016)
- Monkey Kingdom (2015)
- Earth (2007)
- San Andreas (2015)
- Pompeii (2014)
- 10,000 BC (2008)
- Alpha (2018)

Gameschooling Selections for this Unit

Below are some suggested games that you can use to compliment the "Your Land" unit. For descriptions of each of these games please refer to **Appendix I: Resources for Your Land Unit.**

- Ecosystem
- Nature Fluxx
- Wildcraft
- Discover: Lands Unknown
- Dominant Species
- Paleo

- Into the Forest: Nature's Food Chain Game
- Planet
- Photosynthesis
- Bios: Megafauna
- Guess in 10: Animal Planet
- Prehistories

Unit 1 Science Exploration Project

Your Land Science Exploration: Building a Biosphere

(To be completed while you work through Chapters 1-5)

As you work through this unit you will learn many things about the land where your country will exist. You sill begin to think about how the unique placement of your country provides your people with rich ecosystems in which to live and interact. You will start to consider how biomes and ecosystems operate, what the effects of the land formations and weather patterns have upon the cycles of life and biodiversity in your country. How will the land you've acquired be able to sustainably support human inhabitation long term?

Vocabulary

Your should understand the following terms for this project:

- Biosphere
- Ecosystem
- Flora
- Fauna
- pH
- Food Web

Note: You may be wise to wait until after your have started Chapter 2 to complete this project.

Background

Watch the following videos on Biosphere 2

- Inside Biosphere 2: The World's Largest Earth Science Experiment

- Jane Poynter: Life in Biosphere 2

Then explore Biosphere 2's website

- https://biosphere2.org/

Building a Biosphere Overview:

In this project you will be building a model biosphere.

- Start with the basics - soil, air and water. These are the building blocks for any sustainable ecosystem. Then think about what will live in your biosphere. You will need to provide food for the inhabitants inside your enclosed environment.

    - Note 1: If you just throw a bunch of random plants, soil, water and creatures into a glass container and seal it, it is unlikely your biosphere will be successful.. If you want to build a biosphere that will support life, you need to do your research and plan properly.

    - Note 2: Be mindful of the plants and animals that you use. Do not use endangered or threatened species.

- Monitor the interactions within your biosphere and answer the question: What are the ingredients necessary to build a balanced ecosystem?

Note: For an optional extension activity - introduce a change to your biosphere to observe the reaction of the balance of nature to an invasive species.

Required Materials

Clear Container	Lid	Tape
Flora (plants)	Fauna (animals)	Water
Soil	Water and Soil Testing Kits	Other materials as needed

Instructions:

1. Pick an ecosystem to replicate. It can be one of the ecosystems near where you live or one of the ecosystems of your new country that you will learn about in chapter 2.

2. Determine the needs of the ecosystem. This includes the air, water, soil, flora, and fauna. Choose one or two species of flora or fauna as your base organisms for your biosphere.

3. Research the specific ingredients needed to sustain life for your base organisms in your biosphere.
   - Research the environmental needs of your biosphere. How much water will it need? What should the pH of the soil be to support your flora? What does the temperature need to be within the biosphere and how will you achieve that?
   - Decide which members of the food web should be in the ecosystem to keep everything alive. You may need to provide imported food, like worms, for an animal higher on the food chain depending on your particular choices.
   - Figure out the size requirements of your biosphere container. Make sure that your container is big enough to support the food production needs that are required to feed your organisms.

4. Decide how long your biosphere experiment will run

5. Form a hypothesis regarding the outcome of your biosphere

6. Build your biosphere
   - Use a clear, clean container to build your biosphere so that you can monitor the development.
   - Attach a temperature gauge to the inside of the container.

7. Set up your lab notebook and take initial data measurements
   - Test the quality of the soil and water for a beginning reading.
     - Note: You can get simple kits to test nutrient contents and pH levels from most hardware and gardening stores.
   - Temperature
   - Population count of each species of flora and fauna that you include in your biosphere
   - Size/height measurement and general description of each of the flora and fauna that you include in your biosphere. Draw illustrations as needed.

8. Once you populate your biosphere with your chosen ingredients, secure it with a tight fitting lid and seal it with tape.

9. Keep a log of your observations once or twice a day for the duration of your experiment.
   - Try to do your observations at the same time each day

- Measure the following data:
  - Temperature
  - Population count of each species of flora and fauna you included into the biosphere
  - Changes to the size/height of any of the flora or fauna (Dx o not open your biosphere yet. You can estimate the change in size). Draw illustrations as needed.
- At the end of the experiment time open your biosphere and take final data measurements
  - Test the quality of the soil and water for a ending reading.
    - Note: You can get simple kits to test nutrient contents and pH levels from most hardware and gardening stores.
  - Temperature
  - Population count of each species of flora and fauna that you include in your biosphere
  - Size/height measurement and general description of each of the flora and fauna that you include in your biosphere. Draw illustrations as needed.

10. Make the following calculations based on your data
    - The rate of positive or negative growth in your flora
    - The percentage growth or decline in your flora and fauna populations
    - The changes in temperature and soil and water quality

11. Prepare a final report and/or board on your biosphere project. Refer to Appendix VI for information on how to construct a project report and board.

CHAPTER 1

Introducing Your Land

Introducing Your Land

Words Worth Knowing

- Declarative Theory of Statehood

First things first: What is a Country?

You found some land and want to build a country. Fantastic! But, what is a country anyway? Well, it depends on who you ask. There are currently 2 schools of thought when it comes to defining what does and doesn't make a country.

The Declarative Theory of Statehood pretty much agrees with the definition set forth at the Monevideo Convention

The Monevideo Convention: On December 25, 1933, US President Franklin D Roosevelt along with representatives from 18 other countries met in Monteviedo, Uruguay and signed the **Montevideo Convention on the Rights and Duties of States.**

Signers of the **Montevideo Convention** also included representatives from Honduras, El Salvador, Dominican Republic, Haiti, Argentina, Venezuela, Uruguay, Paraguay, Mexico, Panama, Guatemala, Brazil, Ecuador, Nicaragua, Colombia, Chile, Peru, and Cuba.

Words Worth Knowing

- Constitutive Theory of Statehood

*Founded in 301 B.C.E., the country of **San Marino** is thought to be the oldest country in the world.*

Among other things, the **Montevideo Convention** treaty gave a formal definition to "statehood" (or what makes a country). Article 1 of the treaty reads:

The state as a person of international law should possess the following qualifications:

1. *A permanent population;*

2. *A defined territory;*

3. *Government; and*

4. *Capacity to enter into relations with other states.*

The Constitutive theory of Statehood defines a state or country as a person of international law when it is recognized as sovereign by other states. This theory applies regardless of a permanent population or defined territory.

 **Videos Worth Watching**

- What Is A Country? | The MONTEVIDEO CONVENTION And The 4 Requirements Of A STATE

- How are states born? Statehood and its elements

❏ Complete **Worksheet 1.1: Theories of Statehood** In the Workbook

36

A Quick Guide to Geographic Education

In this course we are approaching your geographic learning journey using the **5 themes of geography**. The 5 themes of geography are a framework for learning and teaching this sometimes complex subject.

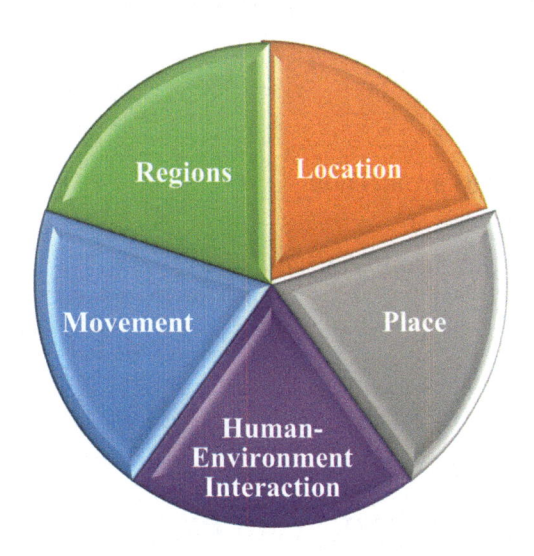

Words Worth Knowing

- 5 Themes of Geography

The 5 themes of geography include:

- **Location**
  - Where are things located?
  - How do we describe where a place is?

- **Place**
  - What makes one place different from another place?

- **Human-Environmental Interaction**
  - What is the relationship between humans and places?
  - How have people changed the environment with their presence?

- **Movement**
  - What are the patterns of movement of people, goods, ideas and information?

The ancient Greek scholar **Eratosthenes** is knows as the "father of geography" Not only was he the fist person to calculate the size of the earth, but he also coined the term geography from the latin roots **"geo"** (the earth) and **"graphein"** (to write).

Words Worth Knowing

- Human Geography

- **Regions**
  - How can things be grouped together and what characteristics do they share?

Websites and Articles Worth Exploring

- The 5 Themes of Geography from Thoughtco
- The 5 Themes in Geography from Worldatlas

Videos Worth Watching

- Five Themes Of Geography (AP Human Geography)
- Five Themes of Geography Fortnite Edition
- Five Themes of Geography: Minecraft Edition

❏ Complete **Worksheet 1.2: 5 Themes of Geography** in the Workbook

What is Human Geography

Human Geography is that particular branch of geography that deals with people and our relationship with each other and the world around us. This branch studies the patterns of human population as it relates to the place and environment in which we live. How has the earth and our physical location and environmental factors in the place we live on the Earth shaped our culture as individual societies? On the other hand, how has our presence here changed the Earth and the ecosystems themselves?

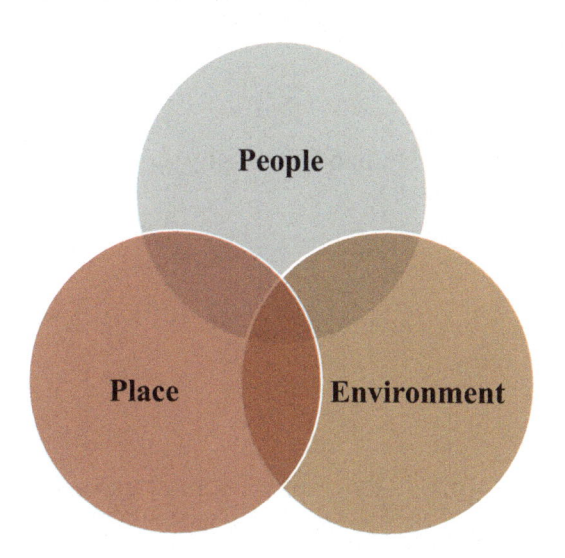

Words Worth Knowing

- Political Geography
- Geopolitics

Political Geography and Geopolitics

Political geography and geopolitics are two sides of the same coin, both of which you will examine in this course. Political geography is a branch of geography that is concerned with how politics shape geography. This could be the defining of borders or the assigning ownership of waterways. In fact anything that deals with the boundaries, possessions and divisions of countries falls under political geography.

Geopolitics, on the other hand, is less a function of geography and more a function of political science or international relations. Geopolitics is concerned with how geographical factors like landforms and access to natural resources influence politics and the relationships between countries or other political actors.

Note: The terms **Political Geography** and **Geopolitics** are very close in definition. Because of this they can and often are used interchangeably in many situations.

Websites and Articles Worth Exploring

- A Short Definition For Human Geography

- Human Geography

- Overview Of Political Geography

- Geopolitics

- Geopolitics Vs. Political Geography Vs. International Relations

Videos Worth Watching

- NGA Explains: What is Human Geography? (Episode 8)

- AP Human Geography Unit 1 Review [Thinking Geographically] *(In fact this whole series is fantastic)*

- Crash Course Unit 4- Political Organization of Space

- Introduction to Political Geography

- What is Political Geography? (1/2)

- What is Political Geography? (2/2)

- What is Geopolitics | A Brief Introduction Geography Lecture

- What is Geopolitics and Why Does It Matter?

National Libraries

A **national library** is a library specifically established by the government of a country to serve as the preeminent repository of information for that country. Common responsibilities of national libraries include:

- Collection, cataloging and preservation of the documents and publications

- Provision of central services to citizens both directly and through other libraries and information centers

- Preservation and promotion of the national cultural heritage

- Acquisition of a representative collection of foreign publications

- Promotion of national cultural policy

- Leadership in national literacy campaigns

The United States does not have an official National Library like many other countries do. However, five US libraries are recognized as being national in scope:

- Library of Congress

- National Agricultural Library

- National Library of Education

- National Library of Medicine

- National Transportation Library

Words Worth Knowing

- National Library

Websites and Articles Worth Exploring

- National Libraries of the World
- United States Libraries and Archives

Videos Worth Watching

- The Library of Congress Is Your Library
- The National Library (of Singapore)
- An Introduction to the National Library of Scotland
- The Bookworms of France's National Library

*The United States has a policy called **Mandatory Deposit.** This requires that any publisher submit two copies of a copyrightable work to US Copyright Office at the Library of Congress.*

Your National Library

Soon you will begin to gather documents and other items related to your new country. Thus, you should start by setting up your national Library. This will be where you keep all the archives, maps, documents, literature, media, and examples of cultural heritage that you create and collect throughout this nation building and administration journey. At the end of each chapter, you will find a National Library page which that tells you where to file your tasks and worksheets for that chapter in your national library. But first you need to set it up.

Task #1: Your First Task

Set up your Binder that will contain your national library

- You will need a 3-ring binder at least 1.5" wide

- Put dividers in your binder for the following sections

    - Guidebook
    - Official Documents
    - Literature / Cultural heritage
    - Promotional material / media
    - Reference

- **Alternative:** if you are going to save this project digitally, create a file folder and use sub-folders to for each of the sections listed.

Chapter 1 Review

The following sections help you review and think about some of the concepts and activities that you performed in this chapter.

Words Worth Knowing Review

The following terms were very important throughout this chapter:

Declarative Theory of Statehood	Constitutive Theory of statehood	5 Themes of Geography	Human Geography
Political Geography	Geopolitics	National Library	

❏ Complete the **Chapter 1 Words Worth Knowing Exercises** in the Workbook

For Discussion

The text describes two models for defining "statehood." Why is it necessary to have models or specific definitions at all for what constitutes the state of being a country?

You as a Citizen

In each chapter going forward, you will have as part of your chapter reviews a section called You as a Citizen.

Throughout the book you are the builder, the creator, and decision maker for your country. But you also need to think through the material from the perspective of a common citizen. Sometimes the questions in the You as a Citizen topics will involve what it would be like as a citizen of the country you are building. Other times you will be asked to consider the information presented in terms of your place in the land and time you actually exist.

CHAPTER 1 REVIEW

Chapter 2

Getting the Lay of the Land

Getting the Lay of the Land

So what is this new land you've happened upon?

Now that you have found your new country, it's time to take a look around. Your country is more than just flat nothingness. It has a shape and a climate and a personality all its own. Grab your sleeping roll and walking stick and head outdoors to discover the land that you claimed.

In this chapter you will establish some basic facts and decide on all of the geographic features that make your country the unique and wonderful place that it is.

Words Worth Knowing

- Cartography
- General Reference Maps
- Outline maps
- Political maps
- Physical maps
- Topographic maps

A **Cartographer** collects and verifies data used in creating maps.

Very soon you will be embarking on a new task and defining the borders of your country. This is likely one of the most important tasks of the course and everything else you do will build from that. However, before you do we want to take a moment and talk about cartography and maps. There are many, many maps in this course, so we want to make sure you have a solid foundation here.

Cartography and Mapmaking

Cartography is the study and practice of making maps. People have been making maps for over 5000 years. Maps are important because they help us make sense of the world and the people, places and landforms therein.

There are 5 broad types of cartography:

- **General Reference Maps** – These are the maps you are probably used to seeing. They include outline maps, political maps, road maps or city or town maps. **Outline maps** show just enough geographic information to permit the understanding of other data. **Political maps** show the geographic boundaries between governmental units such as countries, states, and counties.

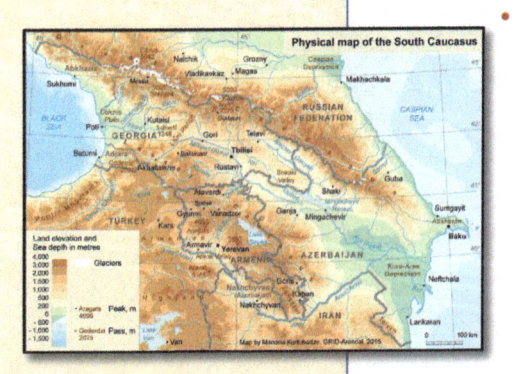

- **Physical or Topographic Maps** – Both of these maps show physical features and elevation changes. Physical maps generally use color to show elevation whereas topographical maps show changes using contour lines

50

- **Thematic Maps** – These maps highlight specific types of information about one topic. Population density maps would fall under this category

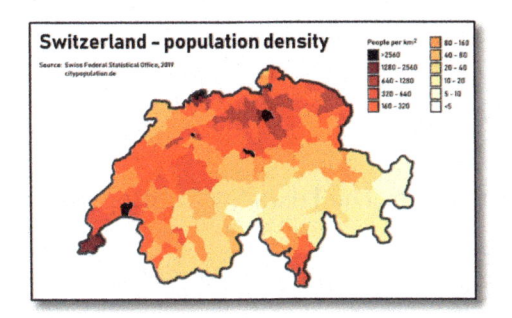

- **Navigation Charts** – These are maps of the ocean (or air) that help with navigation and avoiding accidents.

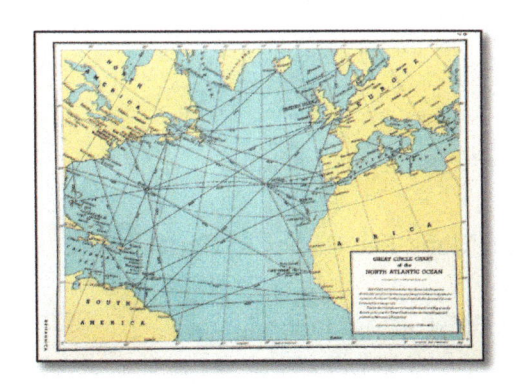

- **Cadastral Maps and Plans** – These maps show details of individual properties

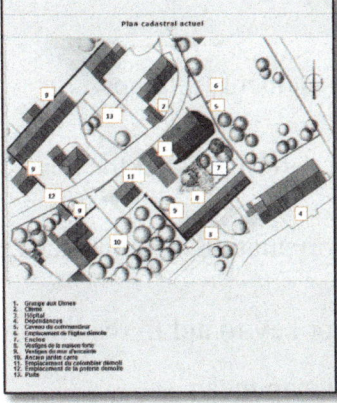

We should note that these are very broad categories. There are many, many more specific types of maps that fall under these categories.

Words Worth Knowing

- Thematic maps
- Navigation Charts
- Cadastral maps

Early mapmakers used to include fake places, called "**paper towns**" in order to trick forgers into copying them and exposing themselves.

Words Worth Knowing

- Title
- Orientation
- Legend
- Grid
- Scale

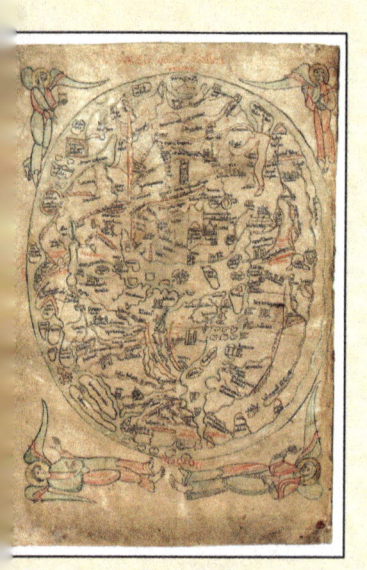

Imago Mundi map

*The oldest surviving map is the **Imago Mundi.** Also known as the Babylonian Map of the World, this map dates back to 700-500 BCE*

Websites and Articles Worth Exploring

- The Fundamentals of Cartography
- Mapping Through the Ages: The History of Cartography
- Cartographer Jobs: Are They Still Relevant In The 21st Century?

Videos Worth Watching

- A Brief History of Cartography and Maps
- Lecture; Maps, Maps, Maps The Basics of Cartography
- How to be a Modern Day Cartographer

Elements of Maps

There are 5 must have elements of maps:

- **Title** - A label that describes what the map shows

- **Orientation** - An orientation symbol such as a Compass Rose

- **Legend** - A chart or key to aid in reading the map. The legend tells what the symbols on the map mean

- **Grid** - The series of lines on a map that match the index.

- **Scale** - Tells what the distance a unit of measure represents in the area shown on the map

Title

Legend

Scale

Orientation   Grid Lines

There are also several other elements that, while not required, you may often encounter on maps. These include:

- **Date -** Tells when the map was made

- **Author -** The person/group who created the map

- **Index -** A collection of major sites and their location on the map

- **Source -** Explains where the author got the information shown on the map

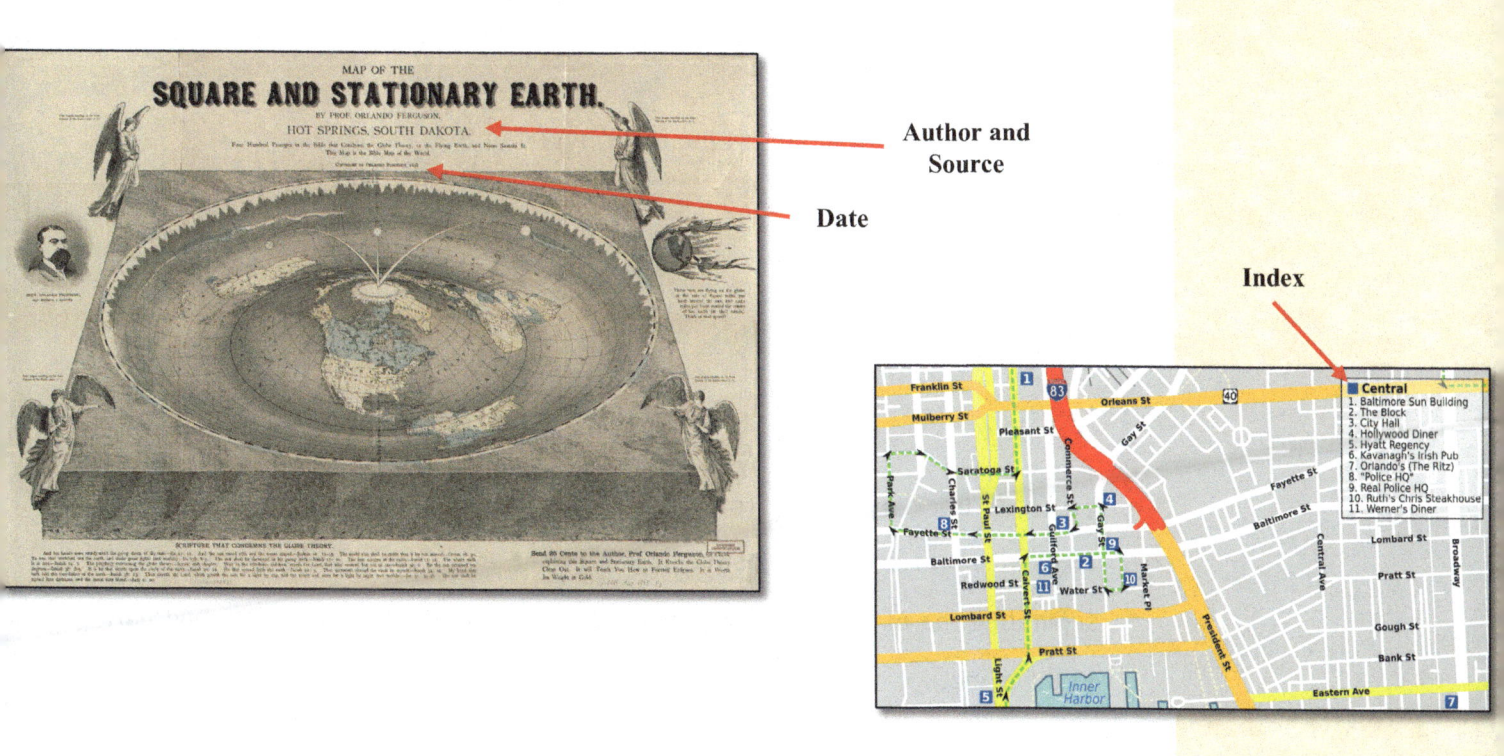

Author and Source

Date

Index

53

Words Worth Knowing

- Latitude Lines
- Equator
- Hemisphere

Websites and Articles Worth Exploring

- Types of Maps
- What are some Different Types of Maps and their Uses
- Types of Maps: Topographic, Political, Climate, and More
- Different types of maps - political and physical
- World Mapper

Videos Worth Watching

- Elements of a Map
- The Map Features Song (Gentleman by PSY)
- 42 Amazing Maps
- Using a Map Scale Song (Line it Up) Fall Out Boy Parody

Latitude and Longitude

Latitude lines are the horizontal lines on a map that run east and west. They measure north and south of the equator. The **equator** is the imaginary line separating the northern and southern hemispheres. (A **hemisphere** is one half of the planet).

Words Worth Knowing

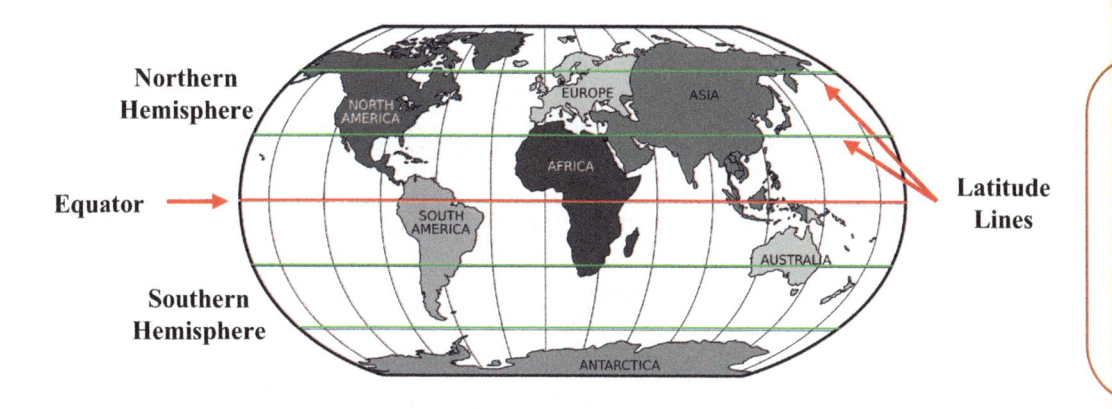

- Longitude lines
- Prime Meridian
- Map projection

Longitude lines are the vertical lines on a map that run north and south. They measure east and west of the Prime Meridian. The **prime meridian** is the line of longitude that is starting point for measuring distance of east and west. It is at 0 degrees longitude. Each 15° of longitude is equivalent to a difference in time of one hour.

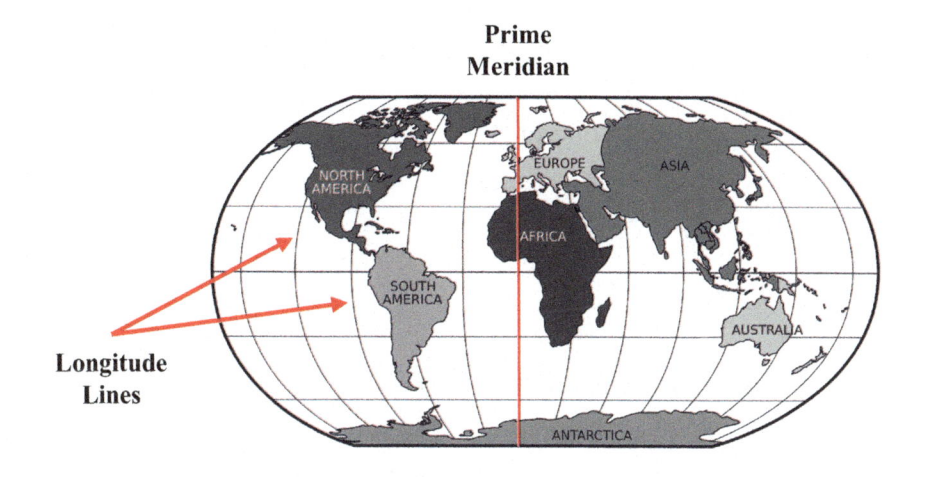

Your **absolute location** is the exact location of a place using latitude and longitude locations

Map Projection

A **map projection** is the method that is used to transfer the measurements of latitude and longitude from a spherical Earth onto a flat or planar surface. All projections of a sphere on a flat plane will distort the surface in some way. The amount of acceptable distortion differs based on the use of the map. Because of this there are several different types of projections like the **Mercator**, the **Stereographic** and the **Robinson**.

The **Mercator projection**, one of the most famous map projections was created by a Flemish cartographer and geographer, Geradus Mercator in 1569

Websites and Articles Worth Exploring

- Latitude, Longitude and Coordinate System Grids
- The Quest for Longitude and the Rise of Greenwich – a Brief History
- Latitude/Longitude Distance Calculator

Videos Worth Watching

- Map Skills: Geography, Latitude and Longitude
- Introduction to Latitude and Longitude
- Latitude and Longitude - Sectional Charts.

Where in the World is Your Country?

It time! Are you ready for the first major decision of the course?

Jigsaw puzzles were invented in the late 18th century to be used specifically in geography classes.

Where is your country?

The first thing you will need to do in this course is decide where the land for your country is located. The planet Earth is a marvelous orb with an infinite combination of landforms, climate conditions, natural resources, and vegetation types. Each of these variations create different concerns for you in the building and running of your country. You have a choice right now as to which of these variations are important to your image of the country you want to build. So, as you think about where your country is, do not forget to consider these things.

The Ground Rules:

You do have some specific limitations and considerations on where you are able to put your country.

- ✓ **Your country must be located on the surface of the Earth**. Its location must make sense. It cannot be on the moon or at the bottom of the ocean or in another dimension.

- ✓ You may choose to create your country on an **island,** a **peninsula**, on the coast, or the inner regions of one of the continents. You can place your country between or bordering real countries. Each choice will have pros and cons later when you begin the actual governance of your country.

- ✓ If you choose to carve your country out of another country or place it between other countries it must be located on a border. **You cannot place your country in the middle of another country.**

57

Other Considerations

If available, look at a globe. If not, find some maps on the internet that will provide you a look at the world as a whole. What are some of the considerations you might consider? Below are some, but they are not everything. And each consideration has both pros and cons associated with it.

✓ **First, do you think your country needs ocean coast or seacoast?** Both these would provide you the natural resources and environmental factors associated with salt water. Sea food would be plentiful, something to be considered when thinking about food sources for your population and potential industry and exports that can grow because you have ports. But access to the ocean or seas also makes it more difficult to defend your country from hostile nations. Your country will be open access to any nation with a navy.

✓ **Pay attention to the size of your country.** As you move through this project you will be filling your country with rural and urban areas as well as natural resources and wilderness areas. As you begin to map out the size of your country make sure that it will be big enough to accommodate these things. On the other hand, you also do not want your country so big that it will be unwieldy and difficult to govern effectively. Think about the difference between tiny countries such as Monaco (2 km^2) or Liechtenstein (160 km^2) and larger countries such as Brazil (8.51 million km^2) or the United States of America (9.63 million km^2). How does size affect things like communication, urban vs rural land distribution, and transportation?

*The area of the United States is so large that you could fit **30 European countries** just inside the continental part of the USA*

- ✓ **What effect will the terrain of an area have?** When you look at the globe to find a good place to build your country you need to consider the terrain. We cannot arbitrarily change the natural land formations simply because we do or don't want them in in our land.

Words Worth Knowing
- Fauna
- Flora

- ✓ **Look at mountain ranges**. Are they difficult to cross? This will have an impact on the transportation and communication systems you will need. But they also provide a barrier against invading armies. Mountain ranges frequently are abundant with natural resources you may want to build industry and possible exports. Would mountains provide vistas and views you could build resorts, parks and other activities that could attract tourists. Tourism can be a huge industry affecting your economy.

- ✓ **Look at the major rivers.** Rivers must be considered as an internal source of transportation and as habitat for **fauna** (animals) and **flora** (plants). But if there are no major rivers in the area you are looking at, does that make the area uninhabitable? Unless you choose an extremely arid region there are means to gather rainwater and smaller rivers, streams, and lakes to rely on.

✓ **Distance from the Equator.** Simply put, the distance from the equator affects the climate of your country. Areas close to the equator are warmer climates. But depending on the area, the warmer climate may create hot barren deserts, or thick, dense rain forests that can impede development. As you move away from the equator, the climates become more tepid with noticeable changes of seasons. How will these climate changes affect your decision? What are the pros and cons of the areas closer to the arctic circle? How will you reap the positive and negative aspects of a variety of the climate, fauna, and flora?

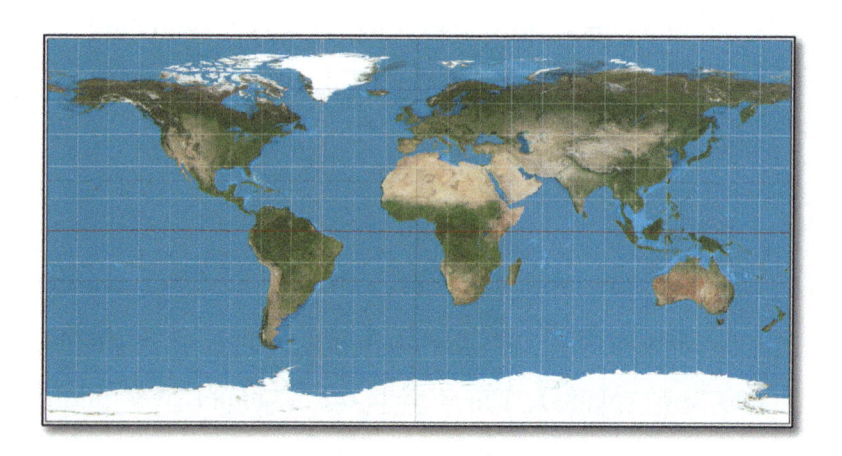

✓ **Don't worry about whether there are people living currently in the location you are putting your country**. For the purposes of this course we will assume that there are no people currently living in the land you claim.

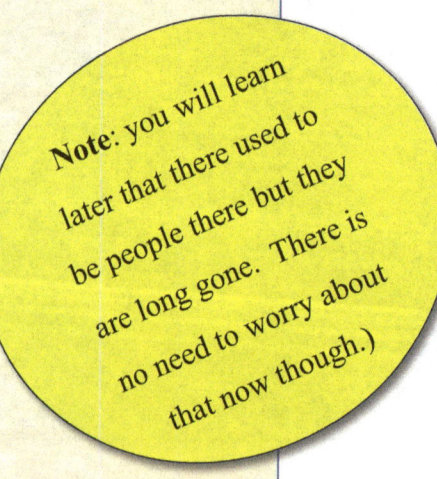

Note: you will learn later that there used to be people there but they are long gone. There is no need to worry about that now though.)

Task #2: Defining Your Borders

Congratulations! You have discovered some unclaimed land. Now that you have claimed it, the first thing you need to do is define your borders. To do this you will start with a basic political map.

☐ **Create a political OUTLINE MAP of your country.**

- Use 1 8.5 x 11 sheet of graph paper.

- Your country must be a polygon. *(Note: While it is true most countries have rounded borders, you will want straight sides for your country to be able to calculate distances and areas later.)*

- Your country should take up <u>at least half of the page</u>

- Label all neighboring countries and major bodies of water.

- Your map for this task must include:

    - a compass rose,

    - a scale. *(Hint: Use the squares on your graph paper to help you define your scale.)*

- You will be using this outline many times throughout this course so make sure that your lines are dark enough to be copied. Because of this, this first map should also **NOT** be colored in. This should be an outline only.

Helpful Information

1 Mile (Mi) = 1.61 Kilometers (KM)

☐ Complete **Worksheet 2.1: How Big is Your Country** in your Workbook

☐ Complete **Worksheet 2.2: Where in the World is your Country?** in your Workbook

Words Worth Knowing

- Atmosphere
- Geosphere
- Lithosphere
- Biosphere
- Hydrosphere

Extension Activity #1: 3D Globe

Objective: Create a 3D model of the Earth showing the Location of your Country

- Label the following on your globe:
    1. The Continents and Oceans
    2. The Equator
    3. The Prime Meridian
    4. The Location of your Country

Earth's 5 Systems

In this course you will be talking a lot about things that are happening in, on, around and above your country. While some of this may be review, we wanted to ensure that you had a solid foundation on which to stand and explore your new country. In that vein, let's take a moment and talk about some of the general properties that make up our planet.

The Earth is comprised of 4 (or 5 or 6) main systems/spheres:

- The **atmosphere** is the blanket of gasses that cover the earth.

- The **geosphere** makes up the interior and surface of the earth. The geosphere can also be called the **lithosphere**.

- The **biosphere** is that part of the planet that can support life.

- The **hydrosphere** is the made up of all of the water on the earth, no matter the state.

- Some scientists also include the **cryosphere** which is the part of the hydrosphere that is made up of frozen water. These ice sheets play an important role in the preservation of our planet and the life on it.

- Some scientists also include the **Ionosphere**. This is the magnetic field that surrounds the earth.

Words Worth Knowing

- Cryosphere
- Magnetosphere
- Ionosphere

Websites and Articles Worth Exploring

- The 17 Spheres of Earth
- Earth's Systems
- Earth's Spheres

Videos Worth Watching

- Earth's Interconnected Cycles
- Introduction to the Spheres of Earth
- Working Together - Earth's Systems & Interactions

❏ Complete **Worksheet 2.3: Earth's Major Spheres** in your Workbook

Words Worth Knowing

- Abiotic factors

About 70% of the Earth's crust is Oceanic crust.

The Geosphere

We will be talking more about some of the earth's sphere's as we move through the chapter. Let's start with the geosphere. The geosphere is made up of all abiotic, or nonliving things inside and on the surface of the earth. Therefore we will just briefly talk here about the The Earth is made up of 5 layers: An inner and outer core, a lower and upper mantle and a crust. The core and the mantle of the earth contain only abiotic factors. **Abiotic factors** are those factors of the earth that are not living such as ricks, minerals and soil.

The crust of the Earth is where all the "stuff" happens. This is where the biosphere begins to interact with the geosphere. The crust is made up of a thicker continental crust and a thinner, but denser oceanic crust.

The Atmosphere

Like the Geosphere, the atmosphere is made up of layers. The Troposphere goes from the surface of the earth to about 7.5 miles up. This layer holds all of the air that both plants and animals breathe. Above that the stratosphere goes up to 31 miles. The ozone layer is located in the stratosphere. From the top of the stratosphere to 50 miles up is the very cold mesosphere. The thermosphere, from 50-330 miles up, contains the ionosphere as well as the aurora borealis that we sometimes see in the sky. Finally, the furthest layer out of the atmosphere is the exosphere. This extends all the way to over 6000 miles above the surface of the Earth.

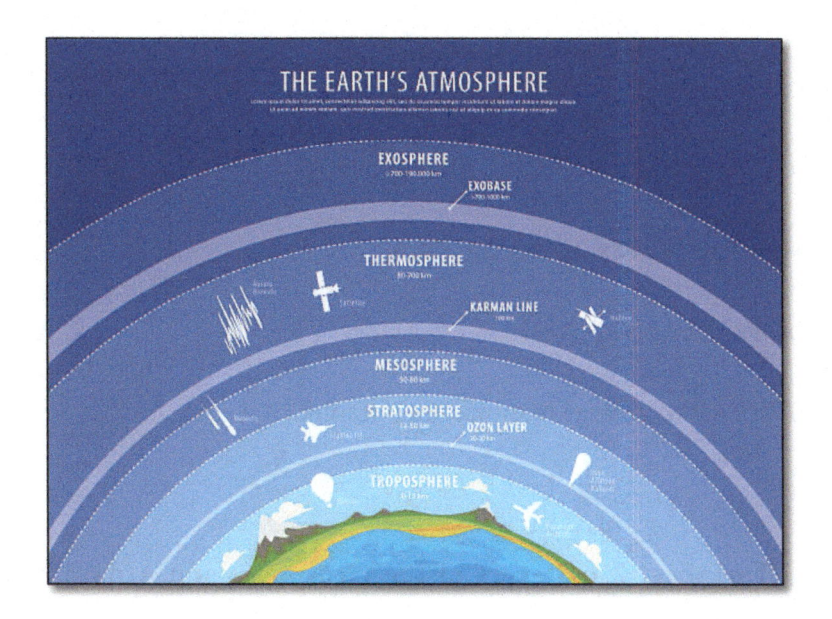

Websites and Articles Worth Exploring

- What Are The Earth's Layers?

- Earth Structure

- Earth's Atmosphere: A Multi-layered Cake

- Atmosphere

- What Is The Atmosphere?

Words Worth Knowing

- Landforms

Videos Worth Watching

- Structure of the Earth| 3D

- Layers Of The Geosphere (Interior Of The Earth)

- 7 Ways We Know What's Inside The Earth

- The Atmosphere

- Reveal Earth's Atmosphere | National Geographic

❏ Complete **Worksheet 2.4: Layers of the Geosphere and Atmosphere** in your Workbook

Landforms and Physical Maps

Landforms are the natural physical features found on the surface of the earth. They are part of the Earth's terrain. Landforms are created as a result of various forces of nature such as wind, water, ice, and movement of tectonic plates. There are many different types of landforms. Often you can see the types of landforms in a given area on a physical map. Remember, physical maps are designed to show the natural landscape features of Earth.

Physical maps show **topography**, or the arrangement of the physical features of a land, either by colors or as shaded relief. Some common color schemes for physical maps include:

- Green to brown to gray color scheme can be used for showing the elevation of the land.
  - Darker greens are used for near-sea-level elevations, with the color grading into tans and browns as elevations increase.
- Shades of blue can be used for rivers, lakes, seas and oceans.
  - Light blue colors are used for the most shallow areas and darker blues for areas of deeper water.
- Glaciers and ice caps are shown in white colors.

Words Worth Knowing

- Topography

Mountain	Plateaus	Valleys	Deserts	Dunes	Islands
Plains	Rivers	Oceans	Loess	Glaciers	Volcano
Isthmus	Peninsula	Delta	Mesa	Waterfall	Geyser
Archipelago	Bluff	Butte	Caves	Beaches	

67

Websites and Articles Worth Exploring

- The Different Types of Landforms

- Physical Maps

- What are some Common Features Shown on Physical Maps?

Videos Worth Watching

- Landforms, Hey!: Crash Course Kids #17.1

- An Introduction to Landforms of the Earth

- Landscapes and Landforms

Considerations for Your Physical Features

So, it's almost time for your next task. In this task you will be determining the landforms and other physical features that make up your new land. As you prepare for this task there are a few things you will want to think about.

✓ **If possible, you want your country to have a nice mix of physical features.**

- **Keep in mind the geographic location of your country. Your physical features must be realistic.** This is where your location decisions from earlier come into play. If your country is in a mountainous region you will need to include mountains in your country.

- **Don't forget about fresh water sources!** Remember that if your country sits on or near the ocean, you will still want at least one source of fresh water – that is unless you plan on importing all your drinkable water.

- **Your physical features will determine your natural resources.** We will discuss these in more detail later in the chapter

- **Your geographic location along with your physical features will help define your weather and climate.** We will also be discussing this more in a few.

A **Geologist** studies the matter that makes up the Earth and other terrestrial planets.

Task #3 Creating Your Physical Map

As you begin to explore your land, the first thing you should do is create an initial physical map. This will let you know where the major geographic features of your country are. This map will be very helpful later on.

While creating your physical map keep in mind the location of your country. If your country is an island you have a bit more freedom with physical features. You still should think about the type of coastlines that you want (i.e. shallow beaches, rocky cliffs, etc.). If your country sits near or between other countries, make sure to take into consideration the physical features of the area where your country is located. Is it in the Alps? Near the ocean? Landlocked?

❑ **Create an initial physical map of your country.**

- Use the **OUTLINE MAP** you made in T1-1 as your guide
- You must use at 3 different types of landforms. Make sure to note and name any major mountain ranges, lakes, rivers or other large features.
- Be sure to include the same compass rose, scale and legend as on your political outline map.

Composition Assignment #1

- **Write an essay discussing the landforms of your country.**
  - Choose at least 3 of the landforms present in your country
  - Explain what each landform is and how it develops or interacts with the other landforms around it. Be sure to include illustrations for each of the different landforms.

Extension Activity #2: 3D Landform model

Objective: Create a 3D model of your country showing the various landforms

- Your model should be on a base larger than your country

- Label the surrounding countries and bodies of water that border your country

- Label the major landforms of your country

Natural Resources

Now that you have defined the boundaries and major landforms in your country it is time to turn your attention to **natural resources**. Natural resources are the materials provided by the Earth that can be used to support life and meet the needs of people. Natural resources come in 2 major types: Renewable resources and Non-renewable resources. A **renewable resource** grows again and comes back again after we use it. For example, wood is a renewable resource. A **non-renewable resource** is a resource that does not grow and come back, or a resource that would take a very long time to come back. For example, coal is a non-renewable resource.

Words Worth Knowing

- Natural resources
- Renewable resource
- Non-renewable resource

```
                    Natural
                    Resources
                   /         \
          Renewable           Non-renewable
          Resources           resources
          /      \           /      |      \
      Plants   Animals   Fossil fuels  Minerals  Soils
```

Natural resources, both renewable and non-renewable, form the base of the real wealth of nations. These are the original materials out of which other items and capital are produced. In fact every person on earth consumes a natural resource, either directly or indirectly. Unfortunately our use of Earth's natural resources has not been the kindest to our planed and has led to a host of environmental issues. We will get more into that in chapter 3. For now we just want you to start thinking about the types of natural resources that will be present in your country.

*People in rich countries consume up to **10 times more** natural resources than those in the poorest countries.*

Words Worth Knowing

- Resource map

In just a bit you will make a **Resource Map** for your country. Resource maps are designed to show the locations of natural resources. They do not show every place that every little thing is located, rather they show the general area or most important places in which you might find the resources (animal., plant, mineral, etc. These locations are denoted using various symbols.

Possible symbols for Resource maps:

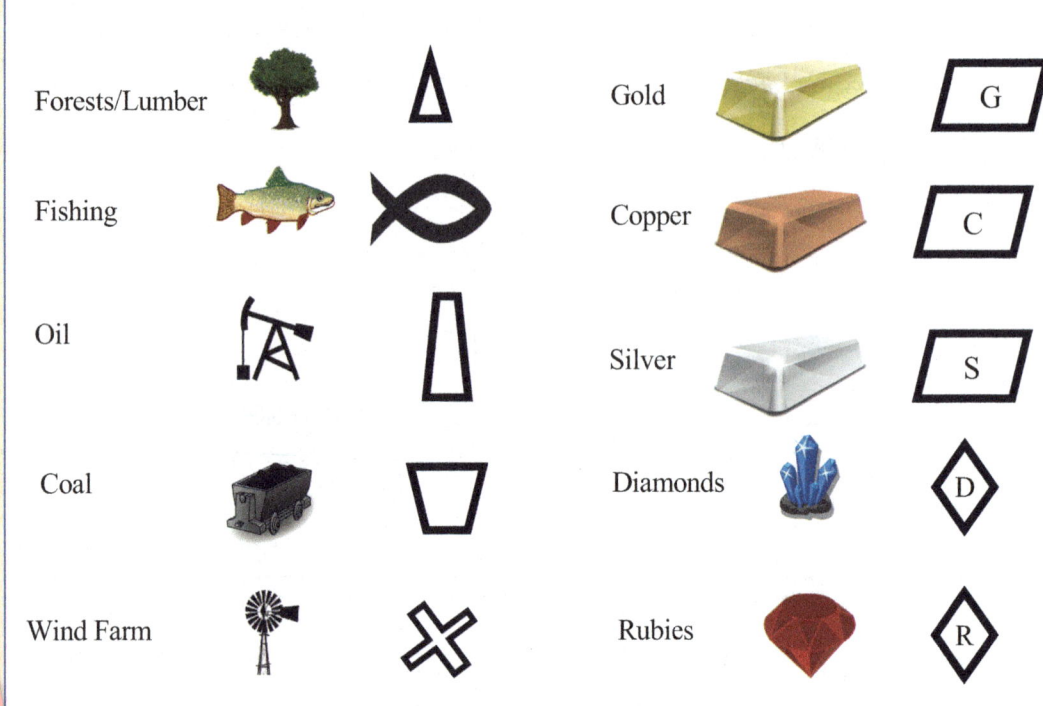

Resource	Symbol	Symbol	Resource	Symbol	Symbol
Forests/Lumber	🌳	△	Gold		G
Fishing	🐟	✠	Copper		C
Oil			Silver		S
Coal			Diamonds		D
Wind Farm		✕	Rubies		R

An <u>Environmental Engineer</u> uses engineering and science to develop solutions to environmental problems.

Websites and Articles Worth Exploring

- Introduction To Natural Resources (NR)

- The Economic Significance Of Natural Resources: Key Points For Reformers In Eastern Europe, Caucasus And Central Asia

- Renewable And Non-renewable Energy Resources Explained

- The House Committee On Natural Resources

- Natural Resource Maps Of The World

Videos Worth Watching

- ESS3A - Natural Resources

- Resources: Welcome to the Neighborhood - Crash Course Kids #2.1

- Going, Going Gone: Natural Resource Depletion

- Exploring Natural Resources

- How to use resource maps

Considerations for Your Natural Resources

You are gearing up for task #4 – creating your resource map. When you embark on that task, though, you will want to keep a few things in mind.

✓ **Your natural resources must make sense in relation to your country's physical geography.** If you chose, in the last task, to make your country predominantly forested then it would not be realistic to list wind power as a natural resource. However, you would be able to mark some forests on your resource map.

✓ **Your natural resources must make sense in relation to your country's geographic location.** Before you list a natural resource on your map, be sure to check the surrounding countries and areas to make sure that the resource could realistically be found in the location where your country sits.

Words Worth Knowing

- Weather
- Precipitation

Task #4 – Your Resource Map

Now it is time to look at the natural resources abundant in your country. Where are the fresh water sources? Is your country forested or mostly grassland or desert? Are there any mineral deposits?

Keep in mind the location, physical features, and climate in your country. The natural resource map must be logical. This map will be helpful as you begin to develop your country later on.

❏ **Create a map showing the locations of all natural resources.**

- Use the **OUTLINE MAP** you made in T1-1 as your guide
- However, make sure to include enough features from your physical map for the natural resources map to make sense.
- Make sure to include a compass rose, a scale and a legend.
- This map should be in color.

❏ Complete **Worksheet 2.5: Natural Resources in your Country** in your Workbook

---

A **Meteorologist** studies individual regional weather trends/patterns over a specific period of time.

Climate Vs Weather

Next on our review of basic information for your country comes your climate and weather. **Weather** is the different events that happen each day in our atmosphere, like rain or snow, hot or cold. When you look outside to see what the temperature and precipitation will be today you are checking the weather. **Precipitation** is any water that falls to earth, whether in liquid or solid form.

Climate, on the other hand, is the average weather in a location over a long period of time. Rather like biomes (which we'll get into in chapter 3) there is some debate as to how many **climate zones** there are. There are 5 major climate zones on Earth according to the **Köppen climate classification system**: Tropical, Dry, Temperate, Continental, and Polar.

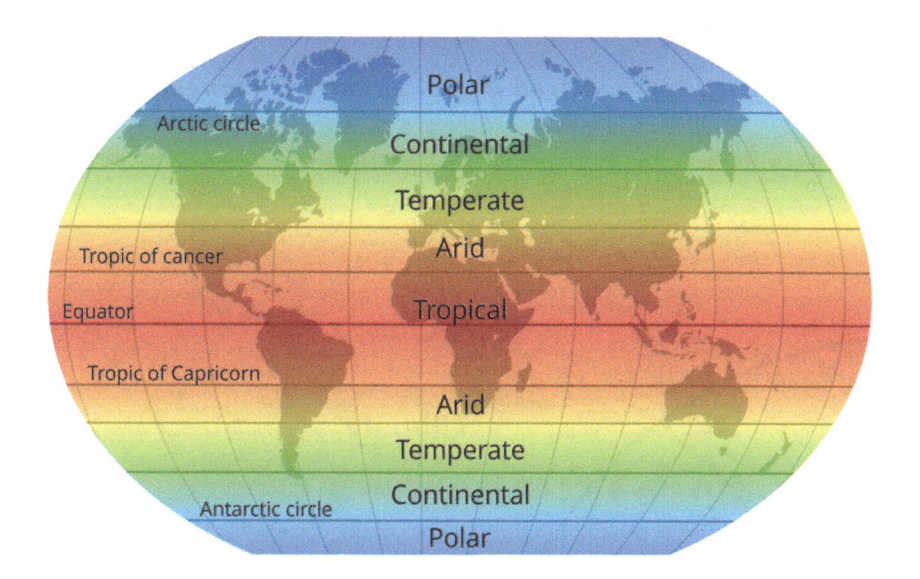

Words Worth Knowing

- Climate
- Climate Zone

A **climatologist** studies large scale weather patterns over a long period of time

- The **Tropical Zone** is the area nearest to the equator. This zone is normally hot and wet

- The **Arid/Dry climate zone** has more evaporation than precipitation. It is very dry and hot most of the year.

- **Mild Temperate zones** have the most distinct seasons. While the length and duration may differ, the countries in this zone can enjoy some predictability in seasonal weather

- **Continental Zones** have wide temperature variations between seasons but often low precipitation

- **Polar zones** are located at the top and bottom of the earth. These zones are typically very cold and dry.

The **Köppen climate classification system** was first published by German-Russian climatologist **Wladimir Köppen** in 1884. It categorizes climate zones throughout the world based on local vegetation.

Many classification lists also include a highland zone. Highlands have unique characteristics based on their elevation. This climate is subject to rapid changes in climate over short distances.

When you think about weather and climate just remember: *__weather__ tells you if it will rain today, __climate__ tells you if your country is prone to be rainy and wet.*

Weather

- Short term measurements
- Daily conditions including temperature and precipitation
- Usually reported as forecasts
- Can change rapidly
- Changes involve shifts in precipitation, winds and clouds

- Precipitation
- Temperature
- Humidity
- Wind Speed and Direction

Climate

- Long term measurements
- State of the atmosphere over years of collected data
- Usually reported as averages
- Controlled by the balance of energy of the earth and its atmosphere
- Influenced by slow changes in the ocean, the land, the orbit of the earth, and the energy output of the sun

Websites and Articles Worth Exploring

- What's The Difference Between Weather And Climate?

- Nasa - What's The Difference Between Weather And Climate?

- What Is The Difference Between Weather And Climate?

- All About Climate

- What Is A Climate Zone?

- Köppen Climate Classification System

- Guide To Determining Climate Regions By County

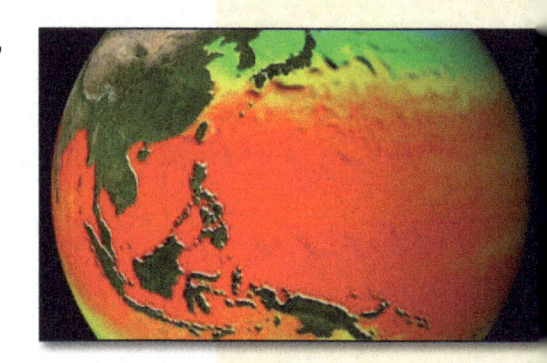

Videos Worth Watching

- Weather vs. Climate (Mike Sammartano)

- Weather vs Climate (CoCoRaHS Educational Series)

- Climates for Kids | Learn about Different Weather and Climate Zones

- Climate Zones of the Earth - The Dr. Binocs Show

- The Koppen-Geiger Climate Classification System

Task #5 – Your Weather Forecast

Few things have more impact on a location and its people than the weather and climate. These two coordinating yet distinct factors decide what can grow where and what people need to survive in a land.

In this task you will take a look at the climate and weather of your country.

❏ Complete **Worksheet 2.6: Understanding your Climate** in your Workbook

❏ Complete **Worksheet 2.7: Monthly Temperature and Precipitation** in your Workbook

❏ **Create and present a 7 day weather forecast for your country.**
- Make sure to include what specific dates of the year your forecast is for
- Create at least one graphic representing your forecast
- Present a 1 minute "Weather Spot" discussing the forecast for the week.

Natural Hazards and Disasters

A **natural hazard** is a threat of an event that could occur naturally and usually has a negative effect on humans. When such an event actually occurs we call that event a **natural disaster.** For example if you lived on the coast of Florida hurricanes may be a natural hazard for your area. However, if a hurricane actually happens and causes harm to people or property, then that singular event would be classified as a natural disaster. In short, the natural hazards inherent to your country could lead to a natural disaster.

Natural Disasters fall into 3 main categories: Geologic Hazards, Atmospheric Hazards, and Other Hazards.

Geologic Hazards Can Include:

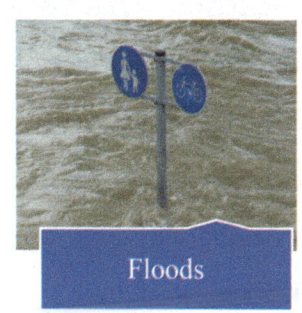

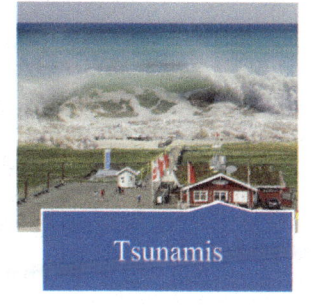

- Earthquakes
- Landslides and Mudslides
- Volcanoes
- Floods
- Tsunamis

Words Worth Knowing

- Natural Hazard
- Natural Disaster

Words Worth Knowing

- Primary Effects
- Secondary Effects
- Tertiary Effects

Atmospheric Hazards Can Include:

Extreme Heat | Lightening | Drought

Tornadoes | Winter Weather | Hurricanes

Other Hazards Can Include:

Wildfires | Infestation | Epidemic

Just like there are three categories of hazards, there are three levels of effects if a natural disaster were to occur. The **Primary Effects** occur as an immediate result of the disaster itself. An example of a primary effect of a hurricane could be a building collapse due to the wind. **Secondary Effects** occur as a result of a primary effect. In the hurricane example, a secondary effect may be the power outages that result from damage to the electrical lines during the hurricane. Finally, **Tertiary Effects** are **long-term effects** that occur as a result of the primary disaster. Still using our hurricane example, the tertiary effects could include loss of habitat due to beach erosion caused by the hurricane.

Assessing Risk

If you live on Earth, you are at risk for a natural hazard. Unfortunately it's a fact of life. How big of a risk you have for which types of hazard, though, depends on several factors including the location, climate and physical features of your country. As the leader of your country it is crucial you be aware of your country's risk information.

Risk information is any information which can influence a decision. It is the foundation for good disaster risk management and mitigation. **Mitigation** is the effort to reduce the impact of a disaster, specifically in regards to the loss of life and property. These are actions that are taken <u>before</u> a disaster occurs. This is how communities and governments protect people and property from natural hazards. Knowing your country's risk information will help you plan later your mitigation and emergency response strategies. After all, *if you don't understand the risk, you can't manage it!*

Words Worth Knowing
- Risk Information
- Mitigation

Risk Information tells the story of...
- **What** disaster might happen
- **When** a disaster may occur
- **Where** a disaster may occur
- **Who** may be affected by a disaster
- **How severe** a disaster may be

Every **$1.00** spent on disaster mitigation is worth **$6.00** in disaster response.

A **Seismologist** studies seismic activities of the Earth such as Earthquakes.

Websites and Articles Worth Exploring

- Natural Disasters And Severe Weather

- Natural Disasters (National Geographic)

- Natural Disasters (Homeland Security)

- Risk Assessment

- Disaster Risk Assessment

- Natural Hazards And Natural Disasters

Videos Worth Watching

- Natural Disasters - Definition & Types

- ESS3B - Natural Hazards

- Natural Disasters

- Integrated Approach To Disaster Risk Management: Prevent, Residual Risk Prepare, Respond, Recover

- Education For Disaster Preparedness

Task #6: Your Disaster Risk Assessment

You've now had a look at the boundaries of your land, the physical features, the climate and the weather. The final part of getting the lay of the land is to assess the disaster risk of your country.

❏ Complete **Worksheet 2.8: Natural Disaster Risk Analysis** in your Workbook

❏ **Prepare a Risk Information Report for your country**
- Choose 2 natural disasters that are a greater risk to your country. Prepare a presentation explaining what the natural disaster is, how it forms, and why your country is at a greater risk for that disaster.

Extension Activity #3 Demonstrating the Effects of Natural Disasters

Objective: Create a 3D model of a building and design a method of demonstrating the effects of a natural disaster on the structure

- The disaster you demonstrate must be one of the two from your risk information report
- Your building must be freestanding prior to the disaster.

Chapter 2 Review

The following sections help you review and think about some of the concepts and activities that you performed in this chapter.

Words Worth Knowing Review

The following terms were very important throughout this chapter:

Cartography	General Reference Map	Outline Map	Political Map
Physical map	Topographical map	Thematic map	Navigation charts
Cadastral map	Title	Orientation	Legend
Grid	Scale	Latitude Lines	Equator
Hemisphere	Longitude lines	Prime meridian	Landforms
Natural Resources	Renewable resources	Non-renewable resources	Resource map
Weather	Precipitation	Climate	Risk information
Mitigation	Flora	Fauna	Map Projection
Atmosphere	Geosphere	Lithosphere	Biosphere
Hydrosphere	Cryosphere	Ionosphere	Abiotic factors
Topography	Climate Zone	Natural Hazard	Natural Disaster
Primary Effects	Secondary Effects	Tertiary Effects	

❑ Complete the **Chapter 2 Words Worth Knowing Exercises** in the Workbook

For Discussion

In this chapter we covered many aspects of physical and climatological nature of your country. Why is it important for leaders to understand the physical and climatological characteristics of their country?

You as a Citizen

As a citizen, what is your responsibility when it comes to your protecting your country's physical land and natural resources?

What is something that you could do to help your family be prepared for one of the natural disasters that your country is at higher risk for.

CHAPTER 2 REVIEW

Your National Library

The following Items should be filed in your national library

- **Guidebook**
    - Sample Weather Forecast
    - Understanding Your Climate
    - Monthly temperature and precipitation
- **Official Documents**
    - Outline Map
    - Physical map
    - Natural Resource map
    - How Big is Your Country
    - Where in the World is Your Country
    - Natural Resources in your Country
    - Natural disaster risk analysis

CHAPTER 3

Checking out the Ecosystem

Checking out the Ecosystem

So, you've hiked and mapped your country's physical features and you know its climate. But a land is more than mountain ranges and rainfall. A land is grasses and trees, flowers and birds, animals and fish.

In this chapter you will you will explore the ecosystem and discover a few of the many plants and animals that call your new country home.

Words Worth Knowing

- Ecological organization
- Biome
- Ecosystem
- Biotic
- Abiotic

Ecological Organization

Ecological organization refers to the relationship of biological organisms to each other and their environments. These relationships can be studied on a large, macro level or a smaller, micro scale. The largest level of organization is the Biosphere. The biosphere is made up of the entire ecosystem of the planet Earth. Beneath the biosphere come biomes. A **biome** is a set of ecosystems that all share similar characteristics.

The **ecosystem** is the main unit of measurement when it comes to ecological organization. It would be like the meter in length measurement. An ecosystem is a community of living organisms that all interact with each other and with their environment in a specific area. Ecosystems include both **biotic** (living) and **abiotic** (nonliving) factors.

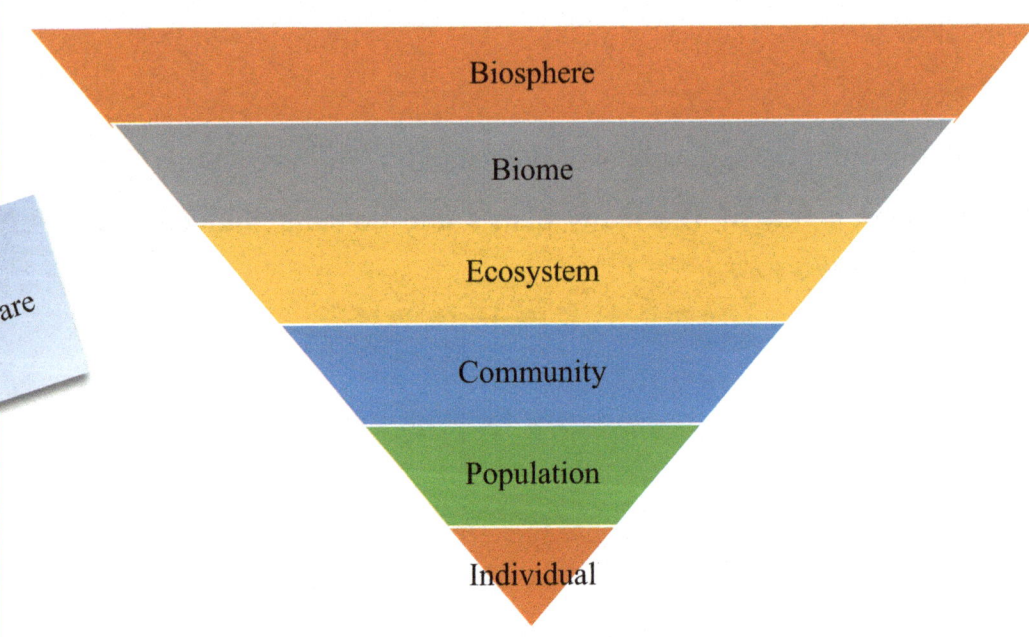

Three-fourths of all ecosystems on Earth are Aquatic.

- Biosphere
- Biome
- Ecosystem
- Community
- Population
- Individual

Within an ecosystem are many communities. **Communities** are the summation of all of the actual populations of species living within a given biome. A **population** includes all members of the same type of organism.

The lowest level of organization is the **individual**. The individual in an ecosystem is one single living organism.

Words Worth Knowing
- Communities
- Population
- Individual

Websites and Articles Worth Exploring

- What Is An Ecosystem?
- Ecosystem: Definition, Examples, Importance – All About Ecosystems
- Levels of organization in an ecosystem

An **Ecologist** studies nature and how living things interact with each other.

Videos Worth Watching

- Ecosystems for Kids
- Ecosystem Ecology: Links in the Chain - Crash Course Ecology #7
- ECOSYSTEM - The Dr. Binocs Show | Best Learning Videos For Kids | Peekaboo Kidz

Biomes

While all of the levels matter, for this course, you will really be concerned with the biomes and populations. So, lets start with biomes.

There are several types of biomes that fall into 5 main categories: Aquatic, Desert, Grasslands, Forests and Tundra.

Different Types of Biomes

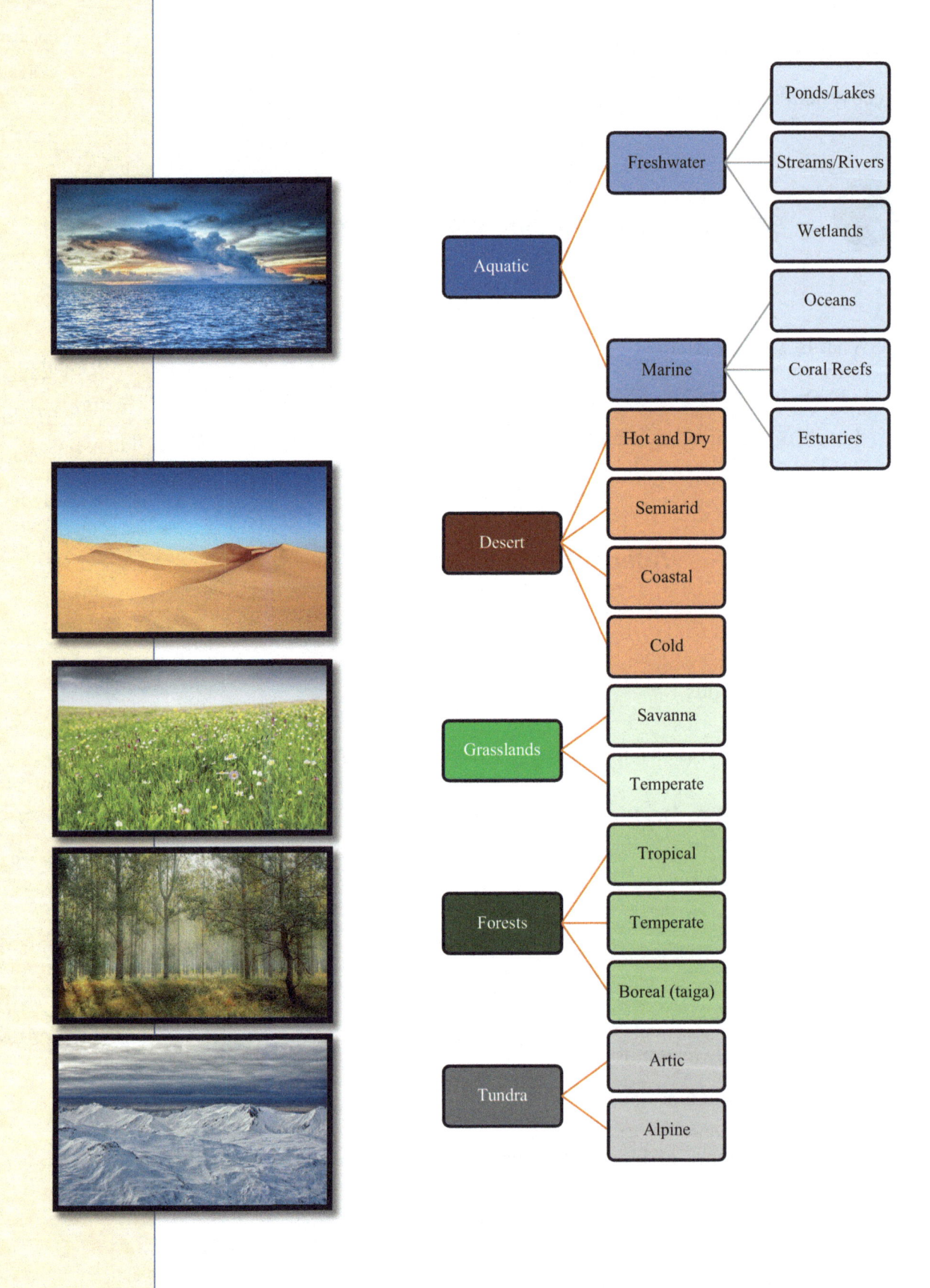

- Aquatic
  - Freshwater
    - Ponds/Lakes
    - Streams/Rivers
    - Wetlands
  - Marine
    - Oceans
    - Coral Reefs
    - Estuaries
- Desert
  - Hot and Dry
  - Semiarid
  - Coastal
  - Cold
- Grasslands
  - Savanna
  - Temperate
- Forests
  - Tropical
  - Temperate
  - Boreal (taiga)
- Tundra
  - Artic
  - Alpine

Considerations for Placement of Your Biomes

The next task involves defining and marking the locations of the biomes in your country. To help you in this task here are a few considerations for your to think about.

- ✓ **Take a look at some of the countries in the same geographic area as your country.** What types of biomes do they have?

- ✓ **Think about the physical features that you mapped in your country.** Do you have any freshwater sources? What kinds of biomes are located around there? What about mountains or valleys?

- ✓ **Consider some of the features from your natural resources map.** Did you include forested areas? Do you have areas suitable for wind farming or mineral mining? What types of biomes are common in areas possessing those resources?

A **Marine Biologist** studies organisms of the ocean in their natural environment.

Biomes move as the climate changes. 10,000 years ago parts of the Sahara Desert in North Africa were lush and green.

Words Worth Knowing

- Taxonomy

Task #7 Defining your Biomes

❑ **Create a map defining the biome areas in your country.**

- Use the **OUTLINE MAP** you made in Chapter 1 as your guide
- Include at least 3 different biomes within your country
- Color each biome a different color.
- Make sure to include a legend showing which color belongs to which biome.
- Include a Compass Rose

❑ Choose at least 3 biomes located within your country and complete **Worksheet 3.1: Biomes in my Country** in your Workbook. (There are 3 copies of this worksheet in your workbook.)

Classification of Populations

As mentioned before the next step down from a biome is an ecosystem. We talk about how we will be using the ecosystem as the main unit of measurement in this course. In fact how you, as the leader of your country, fit your land and people into the existing ecosystem will play a substantial role as you move through the course. However we are going to skip over the ecosystem level right now and approach it again, but from the other direction.

A single individual organism can be identified by its relationship with other organisms. Scientific classification, otherwise known as **taxonomy**, is a system of classifying living things. There are seven major levels of taxonomy: Domain, kingdom, phylum, class, order, genus and species. You can easily remember the taxonomy levels with the Mnemonic "Dear Kevin, Please Come Over For Great Snacks."

There are only 3 domains and 6 kingdoms of living things and all plants, animals bacteria etc. falls under one of these.

"**D**ear **K**evin. **P**lease **C**ome **O**ver **F**or **G**reat **S**nacks!"

- **D**omain
- **K**ingdom
- **P**hylum
- **C**lass
- **O**rder
- **F**amily
- **G**enus
- **S**pecies

All living things share some basic characteristics:
- They are made of cells.
- They respond to stimuli.
- They adapt to their environment.
- They use energy.
- They can reproduce.
- They contain DNA, molecules that contain instructions for life.

Living things:

Domain → Kingdom
- Bacteria → Bacteria
- Archaea → Archaea
- Eukarya → Protista, Plantae, Fungi, Animalia

95

Words Worth Knowing

- Binomial nomenclature

Taxonomy of YOU

Domain	Eukarya	**Organisms**/cells that contain a nucleus inside a membrane
Kingdom	Animalia	**Multicell organisms** that have a nucleus but lack a cell wall (**Animals**)
Phylum	Chordata	**Animals** with a spinal chord
Class	Mammalia	**Chordates** that bear live young and give milk to nourish their young
Order	Primates	**Mammals** with front facing eyes, a collar bone, grasping hands and two types of teeth
Family	Hominidae	**Primates** who stand upright, have a large brain, and use their hands and feet for different purposes
Genus	Homo	**Hominids** with an S curve in their spine (**Humans**)
Species	*Homo Sapiens*	**Humans** with a well developed chin, a thin skull and a high forehead

Species are normally identified by their **binomial nomenclature**. The binomial nomenclature is made up of two names. The first name is the **genus**, the second is the **species**. These two names are usually italicized.

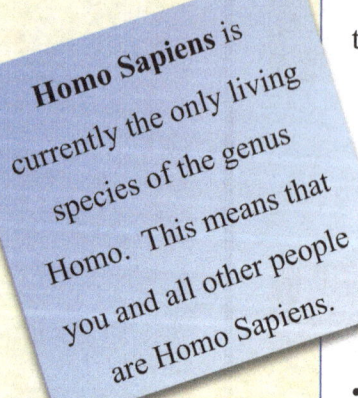

Homo Sapiens is currently the only living species of the genus Homo. This means that you and all other people are Homo Sapiens.

Websites and Articles Worth Exploring

- The Taxonomic Classification System
- Classification system
- Know Scientific Classification for the ASVAB

Videos Worth Watching

- Taxonomy: Life's Filing System - Crash Course Biology #19
- Classification of Life
- Classification of Living Things

Words Worth Knowing

- National symbols

National Symbols

National symbols are very important to national identity. These symbols can be used to foster pride and unity in a nation's population. National symbols can represent something unique and special about a particular country and is often displayed or highlighted on promotional materials as well as at celebrations.

Considerations for Choosing Your National Symbols

In a moment you will be choosing the national symbols for your country. We know, we know – you don't have a government or even any people yet. In the next unit you will be creating some ads to help draw people to your new land. When they get here you want to be able to rally them right away to your national identity. You will be using your national symbols as you begin to create your flag and any propaganda you may be creating. But first, a few things to think about:

97

- ✓ **The plants and animals you choose for your national symbols MUST be native to your country**.

- ✓ **You cannot** claim an invasive species or a mythical creature as your national symbol.

- ✓ **As you are choosing your symbols think about the biomes and ecosystems that you have in your country**. What kinds of animals live there?

- ✓ **Your national symbols, however, do NOT have to all come from the same biome.** Feel free to branch out to different parts of your country (depending on how big you made your country in task #1)

- ✓ **Choose your symbols wisely**. You will be learning a lot more about them in task #10

Task #8 Your National Symbols

For this task you will choose 5 of your country's national symbols

- ❏ Complete **Worksheet 3.2: National Tree Worksheet** in your Workbook

- ❏ Complete **Worksheet 3.3: National Flower Worksheet** in your Workbook

- ❏ Complete **Worksheet 3.4: National Land Animal Worksheet** in your Workbook

- ❏ Complete **Worksheet 3.5: National Aquatic Animal Worksheet** in your Workbook

- ❏ Complete **Worksheet 3.6: National Bird Worksheet** in your Workbook

- ❏ **Create a Poster Highlighting the National Symbols of your country**

Food Chains and Food Webs

A **food chain** shows the feeding relationship between different living things in an ecosystem. Basically it is saying who eats whom in the circle of life. See the food chain below. Notice it breaks the circle of life down into the abiotic factors such as sun, air, water and soil and the biotic factors, the plants and animals.

> **Words Worth Knowing**
> - Food chain
> - Autotrophs
> - Consumers
> - Detritivores

The food chain is further broken down into three tropic levels or categories in the food chain :

- **Autotrophs** – these are the producers, the plants

- **Consumers** – these are the animals who eat the plants (herbivores) or who eat other animals (carnivores). This level is further divided into primary (that's the herbivores), secondary (animals that eat the herbivores) and tertiary (animals that eat other carnivores) consumers. At the very top of the consumer level we have apex predators, animals with no known predators of their own.

- **Detritivores** – these are also known as decomposers. Decomposers eat the remains of other nonliving plants or animals.

Words Worth Knowing

- Food web

A **food web** is similar to a food chain but larger, and combines many food chains into one picture. When you are examining a particular ecosystem it is helpful to use a food web to look at the flow of energy from the abiotic factors through the biotic circle of life and back again. This can tell you a lot about the relationships and interactions in your ecosystem.

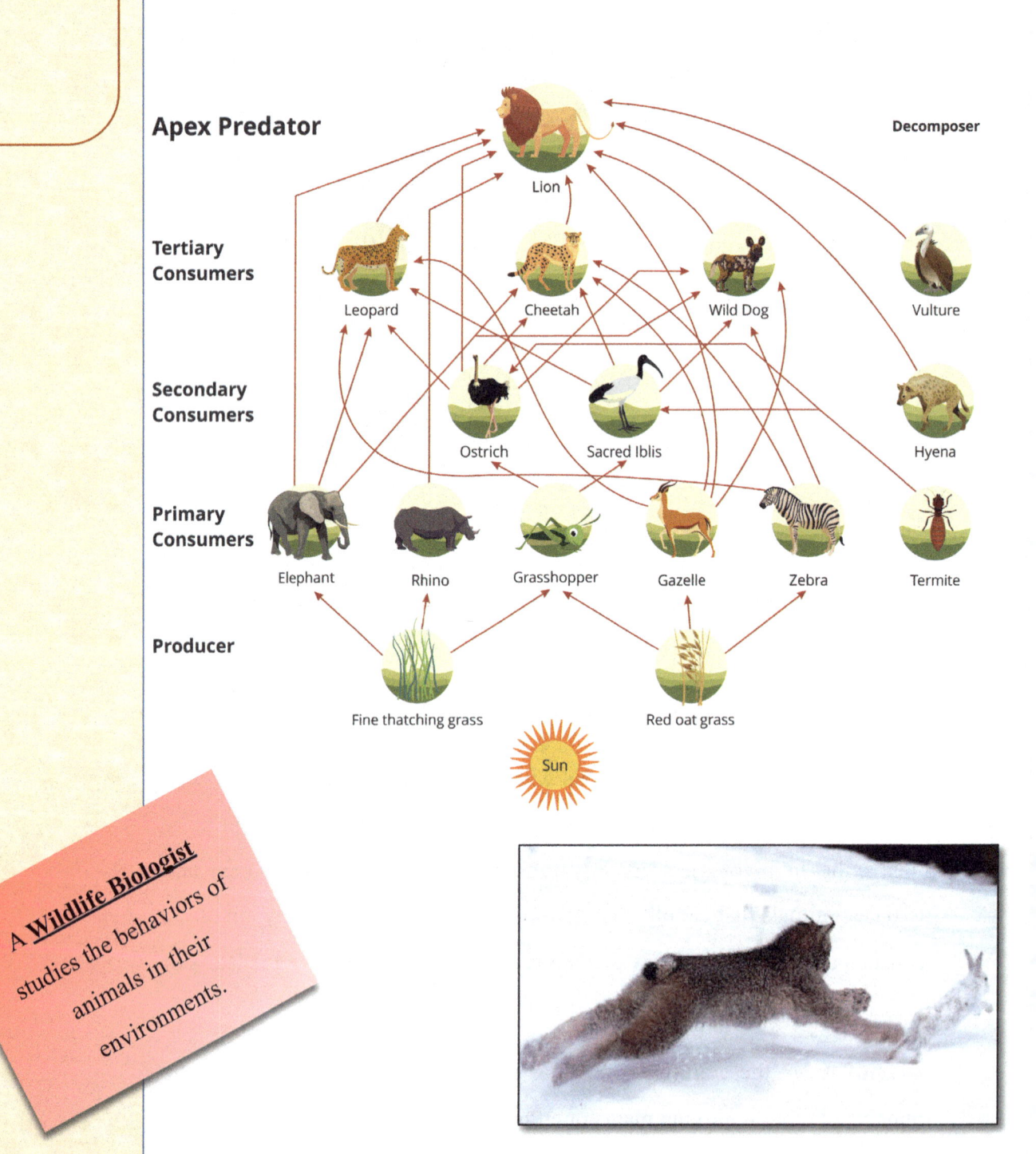

Apex Predator — Lion

Tertiary Consumers — Leopard, Cheetah, Wild Dog

Decomposer — Vulture, Hyena, Termite

Secondary Consumers — Ostrich, Sacred Ibis

Primary Consumers — Elephant, Rhino, Grasshopper, Gazelle, Zebra

Producer — Fine thatching grass, Red oat grass

Sun

A **Wildlife Biologist** studies the behaviors of animals in their environments.

100

Websites and Articles Worth Exploring

- Food Chain
- Food Web: Concept And Applications
- Food Chains & Food Webs
- Food Chains And Food Webs (Wwf)

Videos Worth Watching

- The Food Chain
- Food Chains & Food Webs
- Understanding Ecosystems For Kids: Producers, Consumers, Decomposers - Freeschool
- Food Chains, Food Webs, & Energy Pyramids

Food chains were first introduced in the 10th century by Arab scientist and philosopher **Al-Jahiz.** He wrote about them in his work "**Book of Animals**". Nearly 1000 years later, in **1927**, animal ecologist **Charles Elton** expanded on that idea by first introducing the idea of **food webs.**

Task #9 Your Food Chain and Food Web

☐ Complete **Worksheet 3.7: Food Chains** in your Workbook

☐ **Create a Food Web Diagram for your country.** This can be done using any artistic medium of your choice. Your web must include the following:

- It must include BOTH food chains from worksheet XX
- Either your national Tree or National Flower must be featured in your food web

- Either your National Animal, National Aquatic Animal or National Bird must be featured in your food web
- You must have labels for the following:
  - Producer
  - Primary Consumer
  - Secondary Consumer
  - Tertiary Consumer
  - Detritivore

Extension Activity #4: Ecosystem Diorama

Objective: Demonstrate one ecosystem and food chain found in your country in 3D form

- You may create your diorama either in physical 3D form or digitally using 3D software or a virtual world

- Your diorama must demonstrate one complete food chain from **Worksheet 3.7: Food Chain** to include:
  - Producer
  - Primary Consumer
  - Secondary Consumer
  - Tertiary Consumer
  - Detritivore

- Refer to **Extension Activity #4** in your workbook for additional information or instructions

Chapter 3 Review

The following sections help you review and think about some of the concepts and activities that you performed in this chapter.

Words Worth Knowing Review

The following terms were very important throughout this chapter.

Ecological Organization	Biome	Ecosystem	Biotic
Abiotic	Communities	Population	Individual
Taxonomy	Binomial Nomenclature	National symbols	Food chain
Autotrophs	Consumers	Detritivores	Food Web

❏ Complete the **Chapter 3 Words Worth Knowing Exercises** in the Workbook

For Discussion

In this chapter you learned that an apex predator is at the top of the food chain. Now that humans are in the picture do you think there truly are any apex predators left in your understanding of its definition?

CHAPTER 3 REVIEW

How do you think your arrival and establishment of a country will affect the ecosystem of your new land? What actions might you take as a leader to lessen the impact?

You as a Citizen

As a citizen, what is your responsibility when it comes to your protecting the ecosystem and food webs in your own community?

Your National Library

The following Items should be filed in your national library

- **Guidebook**
    - Biomes Worksheets (3)
    - National Tree, Flower, Land Animal, Aquatic Animal, and Bird Worksheets
    - Food Chain worksheet
    - Food Web
- **Official Documents**
    - Biomes map
- **Promotional material / media**
    - National Symbols Poster (or a picture of it, if larger than will fit)

Chapter 4

Your Previous People

Your Previous People

As you were hiking around your country, checking out the land and the ecosystem you stumbled upon evidence of a previous population. After verifying that whoever lived there before is long gone you have called in some archeologists and anthropologists to help you learn about your country's previous people.

In this chapter you will explore remains of your country's previous people and learn about their civilization and culture. You will be constructing an archaeological report documenting your findings.

Words Worth Knowing

- Anthropology
- Archeology

*An **Anthropologist** studies the customs, cultures and origins of humans.*

*An **Archeologist** studies human history through original documents and artifacts.*

Anthropology vs Archeology

Anthropology is the study of all of the thing that make us human. Through anthropology we learn about how we, as a species, got to where we are today. Studying the past can often help us make decisions about the future.

Archeology is a subset of anthropology that aims to understand the human condition and past cultures through the examination of artifacts and texts. Archeologist uncover and examine the material remains of past civilizations.

Soon you and your team of archeologists and anthropologist will begin digging up the artifacts from your previous people and digging into their culture. Normally, before archaeologists begin an excavation, though, they research the area to better understand the context of the site. Landscape features can help explain where different settlements and artifacts may be found, why people settled in a particular area and how they may have organized their settlement.

Topographic maps are useful tools to understanding an area. Topographic maps show elevation using contour lines. Contour lines can be very close together which identifies a steep, or heavily sloped, area like in mountains. Plains and areas that are flatter have contour lines that are far apart.

Words Worth Knowing

- Topographic maps

Websites and Articles Worth Exploring

- About Archeology

- 10 Archaeological Mysteries That Will Awe You

- What is anthropology

- What is Topography? The Definitive Guide

- Topographic maps: The basics

Videos Worth Watching

Topographic Map

- An introduction to the discipline of Anthropology

- Anthropology 101 | The Science of the Human Species Explained (With Dogs!)

- Archeology – exploring the past with modern technology | DW History Documentary

- Behind the Scenes of the First Excavation of Pompeii in 70 Years

- What is a Contour (Topographic) Map?

- Understanding Topographic Maps

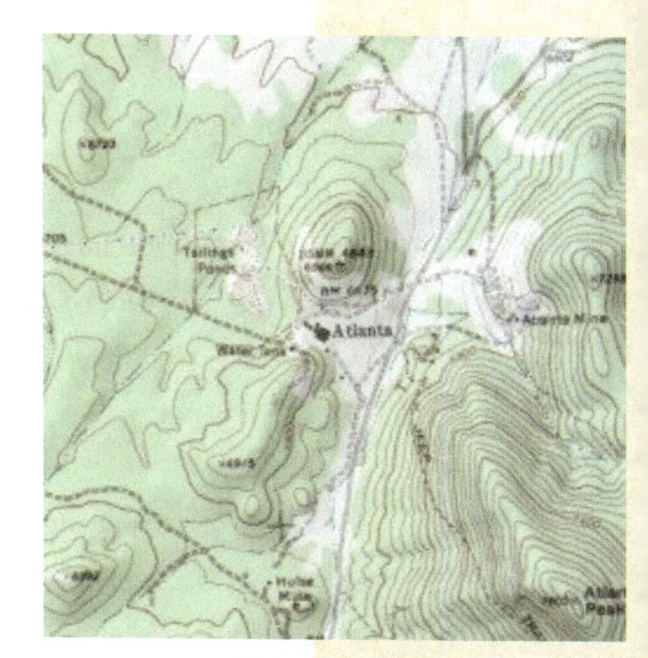

Considerations for your archaeological site

Earlier in this course you made a physical map of your land as a whole. Soon you will be creating a topographical map, which also shows elevation, but using contour lines instead of color. However, instead of showing your entire country, you will be focusing on the specific area(s) where your archaeological discovery takes place. Before you jump into that, though, there are a few considerations for you to think about.

It is believed that the first recorded **archaeological dig** was operated by the last king of Babylon **Nabonidus**. He ruled between 555–539 BCE

- ✓ **Be intentional about the location of your archeological site.** This will be important later when you begin to allocate your land for different purposes

- ✓ **Your archeological site will include locations both inside and outside the remains of a village.** Therefore the area of your site will need to be at least 1 mile by 1 mile to accommodate both locations. However it can be more. You can, however, split your site into more than one location. The total area of ALL the location must equal at least the 1 square mile.

- ✓ **While your site can include areas of water there must be at least some land.** You cannot place your entire site in the middle of a lake or ocean.

- ✓ **Think about the topography of your country.** Where would a past civilization settle? Why would they choose that location over others?

Task #10 Your Topographical Site Map

❑ Create a topographical map of your country using contour lines to show elevation.

- Use the **OUTLINE MAP** you made in Chapter 1 as your guide
- Mark the boundaries of the archaeological site location(s) on your map.
- Make sure to include a legend showing any appropriate symbols or information
- Include a Compass Rose

Words Worth Knowing

- Artifact
- Grid map

Artifact

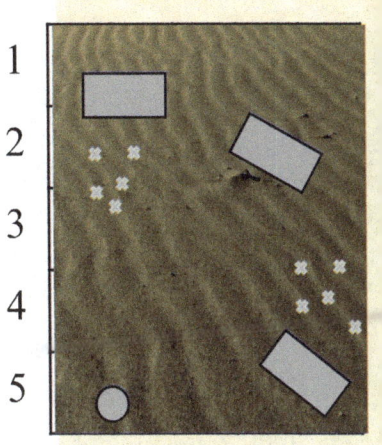

Grid Map

Artifacts

Archeologists learn about the culture of a past people by studying artifacts that are found on the site. An **artifact** is any item that was made or given shape by people. The original location and placement of an artifact can tell a lot about what that artifact might have been used for. This is why archeologists create a grid map of the archaeological site as they work.

A spatial or **grid map** is a square grid that is is laid over the map of the site providing a reference system for marking the location of artifacts. As the team excavates, they record the location of any artifacts they find on the grid and then can refer back to them using coordinates.

Remember, the process of excavation destroys a site completely. If the location of artifacts aren't accurately recorded during excavation it's not like they can be put back where they went. Thus a thorough and accurate grid map is extremely important.

Websites and Articles Worth Exploring

- Mapping the Site
- Establishing a Site Grid

Videos Worth Watching

- Archaeological Methods: Set up a 1m grid square
- HOW TO DIG: Archaeological Excavation Methods
- Field Mapping, GIS, and Continuity - Dig Deeper, Episode 28

A few Considerations for Your Grid Map

Your next task involves creating a grid map of your archaeological dig site. This will include "placing" your discovered artifacts around your site and referring to them in by grid location. But first, a little bit of information that may prove helpful for this task.

✓ If you split your archaeological discovery into multiple areas on the last task, you need to designate one of the areas as the "main" village dig site.

---

*Archaeologists use **geophysical survey** which uses electricity and magnets to find tiny differences in the earth. This creates a map of potential archeological artifacts underneath.*

*Archaeologists also use **drones** to take aerial photographs of potential sites. This can show things like cropmarks and other clues to past human activity. .*

- You will be assigned a data set based on some of the decisions that you made previously in the course. This data set will specify a number of small, medium and large artifacts that your team has "found" at your dig site.
    - Examples of **small artifacts** include: pieces of stone axes or tools, broken pieces of clay pots, arrowheads  
    - Examples of **medium artifacts** include: whole pots or bowls, larger stone tools or weapons; bone tools; ritual items or figurines 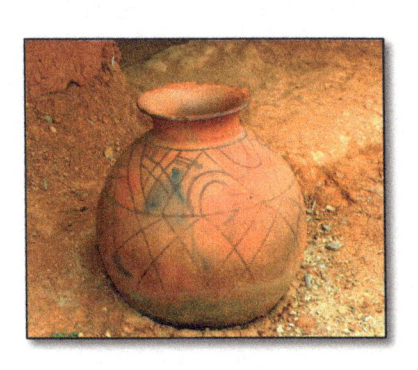 
    - Examples of **large artifacts** include: structures or parts of structures like houses or ritual areas, preserved clothing; boats or crafts (depending on location)

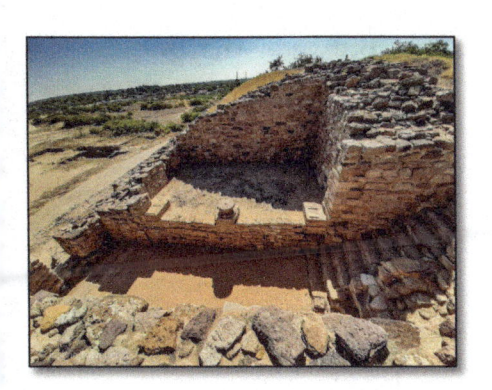

✓ Artifacts can be made from several different materials: bones, clay, stone, metals. You may want to do a little research into the types of indigenous people that may have once inhabited lands with similar characteristics as yours. Also think about the ecosystems near where your village dig site sits. What types and materials of artifacts would logically be in that type of area?

Task #11 Your Grid Map

You have begun to excavate your main village dig site. As you do so it is important to create a record of exactly where you found each of your artifacts. For this task you will be creating a grid map showing the locations of everything that your team has found so far during the dig.

❑ Complete **Worksheet 4.1: You Artifact Data Set** in your Workbook

❑ Refer to Data Set 1 in Appendix V and find the list of artifacts that you found at your main dig site.

❑ Create a Grid map of your dig site.

- Mark the location of each artifact from your data set on your grid map.
- Label the grid lines across the top and down the side
- Include a scale showing the distances between the grid lines

❑ Complete **Worksheet 4.2: Artifact Location Record** in your Workbook

❑ Complete **Worksheet 4.3: Artifact Record** in your Workbook based on one of your medium artifacts from your artifact location record

Extension Activity #5 Examining An Artifact

Objective: Create an artifact that could have been unearthed during your archaeological dig

- Using clay or a similar medium, construct one of the medium sized artifacts that could have been found at your archaeological dig site.

- The artifact should either be the artifact you used on **Worksheet 4.3: Artifact Record** or you will need to complete a new Artifact Record. An extra worksheet has been provided in your workbook for you.

Using Artifacts to Tell a Story about People

Now that you have your artifacts and basic information from your main dig site it's time to start researching and really thinking about what types of people may have once occupied your land. Who were they? How did they live? What was their culture like?

Websites and Articles Worth Exploring

- The Power of Artifacts to Elevate the Story

- Looking at Artifacts, Thinking about History

- Archaeologists find vast network of Amazon villages laid out like the cosmos

Words Worth Knowing

- Culture

Types of Culture

- Archaeologists find vast network of Amazon villages laid out like the cosmos
- Social Life
- Life In Ancient Cities

Videos Worth Watching

- Archaeological Sites: Mapping Alpine Villages
- What Archaeological Sites Used To Actually Look Like
- The Birth of Civilization - The First Farmers (20000 BC to 8800 BC)
- Amazing Viking Age Village

Types of Culture

Culture is the customs, traditions, beliefs and values that a group of people share. Basically it is the TOTAL way of life shared by members of a society. A people's culture includes language, what they do, eat, make, believe, and how they dress. Groups that share these traits are called a cultural group

*Lasting from 6th century BC to the 5th century AD, the **Roman civilization** is thought to be the most powerful ancient culture.*

Culture can be divided into two main categories: **Material culture** and **non-material culture**. Material culture is tangible. It has a physical reality. These are the things that a culture has made. Non-material culture are those things that don't have physical reality. Examples of this include values, beliefs, religion, music, art, government.

Words Worth Knowing

- Material culture
- Non-material culture

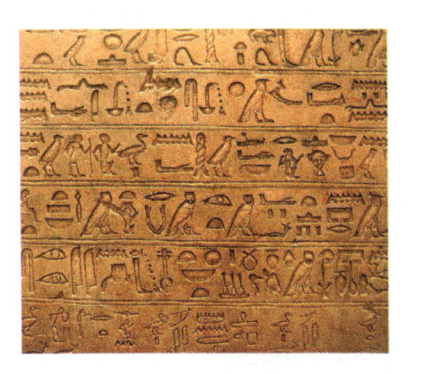

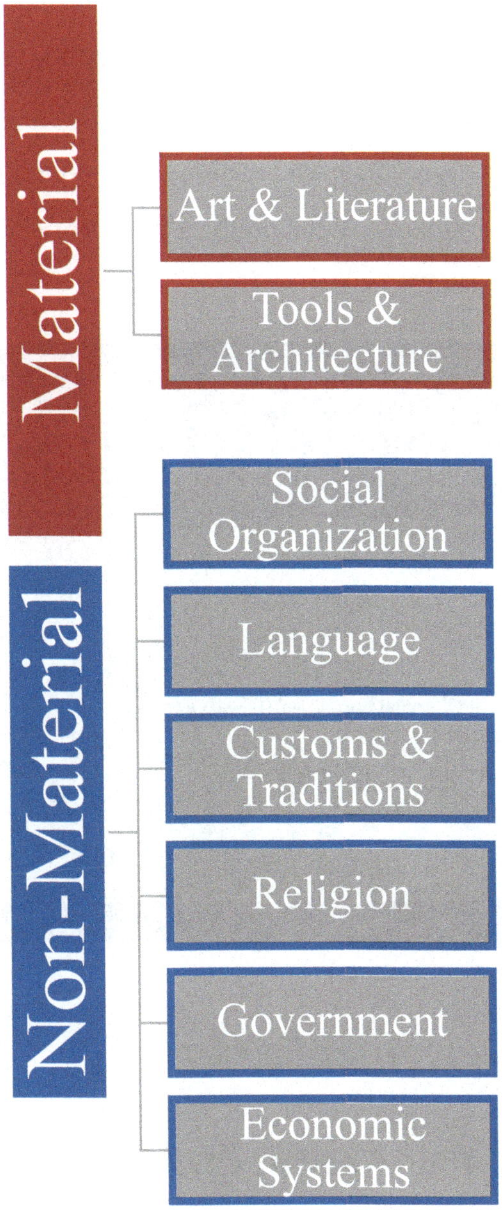

Material
- Art & Literature
- Tools & Architecture

Non-Material
- Social Organization
- Language
- Customs & Traditions
- Religion
- Government
- Economic Systems

Words Worth Knowing

- Cultural Transmission
- Cultural Narratives

Passing on culture

Cultural transmission is the act of passing the culture and cultural elements of a people from one person or group to another. This is how we pass the elements, both material and non-material of our lives on to the generations that come after us. One method of cultural transmission is through the use of cultural narratives. **Cultural narratives** are the stories that make up a culture. These stories help a population assign meaning to its existence, educate its people about the values and norms of the group, and strengthen its shared identity. Cultural narratives take many forms from creation stories to folktales. Think about the folktales in the chart below. What do these stories or tales tell your about the culture that created them?

Types Of Folktales

Myths	Fables	Tall Tales	Legends	Fairy Tales
• Midas Touch • Daedalus • Demeter And Persephone	• Tortoise And The Hare • The Fox And The Crow • The Ant And The Grasshopper • The Lion And The Mouse	• Paul Bunyan • Annie Oakley • Davy Crocket • Pecos Bill	• King Arthur • Robin Hood • Johnny Appleseed • Trojan Horse	• Cinderella • Snow White • Sleeping Beauty • The Little Mermaid

Professional Storytellers tell stories in exchange for food, lodging or money. They were also called *bards*, *skalds* and *troubadours* depending on the country.

Considerations for the Cultural Narratives of Your Ancient People

We are going to talk and explore much more about culture in the next unit, but for now lets take a look at some of the various ways that people pass on their culture and how we can learn about and understand people and cultures that have come before us. Think about the archaeological site that you uncovered on your land.

- ✓ **Consider the answers you listed in Worksheet 4.2: Artifact Location Record and Worksheet 4.3: Artifact Record.** What do your artifacts and their locations tell you about the way your ancient people lived?

- ✓ **Don't forget about the global position of your country as a whole.** What kinds of peoples lived in the surrounding areas? Think about the Mayans of South America or the Vikings of northern Europe or the native people of islands of the Pacific?

- ✓ **Think about the biomes and ecosystems present in your country**. How would ancient people have had to adapt to live in their environment? How might that have shaped the material and non-material culture that made up their society?

☐ **Complete Worksheet 4.4 Decoding your Ancient People in your Workbook**

Extension Activity #6 Model Village

Objective: Represent the culture and architecture of your ancient people by creating a visual representation of the village your country in 3D form

- You may create your diorama either in physical 3D form or digitally using 3D software or a virtual world

- Your model should include several structures as well as a bit of the surrounding area (farmland, forests, etc)

- Your model should illustrate the social structure and housing decisions that you made in **Worksheet 4.4 Decoding your Ancient People**

Composition Activity #2 Ancient Culture's Fable

Create a fable based on the people native to your country. The fable must include the following elements:

- Your fable must be at least one page long

- It must include only animals/plants that are native to your ecosystem

- It must have a clearly spelled out moral or lesson

Task #12: Passing on Ancient Cultures

Choose a method in which your ancient people passed on their culture. If they were literate, perhaps they passed it on through books and writing or hieroglyphics. If not, perhaps they pass it on orally or through art.

❑ Illustrate how your ancient people would have passed on the fable you created in **Composition Activity #2: Ancient Culture's Fable** through either literature, art, oral or creative expression. If you didn't complete the composition activity choose a fable common to an ancient culture and illustrate it in the manner of your people.

- **If you choose literature:**

    - Complete **Worksheet 4.5 Ancient Language Cryptogram** in your Workbook (*Alternately if you choose to have pictures or symbols stand for phonetic sounds or whole words, create a cryptogram-like reference list for your symbols.. Be sure to include a couple of reference phrases or sentences.*)

    - Write the first paragraph of your myth or fable in the written language that you created.

- **If you choose art:**

    - Create a painting, sculpture, or other artwork that represents the fable

- **If you choose oral or creative expression:**

    - Present your fable through either an oral reading or dance presentation.

    - Record your presentation.

Chapter 4 Review

The following sections help you review and think about some of the concepts and activities that you performed in this chapter.

Words Worth Knowing Review

The following terms were very important throughout this chapter.

Anthropology	Archaeology	Topographic map	Artifact
Grid map	Culture	Material culture	Non-material culture
Cultural transmission	Cultural narratives		

❏ **Complete the Chapter 4 Words Worth Knowing Exercises in the Workbook**

For Discussion

This chapter looked at the discovery of ancient people and explored how ancient people may have existed on the land.

Why do you think it is important to learn about people who may have occupied your land before you? How might knowing about your previous populations change some of the decisions you may be faced with making as a leader in your country?

You as a Citizen

Archaeologists and anthropologists are continually finding and exploring sites of ancient civilizations. These may include the ruins of villages or even tombs and burial sites. How do we, as citizens and as a society balance our need to discover and learn from past people with the obligation to be culturally responsible and respectful of these, sometimes sacred sites?

Your National Library

The following Items from this chapter should be filed in your national library

- **Guidebook**
    - Topographical Site Map
    - Grid map

- **Literature / Cultural heritage**
    - Main site artifact list
    - Artifact record
    - Decoding your ancient people
    - Ancient people fable
    - Passing on ancient cultures deliverable

CHAPTER 5

Announcing Your Country

Announcing Your Country

It's all starting to come together now. You have land. You've explored it all and become familiar with its distinctive terrain, ecosystems, and weather. You even discovered some ruins and learned all about the people who lived here long ago. Now its time to announce your budding country to the World so that you can begin to bring new people to your land.

In this final chapter of this unit you will be naming your country, designing its flag and planning its debut on the world stage. You will also complete some unit wrap-up activities.

Words Worth Knowing

- Toponymy

Country Names

The time is finally here. It's time to name your country. **Toponymy** is the study of place names. As with everything else you are discovering, naming a country isn't as simple as just pulling a random word out of a hat. There is a little bit of logic in it. Did you know… Most countries in the world are named after one of four things:

1. **An important person with some connection to the country or its history**
   - Bolivia, named after revolutionary Simon Bolivar.

2. **A directional description of the country**
   - Norway means "North Way" in old Norse.

3. **A tribe or ethnic group**
   - Turkey, named after the Turkish people.

4. **A feature of the land**
   - Niger is named after the Niger River, which flows through several countries in West Africa.

Websites and Articles Worth Exploring

- This Enlightening Map Shows The Literal Meaning Of Every Country's Name

- The Four Things Almost Every Country In The World Is Named After

- The Social And Cultural Value Of Place Names

The **United Sates of America** got its name in 2 ways. "America" is named after the Italian explorer Amerigo Vespucci who introduced the idea that the land Columbus bumped into was actually a separate continent and not India. Then on September 9, 1776, the Second Continental Congress added "**The United States**" to the official title making it formally the "United States of America".

Videos Worth Watching

Words Worth Knowing
- Vexillography
- Vexillologist

- Country Names Explained
- Learn Countries Of The World | All 195 Countries Of The World - World Geography With Pictures

❏ Complete **Worksheet 5.1 What's in a Name?** in your Workbook

Flag Design

Along with a name, your new country will need a flag. A flag will help your country be easily recognizable and give your people (when they get here) a banner to rally behind. The art of flag-designing is called **vexillography** and a person who studies flags is a **vexillologist.**

There are five basic principles to flag design. Keeping these in mind will help your flag be recognized and understood without being overly busy or meaningless. The principles are:

1. **Keep It Simple.** Your flag should be simple enough that a child of your country could draw or color it from memory.

2. **Use Meaningful Symbolism.** Your flag's colors, patterns or images should signify something meaningful about your country or its values

3. **Use 2 or 3 Basic Colors.** Make sure the colors on your flag contrast well and are fairly standard colors. You want the colors of your flag to be able to be colored from a standard box of crayons

4. **No Lettering or Seals.** Never use writing of any kind on your flag.

June 14 is known as **Flag Day**. It was established in 1916 to celebrate the date in 1777 when the United States approved the design for its first national flag.

5. **Be Distinctive or Be Related.** Try not to copy other flags. However, it is acceptable to use similarities to show connections to other countries.

Flag colors are also very important to the identity of a country. In some instance the colors can refer to the colors of nature, such as blue for water or sky and green for grasslands or forest. However there are many other meanings also associated with flag colors.

> The flag of every country in the world is **rectangular** with only 3 exceptions. Switzerland and the Vatican City have square flags. Nepal's flag is made up of 2 triangular shapes.

Websites and Articles Worth Exploring

- Parts Of A Flag
- Good Flag, Bad Flag
- Country Flags Of The World

Videos Worth Watching

- Vexillology - Basic Principles Of Flag Design
- History Of The U.S. Flag, In Paper
- Flag This!

Common Flag Colors and their meanings

	Color	Meaning
	Black	Signifies determination, ethnic heritage, the defeat of enemies, death or mourning
	White	Signifies peace, purity and harmony, and innocence. It can also represent surrender in times of battle.
	Red	Signifies power, revolution, vibrancy, valor, heartiness, courage, determination or war/bloodshed. It can also be represent an alert of danger.
	Blue	Signifies determination, liberation, alertness and good fortune, freedom, vigilance, perseverance, justice, prosperity, peace, and/or patriotism.
	Green	Signifies agricultural influence, prosperity, fertility, youth or hope.
	Yellow (or Gold)	Signifies wealth, energy, the sun, happiness or justice.
	Orange	Signifies courage or sacrifice.

❑ Complete **Worksheet 5.2 Designing your Flag** in your Workbook

National Mottoes

National Mottoes are a few words or short phrases used to represent a country. There are many reasons why countries choose the mottos they do. National mottoes can help describe the intent or motivation of the country. They can bring enthusiasm and a sense of patriotism to the people. Mottoes also

---

Words Worth Knowing

- National Mottos

You often find **national mottoes** included on a country's coat of arms, coins or banknotes.

represent what a nation stands for or strives for. For example the national motto of Greece is **Ελευθερία ή θάνατος** which means "Freedom or Death". Another example of a national motto is the motto of Swaziland which is **Siyinqaba** which means "We are the fortress". The national motto of the United States of America is "In God We Trust".

Since you will soon want to encourage people to come live in your country it is a good idea to create a motto to go along with your new name and flag.

Websites and Articles Worth Exploring

- The (Brief) Stories Behind 15 National Mottoes
- How to Make a Motto

Videos Worth Watching

- How Did "In God We Trust" Become the National Motto? | Billy Graham | American Experience | PBS
- 30 Best NATIONAL MOTTOES from Around the World || Country Motto || national motto

Considerations for creating your country's motto

✓ **Your motto doesn't necessarily need to be witty as long as it is a good reminder of your values or goals for your country**

✓ **Keep your motto short and easy to remember.**

✓ **Make sure your motto strikes the right chord within you.** Does it give you a sense of pride and ownership for your country. Remember: if your motto doesn't inspire you, your country's leader, it's doubtful it will inspire your people.

✓ **Boost your motto's power with a rhyme or alliteration.**

❏ Complete **Worksheet 5.3 Choosing a motto** in your Workbook

Task #13: Announcing Your Country

Great News!! You have claimed your land and you have established some of the basic information about your new country. You have also picked out a name, designed your flag and chosen a motto. Now it is time to formally announce your new country to the world

1. **Create a Press Release introducing your new country to the world.**

    - Use 1 8.5 x 11 sheet of blank paper.

    - Your press release must include:

        - The name of your country,

        - Your flag,

        - Your motto.

    - Your press release must be in color

Chapter 5 Review

The following sections help you review and think about some of the concepts and activities that you performed in this chapter.

Words Worth Knowing Review

The following terms were very important throughout this chapter.

Toponymy	Vexillography	Vexillologist	National Mottoes

❑ Complete the **Chapter 5 Words Worth Knowing Exercises** in the Workbook

For Discussion

How did your knowledge of the physical and ecological makeup play into your decisions as you created your country's name, flag and motto?

You as a Citizen

There is no You as a Citizen for this chapter.

CHAPTER 5 REVIEW

Your National Library

The following Items from this chapter should be filed in your national library

- **Guidebook**
    - What's in a Name
    - Designing your Flag
    - Choosing a Motto

- **Promotional material / media**
    - Press Release

Unit Review

Unit 1: Your Land

Your Land Words Worth Knowing Review

Choose **at least 20** Unit 1 Words Worth Knowing Review words from the tables below. Write a short essay, scene or story that uses each of the words in context. You may include labeled illustrations as well.

- You must include **at least 3 terms from each list**

Chapter 1 Words

Declarative Theory of Statehood	Constitutive Theory of statehood	5 Themes of Geography	Human Geography
Political Geography	Geopolitics	National Library	

Chapter 2 Words

Cartography	General Reference Map	Outline Map	Political Map
Physical map	Topographical map	Thematic map	Navigation charts
Cadastral map	Title	Orientation	Legend
Grid	Scale	Latitude Lines	Equator
Hemisphere	Longitude lines	Prime meridian	Landforms
Natural Resources	Renewable resources	Non-renewable resources	Resource map
Weather	Precipitation	Climate	Risk information
Mitigation			

UNIT 1 REVIEW

Chapter 3 Words

Ecological Organization	Biome	Ecosystem	Biotic
Abiotic	Communities	Population	Individual
Taxonomy	Binomial Nomenclature	National symbols	Food chain
Autotrophs	Consumers	Detritivores	Food Web

Chapter 4 Words

Anthropology	Archaeology	Topographic map	Artifact
Grid map	Culture	Material culture	Non-material culture
Cultural transmission	Cultural narratives		

Chapter 5 Words

Toponymy	Vexillography	Vexillologist	National Mottos

For Discussion

As you worked through the initial development of your country in this unit, what do you think were the most important questions that you asked yourself? How did these questions help you make choices about the location and topography that you chose?

Check Your Understanding

Review Questions

1. Name two types of maps that you created in this unit and discuss what kind of information you get from each type. Why do you think someone would need so many different types of maps as opposed to having all of the information on a single map?

2. Describe the relationship between climate and ecosystems. How did the climate that you chose for your country impact your decisions for the plants and animals that you chose for your national symbols?

3. What is the difference between renewable and non-renewable resources? Why is it important for a country to have both types?

4. What physical features will have the greatest impact on your country's chances for success and why?

5. Based on the what you have defined in your topography and ecosystem, what kind of adaptations or accommodations would people need possess or develop to survive on your country and why?

6. What is the difference between an archaeologist and an anthropologist. As a leader why would it be a good idea to have either or both on your team as you begin to develop and create your new country?

Current Events in Your World:

Disaster Research Project

❑ Investigate 2 different recent (within the last 5 years) natural disasters.

- For each disaster learn about it from at least 2-3 different news sites. These can be magazines, websites, radio, or television.

❑ Prepare a presentation covering and comparing the two disasters. Your presentation should cover the following points:

- When and where did the disaster occurred?
- What kind of impacts did the disaster have on the land?
- What kind of impacts did the disaster have for the people?
- Compare and contrast the governmental and community response for each of the two disasters
- How did the coverage of the disaster by the media affect your opinion of the causes, effects, and/or responses to the disasters?

UNIT 1 REVIEW

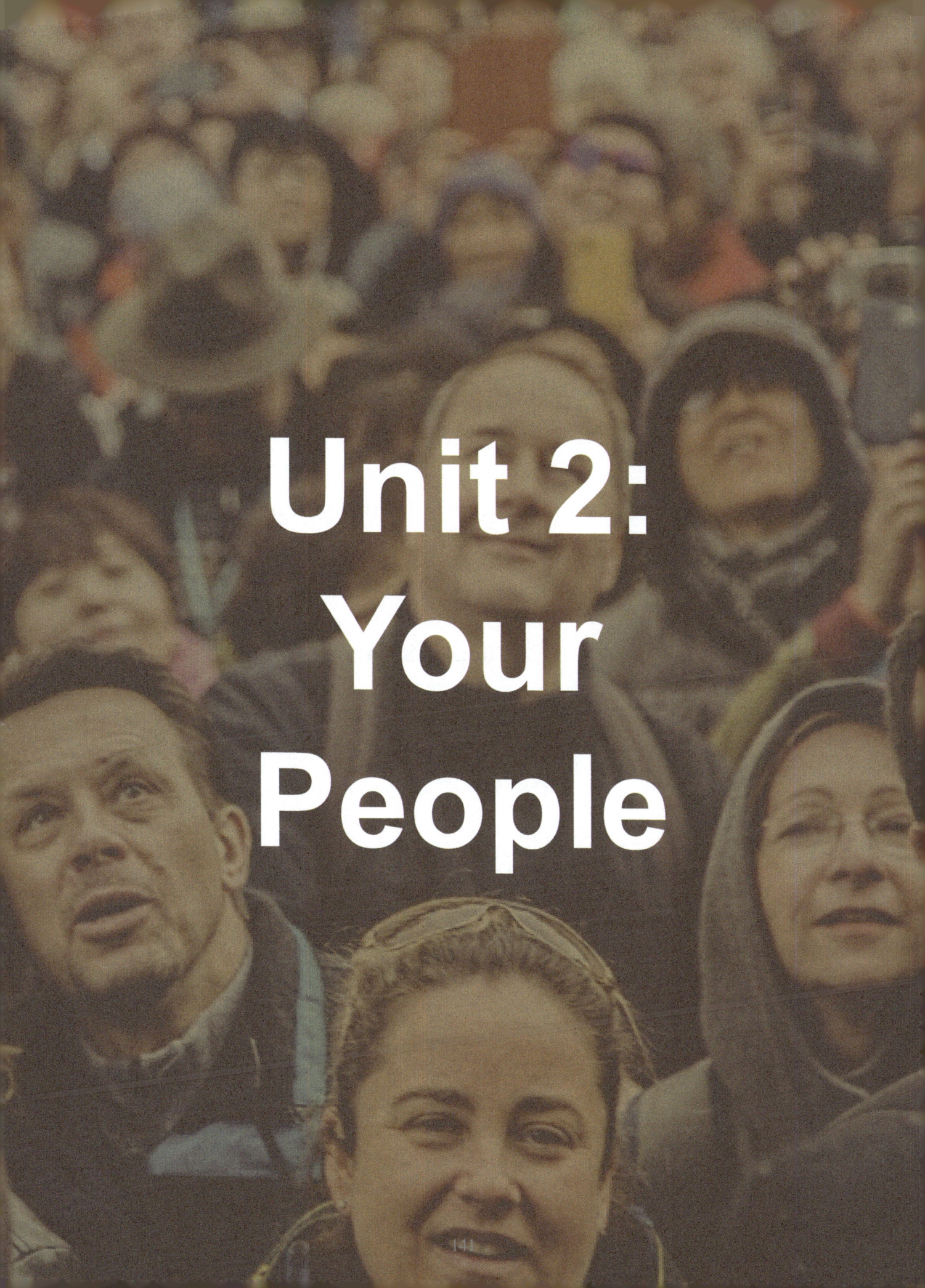

Unit 2: Your People

Contents of Unit 2: Your People

Chapter 6: Growing Your Population

Chapter 7: Establishing Your Unique Culture

Chapter 8: Meeting your People

Unit Overview

Congratulations!!

You have explored your new country, defined your borders and learned all about the trees, grasses, birds, fish and 4-legged beasts that inhabit your lands. You have even completed an archaeological dig and learned about the people that used to live on your land. You have been very busy. Your investors are pleased and ready to help you grow your country.

However, to have a country you need more than just plants and animals. Remember, there are 4 things you need to be a country. The first was land. You've got land. Now its time go get some people.

In Unit 2 you will entice some people to come to your land. You will take a look at land allocation and decide where you will put them all. You will also learn all about the makeup of your population and meet the people who arrive and settle in your country.

Books Worth Reading with this Unit

Below are some suggested books that you can use to compliment the "Your People" unit. For descriptions these books please refer to **Appendix II: Resources for Your People Unit.**

- ## Informational
    - *Open Borders: The Science and Ethics of Immigration* by Bryon Caplain
    - *The Culture Code: An Ingenious Way to Understand Why People Around the World Live and Buy as They Do* by Clotaire Rapaille
    - *Counting Americans: How the US Census Classified the Nation* by Paul Schor
    - *The Sum of the People: How the Census Has Shaped Nations, from the Ancient World to the Modern Age* by Andrew Wilby
    - *The Usborne Encyclopedia of world religions* by Susam Meredith
    - *This Land Is Our Land: A History of American Immigration* by Linda Barrett Osborne

- ## Literature
    - *Gulliver's Travels* by Jonathan Swift
    - *Census: a Novel* by Jessie Ball
    - *The Jungle* by Upton Sinclair
    - *Ink Knows No Borders: Poems Of The Immigrant And Refugee Experience* by Patrice Vecchione

Movie Selections for this Unit

Below are some suggested movies that you can use to compliment the "Your People" unit. For descriptions of each of these movies as well as parental guidance ratings please refer to **Appendix II: Resources for Your People Unit.**

- Live And Become
- Persepolis
- Gangs Of New York (2002)
- A Day Without A Mexican (2004)
- The Joy Luck Club (1993)
- My Big Fat Greek Wedding (2002)

- Minari
- The Namesake (2007)
- An American Tail (1986)
- The Godfather (1972)
- The Kite Runner (2007)
- The Terminal (2004)

Gameschooling Selections for this Unit

Below are some suggested games that you can use to compliment the "Yout People" unit. For descriptions of each of these games please refer to **Appendix II: Resources for Your People Unit.**

- Passport to Culture
- Where in the World

- Ticket to Ride
- Culturetags

Unit 2 Science Exploration Project

Your People Science Exploration: Designing a Sustainable Farm using Agroecology

(To be completed while you work through Chapters 6-8)

As you work through this unit you will learn many things about the people who will come to live in your country. You will make decisions about how to allocate your land and where your people will live. You will begin to consider issues like how will you feed all of your people. How can you accommodate a sudden population without doing irreparable damage to the land itself? How will you maximize the resources that your land has provided to give your people the best quality of life?

Vocabulary

You should understand the following terms for this project:

- Agroecology
- Sustainable agriculture
- Regenerative farming
- Biodiversity

Background

Watch the following videos on Agroecology

- Can we create the "perfect" farm? - Brent Loken

- The 10 Elements Of Agroecology: Enabling Transitions To Sustainable Agriculture And Food Systems

- Agroecology: Farmer's Perspectives

- Regenerative Farming In Kenya | Circular Food Systems In East Africa 1/5

Then explore these Agroecology websites

- What Is Agroecology?

- Agroecology Knowledge Hub

Note: For an optional extension activity – how can you use drone technology to help you monitor the health of your agricultural land?

Designing a Sustainable Farm using Agroecology Overview:

In this project you will be designing a sustainable farm for your people.

- Start with the basics – what kinds of crops will grow best in your country?

- Design a farm using the principles of agroecology and regenerative farming
    - Your farm should produce enough yield to provide food for 150 people.
    - Develop a crop layout and rotation plan that will enable you to meet the supply demand while minimizing the environmental impact to the land

- Choose two crops that you feel will compliment each other when planted together for the best overall maintenance of soil health

Required Materials

3 trays or flower pots	Soil, mimicking the composition of your chosen ecosystem	Water
Seeds or plants of two different varieties	soil testing kits	Soil Moisture Meter

Instructions:

1. Choose one of the ecosystems in your new country to replicate for the location of your farm

2. Research the environment and the specific types of crops that grow best in that environment. What are the agricultural needs and benefits of the environment. What is the soil like? What does each crop need to survive? Which crops may work best together or which crops should be in alternating growing seasons?

3. Design a farm for your country based upon your findings. Your design should include:

    - A map of your country showing the location of the farm
    - A map of the layout of the farm showing the locations of any crops. Also label the location of any buildings or structures
    - An explanation of the planting schedule and techniques

4. Choose two plants from your concept farm to test and decide how long your farming experiment will run.

5. Form a hypothesis regarding the outcome of the health of the soil with the crops planted apart or together

6. Design your experiment.
    - Recreate as close as possible the soil composition of your chosen ecosystem. This includes the level of soil moisture as it would be in that biome.
    - Fill all three pots or containers with the same amount of your soil.
    - Label one pot with crop A, one pot with crop B and one pot A+B

7. Set up your lab notebook and take initial data measurements
    - Test the quality of the soil for a beginning reading.
        - Note: You can get simple kits to test nutrient contents and pH levels from most hardware and gardening stores.
    - Test the level of moisture in the soil with the moisture reader
        - Note: You can get simple moisture readers from most hardware and gardening stores

8. Plant your crops (each one separately and both together) and place together in a sunny location.

9. Take initial plant data measurements including size/height measurement and a general description of each of the plants. Draw illustrations as needed.

10. Make sure to track and measure each time your water your plants. Water them all at the same time with the same amount according to the average rainfall of the location where you would put your farm

11. Keep a log of your observations once a day for the duration of your experiment.
    - Try to do your observations at the same time each day
    - Measure the following data:
        - Soil nutrient level
        - Soil pH
        - Moisture level
        - Plant size/height measurements

12. Make the following calculations based on your data
    - The changes in nutrient level, pH and moisture level of your soil
    - The growth or decline of the plants in the different containers

13. Prepare a final report and/or board on your farm project. The report should not only include the results of your experiment, but also your maps and plans for the farm itself from step 3.
    - Refer to Appendix VI for information on how to construct a project report and board.

CHAPTER 6

Growing Your Population

Growing Your Population

Great news! A year has passed since you first discovered your unclaimed land. And what a year it has been. You have trekked your territory from one end to the other, explored your ecosystem and gotten to know your new country. But now it is time to take your country to the next step.

In this chapter you will look at ways to increase your population. You will invite new people to your country and get them settled in.

Words Worth Knowing

- Allocation
- Scarcity
- Opportunity Cost

A Land Surveyor measures land features based on specific reference points. The surveys he creates often lead to the creation of maps.

Land Allocation

Before you can invite and receive your new population you will need to make some decisions on where you will put these new people. This is where land allocation comes in. **Allocation** is the process by which a government decides how to use a parcel of land. Due to scarcity, it is important to make the best use of the land and resources available in your country.

Scarcity is an economics term that refers to when the demand for a resource is greater than the supply of that resource. Just like the renewable and non-renewable natural resources that you explored in chapter 2, the territory of your land itself is a scarce resource. There is only so much square footage that your are working with. Now depending on the choices you made in designing your initial political map, your land may be comfortably big or quite small, bit the area is still finite. Therefore, you need to carefully consider how you want to use each and every square mile. Designating more land to one area means that there is less land available for another use. This loss of potential gain from other alternatives when one option is chosen is called an **opportunity cost**.

There are many levels and types of land allocation from large scale to small. For this chapter, though you will focus on large scale, general allocation of the land your country occupies.

Choices for Land Allocation

You will have **4 choices** in this course for land allocation. Remember this is not an all or nothing decision. For your country to be successful you need to include include a bit of all four of these choices. However, the ratios and percentages of each how much of each type you allocate are up to you.

Choices for Land Allocation

Urban

Agriculture

Resource Collection

Natural State

Words Worth Knowing

- Urban
- Agriculture

You can designate land for urban areas. Urban lands are your cities. For this course you will assume that any manufacturing activities will take place in urban development areas. If you give the majority of your land allocation to urban development you have to import more food, but you can hold more population and your ability to manufacture goods increases.

You can designate land for agriculture. Agricultural lands are designated for food and textile production. This includes both farming and ranching activities. Remember you will need to feed the population that will soon be arriving. If you give the majority of your land allocation to agriculture you will lack in manufacturing/industrialization capabilities. However you will be able to feed your expanding population with less need to import.

An **Urban Planner** makes plans and policies for the controlled use of urban and rural land, and advises factors affecting land use.

Words Worth Knowing

- Ratio

You can designate land for natural resource collection. This would include mining, forestry, fishing, etc. Remember the natural resource map you made in the last unit? You can only mine for resources on land designated for resource collection. If you give the majority of your land allocation to natural resource collection you will have more resources to export. However, you may have to import food and other goods. Also, depending on the type of resource you're collecting (renewable vs non-renewable), you may risk overcollection of your natural resources and they may run out

Forestry resource collection products make up **47%** of all raw materials used in manufacturing in the United States

You can designate land to be left in the natural state. This would include your national forests and parks. Also, if there are any of your archaeological sites from chapter 4 that your want to preserve they would need to be designated as natural state use. . There is a reason that you mapped the locations of your archaeological sites. If you give the majority of your land to natural state, mother nature and the cultural identity of your people will be happier. However, there may not be enough room to hold your new population when it arrives. There also may not be enough farm and ranchland available to feed them all.

The **Golden Ratio (1:1.618)** is a special mathematical pattern that is often found in nature. It is derived from the Fibonacci Sequence

A Note About Ratios and Percentages

A **ratio** shows the relationship between two or more items. Ratios can either be written as a ratio notation (2:5) or as a fraction (2/5). Ratios are also usually simplified. For example, if you allocated 12,000 square miles of urban development land and 43,000 square miles of agriculture land your ratio of urban to agriculture would be **12:43 urban to agriculture** or **12/43 urban to agriculture**. Don't forget when expressing ratios to label which number goes with which part.

A **percentage** is a figure that shows the proportion of a part to a whole. Percentages are similar to ratios, but instead of comparing two parts of a whole against each other, percentages compare one part against the whole itself. When you want to convert a ratio to a percentage, you must first find the value of the whole. Once simplified, the percentage ratio must always be out of 100. The formula to convert the fractional ratio to a percentage is

$$(\text{Part} \div \text{Whole}) \times 100$$

Graphs help us visualize information quickly and easily. They can reveal trends and comparisons as well as show the relationships between variables and groups of statistical information. A **pie chart** is a special type of graph that shows the relationship of several parts to the whole. To create a pie chart you need to first know the percentages of each of the parts. Then you can create wedges of the pie for each of the relative percentages. Remember: when you add all of the parts together they should equal 100% or one whole.

Words Worth Knowing
- Percentage
- Graphs
- Pie Chart

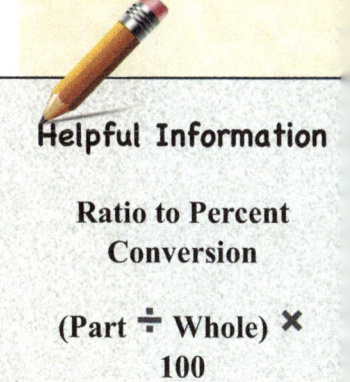

Helpful Information

Ratio to Percent Conversion

$$(\text{Part} \div \text{Whole}) \times 100$$

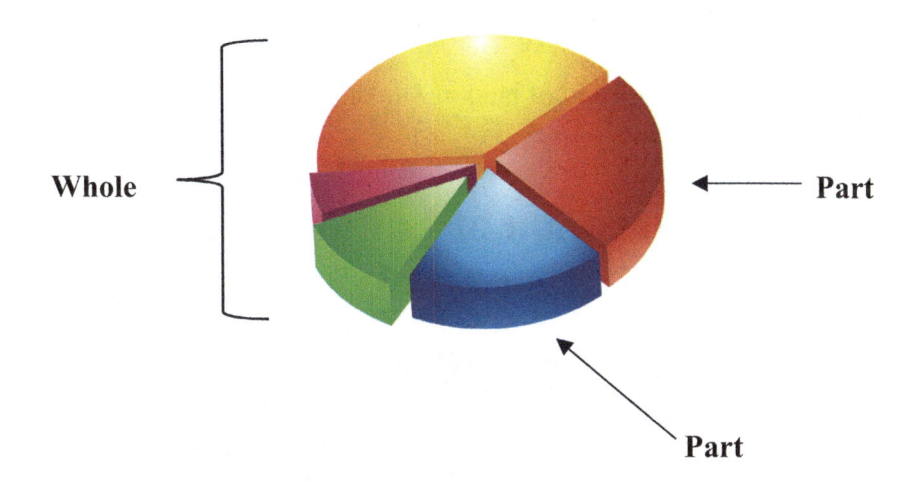

All **graphs** are **charts** but not all **charts** are **graphs**. Charts can also present information in the form of *tables* and *diagrams*.

Consider this example:

Student X creates a country with a total area of 72,000 square miles. She allocates the land in the following ways:

- 36,000 square miles for agriculture

- 20,000 square miles for urban development

- 10,500 square miles for resource collection

- 5,500 square miles for natural state

38% of all the land in the world is used for agriculture while only about 3% of the land is considered urban.

The ratio of urban development to agriculture land would be 20,000 (urban) to 36,000 (agriculture). This would be simplified as low as it could go and could be expressed as 5:9 urban to agriculture or 5/9.

The percent of land allocated to agriculture, remember, is expressed as part of a whole. The total amount of land, remember is 72,000 square miles. Therefore the ratio of agriculture land to the total amount of land is 36,000:72,000. Expressed as a percentage this would be

$$(36,000 \div 72,000) \times 100 = 50 \text{ percent or } 50\%$$

The pie chart showing the allocation of land in Student X's country would look like this:

Allocation of Land in the Country

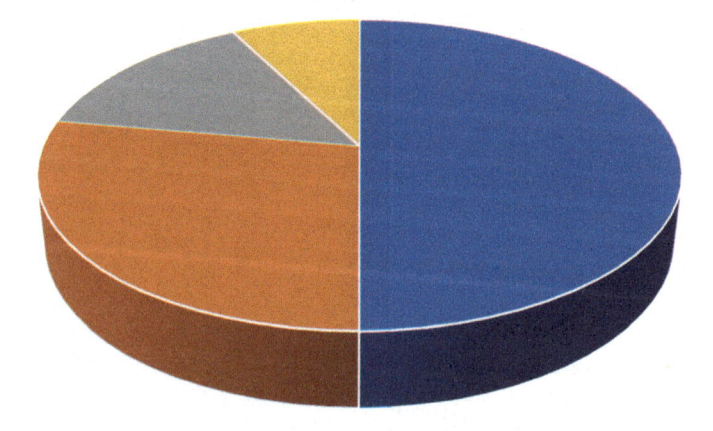

■ Agriculture ■ Urban ■ Resource Collection ■ Natural State

Websites and Articles Worth Exploring

- Ratios

- Ratios and Fractions and How They Relate to Percentage

- Pie Chart

Videos Worth Watching

- Land Use & Characteristics In Urban Areas (9:39)

- Video 14: Land Use - Agriculture

- The Top Agricultural Producing Countries 1960 To 2016

- How Much To Plant Per Person For A Year's Worth Of Food

- What Is Mining - More Science On The Learning Videos Channel

- Sustainable Wood From Sustainable Forests

- Who Owns The "Wilderness"? - Elyse Cox

- What Is A National Park?

- Every Type Of Us National Park, Explained

- Introduction To Ratios | Ratios, Proportions, Units, And Rates | Pre-algebra | Khan Academy

- Math Antics - What Are Percentages?

- Drawing Pie Charts By Hand

- How To Create A Pie Chart In Excel (With Percentages)

Considerations for the Ratios in your Land Allocation

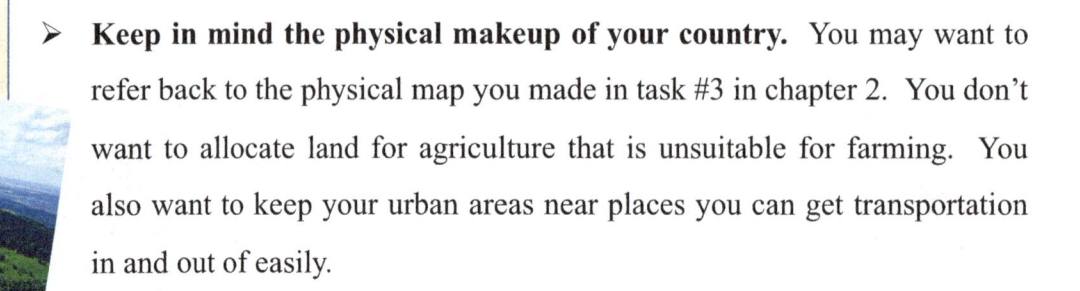

➢ **Keep in mind the physical makeup of your country.** You may want to refer back to the physical map you made in task #3 in chapter 2. You don't want to allocate land for agriculture that is unsuitable for farming. You also want to keep your urban areas near places you can get transportation in and out of easily.

➢ **You may also want to refer back to your natural resource map you created in Task #4 in chapter 2.** As you move through this course and onto the world stage you will want to be able to trade with other countries. To trade you need resources. You want to ensure you allocate sufficient resource collection lands to allow your country to be able to trade to things that your people need.

Land is one of the only resources that has virtually no cost of production.

➢ **Remember what your learned about the ecosystems of your country.** Are there any endangered species living in these areas? Also, as mentioned, you want to preserve at least one of your agricultural sites to feed your new population's growing cultural identity.

➢ **Think about where your people will live.** People can live in small numbers on agricultural and resource collection land. However, the many more people can live in a smaller area on lands designated for urban use. Also, your urban areas will be where your manufacturing is. The type and amount of manufacturing capabilities may play a part in the types of trade deals in your country's future.

- **Remember, land allocation is a very complicated subject.** There are many more different types of land use than we have the time for in this course. These 4 designations are an over-simplification of the allocation land designed to get you thinking about how we use one of our most valuable resources – space.

- Finally, your decision about how you allocate your land will make a difference in who shows up when you advertise for additional population and where you will put them. **This will affect the future economy of your country**.

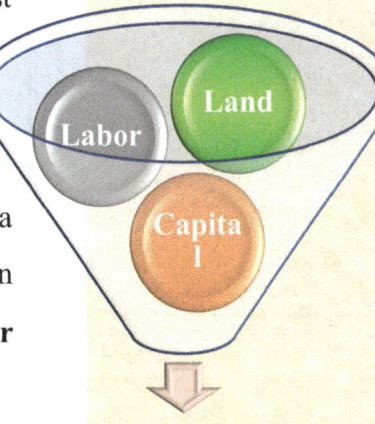

Production

Task #14: Land Allocation

Take a look at the different maps of your land you created in chapter 2. In this task you will decide how much of that land you want to allocate to urban development (cities), agricultural development (farmland/ranchland), natural resource collection activities (logging, mining, fishing, etc.) or keep in its natural state. Keep in mind the different resources and physical makeup of your land.

☐ **Create a land allocation map**

- Use the **OUTLINE MAP** you made in Chapter 2 as your guide
- However, make sure to include enough features from your physical map in chapter 2 for the land allocation map to make sense

---

The three factors of production in economics are Land, Labor and Capital. In this trifecta land is considered to be the "original and inexhaustible gift of nature".

Words Worth Knowing

- Immigrant
- Conquer
- Annex

- Using 4 different colors, shade the areas intended for urban, rural, collection activities, or natural state. **Your entire country should be shaded one of the 4 colors**

- You cannot just evenly distribute the land allocation. You must give at least slight preference to one of the 4 areas

- Make sure to include a compass rose, a scale and a legend.

❑ Complete **Worksheet 6.1 Land Allocation Worksheet** in your Workbook

Attracting a Population

You've decided where you are going to put your new people. Now you just need some people to come over. There are a few ways to attract (or acquire) a population for your new country.

Over **1 million people** immigrate to the United States each year. That's more than the total population of the 5 smallest countries combined.

- **Offer land, or money/jobs**:
  - Many countries offer free land to new immigrants. An **immigrant** is a person who comes to live permanently in a foreign country. This land would usually serve a purpose, like farmland.

Note: Since you do not yet have a large military, you will not be able to exercise the option to conquer or annex a neighbor.

- **Conquer** or **annex** a neighbor:
  - When a country conquers another, it is taken by force. Annexing a country is a more peaceful option of taking control by absorbing the other country's land and population into your country.

- **Welcome refugees**:
    - Refugees are people who are in danger in their own country. By offering them safety, you are saving their lives and gaining a population of your own.

> ### *Words Worth Knowing*
> - Refugees
> - National Debt

Something to think about… However you choose to attract a new population will have a cost. Not just an opportunity cost, but an actual economic cost. Remember, while you have a few backers, you don't have an ongoing basis for funding yet. Thus, whichever choice is made you will be creating **National Debt.** Your national debt is the total amount of money that your country's government has borrowed. Just like in life, at some point your country's debts will have to be dealt with.

Websites and Articles Worth Exploring

- Immigration
- How The United States Immigration System Works
- Conquest
- Annexation
- Refugees (UNHCR)
- Refugees (UN)
- National Debt
- The U.S. National Debt And How It Affects You

Videos Worth Watching

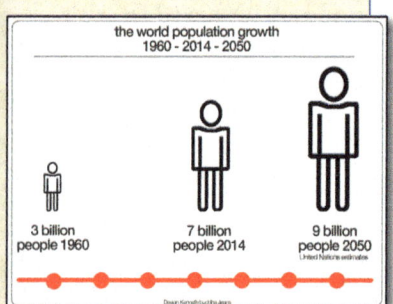

- Why Do People Migrate?! (Push & Pull Factors: Ap Human Geo)
- U.S. Immigration | Let's Talk | NPR
- The Economics Of Immigration: Crash Course Econ #33
- Annexation
- What Does It Mean To Be A Refugee? - Benedetta Berti And Evelien Borgman
- Who Is A Refugee?
- Understand The Immigration System In 8 Minutes
- Understanding The National Debt And Budget Deficit
- Deficits & Debts: Crash Course Economics #9
- National Debt

Around 90% of all the people on earth live in the northern hemisphere.

Task #15: Attracting Your Population

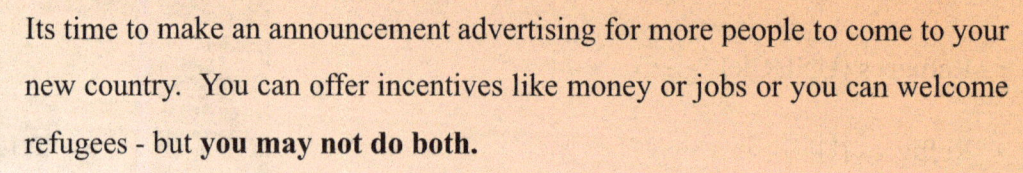

Its time to make an announcement advertising for more people to come to your new country. You can offer incentives like money or jobs or you can welcome refugees - but **you may not do both.**

If you choose to offer land or money:

❑ Create a flyer for your country.
- This flyer should tell what you are offering (land area, dollar amount, job type, etc.) as well as other perks you might offer to your citizens.

- Make your flyer creative- you want as many people to come as possible!
- Don't promise more than you can give, unless you want an immediate revolt. For example, if you don't have any farmland on your map, don't offer that.

If you choose to welcome refugees:

❏ Create an announcement that will let these people know that they are welcome in your country. Again – Make your flyer creative.

- In your announcement, make sure to include what resources (if any) you will offer to refugees. Many of these people are in desperate need of food and healthcare, so these might be good incentives for them to come to your country, in addition to safety from persecution.

More on Charts and Graphs

Pie charts are not the only way to represent your data. Once your people get here you will want to be able to look at and understand just who arrived and what is the new makeup of your population. You will need to be able to think about your people statistically, not just culturally. **Statistics** is the science that deals with the collecting, analyzing, interpreting and presenting of data. As a leader you will use statistics about your land and your people to help you make decisions that will guide the future of your country. Here are a few other types of graphs you will be encountering (and using) shortly.

Words Worth Knowing

- Statistics

A **Statistician** gathers, analyzes, and interprets data to help solve real-world problems.

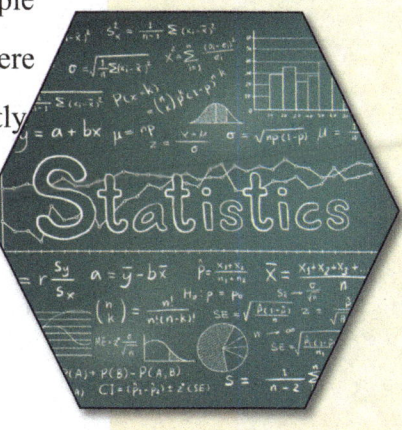

Words Worth Knowing

- Bar graph
- Line graph

Note: Many computer programs such as Microsoft Excel can make the process of making graphs and charts easier.

Bar Graphs

A **bar graph** can also be called a bar chart. This type of graph shows data using bars of different heights. There are four different types of bar graphs: vertical bar graphs, horizontal bar graphs, stacked bar graphs, and grouped bar graphs.

Types of Bar Graphs

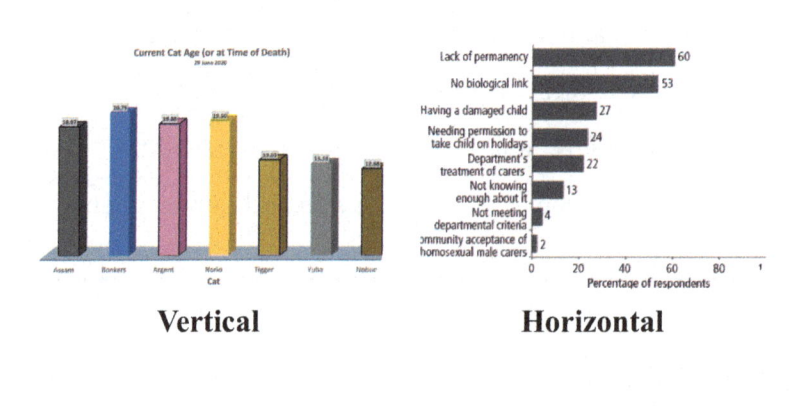

Vertical

Horizontal

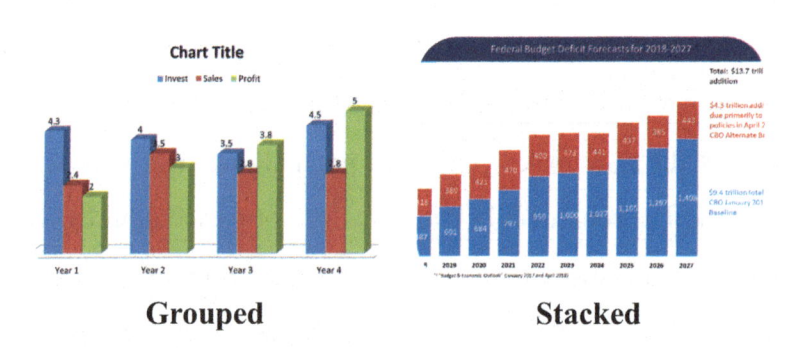

Grouped

Stacked

Line Graphs

A **line graph** is used to show changes in something over a period of time. These can be used to show the changes in just one element with a simple line graph. You can also show the changes in a group of related elements with a compound line graph.

Line Graph

(Graph showing Group 1 and Group 2 across Item 1 to Item 4, values ranging 0 to 6)

Words Worth Knowing

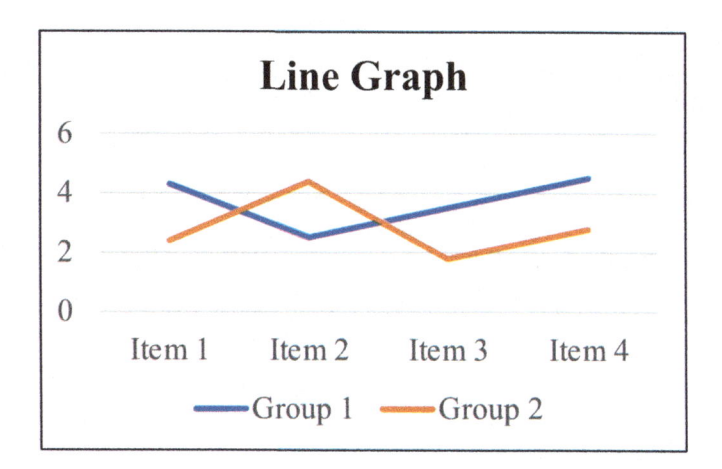

- Pictograph

Pictograph

A **pictograph** (or picture graph) uses symbols and pictures to represent data. It can be a more visually striking way of representing data than using a bar graph. The key to pictographs, though, is to make sure the picture or symbol used matches the type of data you are representing.

Pictograph

Item	Number of Items
Item 1	★ ★ ★
Item 2	★ ★
Item 3	★
Item 4	★ ★ ★ ★

Websites and Articles Worth Exploring

- Using and Handling Data
- Which Type of Chart or Graph is Right for You?

*In a bar, line and pictograph graph, you will find a **horizontal axis (x)** and a **vertical axis (y)**. The horizontal axis contains the line of figures or data arranged along the bottom. The vertical axis contains the figures or data that are arranged from top to bottom at the side of the graph.*

Words Worth Knowing

- Population Density
- Population density map

Videos Worth Watching

- Charts Are Like Pasta - Data Visualization Part 1: Crash Course Statistics #5
- Which Is The Best Chart: Selecting Among 14 Types Of Charts Part I
- Which Is The Best Chart: Selecting Among 14 Types Of Charts Part II

Population Density

Population density refers to the number of people who live in a specific area. It is usually expressed as the number of people per square mile or square kilometer of land area

*The **population density of Earth** as a whole is about 38 people per square mile.*

A **population density map** can show the population density of an area in a couple of different ways. The first is by coloring regions based on the number of people living in each area. Another method is to put a dot on the map for every X number of people. Both methods can give you a quick snapshot into where the majority of people are located in an area.

*Nearly **90%** of Earth's population live on only about **10%** of its land.*

Websites and Articles Worth Exploring

- Population Density

- Understanding Population Density

- Our World in Data: Population Density

- How to Create a Population Density Map

Videos Worth Watching

- Population Density

- Population Densities (AP Human Geography)

- World Population

- Population Density Map Introduction

Asia is the most densely populated continent with nearly 260 people per square mile.

Congratulations!! Your population growth strategy was a success!! Now let's see who has arrived to become your new citizens.

The population density of the United States is 94 people per mi²

Task #16: Receiving your Population

❏ **Refer to the table below to find out which group of immigrants you receive.** This is based on your answers on **Task #14: Land Allocation** and your choices on **Task #15: Attracting a Population**.

| | Attracting a Population Choices ||
Land Allocation Percentages	Offer Land or Money/Jobs	Welcome Refugees
Highest Percentage to Urban Development	Group 1	Group 5
Highest Percentage to Rural Use	Group 2	Group 6
Highest Percentage to Resource Collection	Group 3	Group 7
Highest Percentage to Natural State	Group 4	Group 8

❑ Look up your data set based on your group number in **Appendix V**

❑ Complete **Worksheet 6.2 Analyzing your Population** in your Workbook

❑ Create the following charts on a separate sheet of paper based on your Total Population:

1. A **pictograph** showing the total number of men, women and children in your population

2. A **pie graph** showing the percentage of men to women to children.

3. A **pie graph** showing the national origins of your Total population. Include the percentages for each

4. A **bar graph** showing the respective levels of education. For this question, assume that your indigenous people have no formal education.

5. A **pie graph** showing the percentages of education levels of your population

Helpful Information

Ratio to Percent Conversion

(Part ÷ Whole) × 100

❑ Create a population density map showing the location of your total population.

- Use the **OUTLINE MAP** you made in Chapter 1 as your guide and be sure to have your land allocation map handy for reference

- Decide whether you will use the dot method or the color method

- Place your population on your map, following the following rules
    - Areas designated natural state cannot have people living there.
    - Areas designated agriculture can have no more than 1000 people per square mile
    - Areas designated resource collection can have no more than 2500 people per square mile
    - Areas designated urban should have >2500 people per square mile.

Helpful Information

Population Density

Total population ÷ area of land (in mi^2 or km^2)

Extension Activity #6: Population Density in 3D

Objective: Create a 3D representation of your population density

- Construct a 3 dimensional representation of the population map that you created in task #16

- You may use any medium of your choice either physical such as clay or Lego or virtual in a 3D modeling world or environment.

- Refer to **Extension Activity #5** in your workbook for additional information or instructions

Composition Activity #3 Immigrant Letter Home

Write a letter from the head of one of your new immigrant families to their relatives in their previous country:

Words Worth Knowing

- Census

- Your letter must be at least one page long
- In your letter you must:
    - Describe each member of the family
    - Tell what your immigrant's life was like prior to arriving in your country
    - Describe the events that led to your immigrant arriving in your country
    - Give your immigrant's first impressions upon arriving in your country.

Your Census

Boy, time flies when you're growing a country. 4 years have passed since you first advertised for a new population. Your total Population has grown by 20%. As you near your country's 5th anniversary its time to take stock of your people. You will do this by taking a census.

A **census** is a way of calculating, acquiring and recording information about the members of a given population.

There are 4 essential features of a census:

- Each individual in a census is counted separately.
- The census covers a defined area and includes every person present or living within that area.
- Each item in the census is counted with respect to a defined point of time.
- The census is taken at regular defined intervals, usually every 10 years.

*The first **Federal Population Census** in the United States was taken in 1790, and has been taken every ten years since. It is mandated by **Article I, Section 2 of the Constitution**.*

Sample Data

Because the figures and data in a census can be so huge, it is often easier and preferable to work with sample data. **Sample Data** is a representative subset of your Total Data Set.

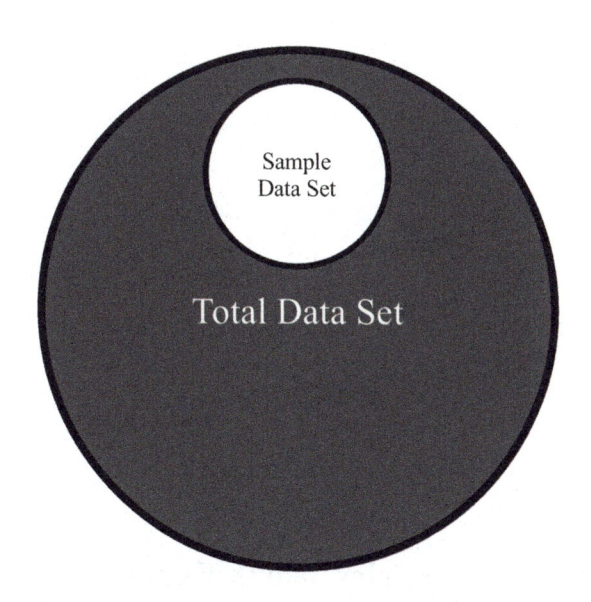

Sample Data Set

Total Data Set

Words Worth Knowing
- Sample Data
- Multiplier

Helpful Information

Total Population

Sample Data ✕ Multiplier

To illustrate how the sample data relates to the total data set, statisticians use a multiplier. A **multiplier** is the number that you would multiply your sample data by to get to your total data figure. It is found by dividing a known total data figure by a known sample data figure.

Statistical inference is when statisticians make inferences about a **population** from **sample data.**

Consider This Example:

Say you want to know how many red cars are in a total set of 30,000 cars. You went and looked at 30 random cars, 7 of which were red.

Helpful Information

Total Population

Sample Data ✖ Multiplier

Taking a census is not a cheap undertaking. It cost nearly $13 billion to carry out the 2010 census in the United States.

*An **Actuary** analyzes statistics to help understand the cost of different changes, risks and uncertainty.*

Your Total data set = 30,000

Your Sample Data set = 30

30,000 / 30 = 1,000

Your Multiplier would be 1000.

The approximate number of red cars in the total data set would be

7 X 1,000 = 7,000

Websites and Articles Worth Exploring

- Census
- What Is A Census And What Kind Of Data Is Collected?
- Census Records
- How To See The Bigger Picture With Data Sampling
- A Peek At Data Sampling Methods
- Population Vs. Sample | Definitions, Differences & Examples

Videos Worth Watching

- What's The U.S. CENSUS + Why's It SO IMPORTANT?

- Why have a Census?

- Introduction to sampling distributions | Sampling distributions | AP Statistics | Khan Academy

- Population vs Sample

- Using a Sample to Make Predictions about a Population

> The **Hollerith Machine**, invented by Herman Hollerith was used to tabulate the 1890 census. This is considered one of the first computational devices.

Task #17: Taking a Census

It's time to take the first census in your country. Remember, in the nearly 5 years since your initial people arrived your population has grown by 20 percent.

❏ Assuming that all groups of your total population increased equally, calculate your new total population. You will need this number to complete the Making Sense of Your Census Worksheet in a moment.

❏ Take a look at the **Worksheet 6.3 Census Form** in your Workbook. Notice the types of questions asked on the form. These will be the questions answered in the data sets you will receive.

❏ See the table below to find out which two census data sets you receive. Each data set contains 10 records. These 20 records will make up a representative sample of your entire new population. The census data sets are located in Appendix 3. You may get the same data set twice. That's okay, just treat them like 2 different sets.

- Your **first data set** will be the Month (#) of your birth. i.e. January = Data set 1, February = Data set 2, etc.

- You **second data set** will be the day of your birth using the below table.

Day of Birth	1-3	4-5	6-8	9-10	11-13	14-15	16-18	18-20	21-23	24-25	26-28	29-31
Data Set #	1	2	3	4	5	6	7	8	9	10	11	12

❑ Complete **Worksheet 6.4 Making Sense of your Census** in your Workbook

❑ **Create the following charts on a separate sheet of paper based on your Total Population:**

1. A pie chart representing the gender makeup of your country
2. A bar chart representing the age makeup of your country.
3. A bar chart representing urban to rural population amounts (hint: look at the amount of land each household occupies)
4. A pie chart representing the work status of your population

Chapter 6 Review

The following sections help you review and think about some of the concepts and activities that you performed in this chapter.

Words Worth Knowing Review

The following terms were very important throughout this chapter.

Allocation	Scarcity	Opportunity Cost	Urban
Agriculture	Ratio	Percentage	Graphs
Pie Chart	Immigrant	Conquer	Annex
Refugees	National Debt	Statistics	Bar graph
Line graph	Pictograph	Population density	Population density map
Census	Sample data	Multiplier	

❏ Complete the **Chapter 6 Words Worth Knowing Exercises** in the Workbook

For Discussion

- How do you think the choices that you made in land allocation as well as your choices for attracting a new population will affect your ability to pay off your initial National Debt?

CHAPTER 6 REVIEW

- How does the education levels of your population affect the standard of living in the different land allocation types? Which type would have the highest need for skilled trade? What about laborers? Where would college degrees be the most useful? Or is the distribution of education levels of your population unrelated to the type of land allocation?

You as a Citizen

- As a citizen what would be some of the first things you would need/want to do upon immigrating to a new country?

- What are some things that you can do in your own community to help newcomers feel more welcome?

Your National Library

The following Items from this chapter should be filed in your national library

- **Guidebook**
    - Making Sense of your Census
    - Graphing your Census Data Graphs

- **Official Documents**
    - Land Allocations and Land Allocation Map
    - Population Density Map
    - Analyzing your Population
    - Graphing your Population Graphs

- **Promotional material / media**

    - Attracting a Population Flyer (*)

    - Announcement for refugees (*)

* Whichever of these you completed in task #15

CHAPTER 6 REVIEW

CHAPTER 7

Crafting your Unique Culture

Crafting Your Unique Culture

Its never easy to blend the old and the new. Over the last several years your new citizens have arrived and your country has grown and flourished. The immigrants from the different originating countries have had to learn to live together in harmony.

Now you are starting to see the fruits of your unique blending of people – a brand new culture all your own. This culture is unique to your country and complete with everything that makes a culture wonderful.

In this chapter you will discover some of the stories and traits that encompass your new, unique culture.

Words Worth Knowing

- Cultural Blending
- Cultural Diffusion

A *Sociologist* studies human behaviors and interactions within societies.

There are five different **types or methods** of cultural diffusion:
- Expansion
- Contagious
- Hierarchical
- Stimulus
- Relocation

A Brief Culture Refresher

Material
- Art & Literature
- Tools & Architecture

Non-Material
- Social Organization
- Language
- Customs & Traditions
- Religion
- Government
- Economic Systems

Remember when we discussed culture back in chapter 4? You learned that culture can be material and non-material. In that chapter, you were concerned with the culture of the ancient people that used to inhabit your land. In this chapter, you will be looking at culture through the lens of the people that currently live in your country. As you work through the chapter think about the different aspects of a country that serve to unite a people. How will your new country go from just groups of immigrants from different places to one people under your flag with a shared cultural identity? And how will this new, shared culture then help you better understand the path forward that you want your country to take and its future?

Cultural Diffusion and Blending

Cultural blending refers to the cultural changes groups experience after interacting with other groups or cultures. A main component of blending is cultural diffusion. **Cultural diffusion** is the spread of cultural beliefs and social activities from one group of people to another. Cultural diffusion can be seen ins several aspects of life:

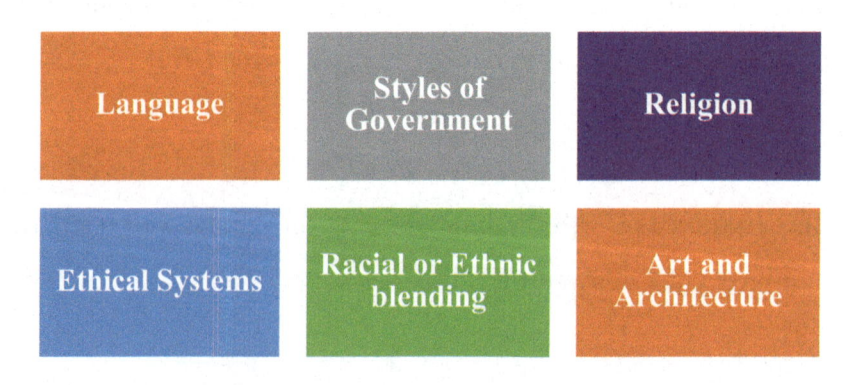

Language	Styles of Government	Religion
Ethical Systems	Racial or Ethnic blending	Art and Architecture

Websites and Articles Worth Exploring

- Cultural Blending Case Study

- What Should Cultures Do To Benefit From Cultural Blending?

- 12 Examples Of Cultural Diffusion

Videos Worth Watching

- What Is Cultural Diffusion?

- Cultural Diffusion Rap

- Effects Of The Diffusion Of Culture [AP Human Geography Unit 3 Topic 8] (3.8)

- A Blending Of Cultures

Words Worth Knowing

- National Landmark

Devils Tower, the first National Landmark, was designated as such by President Theodore Roosevelt on **September 24, 1906.** It is a geological features in the black hills of Wyoming and considered sacred to the Native American tribes in the area.

National Landmarks

Most countries have a natural or historical site that is important to the people who live there. This may be a physical feature such as a waterfall, mountain or tree. This could also be an archaeological site such as some cave paintings or ancient statues. Often there are stories of these landmarks woven into the cultural fabric of the population. These sites usually become national landmarks. A **national landmark** is a historic property that illustrates the heritage or cultural identity of a people. Establishing a national landmark is a great way to honor the blending of your people into a unique culture.

Established on August 25, 1916 by then President Woodrow Wilson, the **National Park Service** manages all national parks, most national monuments, and other natural, historical, and recreational properties within the united states.

Websites and Articles Worth Exploring

- The USA's 21 Most Popular Landmarks and Monuments
- National Historic Landmarks Program
- National Natural Landmarks

Videos Worth Watching

- America's Most Important Landmarks
- National Natural Landmarks Program

Task #18: Your National Landmarks

❏ Design two national landmarks for your country
  - Only one of these may be a result of your archaeological digs or sites. The other must be a physical feature of your land.

❏ Mark the location of the sites on your physical map that you made in task #3. If you no longer have that map, you need to redraw it.

❏ Complete **Worksheet 7.1: National Landmark** in your Workbook for each landmark (there are 2 worksheets provided)

❏ Design a poster, flyer, or pamphlet advertising your national landmarks

Composition Activity #4 Legend of the Landmark

Write a legend from the point of view of your new people and culture about your physical feature national landmark.

- Your legend must illustrate why the site has such meaning to your people.
- Your legend must be at least one page long.

Words Worth Knowing

- Custom
- Tradition

Customs and Traditions

When a blended family joins together, each member brings a bit of their own heritage with them. They do this through the practice of the customs and traditions of their ancestry. A **custom** is a widely accepted way of behaving or doing something that is specific to a particular people, place, or time

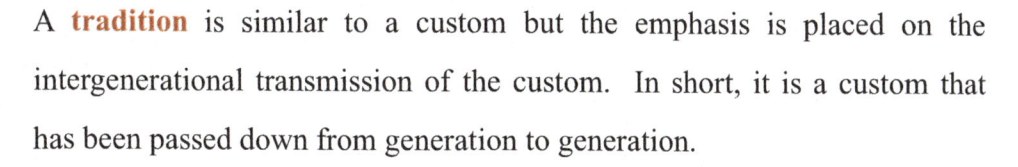

A **tradition** is similar to a custom but the emphasis is placed on the intergenerational transmission of the custom. In short, it is a custom that has been passed down from generation to generation.

The same is true for the people of your country. All of the places from which your new populations came have customs and traditions to which they hold dear. It is through the blending of these traditions that your new cultures can be born and flourish. A unique blended culture will have both old customs picked up from the ancestry of the people as well as new customs and eventually traditions specific to the new culture.

The town of **Bruñol** in Spain holds a traditional **La Tomatina Festival** each year. During the festival, which has been going on since 1945, crowds of people throw tomatoes at each other in a massive food fight.

Websites and Articles Worth Exploring

- American Culture: Traditions And Customs Of The United States
- The Importance Customs In Society
- Difference Between Custom And Tradition

Videos Worth Watching

- Difference Between Customs And Traditions
- 10 Interesting Traditions Around The World That Are Still Practiced Today
- Preserving The Ways - Culture And Traditions

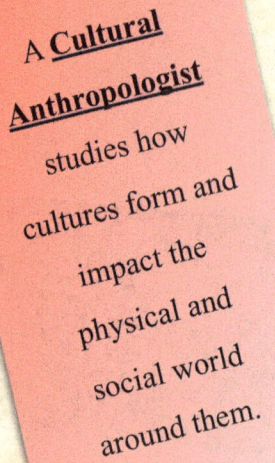

A **Cultural Anthropologist** studies how cultures form and impact the physical and social world around them.

Task #19: Embracing new customs

❑ Research one custom or tradition from each of your immigrant countries (if you have 3 countries you can pick 2 for this task).

❑ Complete **Worksheet 7.2: Immigrant Customs or Traditions** in your Workbook for each country (there are 2 worksheets provided)

❑ Create one custom that is new for your people. This customs should have aspects of the history of all of your peoples original countries.

❑ Complete **Worksheet 7.3: New Custom** in your Workbook

Extension Activity #7: Embracing your Custom

Objective: Demonstrate the observance of your people's new custom or tradition

Demonstrate your new custom in one of the following ways

❑ Create a diorama of a family observing the custom or tradition

❑ Act out the observation of the custom or tradition

❑ Create a comic strip of a family acting out the custom or tradition

Words Worth Knowing
- Social Values
- Social Norms
- Social Role

Social Values

Social values are a set of principles that are generally accepted by a group. These are the communal ideals that are created by the dynamics between the traditions and customs of a people. They form the standard of what is considered good and just by the society. An example of a social value in the United States might be the idea of individuality and independence. These are the abstract ideals of your culture.

Social Norms

Social norms are the unwritten rules, beliefs, attitudes, and behaviors considered acceptable in a particular group or culture. They give people an idea of how to behave in their society. **Social norms are the values of a society made specific.** They are often a function of a person's social role. A **social role** is the part that a person plays in a given social group. Based on the norms of the culture, each community member understands the nature of how to act out their social role. Social norms serve the following major functions:

> The **Social Norms Theory,** first used by Perkins and Berkowitz in 1986, seeks to use and understand environmental and interpersonal influences in order to change individual and social behavior.

Words Worth Knowing

- Folkways
- Mores
- Taboos
- Laws

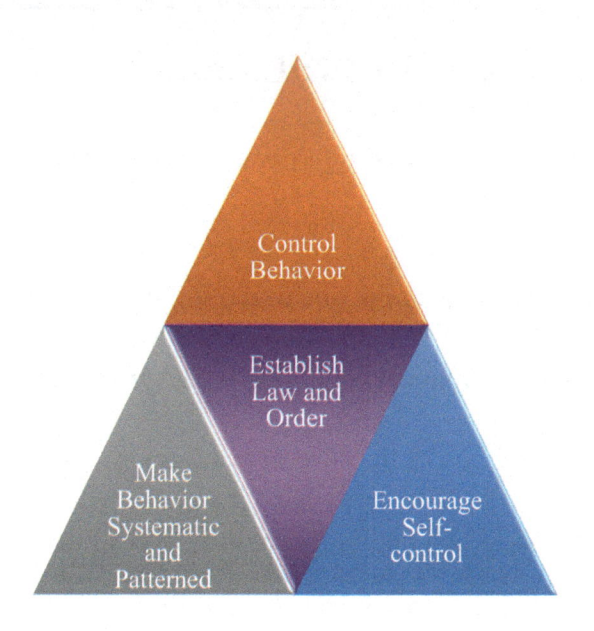

There are four main types of social norms:

Folkways

Folkways stem from and organize the understanding of casual interactions between people. They emerge from repetition and routines. Folkways are considered less socially crucial than mores or taboos.

Mores

Mores structure moral and ethical behavior of a culture. They deal with the difference between right and wrong

Taboos

Taboos are behaviors with strongly negative connotations within a culture. Taboo violations usually result in extreme disgust within the community. Many taboos are codified into laws.

Laws

Laws are social norms that are formally inscribed by local, state or federal government. We will go in great depth into laws in the next unit.

Evolution of a Social Norm

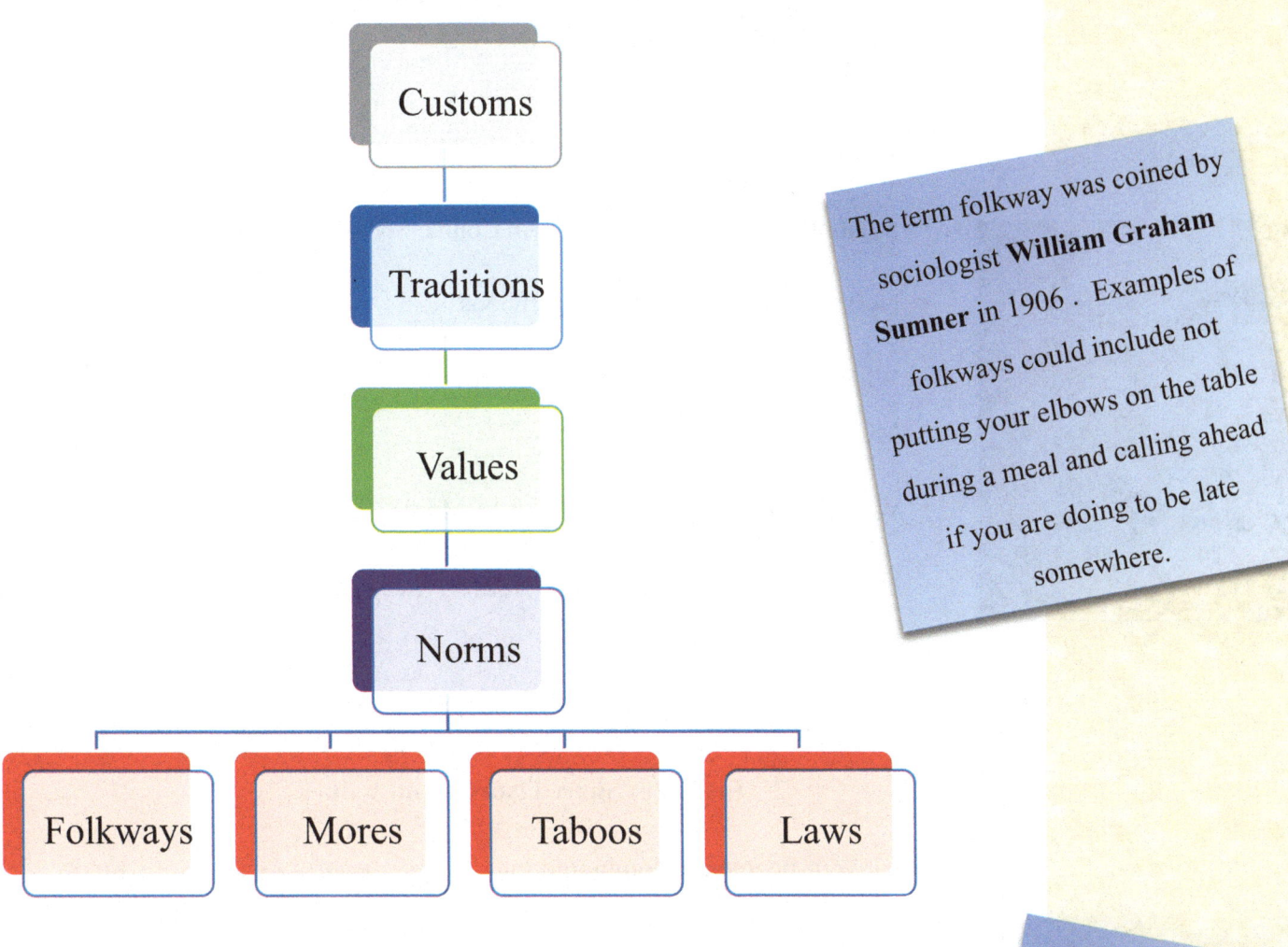

- Customs
- Traditions
- Values
- Norms
  - Folkways
  - Mores
  - Taboos
  - Laws

> The term folkway was coined by sociologist **William Graham Sumner** in 1906. Examples of folkways could include not putting your elbows on the table during a meal and calling ahead if you are doing to be late somewhere.

Websites and Articles Worth Exploring

- Values And Norms Of Society: Conformity, Conflict And Deviation In Norms
- What Is The Difference Between Norms And Values
- Why Do We Follow The Behavior Of Others?
- The 4 Types Of Norms (Folkways, Mores, Taboos & Laws)
- Folkways, Mores, Taboos, And Laws

> The idea that it is not acceptable or mainstream to abuse hard drugs such as heroin and cocaine is an example of **cultural mores.** Another example might be the expectation of timely repayment of one's debts.

Videos Worth Watching

- 1 Culture Norms And Values
- Symbols, Values & Norms: Crash Course Sociology #10
- Norms, Mores, Folkways And Taboos
- What Is Normal? Exploring Folkways, Mores, And Taboos | Behavior | MCAT | Khan Academy
- What Are Social Norms? (Folkways, Mores, Taboos)
- How Do Perceptions Of Social Norms Affect Our Behavior? Featuring Dr. Margaret Tankard

*Many anthropologists believe that there are a few **universal taboos**. Among them are incest, cannibalism, and killing one's parents.*

Task #20: Shared Norms and Values

Now that your people are combining into a single beautiful culture, it's time to look at a few of the values and norms that they share.

☐ Complete **Worksheet 7.4: Shared Values** in your Workbook

☐ Complete **Worksheet 7.5: Shared Mores** in your Workbook

☐ Complete **Worksheet 7.6: Shared Folkways** in your Workbook

☐ Complete **Worksheet 7.7: Shared Taboos** in your Workbook

☐ Create a presentation describing the new shared culture of your people.

In your presentation your should discuss at least:
- One custom
- One Value
- One More
- One Folkway
- One Taboo.

Chapter 7 Review

The following sections help you review and think about some of the concepts and activities that you performed in this chapter.

Words Worth Knowing Review

The following terms were very important throughout this chapter.

Cultural Blending	Cultural Diffusion	National Landmark	Custom
Tradition	Social Values	Social Norms	Social Role
Folkways	Mores	Taboos	Laws

❑ Complete the **Chapter 7 Words Worth Knowing Exercises** in the Workbook

For Discussion

- How do you think the rapid rise in technology has affected culture and how people perceive culture?

- Is it possible to promote inclusiveness while still honoring cultural heritage and ancestry? Why or why not?

CHAPTER 7 REVIEW

You as a Citizen

- What are some folkways, mores and taboos in your own culture? Do you feel they are still relevant to the times?

Your National Library

The following Items from this chapter should be filed in your national library

- **Guidebook**
    - National Landmark map and worksheets

- **Official Documents**
    - Shared Values
    - Shared Mores
    - Shared Folkways
    - Shared Taboos

- **Literature / Cultural Heritage**
    - Legend of the Landmark
    - Immigrant customs or traditions
    - New Custom

- **Promotional Material / Media**
    - National Landmark poster, flyer or pamphlet (or a picture of it)
    - Shared culture presentation

Chapter 8

Meeting Your People

Meeting Your People

Congratulations! Your country is flourishing! Your budding land still stands as beautiful as ever and the people are happy. They are bonding together as one new, unique culture.

The time has arrived. Your county's anniversary is only a few months away. You have decided that you would like to hold and anniversary celebration, set your first national holiday and address your citizens.

In this final chapter of this unit you will be planning your country's national holiday. In addition, you will be crafting and delivering a keynote address for your National Holiday Festival. You will also complete some unit wrap-up activities.

Words Worth Knowing

- National Holiday
- Federal Holiday

In 1870 Congress granted the **first four federally designated national holidays** in the United States by granting paid time off to federal workers for New Year's Day, Independence Day, Thanksgiving Day, and Christmas Day

National Holidays

A **national holiday** is a holiday celebrated throughout the country. They are generally intended to allow people to celebrate or commemorate an event of cultural, historical or religious significance. National holidays are often established or sanctified through the country's government. A holiday that has been officially declared a public holiday by the government is called a **federal holiday**. Often federal and many other workers get the day off in observance of their country's national holiday. The United States currently has 12 permanent federal holidays. While these holidays technically are only applicable to federal workers, they are observed by the population as a whole as national holidays and thus opportunities for national remembrance or celebration. These 12 holidays are:

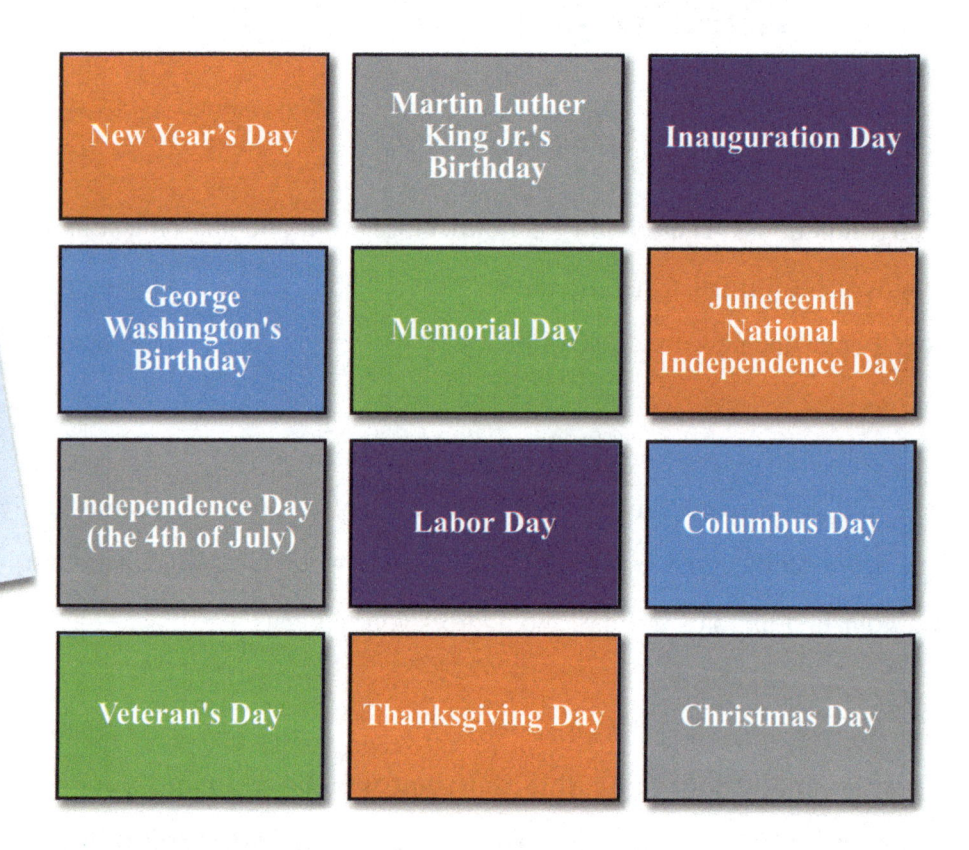

New Year's Day	Martin Luther King Jr.'s Birthday	Inauguration Day
George Washington's Birthday	Memorial Day	Juneteenth National Independence Day
Independence Day (the 4th of July)	Labor Day	Columbus Day
Veteran's Day	Thanksgiving Day	Christmas Day

You don't have a full formal government yet (so far its just you leading your people) so you can't technically legislate a federal holiday, however, as the de facto leader you will soon be calling for your country's first national holiday.

Websites and Articles Worth Exploring

- Federal Holidays: Evolution And Current Practices
- The History And Timeline Of Federal Holidays In The US
- How To Create Holidays And National Days

*Iran celebrates **27 National Holidays** a year – the most of any country in the world.*

Videos Worth Watching

- The Importance Of National Holidays
- History Of Holidays In The United States
- My Own National Holiday
- Most Celebrated Holiday Comparison

*An **Event Planner** helps plan and run events, and ensures everything related to the event is taken care of, from conception to preparations to day-of logistics.*

Task #21: Your National Holiday

You have decided that your country needs a holiday to bring the people together in celebration. In addition, your people want a grand festival to mark the occasion. This festival should highlight the cultures of all your people.

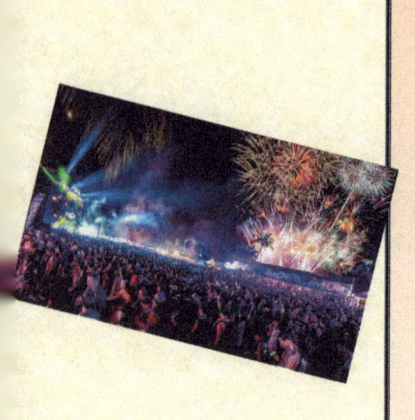

❏ Choose a holiday for your country. This must be unique to your country (it can't be Christmas, Valentines Day or any currently recognized holidays)

❏ Complete **Worksheet 8.1: National Holiday** in your Workbook

❏ Design a grand celebration in your major city to commemorate the holiday.

1. **Choose a date, name and theme for the celebration.** This will be your first national holiday.

2. **Create a schedule of events.** Your schedule should include at least 3-5 activities highlighting the many cultures and traditions that make your country uniquely yours. Include a short description with each activity.

3. **Design a flyer announcing the celebration.** Your flyer must include:

    1. Name, date and location of festival
    2. This year's theme
    3. Any activities

A **journalist** investigates, collects, and presents information as a news story.

Composition Activity #5: Newspaper Article about the Festival

Write a newspaper article reporting on the festival from the viewpoint of a reporter in your country.

- The article should be at least 500 words long and highlight at least one of the major activities of the festival

- The article should include quotes and statements from at least 3 fictional residents of your country

Public Speeches

Public speaking, also called oration, is the art of presenting before a live audience. The art of public speaking is one of the most important soft skills a leader can possess. Good public speaking allows you to form connections, influence decisions, and motivate change in the world around you. There are many types of speeches but here are four major types of public speeches that you, as a leader, may be called to give.

> **Words Worth Knowing**
> - Public Speaking
> - Ceremonial speeches
> - Demonstrative speeches

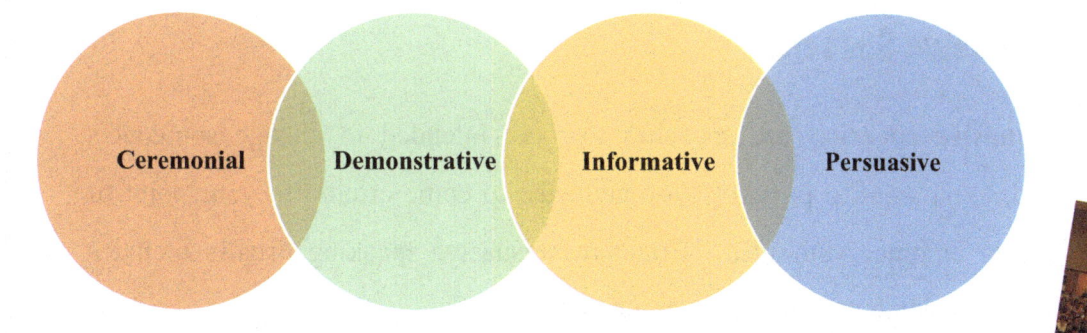

- Ceremonial
- Demonstrative
- Informative
- Persuasive

Ceremonial Speeches

Ceremonial speeches include speeches given on a special occasion. These types of speeches are usually brief and focused on the occasion itself. Ceremonial speeches should include personal touches or anecdotes to help build a connection to your audience.

Demonstrative Speeches

Demonstrative speeches are speeches that explain how to do something. Perhaps you have a new process or technology that you need your people to understand or use. This is where you would use demonstrative speaking skills. In a demonstrative speech you should strive to be as clear as possible, avoiding the use of slang or jargon. Demonstrative speeches also often employ the use of visual aids to help with understanding.

> **Glossophobia**, the fear of public speaking, affects nearly 75% of people. That's more than any other phobia.

Words Worth Knowing
- Informative speeches
- Persuasive Speeches

Informative Speeches

Informative speeches are speeches that are intended to merely give information about something. The ability to be able to clearly give information is a crucial skill for leaders. Informative speaking skills help build credibility and facilitate conversations with both your common people and other leaders.

Persuasive Speeches

Persuasive speeches are speeches that are intended to change someone's mind. You want to persuade you audience to come around to your point of view or embrace your idea. Effective persuasive speaking usually includes emotional elements and strong language

*The Guinness World record for the **longest speech** is held by Dr. Ajay Shesh. He spoke about how to be a better person for **over 60 hours.***

Websites and Articles Worth Exploring

- Public Speaking
- The 4 Types Of Public Speaking
- The Top 10 Famous Speeches That Stand the Test of Time

*A **Speech Writer** creates and edits speeches for other people to give.*

Videos Worth Watching

- What is Public Speaking?
- What is Public Speaking? | Factors of Public Speaking

- Public Speaking 8: Types of Speeches

- 4 types of Audience for your Speech

Task #22: Your Festival Address

- ❏ Create and deliver a 10 minute presentation about your country.

    - Your speech should include:

        - A brief history of the founding of your land

        - Some highlights about what makes the land and ecosystem special

        - Some highlights about what makes the people special

        - Some thoughts and hopes for the future of your country

    - Your speech should include aspects of both ceremonial speeches and informative speeches.

The **State of the Union Address** is an annual speech given by the president to Congress that discusses major issues facing America and its people.

Chapter 8 Review

CHAPTER 8 REVIEW

The following sections help you review and think about some of the concepts and activities that you performed in this chapter.

Words Worth Knowing Review

The following terms were very important throughout this chapter.

National Holiday	Federal Holiday	Public Speaking	Ceremonial Speeches
Demonstrative speeches	Informative speeches	Persuasive speeches	

❑ Complete the **Chapter 8 Words Worth Knowing Exercises** in the Workbook

For Discussion

- How do regular speeches by leaders help foster a sense of belonging and trust among the population?

You as a Citizen

- What was the last speech you heard that you either enjoyed or were motivated by? What was it about the speech that made it successful?

Your National Library

The following Items from this chapter should be filed in your national library

- **Guidebook**
    - National Holiday Information

- **Promotional Material / Media**
    - National Holiday Festival Schedule
    - Flyer announcing the Festival
    - Newspaper Article about the Festival
    - Festival Address

CHAPTER 8 REVIEW

Unit Review

Unit 2: Your People

Your People Words Worth Knowing Review

Choose **at least 20** Unit 2 Words Worth Knowing Review words from the tables below. Write a short essay, scene or story that uses each of the words in context. You may include labeled illustrations as well.

- You must include **at least 3 terms from each list**

Chapter 6 Words

Allocation	Scarcity	Opportunity Cost	Urban development
Agriculture	Ratio	Percentage	Graphs
Pie Chart	Immigration	Conquer	Annex
Refugees	National Debt	Statistics	Bar graph
Line graph	Pictograph	Population density	Population density map
Census	Sample data	Multiplier	

Chapter 7 Words

Cultural Blending	Cultural Diffusion	National Landmark	Custom
Tradition	Social Values	Social Norms	Social Role
Folkways	Mores	Taboos	Laws

UNIT 2 REVIEW

Chapter 8 Words

National Holiday	Federal Holiday	Public Speaking	Ceremonial Speeches
Demonstrative speeches	Informative speeches	Persuasive speeches	

For Discussion

Based on what you've learned and done in this unit, as a leader, how do you take your people from feeling like immigrants to feeling like citizens? How do you build that sense of community and pride that a country needs to grow and flourish?

Check Your Understanding

Review Questions

1. What is the difference between population distribution and population density? Why is it useful to know both of these statistics?

2. What 3 additional questions would you add to your next census and why?

3. How do the different types of folktales contribute to the passing on of norms and values?

UNIT 2 REVIEW

4. In the next unit we will begin creating a government. How can understanding the culture of a population help with the task of creating a government?

5. How do you think the data derived from your census will help as you begin drafting social policy later in the course?

Current Events in Your World:

Famous Speech Research

❏ Look up and watch or read transcripts from two world leaders.

❏ Prepare a presentation comparing and contrasting the two speeches. The presentation should include
- Some background information about each of the leaders and the occasion and nature of the speech.
- A short summary of each speech
- A determination of which speech you feel was more successful in achieving its purpose and why.

Unit 3: Your Government

Contents of Unit 3: Your Government

Chapter 9: Creating your Government

Chapter 10: Creating Your Economic System

Chapter 11: Fleshing Out your Governmental Infrastructures

Chapter 12: Making Hard Choices with your Priorities

Unit Overview

You have a country… almost.

Without a government in place, society quickly descends into anarchy and ruin. It becomes easy prey for outside forces and will soon be lost to conquest or annexation. That is not the future you want for your people. To avoid that, its time to design the system of bones that hold up your country – your government!

In Unit 3 you will learn what it takes to create and sustain a functioning government. You will choose a government type, create and enforce laws, understand your economy and flesh out your infrastructure

Books Worth Reading with this Unit

Below are some suggested books that you can use to compliment the "Your Government" unit. For descriptions these books please refer to **Appendix III: Resources for Your Government Unit.**

➢ Informational

- *Words That Built a Nation: Voices of Democracy That Have Shaped America's History* by Marilyn Miller

- *A Kid's Guide to America's Bill of Rights: Curfews, Censorship, and the 100-Pound Giant* by Kathleen Krull

- *Constitution Translated for Kids* by Cathy Travis

- *Understanding Politics & Government* by Alex Frith

- *This Is Our Constitution: What It Is and Why It Matters* by Khizr Khan

- *The Cabinet: George Washington and the Creation of an American Institution* by Lindsay Chervinsky

➢ Literature

- *1984* by Orson Wells

- *Animal Farm* by George Orwell

- *Brave New World* by Aldous Huxley

- *Fahrenheit 451* by Ray Bradbury

Movie Selections for this Unit

Below are some suggested movies that you can use to compliment the "Your Government" unit. For descriptions of each of these movies as well as parental guidance ratings please refer to **Appendix III: Resources for Your Government Unit.**

- Bridge Of Spies (2015)
- Milk (2008)
- The Supreme Court Miniseries (2007)
- Lincoln (2012)
- Wag The Dog (1997)
- Mr. Smith Goes To Washington (1939)
- Thank You For Smoking (2005)

- Dave (1993)
- All The President's Men (1976)
- 12 Angry Men (1957)
- Selma (2014)
- Vice (2018)
- The Butler (2013)
- The Wolf Of Wall Street (2013)

Gameschooling Selections for this Unit

Below are some suggested games that you can use to compliment the "Your Government" unit. For descriptions of each of these games please refer to **Appendix III: Resources for Your Government Unit.**

- Constitution Quest
- Campaign for President
- Diplomacy
- Chronology
- Corinth

- Election Night
- Professor Noggins Presidents of the United States
- Monopoly House Divided
- Race to the White House
- Mystic Market

Unit 3 Science Exploration Project

Your Government Science Exploration: Evaluating Renewable and Non-renewable Fuels

(To be completed while you work through Chapters 9-12)

Over the course of this unit you will be creating your government and building your economy. One major factor of a sustainable economy is the transportation and movement of raw materials and finished goods. To do this you need power. But which form of power is most effective and sustainable for your people?

In the first unit you learned about the difference between renewable and non-renewable resources. In the last unit you allocated some of your land to collecting some of your country's resources. Now let's put your knowledge to the test.

Vocabulary

Your should understand the following terms for this project:

- Renewable resource

- Non-renewable resource

- Fossil Fuel

- Biofuel

- Agrofuel

Background

Watch the following videos on different types of fuels

- Fossil Fuels For Kids | Learn All About Fossil Fuels, What They Are, And Where They Come From

- Will Fossil Fuels Run Out? | Earth Lab

- 300 Years Of FOSSIL FUELS In 300 Seconds

- What Are Biofuels And Where Are They Going?

- Biofuel Instead Of Coal And Oil - How Promising Are These Renewable Resources? | DW Documentary

- Ethics Of Biofuels-corn As Agrofuel?

- How To Make Biodiesel At Home In 5 Minutes..! | Biofuel From Used Vegetable Oil / Cooking Oil

Then explore these websites

- Fossil Fuels

- Fossil

- Biofuel Basics

- Biofuels Explained

- Agrofuels

- Energy

Evaluating Renewable and Non-renewable fuels Overview:

In this project you will be discovering whether a renewable fuel produces the same level of energy as an equivalent amount of nonrenewable fuel.

Required Materials

Ring Stand	Soda Can, Cleaned With The Top Removed (Or Glass Beaker)	Tray Or Dish To Contain Fire	Cotton Balls
Medicine Dropper	Lighter	Scientific Thermometer	Timer
Measuring Cup	Water	Baking Soda (To Extinguish Fires If Needed)	Moist Paper Towels
Vegetable Oil	Olive Oil	Motor Oil	

Instructions:

1. Research the following:
    - What kinds of fossil fuels are available in your country? How much does it cost to harvest each resource?
    - What are your country's agriculture resources? How much corn or other oil making vegetable does it take to make one cup of vegetable oil

2. Form a hypothesis regarding which type of fuel will increase the temperature of the water by the greatest amount.

3. Design your experiment.

    - Using your materials, design an experiment that tests how much the same amount of oil, applied to a cotton ball and lit on fire, will increase the temperature of a set amount of water.

4. Set up your lab notebook and take initial data measurements

    - Measure out the same amount of water into your can or beaker for each test

        - Take the initial temperature of the water prior to each test

    - Measure out the same amount of oil onto each cotton ball

5. Perform the experiment keeping a log of your observations

    - Place the container of water on the ring stand and place the oil soaked cotton ball in the tray beneath the container

    - Light the cotton ball on fire and start the timer.

    - Measure the temperature of the water at 1 minute increments until the cotton ball burns out.

6. Repeat the test twice with each type of oil

    - Vegetable oil

    - Olive oil

    - Motor oil

7. Make the following calculations based on your data

    - The total change of the water temperature over the duration of the test

    - The percent change over time per minute

8. Prepare a final report and/or board on your fuel project. The report should not only include the results of your experiment, but also the application your results could have on energy use and consumption

   • Refer to Appendix VI for information on how to construct a project report and board.

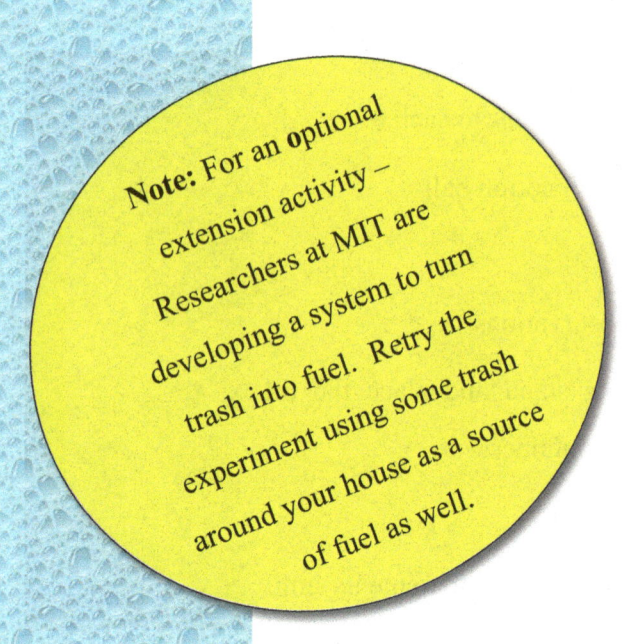

Note: For an optional extension activity – Researchers at MIT are developing a system to turn trash into fuel. Retry the experiment using some trash around your house as a source of fuel as well.

Chapter 9

Creating Your Government

Creating Your Government

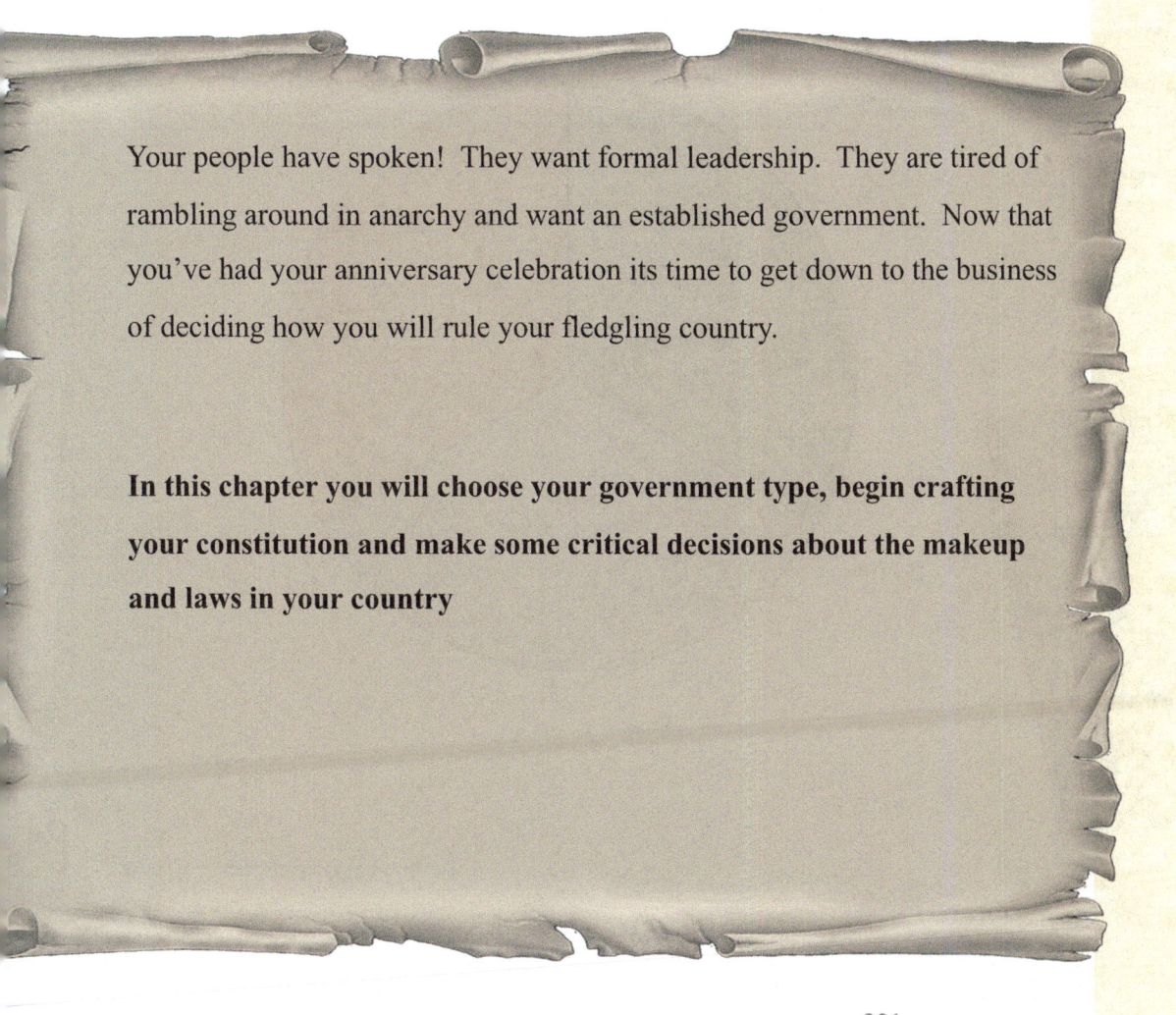

Your people have spoken! They want formal leadership. They are tired of rambling around in anarchy and want an established government. Now that you've had your anniversary celebration its time to get down to the business of deciding how you will rule your fledgling country.

In this chapter you will choose your government type, begin crafting your constitution and make some critical decisions about the makeup and laws in your country

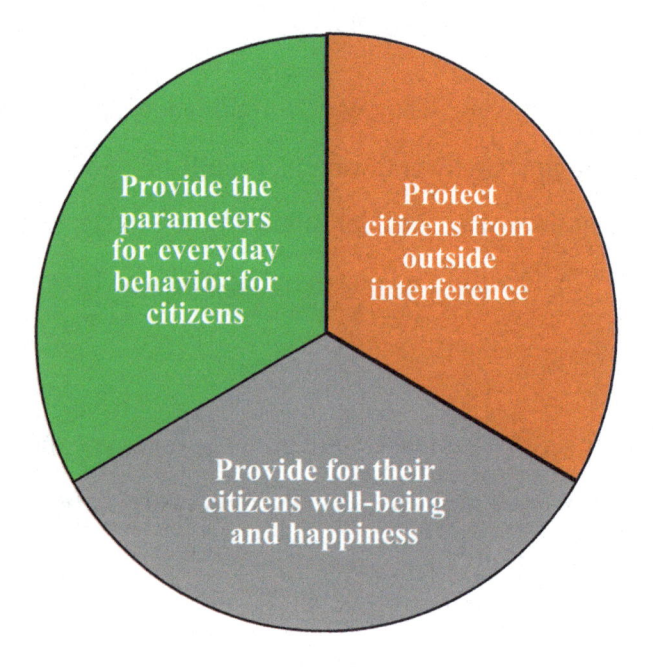

Words Worth Knowing

- Government

What is a Government

You are now ready to start formally creating a government for your people. But what does that mean? What exactly is a government and what does it do? How do you know what kind of government you want or need based on the desires of your people and your priorities and values for your country?

A **government** is the system of rules and the people who make and administer them. Governments provide three essential functions in a country:

1. They provide the parameters for everyday behavior for citizens,

2. They protect citizens from outside interference, and

3. They often provide for their citizens well-being and happiness.

The first known government ever was established in Sumeria in the 4th century BCE. The Sumerians at the time were ruled by a priestly governor or king.

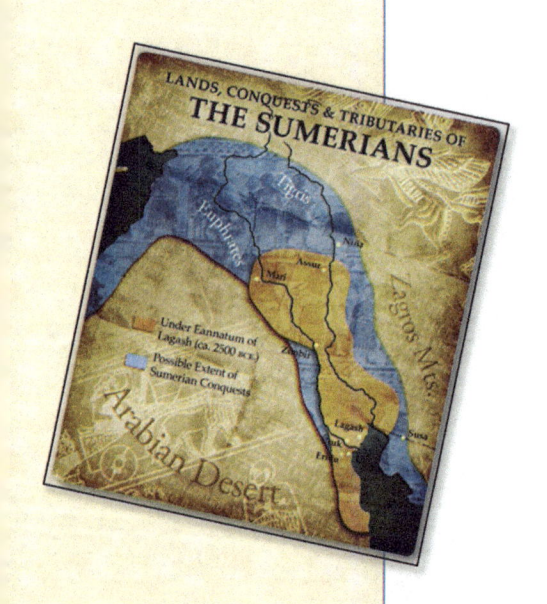

Governments don't operate just because they want to. There are a few requirements to cement the legitimacy of a country's ruling power.

Words Worth Knowing

- Sovereignty
- Legitimacy
- Jurisdiction

First, the country that a government rules must have sovereignty. **Sovereignty** is the power that a country or group has to govern itself or another country or state. The country must be free from the external control of another country.

Second, a government must have legitimacy. **Legitimacy** means that the people accept the government's power. This doesn't mean that the people have to like it, they must only accept that the government is the ruling power.

Third, the government must have jurisdiction over the land which it claims to govern. **Jurisdiction** means that the ruling body has the right or power to exercise authority over a territory or people. Anybody can call themselves a government. However, without sovereignty, legitimacy and jurisdiction in place, their words are meaningless.

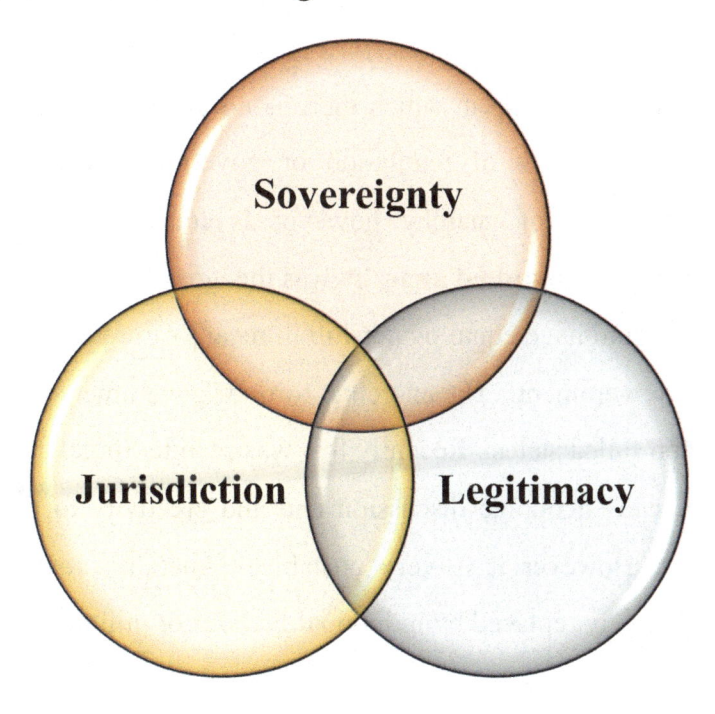

Words Worth Knowing

- Anarchy
- Communal anarchy

Types of Government

There are four major types of governments. These are based on who is ruling the country. The types range from being ruled by no one, to being ruled by one person or a few people, to being ruled by many people or everyone. Each has factors that make it enviable in certain circumstances.

Anarchy
- Ruled by None

Autocracy
- Ruled by One

Aristocracy
- Ruled by a Select Few

Democracy
- Ruled by Many

Karl Marx (1818-1883) was a German philosopher who cowrote the **Communist Manifesto**. This book is one of the cornerstones of Marxism and was a call for workers of the world to unite.

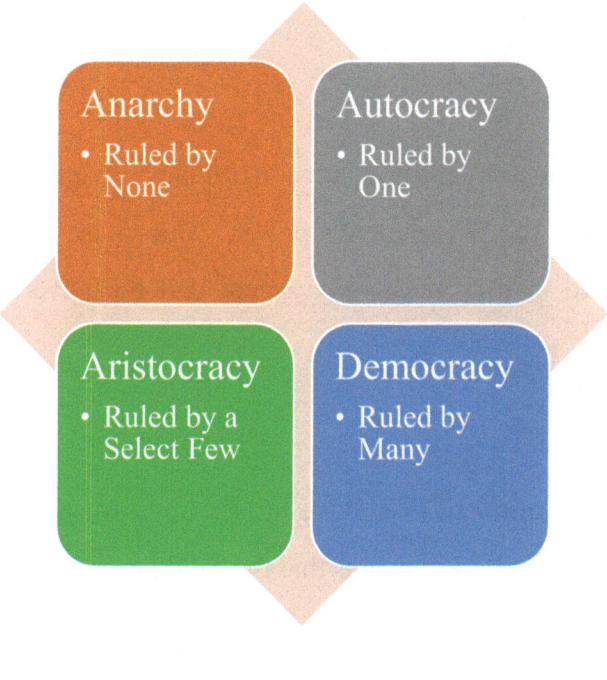

Anarchy

Anarchy is a system or group in which there is no governing authority. It is the belief that every form of regulation or government is immoral and unnecessary. The basis of anarchy however is founded in the idea of Communal Anarchy. **Communal anarchy** was the goal of Karl Marx in which citizens would have equal ownership in means of production and have no need to form government. The anarchist form of government can be found in revolutions and failed states. Recently this was seen in Somalia from 1991-2006. Anarchy can encourage discussion and add creativity to the problem solving process. However it is very unstable. Anarchy creates a power vacuum which is easily replaced by individual factions or military regimes.

Pros and Cons of Anarchies

Pros	Cons
➢ Individual has absolute liberty ➢ It adds creativity to problem-solving process ➢ Encourages discussion to find common ground ➢ Allows for individual privacy	➢ Unsustainable ➢ Creates power vacuum and is commonly replaced by a military regime ➢ Creates followers, allowing factions to move into power

Words Worth Knowing

- Autocracy
- Monarchy
- Absolute Monarchy

Autocracy

Autocracy is a system of government where one person has all of the power. This is one of the oldest types of government. There are two main types of autocracies: a Monarchy and a Dictatorship.

Monarchy

A **monarchy** is a type of autocracy where one individual maintains executive authority via divine right (king, queen, czar, emperor, etc.) Usually one has to be born into the ruling family to rise to power.. Historically, rule in a monarchy has primarily been passed via patrilineal inheritance, through the father's bloodline. There are two main types of monarchies.

In an **absolute monarchy** the monarch has unlimited power to rule his or her people and the right to rule comes directly from God and the dominant religious institution. Some examples of absolute monarchies include:

The record for the longest reigning monarch in history goes to King Louis XIV or France. He ruled for 72 years, from 1643-1715.

A **Monarch** is a sovereign head of state in an Autocracy form of government. They have also been known as Kings, Queens or Emperors.

Words Worth Knowing

- Constitutional Monarchy

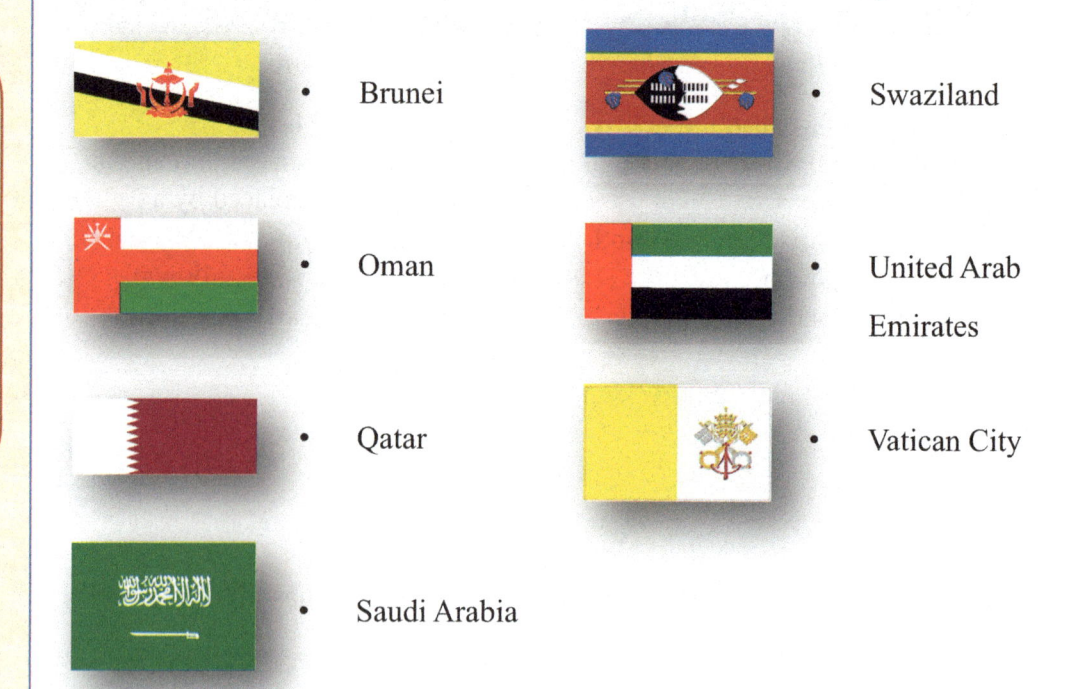

- Brunei
- Oman
- Qatar
- Saudi Arabia
- Swaziland
- United Arab Emirates
- Vatican City

A **constitutional monarchy** is one where monarchs share governmental powers with elected legislatures and often serve as ceremonial executive leaders of their government. In a constitutional monarchy the right to rule comes partially from inheritance and partially from the will of the people. Examples of constitutional monarchies include:

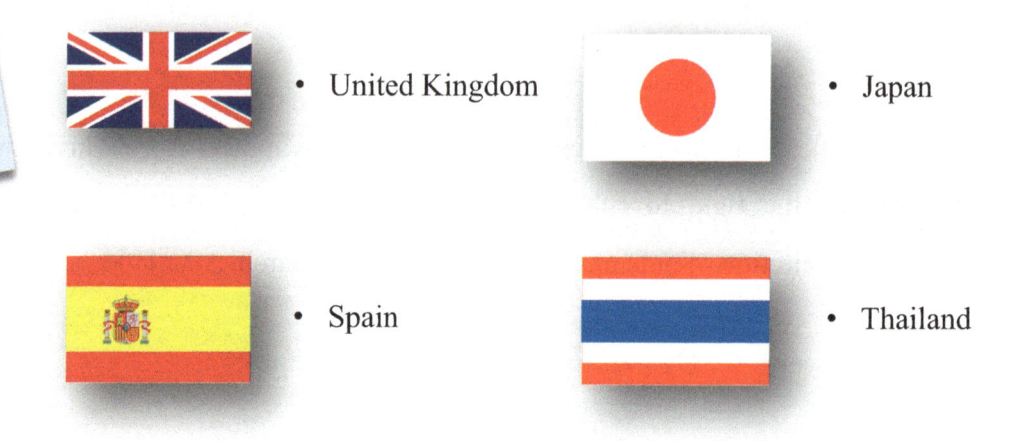

A **Parliament** is a legislative body of government. The main difference between a parliament and a congress is that a congress is separate from the executive branch while a parliament is part of it.

- United Kingdom
- Spain
- Japan
- Thailand

Pros and Cons of Monarchies

Pros	Cons
➢ Swift action	➢ People do not have the right to remove a monarch.
➢ Low cost to upkeep	
➢ Long-term consistency/ relationships	➢ Monarchs may not care about certain people (especially the poor)

Words Worth Knowing

- Dictatorship

Dictatorship

A **dictatorship** is a type of autocracy where one individual maintains executive authority via force. In a dictatorship the government controls all social, political and economic aspects of life within their country. This control is often gained and maintained through establishing a police state with martial law and controlled borders. Any opposition to the rules or laws established is quickly silenced. Examples of dictatorships include:

Cuba 　　　　　　　　　Algeria 　　　　　　　　　North Korea

Pros and Cons of Dictatorships

Pros	Cons
➢ Very quick to act	➢ Lots of oppression, and dictators often do not care what the people want/think.
➢ An effective dictator can get a lot done.	
➢ No disagreement in government	➢ People often have little to no freedom
	➢ Dictator can become too powerful and out of control

A **Dictator** is a person with absolute control over a country, usually obtained and maintained by force.

Words Worth Knowing

- Oligarchy
- Theocracy
- Plutocracy
- Aristocracy

Oligarchy

An **oligarchy** is a system of government where the country is ruled by a very small group of people who make decisions for everybody. This small group holds power due to influence gained by their social status, military position, wealth or even education. Some examples of countries with oligarchies include:

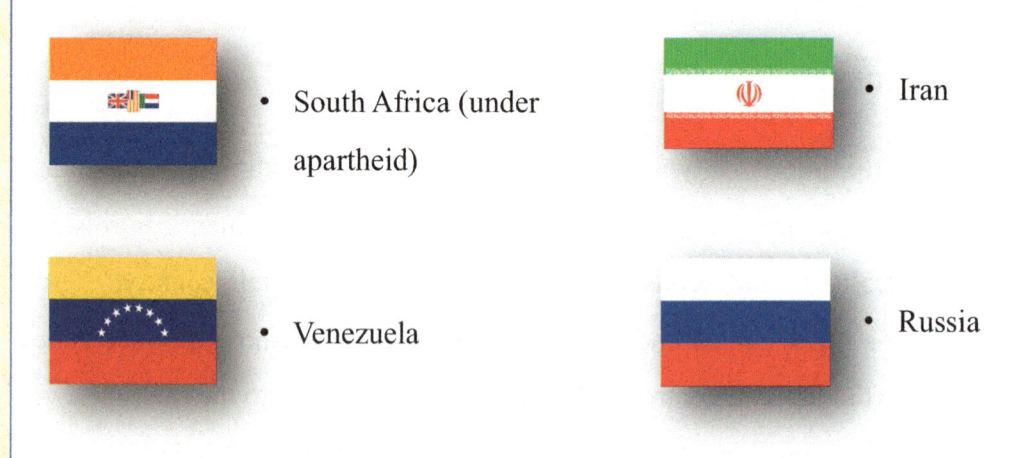

- South Africa (under apartheid)
- Venezuela
- Iran
- Russia

There are many different types of oligarchies. Some of the most common are:

- **Theocracy** - a government ruled by a religious leader or leaders. Theocratic governments have a clergy member as leader and use religious law to rule the people

- **Plutocracy** - government ruled by the wealthy either directly or via monetary influence of representatives

- **Aristocracy** – government in which power is in the hands of a privileged few

Additional Oligarchy Types

Band Society
- Based on small (usually family) unit with a semi-informal hierarchy, with strongest (either physical strength or strength of character) as leader

Noocracy
- Government ruled by wise people or philosophers

Gerontocracy
- Government form with rule by elders

Kleptocracy
Exists to increase the personal wealth and political power of its officials, a government so corrupt, that there remains no pretense of honesty.

Technocracy
The rulers are people with technical or elite expertise and have a lot of technical and scientific knowledge

Kritarchy
- Rule by judges

The **band society** form of oligarchy has been around for hundreds of years. Some examples throughout history include the Inuit of northern North America, the Shoshone of the Great Basin, the Bushmen of southern Africa, and some groups of Indigenous Australians.

Pros and Cons of Oligarchies

Pros	Cons
➤ Consolidates power with those who have expertise	➤ Encourages income inequality.
➤ Encourages citizens to focus on their own endeavors rather than "what-ifs"	➤ Difficult to move past status-quo
➤ Conservative – difficult for a single person to drive the government into risky ventures	➤ Conflict between those who are in the elite group and those who are not

Words Worth Knowing

- Democracy
- Direct Democracy
- Representative Democracy
- Constituent

Direct Democracy
Switzerland – *sort of*

Representative Democracy
United States of America

The first examples of **direct democracy** can be found in the **ancient Greek city-state of Athens**, where decisions were made by an Assembly of some 1,000 male citizens.

Democracy

A **democracy** is a system of government where the power is held by the population itself. The people vote on rules, laws and spending. There are two main types of democracies.

In a **direct democracy** ALL citizens vote on EVERYTHING. This system only really works in very small settings such as local governments. Switzerland is probably the closest modern government to a direct democracy. While not fully direct, the citizens there have more power than in a representative democracy.

In an indirect or **representative democracy** the voting citizens still hold sovereign power. However, instead of voting on everything, the citizens vote for representatives. These representatives then vote on behalf of their constituents. A **constituent** is a voting member of the community which an elected official represents. The United States of America is an example of a representative democracy.

Pros and Cons of Democracies

Pros	Cons
➤ Everyone has equal say ➤ Keeps people vested in their government ➤ Government can provide jobs ➤ Government can provide social benefits as determined by the voters	➤ Collecting votes can be difficult ➤ Majority rules -- Minorities often underrepresented ➤ Slow to react to emergencies

What Kind Of Government Is It?

Deciding and understanding the type of government a country has can sometimes be a grey area. There are some overlaps. For example the Vatican City could be classified as an absolute monarchy or a theocracy. It depends on whether you consider it as being led by the catholic church or by the Pope himself. China could be considered an absolute monarchy, an aristocracy, a dictatorship or a one party democracy depending on your viewpoint.

Vatican city

China

Considerations for Choosing Your Government

There are a few questions to consider, though, when trying to make a type of government determination.

- How many people are making decisions?

- How does the leader come into power or which group has the power?

- How much actual power does the leader possess?

- Who actually votes and makes the laws?

A **Politician** helps propose, create, and support laws that govern a land and people.

There are pros and cons to all different types of government. Think about your people and your land…

- Are your people spread out over a large area of land or clustered in a small geographic area

- What are the values and norms of your people? Do they need a strong hand to guide them? Do they prefer to be left alone to do their own thing?

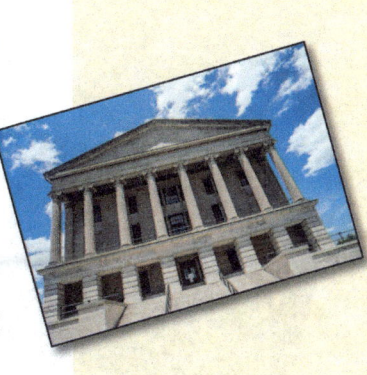

- How close are you to your neighbors? What kind of countries are they? This will matter more in the next unit when we look at your global positioning. However the choices you make here will impact the type of choices you are able to make then.

Websites and Articles Worth Exploring

- What is Government

- What is Government (2)

- Forms Of Government, 2018

- Types of Government

- Understanding Types of Government

Videos Worth Watching

- What is Government?

- The Purpose of Government

- What is a Government and Why Do We Need One?

- Every Type of Government Explained

- POLITICAL SYSTEMS 101: Basic Forms of Government Explained

Task #23: Choosing Your Government

☐ Use the Choose Your Government Flow Chart in Appendix 4 to help you choose a government type.

☐ **If you chose Dictatorship:**

  ☐ Complete **Worksheet 9.1: My New Government – Dictatorship** in your Workbook

☐ **If you chose Absolute Monarchy**

  ☐ Complete **Worksheet 9.2: My New Government – Absolute Monarchy** in your Workbook

☐ **If you chose Constitutional Monarchy**

  ☐ Complete **Worksheet 9.3: My New Government – Constitutional Monarchy** in your Workbook

☐ **If you chose Theocracy**

  ☐ Complete **Worksheet 9.4: My New Government – Theocracy** in your Workbook

☐ **If you chose Plutocracy**

  ☐ Complete **Worksheet 9.5: My New Government – Plutocracy** in your Workbook

☐ **If you chose Oligarchy**

  ☐ Complete **Worksheet 9.6: My New Government – Oligarchy** in your Workbook

☐ **If you chose Direct Democracy**

  ☐ Complete **Worksheet 9.7: My New Government – Direct Democracy** in your Workbook

☐ **If you chose Representative Democracy**

  ☐ Complete **Worksheet 9.8: My New Government – Representative Democracy** in your Workbook

Words Worth Knowing

- Principle

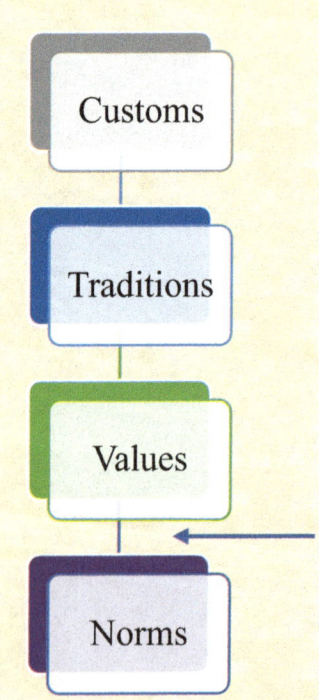

Composition Activity #6: Researching your closest neighbor

Who is your country's closest physical neighboring country? Research that country and write an essay comparing that country's government to your own.

- The essay should include an overview of the neighboring country to include the name, location and a little bit of history.

- The essay should discuss why each government benefits or harms the population of each country.

- The essay should make and defend a determination about which government has the potential to be more successful.

Values to Principles

As a quick review, a **law** is a rule recognized and maintained by the government to regulate the human behavior and conduct in a society. A **law**, at its very foundation, is conceived and derived from **values**. These **values** serve to inform and underpin a rational and fair expectation of *how power should be organized, exercised and controlled* at a private and public level.

Similar to values are a country's guiding principles. A **principle** is a fundamental truth that serves as the foundation for a system of belief or behavior. Principles are more stern and unyielding rules that are based on the values of a people. If you remember the flow chart from chapter 7, principles would be a half-step in between values and norms.

Customs → Traditions → Values → Principles → Norms

The United States founding fathers based their government based on 7 guiding principles:

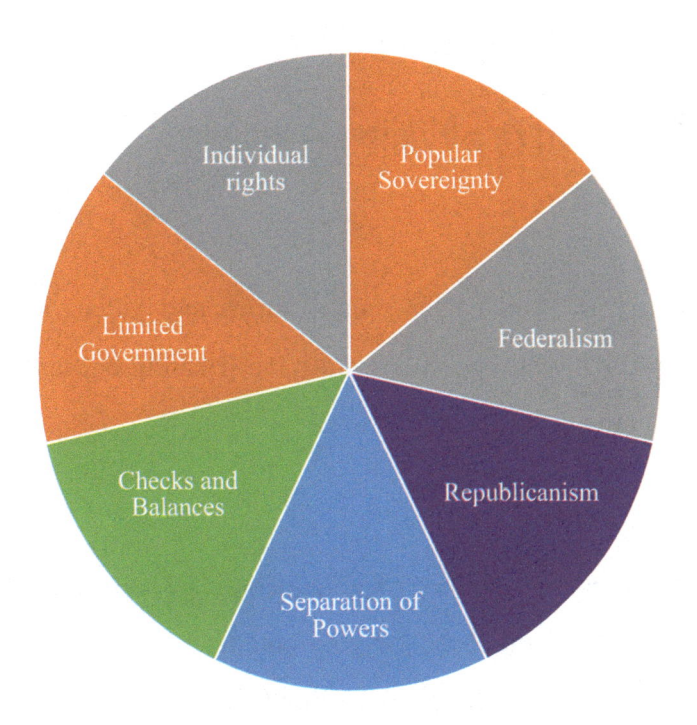

However...

Not all governments have the same principles. For example, here are some principles common to **dictatorships**:

1. In a dictatorship there is one party and one leader

2. In a dictatorship you are not free to speak your mind

3. In a dictatorship the country is entirely controlled by the leader (the dictator)

4. Most dictators try to convince their country that they (the people) are supreme to all other countries

There are 10 men considered one of the principle **founding fathers** of the United States of America. They are: John Adams, Samuel Adams, Benjamin Franklin, Alexander Hamilton, Patrick Henry, Thomas Jefferson, James Madison, John Marshall, George Mason, and George Washington.

Considerations For Your Country's Guiding Principles

- Remember when you created your shared norms and Values list back in chapter 7 (*Task #20*)? Well hopefully you have it handy because you will need it here and in the tasks to come.

- Think about the norms and values of your people. Then think about the type of government that you chose for your country. How will this type of government meet the needs of your population?

Task #24: You Country's guiding principles

❏ Identify 5 principles that will aid in the creation and progress of your government towards its goals. Keep in mind the type of government that you chose in task #23

❏ Prepare a presentation outlining each principle along with the following information:
- State the principle
- Explain why you chose that principle
- Explain why that principle is consistent with the type of government your country has.
- Explain why that principle reflects the values of your people.

Principles to Goals

Goals are things that a country aims to achieve. They are based on the country's guiding principles. Principles point the direction to the goals which provide the benchmark for how a country delivers upon the values of the people.

In the United States the goals of the country are laid out in the preamble to the constitution. A country's **constitution** is a document which outlines the principles, goals and laws that govern the land and people within its borders. The **preamble** of the constitution is the introductory part that states its purpose, aims, and justification.

Take a look at the Preamble of the Constitution of the United States of America:

> *"We the People of the United States, in Order to **form a more perfect Union, establish Justice, insure domestic Tranquility, provide for the common defense, promote the general Welfare, and secure the Blessings of Liberty to ourselves and our Posterity**, do ordain and establish this Constitution for the United States of America."*

Words Worth Knowing
- Goals
- Constitution
- Preamble

Although the **Preamble** is the first part of the constitution, it was the last article added to it.

What is the Goal?	What does it mean?
Form a more perfect union	The states need to work together as a unified nation
Establish justice	To create laws and a system to solve disputes
Insure domestic tranquility	To make sure we have peace in our homes
Provide for the common defense	To be able to raise troops for our national defense
Promote the general welfare	To make sure we are happy and healthy
Secure the blessings of liberty to ourselves and our posterity	To make sure we have and remain a free country

Websites and Articles Worth Exploring

- Principles and Virtues

- Aims and values

- We the People

Videos Worth Watching

- Principles of the Constitutional American Government - Civics SOL

- Principles of the Constitution

- American Fundamental Ideals, Values and Principles: The Basics of Constitutional Government, Part 13

- The Preamble of The Constitution Schoolhouse Rock

- The Preamble to the Constitution | US Government and Politics | Khan Academy

Task #25: You Country's Goals

☐ Create a list of at least 3 goals for your country. For each goal:

1. State the goal
2. State why that goal is important to your country
3. State how that goal does or does not support one of the **principles** of your people.

Composition Activity #7: The Preamble to your Constitution

Remember, the **Preamble** sets forth the goals and purposes for your country. Write a preamble for your governing document.

- Your preamble should be in narrative form.

- Your preamble should consist of:
    - The major goals for your country (from Task #25)
    - At least 3 principles that will help your country achieve those goals (from Task #24)
    - A statement describing your country's core values and explaining about how your values and principles led to the creation of this government and constitution

Words Worth Knowing

- Right
- Natural Right
- Legal Right
- Bill of Rights

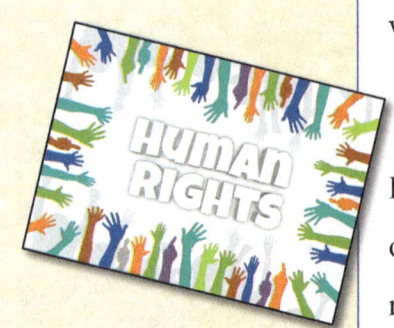

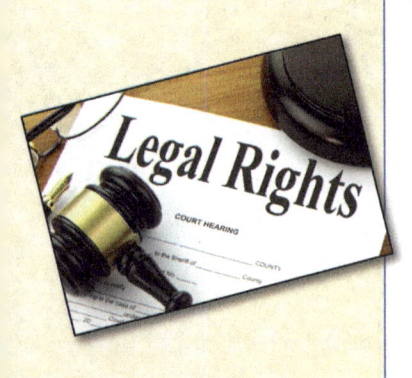

The Rights of Your Citizens

A **right** is a legal or social entitlement afforded to people based on a predefined convention. There are two main types of rights. A **natural right** is an entitlement derived from human nature or God. These are the fundamental rights that are considered universal. In the United States, life, liberty and the pursuit of happiness are considered natural rights. A **legal right** is an entitlement that is based on the norms of the society in which a person lives. These types of rights are usually afforded to citizens of a country. The right to vote or the right to own a gun may be considered legal rights in America.

In America many of these natural and legal rights are immortalized int the Bill of Rights. The **Bill of Rights** spells out the American citizens rights as they relate to the government. This is contained in the first 10 amendments to the constitution.

Websites and Articles Worth Exploring

- Natural Rights
- Human rights and natural law
- What Are Natural Rights?
- The Bill of Rights: What Does it Say?
- Bill of Rights Overview

Videos Worth Watching

- What is the Difference Between Natural Rights and Legal Rights?

- John Locke, Natural Rights

- How are Natural Rights Related to Just Laws? [No. 86]

- Why wasn't the Bill of Rights originally in the US Constitution? - James Coll

- The Bill of Rights: Every Amendment, Why it's important, and How it limits the government

> There were originally 12 amendments to the **Constitution**, however the first 2 were never ratified. The Bill of Rights as we know it actually contains amendments 3 through 12.

Task #26: Your citizens legal rights

☐ Complete **Worksheet 9.9: Natural Rights** in your Workbook

☐ Complete **Worksheet 9.10a-b: Official Choices** in your Workbook

☐ **Complete either option 1 or option 2**

- **Option 1**: Create a list of 5 **legal rights** that you will include in your constitution. For each right:

    1. State the right

    2. State who this right applies to (ie all citizens, all people, etc.)

    3. Give an explanation about why this right is important.

Words Worth Knowing

- Article

- **Option 2**: If your government is such that your citizens have no rights, write an explanation defining your stance on citizen rights. Include at least 3 rights that you are withholding from your citizens and why.

❏ Compose a Bill of Rights document for your country.

Extension Activity #8: Your Beautiful Bill of Rights

Objective: To create a creative method of displaying one of your country's founding documents.

America's original constitution and bill of rights were written on parchment paper using a quill pen. Design a creative way to write and display one of your country's founding documents.

- You may choose to write either your bill of rights or your preamble
- You may create parchment paper and ink or choose another creative way to display the words

Articles

An **article** describes how your government is set up. Who has what powers and/or responsibilities? How are they governed? Most governing documents of countries begin with a series of articles that lay the groundwork for the rest of the governmental framework.

Websites and Articles Worth Exploring

- The Constitution: Articles
- U.S. Constitution
- United States Constitution: How It's Organized

> It's against the law to chew gum in **Singapore**. In fact, no gum is bought or sold here. The law is said to be in place to keep public spaces clean.

Videos Worth Watching

- The US Constitution - Breaking Down the Articles
- The Articles and the Constitution (US History EOC Review - USHC 1.4)

❏ Complete **Worksheet 9.11a-b: Your First 6 Articles** in your Workbook

> A **Lawyer** advises and represents clients regarding matters of the law in courts, before government agencies, and in private legal matters.

Norms and Laws

Norms are formed based on the values and principles of a people. Remember those different types of norms from the last unit? Here's a little refresher:

Norms	
Folkways	Right vs. Rude
Mores	Right vs. Wrong
Taboos	Right vs. Forbidden
Laws	Right vs Illegal

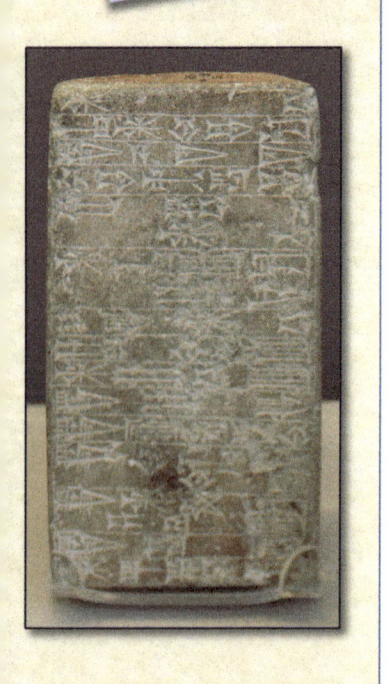

Laws generally follow a set of characteristics. These characteristics help separate a law from the other types of norms such as a more or folkway.

8 Characteristics of Law

1. It is a set of rules.
2. It regulates the human conduct
3. It is created and maintained by the state.
4. It has certain amount of stability, fixity and uniformity.
5. It is backed by coercive authority.
6. Its violation leads to punishment.
7. It is the expression of the will of the people and is generally written down to give it definiteness.
8. It is related to the concept of 'sovereignty' which is the most important element of state.

The **Code of Hammurabi** is the oldest written set of laws. Legend has it the laws, which were carved in huge stone slabs, were given to Hammurabi, the King of Babylon, by Shamash, the God of Justice.

Websites and Articles Worth Exploring

- How Laws Are Made and How to Research Them

- How Our Laws Are Made

- Making Laws

Videos Worth Watching

- How a Bill Becomes a Law: Crash Course Government and Politics #9

- Government Class: How Laws Are Made

- A Few of the Most Interesting Parts of The US Constitution

- The U.S. Constitution, EXPLAINED [AP Government Required Documents]

The *Statutes at Large* is a large compendium (set of books) that includes all the federal laws passed by the U.S. Congress

❑ Complete **Worksheet 9.12: Your Laws #1** in your Workbook

❑ Complete **Worksheet 9.13: Your Laws #2** in your Workbook

❑ Complete **Worksheet 9.14: Your Laws #3** in your Workbook

❑ Complete **Worksheet 9.15: Your Laws #4** in your Workbook

❑ Complete **Worksheet 9.16: Your Laws #5** in your Workbook

❑ Complete **Worksheet 9.17: Your Laws #6** in your Workbook

❑ Complete **Worksheet 9.18: Your Laws #7** in your Workbook

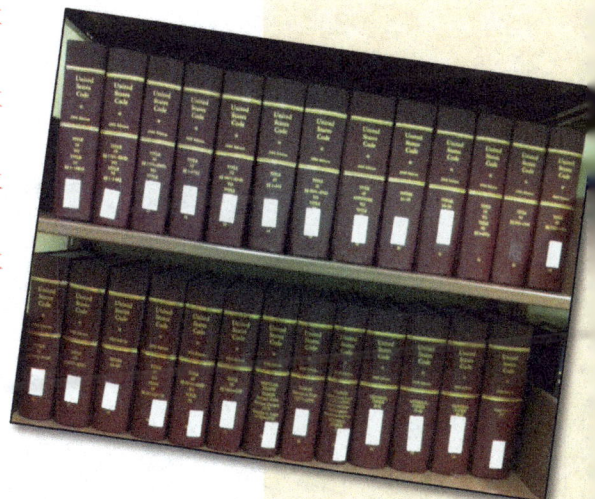

Task #27: Creating Your Constitution

Now that you have all of the pieces decided on its time to create the constitution for your country. *(Note: if your country is a dictatorship or other type of system that doesn't have a constitution you will still do this task. The same sections will apply in a "governmental document" for your country)*

> Only **27 amendments** to the constitution have actually been ratified out of the 33 passed by congress and over 11,000 proposed amendments.

❏ Create a Constitution document for your country. This document should be typed with clearly defined sections. Your constitution should consist of 3 parts:

- The **Preamble** sets forth the goals and purposes for your country. Include the preamble you developed in **Composition Activity #7: The Preamble to your Constitution**

- The **Articles** describe how your government is set up. Use the articles that you created in **Worksheet 9.11a-b: Your First 6 Articles**

- The **Amendments** should list the rights and laws of your government. This section should include:

    - The bill of rights that you created in **Task #26: Your citizens legal rights**

    - The laws that you created in Worksheets **9.12: Your Laws #1** through **9.18: Your Laws #7**.

Chapter 9 Review

The following sections help you review and think about some of the concepts and activities that you performed in this chapter.

Words Worth Knowing Review

The following terms were very important throughout this chapter.

Government	Sovereignty	Legitimacy	Jurisdiction
Anarchy	Communal Anarchy	Autocracy	Monarchy
Absolute Monarchy	Constitutional Monarchy	Dictatorship	Oligarchy
Theocracy	Plutocracy	Aristocracy	Democracy
Direct Democracy	Representative Democracy	Constituent	Principle
Goals	Constitution	Preamble	Right
Natural Right	Legal Right	Bill of Rights	Article

❏ Complete the **Chapter 9 Words Worth Knowing Exercises** in the Workbook

CHAPTER 9 REVIEW

For Discussion

- "Consent of the Governed" is a condition thought by many to be a requirement for any legitimate government. What does consent of the government mean and how does it apply to the many decisions that you made concerning your government and its formation? Is it possible to rule without the consent of the governed?

You as a Citizen

A **Duty** is something that a citizen is required to do by law. A **Responsibility** is something that a citizen should do, but is not required by law.

- What are 5 Duties that you have as a citizen of your country?

- What are 5 Responsibilities that you have as a citizen of your country?

Your National Library

The following Items from this chapter should be filed in your national library

- **Guidebook**
    - Your Country's Guiding Principles
    - Your Country's Goals

- **Official Documents**
    - My New Government Worksheet
    - Your Constitution

- **Literature / Cultural heritage**
    - Your Closest Neighbor Essay

- **Promotional material / media**
    - Your Beautiful Bill of Rights

CHAPTER 10

Creating Your Economic System

Creating Your Economic System

A government and a country does not exist on goodwill alone. It needs an economy. An economy encompasses all of the activity related to production, consumption, and trade of goods and services. It applies to everyone from individuals to corporations to governments. The economy of a particular country is influenced by its culture, laws, history, and geography, among other factors. For this reason, no two economies are identical.

In this chapter you will make decisions about your country's economy. How does your government make money? What does it's money(currency) look like? How does it spend the money your government takes in?

Words Worth Knowing

- Economy
- Supply
- Demand
- Law of Supply and Demand

Ancient formal economies date as far back as the Bronze Age (4000-2500 BCE)

A Political Economist deal with the allocation of scarce resources and researches how public policy will affect the economy.

What is an economy

In the last chapter you learned about governments, types of governments and politics as a function of who makes the rules. In this chapter we will shift slightly and look at your government through the lens of markets and economic structures. Keep in mind as you work through this chapter that the line between politics and economics is a thin/blurred one.

To do this lets start by looking at what an economy is and what the different types of economies are. An **economy** is the wealth and resources of a country particularly when it comes to the production and consumption of goods and services. Economies are how countries address the issue of scarcity. Remember, scarcity occurs when the demand for a good or aa service is greater than the supply of it.

You country only has so many resources. This may be natural resources through your resource collection allocation areas, food resources through your country's agriculture activities, finished goods produced in your country's factories, or even human capital if the form of production or service workers. Regardless of what it is your country can produce, the **supply** of that thing, the total amount that can be offered to consumers, is limited.

Demand is the amount of something that your consumers are willing to by at given price. As a good or service becomes more or less scarce and the price goes up or down, the consumers' demand for that product shifts. This relationship between what people want and what is available to them is called the **Law of Supply and Demand**.

Economic Jobs of a Government

There are six main jobs of a government when it comes to the economy of a country:

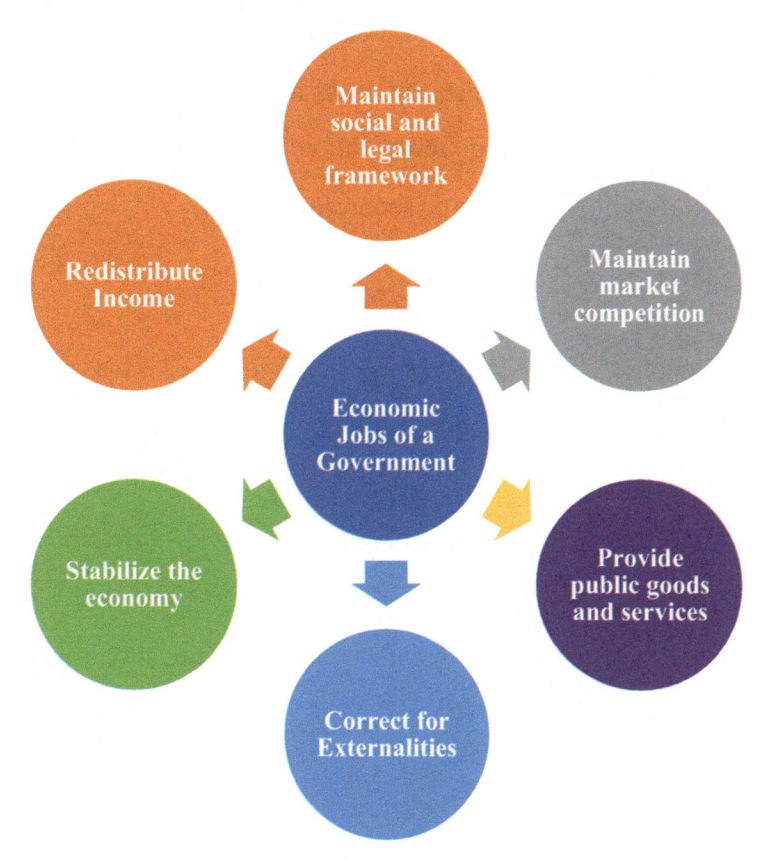

- Maintain social and legal framework
- Maintain market competition
- Provide public goods and services
- Correct for Externalities
- Stabilize the economy
- Redistribute Income

1. A government should maintain the social and legal framework. This defining and enforcing property rights as well as establishing and maintaining a monetary system.

2. A government should maintain competition in the market. This could mean regulating monopolies or creating antitrust laws

3. A government should provide public goods and services. This applies to those goods and services which your people need but are not available in sufficient quantities in the market due to scarcity.

In addition to early laws, the Code of Hammurabi specified norms and outlined rules for economic activity in Babylon.

255

Words Worth Knowing

- Externality
- Unemployment
- Inflation
- Economic System

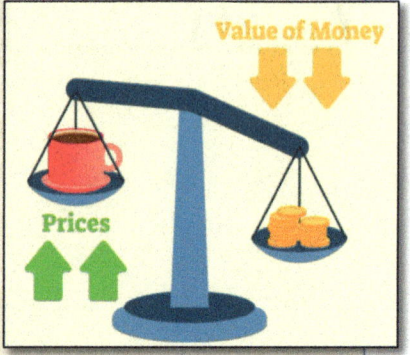

4. A government should correct for externalities. An **externality** occurs when the costs or benefits of a transaction falls outside of the producer/consumer relationship. Externalities can be either positive or negative depending on the situation. Perhaps the production of a good produces large amounts of environmental pollution or the consumption of a good allows for a higher general education level. As a government you want to maximize the positive externalities while minimizing the negative ones.

5. A government should help stabilize the economy. This involves minimizing both unemployment and inflation and promoting economic growth. **Unemployment** occurs when there are not enough jobs for those of your citizens who are both able and wanting to work. **Inflation** is the increase in the price of goods and services relative to the value of your nation's currency. Both unemployment and inflation have negative impacts on your country's economy.

6. A government should help redistribute income. Redistributing income involves shifting wealth from those with higher incomes to those with lower incomes. You don't want a country with one percent mega rich and 99 percent starving masses.

The first reported unemployment rate in the United States was 8.8% in April of 1940.

Types of Economies

Economies function based on the tenets of a countries economic system. An **economic system** is the system by which money, industry, and trade are organized in a country. These systems regulate how much of a country's economy is controlled by the government and how much is left up to the law of supply and demand. There are four main types of economic systems: traditional, command, market and mixed.

A **traditional economic system** is based on goods, services and work that follow traditions or customs. This is one of the oldest economic systems and many of the prices are set according to values established through barter or trade.

A **command economic system** is based on strong governmental controls. The government sets the price on goods and services and there is very little freedom of choice.

A **market economic system** is based on the idea of a free market. A **free market** is one in which prices are set by the law of supply and demand with no government interference.

A **mixed economic system** combines aspects of both a market and a command system. The economy generally operates as a free market, however there are some governmental controls that keep prices from fluctuating too far in one direction or the other.

> **Words Worth Knowing**
> - Traditional Economic System
> - Command Economic System
> - Market Economic System
> - Free market
> - Mixed Economic System

*The **United States** is considered a **Mixed Economy***

Pure Government Control ← **Command** — Mixed — **Market** → Pure Free Market

*No pure **free market** economies exist currently although **Singapore's** economy comes the closest.*

Words Worth Knowing

- Economic ideology

Type of Economy	Traditional	Command	Market	Mixed
Controlling Sector	Traditions & Customs	Government/ Public Sector	Private sector	Both public and private sector
Price Determination	Barter or trade	Government sets price	Price mechanism such as law of supply and demand	Price mechanism system but regulated by the government
Freedom of Choice	Freedom as long as resources are available to produce	No freedom of choice	Consumers and producers have complete freedom of choice	Limited freedom of choice within governmental controls
Associated With	Tribal or aborigine societies	Socialism; Communism	Capitalism	Multiple
Pros	Less threat to the environment. No waste	Low levels of unemployment; Allows for motivators other than profit	Greater innovation due to free flow of ideas; Greater efficiency; Greater chance of wealth.	Same as with market economy
Cons	Dependent on seasons and weather	Lacks innovation; Supply of goods may not match demand; Fosters the growth of black markets	Greater inequality among citizens; Profit is the only motivator; Greater chance of poor working conditions	Possible waste of resources; Economic decisions might get delayed in execution in the private sector

Economic Ideologies

An **economic ideology** is a set of views that form a basis about how an economy should function withing the relationship between the government and the people. These are also sometimes political philosophies or ideologies. There are four major types of economic ideologies that you should be concerned with for this course. (although there are many others as well as subtypes): capitalism, fascism, socialism and communism.

Words Worth Knowing

- Capitalism
- Fascism
- Socialism
- Communism

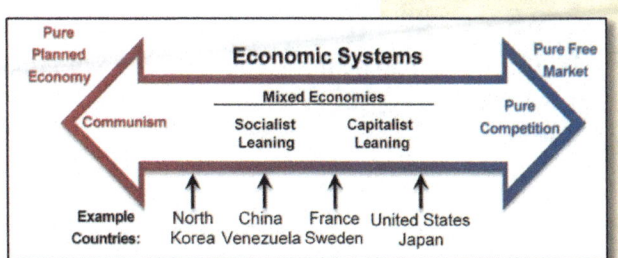

Capitalism is an ideology which the means of production, distribution and exchange should be regulated by private ownership and the law of supply and demand. This is the basis of a free market system.

Fascism is an ideology which advocates that the nation and often race are placed above the individual. A fascist economy is characterized by severe economic and social regimentation, and forcible suppression of opposition.

Socialism is an ideology which advocates that the means of production, distribution, and exchange should be owned or regulated by the community as a whole. In a socialist economy, every member of society theoretically has equal ownership of the factors of production and an equal share of the economic output.

Communism is an ideology which advocates communal means of production, distribution and exchange similar to socialism. However, in communism, the output is divided according to need. Communism is closely linked to the writings of Karl Marx in his work The Communist Manifesto.

**Adam Smith,
Early Capitalist**

**Charles Fourier,
Early Socialist**

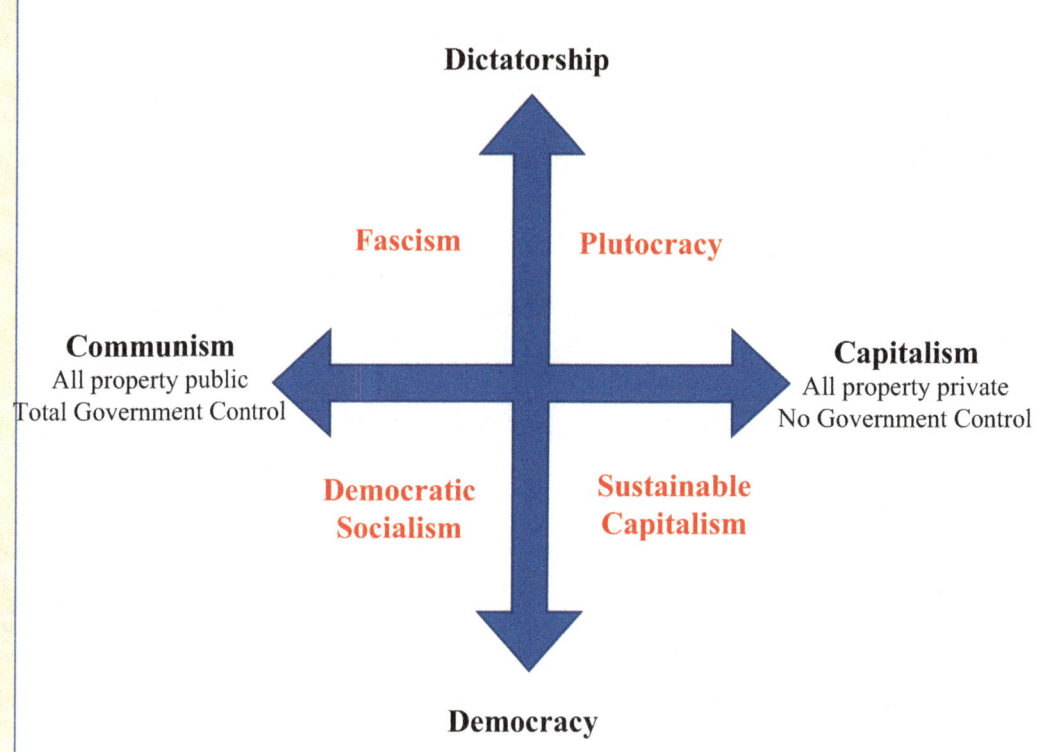

Dictatorship

Fascism **Plutocracy**

Communism　　　　　　　　　　　　**Capitalism**
All property public　　　　　　　　　All property private
Total Government Control　　　　　No Government Control

Democratic　　**Sustainable**
Socialism　　　**Capitalism**

Democracy

Websites and Articles Worth Exploring

- Economy

- Law of Supply and Demand

- What is an Economic System?

- Economic Systems

- 4 Types of Economic Systems

- Capitalism, Socialism, or Fascism? A Guide to Economic Systems and Ideologies

- Make sure that your currency design is easy to use. Your bills and coins should be big enough to be easily recognizable yest small enough to fit inside a wallet or pocketbook. The ratios between different denominations in your money should make sense and be simple to calculate.

- Make sure that your currency design is appealing and easy to understand. You don't want your citizens mistaking one unit for another. You want your money to be readable and make sense to as many people as possible. Arrange the content and design elements in a way that highlights the most important information and removes unnecessary complexity

- Make your currency visually appealing. There is actually a thriving market for collectible coins and bills. You want your currency to stand out among the currency of other nations

The penny costs more to manufacture than it is made.

Other Considerations for Designing Your Currency

- Often a country's currency pays homage to the country's heritage or other national symbols. Think about what you know about your country, its land and its people. How can you incorporate those features into your nation's currency?

- A country's money is yet another way to build comraderies and a sense of pride among your people. What kind of emotions do you want your money to evoke and how can you design your bills and coins to accomplish that?

- Think about the orientation of your money. How do you want it to fit in a wallet? How would you like your money to fit into an ATM or other electronic devices.

Cash money makes up only about 8% of the world's currency.

Words Worth Knowing

- Exchange Rate

The US Dollar acts as the **unofficial global reserve currency**, held by nearly every central bank and institutional investment entity in the world.

A **Banker** manages financial accounts and gives financial advice on matters related to savings, investments, loans, and securities

Exchange Rates

An **exchange rate** is the value of one nation's currency versus the currency of another nation or economic zone. The 6 most popular currencies for trading are:

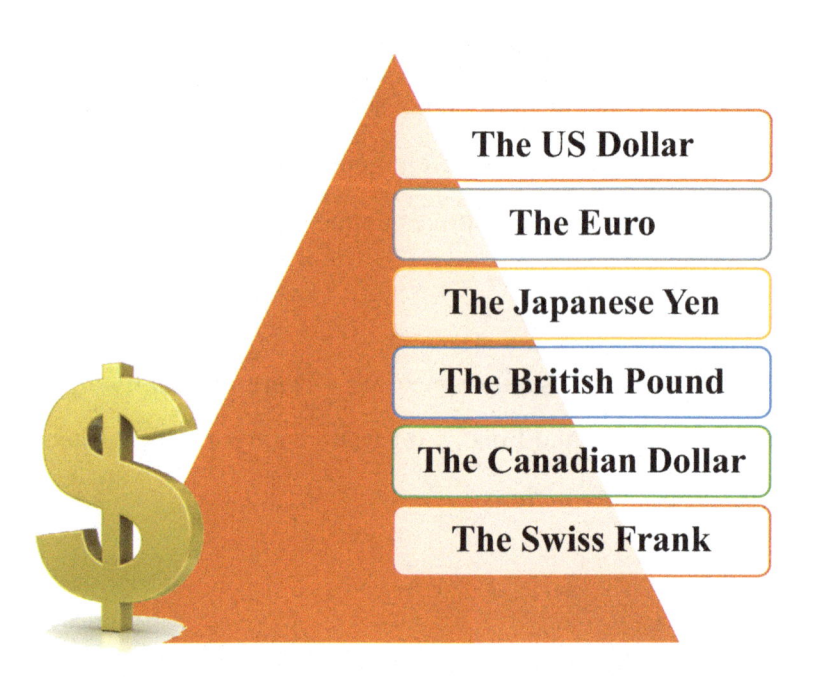

- The US Dollar
- The Euro
- The Japanese Yen
- The British Pound
- The Canadian Dollar
- The Swiss Frank

Actual exchange rates can sometimes fluctuate daily. For this reason, whenever you complete a task or worksheet that deals with exchange rates, be sure to list the date that you looked up the rate. Now, since your country has progressed past the point of subsisting on barter and trade, its time to create your country's currency.

Calculating Money Using Exchange Rates

When you look up an exchange rate you will find a decimal number. For example the US dollar to Euro exchange rate could be .95. This would mean that one US dollar (the base unit of the currency of the United States of

America) is worth .95 Euros (the base unit of the European Unit). *Calculating money using exchange rates works the same way that calculating metric to American measurements did in unit 1.*

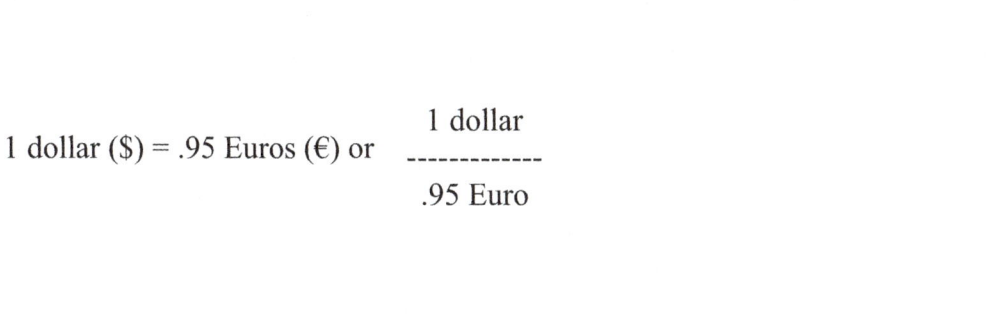

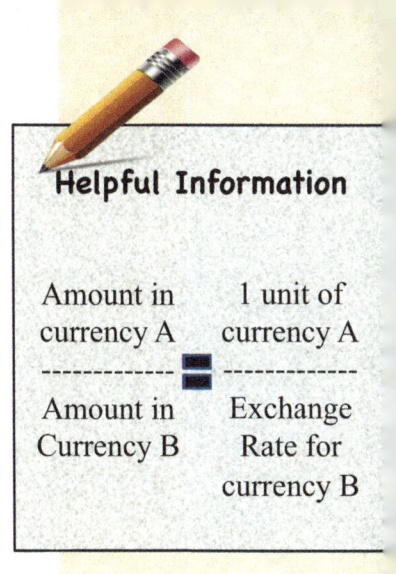

1 dollar ($) = .95 Euros (€)   or $\dfrac{1 \text{ dollar}}{.95 \text{ Euro}}$

Helpful Information

$$\dfrac{\text{Amount in currency A}}{\text{Amount in Currency B}} = \dfrac{1 \text{ unit of currency A}}{\text{Exchange Rate for currency B}}$$

Example 1: So how would you find out how many euros a $5.67 sandwich would cost?

$$\dfrac{5.67}{X} = \dfrac{1 \text{ dollar}}{.95 \text{ Euro}}$$

1 * (X) = 5.67 * .95

X = €5.38

A sandwich that cost $5.67 in American dollars would cost €5.38 in Euros.

Example 2: How much would a shirt that cost €35.81 cost in American dollars?

$$\dfrac{X}{35.81} = \dfrac{1 \text{ dollar}}{.95 \text{ Euro}}$$

.95 * X = 1 * 35.81

$$X = \dfrac{35.81}{.95}$$

As of 2022 the **Iranian Rial** was the lowest valued currency in the world. The most stable currency title belongs to the **Swiss Franc.**

Iranian Rial

Swiss Franc

X = 37.69

A shirt that costs €35.81 would cost $37.69

*The **US Bureau of Engraving** and Printing uses 9.7 tons of ink a day.*

Websites and Articles Worth Exploring

- Currency Design: Designing The Most Desirable Product
- 20 examples of the world's best currency design
- What Money Should Look Like
- The Seven Denominations
- How Coins Are Made: The Design and Selection Process
- Exchange Rate Definition
- Read and Calculate Currency Exchange Rates
- Currency Converter
- Foreign Exchange Rates for U.S. Dollars

***Queen Elizabeth II** has been featured on more coins and banknotes than any other person*

Videos Worth Watching

- Money Marvels - Design Your Own Banknote
- World's Coolest Banknotes 2021 - Voted By You!
- How Money Is Made | How Stuff Is Made | Refinery29
- Minting My Own Currency
- The United States Currency System

- Currency Exchange Introduction

- How Exchange Rates Are Determined

- Currency Exchange Rates - How To Convert Currency

Task #30: Creating Your Currency

❏ Create a new currency, or money system, of your own. You must include at least 4 bills and 4 coins in your system. Make sure there is one bill that is worth a base of 1 of your currency. The other bills should be a multiple of your "1" and the coins should each be a fraction of your "1".

- On separate paper, draw a picture of the front and back of each coin and bill in your new currency.

- Label each bill and coin with its name.

❏ Complete **Worksheet 10.1: Currency Inventory** in your Workbook

❏ Complete **Worksheet 10.2: Item Costs** in your Workbook

Helpful Information

$$\frac{\text{Amount in currency A}}{\text{Amount in Currency B}} = \frac{1 \text{ unit of currency A}}{\text{Exchange Rate for currency B}}$$

Extension Activity #9: Minting Your Money

Create a 3D set of your national currency. Your currency should meet the following requirements:

- Both your bills and your coins should be 2-sided

- Your bills can be made out of cloth, paper, posterboard or any similar material.

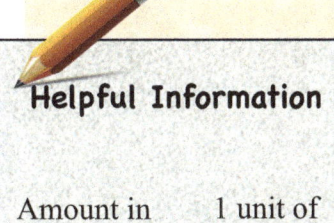

Words Worth Knowing

- Tax
- Tax rate
- Income tax

- Your coins can be made out of clay, wood, cardboard or any similar material.
- You should create enough coins and bills to make change for a fictitious purchase.

Taxes

Taxes are one of the major ways that a country makes money. A **tax** is a charge usually of money imposed by the government or other authority on persons or property for public purpose. The level (usually a percentage) that a government taxes a person, business or item is known as a **tax rate**. Most taxes fall into one of three categories:

A **Tax advisor** helps clients save money by making wise financial decisions about tax-related issues.

Taxes on Income   **Taxes on Property**   **Taxes on Goods and Services**

Taxes on Income

Income tax is a type of tax that applies to personal and business revenue and interest income. In most cases, income tax brackets are progressive, meaning that the greater the income, the higher the rate of taxation. For example in the United States the income tax rate may be anywhere from 10% to 37% of your income depending on what tax bracket a person falls into.

The top **1%** of Americans account for over **38%** of the country's total income tax revenue.

Taxes on Property

Property tax is a tax that is imposed on the value of real estate or other personal property. Property taxes are usually imposed on a recurring basis. Property tax rate is usually based on the assessed value of the property. For example, the tax rate on a house may be .87% of the value of the house.

Taxes on Goods and Services

Taxes on goods and services, also known as **sales tax** impose a tax on a percentage of the sales price of a particular item. Rates can vary between jurisdictions and the type of item bought. Tax rates on goods and services can sometimes vary by type of good and location. For example sales taxes can vary between 3% and 7% and may not include some items such as food. Items like tobacco products and alcohol are often taxed at a much higher rate.

Words Worth Knowing

- Property tax
- Sales tax

Property tax is also known as an **ad valorem** tax. Ad Valorem is Latin for "according to the value"

Websites and Articles Worth Exploring

- Taxes
- What Are Taxes?
- The Three Basic Tax Types

Videos Worth Watching

- Taxes: Crash Course Economics #31
- Types of Taxes in the United States

- What If People Stopped Paying Taxes?

- The 4 Main Types of Taxes We Pay

Considerations for Taxation:

> Most **sales tax** in the United States is governed at the State, not the federal level.

- Remember the big differences between the main types of taxes:

    - Income taxes primarily affect **any wage earners**. This takes from the money people **earn**.

    - Sales taxes primarily affect **consumers**. This takes from the money people **spend**.

    - Property taxes primarily affect those who **possess things** of value. This takes from the **value of things that people own**.

- If you set your taxes to low your government will not have the money to adequately fund infrastructure projects, along with education, healthcare, defense or social programs. This could cause civil unrest due to the decline in your government's ability to support and defend its people.

> In the United States, **Tax evasion**, the illegal non-payment or under-payment of taxes, is a **federal crime** than can be punishable with 5 years in prison and up to a $100,000 fine for individuals.

- If you set your taxes too high your people will start buying less because they have less income. Thus less goods will be sold and less taxes collected. This could cause civil unrest due to the decline in the purchasing power and standard of living of your people.

Allocation of Funds

Once your government takes in money, you will have to decide how to allocate it. **Allocation** involves the distribution of funds for a specific organizational unit or function. It is important to find the correct balance of allocation of your taxes. Too much of your budget spend in one area means a reduction in the availability of funds in others.

Governments usually outline their priorities and allocations of the country's income in their **national budget**, also called a federal budget. There are many different sectors to which a government can allocate its money. However, for the purposes of this course we will focus on seven specific categories.

Words Worth Knowing

- Allocation
- National Budget

Allocation of Funds:
- Defense
- Social Programs (food stamps, welfare, etc.)
- Education
- Healthcare
- Infrastructure
- Research/Technology
- Administration (leaders, salaries, expenses, etc.)

A **Budget analyst** prepares budget reports, monitors spending, and makes recommendations for money allocation.

Websites and Articles Worth Exploring

- Federal Spending: Where Does the Money Go
- Budget of the U.S. Government
- Federal Budget

Videos Worth Watching

- How does the National Budget work?
- Government Budgets and Fiscal Policy | IB Macroeconomics
- Monetary and Fiscal Policy: Crash Course Government and Politics #48
- U.S. Federal Budget Process 101
- What If The US Budget Was Only $100 - How Would It Spend It?

Considerations for Allocations of Funds

- **If your focus your money on Defense:** your people will feel safer, however it could be considered a sign of aggression by your neighboring countries.

- **If you focus your money on Social Programs (food stamps, welfare, etc.):** it will ensure that more of your people have what they need to survive, however it may foster a sense of entitlement among your people and reduce motivation and productivity.

- **If you focus your money on Education:** it will increase your country's potential for innovation and technological growth in the future, however it may reduce the availability of funds for current needs.

- **If you focus your money on Healthcare:** your people will live longer and more productive lives, however your population growth may outpace the ability of your infrastructure to keep up or may reduce the overall standard of living due to scarcity of resources.

- **If you focus your money on Infrastructure (building/maintaining roads, bridges, power and water systems, etc.):** the foundation for your country's physical and economic growth will be strong, however your people's standard of living may still go down due to poor access to health, education and social programs.

In 2019, **nearly 60%** of the budget in the United states was allocated for **Social Security** and other income support programs.

- **If you focus your money on Research/Technology:** your country will be better able to compete on a global scale for resources and reputation, however your people may not be able to see the benefits of the spending due to the slow progress of innovation.

- **If you focus your money on Administration (leaders, salaries, expenses, etc.):** your strong leadership may result in a government better suited to react to global issues, however your people may think they are just paying for overhead without seeing any tangible benefits to quality of life.

To keep your nation going, you must now create a national budget. First you must determine how you will collect money from your citizens. Then, you must allocate these monies based upon the needs of your country. As you are doing so, keep in mind what you learned about your population through your census in Chapter 6 as well as the guiding principles of your new government that you outlined in Chapter 9.

Task #30: Your National Budget

❏ Create a tax system that will help your nation collect money to maintain essential systems and services:

❏ Complete **Worksheet 10.3: Taxing Goods and Services** in your Workbook

❏ Complete **Worksheet 10.4: Property and Income Tax** in your Workbook

❏ Decide how you will spend the money that comes in

- Create a pie chart showing what percentage of your country's income will be allocated to each of the following areas:

  - Defense
  - Social Programs (food stamps, welfare, etc.)
  - Education
  - Healthcare
  - Infrastructure (building/maintaining roads, bridges, power and water systems, etc.)
  - Research/Technology
  - Administration (leaders, salaries, expenses, etc.)

❏ Create a National Budget document outlining how you will collect and spend funds.

Composition Activity #8: Defending Your National Budget

Compose an essay defending your National Budget and the choices you made. Your essay should answer the following questions:

- Why did you make your particular choices regarding taxation? How will those choices affect the standard of living for your people?

- What categories did you allocate the most money to? The least? Why did you set those particular priorities? How will this affect the standard of living for your people?

- What do your choices reveal about the overall priorities of your country?

Chapter 10 Review

The following sections help you review and think about some of the concepts and activities that you performed in this chapter.

Words Worth Knowing Review

The following terms were very important throughout this chapter.

Economy	Scarcity	Supply	Demand
Law of Supply and Demand	Externality	Unemployment	Inflation
Economic System	Traditional Economic System	Command Economic System	Market Economic System
Free Market	Mixed Economic System	Economic Ideology	Capitalism
Fascism	Socialism	Communism	Currency
Universal Design	Denomination	Exchange Rate	Tax
Tax Rate	Income Tax	Property Tax	Sales Tax
Allocation	National Budget		

❑ Complete the **Chapter 10 Words Worth Knowing Exercises** in the Workbook

For Discussion

- How did your country's economic system and ideologies that you chose affect your decisions of where to allocate your resources in your National Budget?

You as a Citizen

- As a citizen, what responsibilities do you have when it comes to protecting the economic wellbeing of your country as a whole?

Your National Library

The following Items from this chapter should be filed in your national library

- **Guidebook**
    - Currency Inventory and Item Costs
    - Picture of 3D set of your Currency

- **Official Documents**
    - Article VII of your Constitution
    - National Budget

- **Promotional material / media**
    - Defending your National Budget Essay

CHAPTER 10 REVIEW

CHAPTER 11

Fleshing out your Governmental Infrastructure

Fleshing out your Governmental Infrastructure

So now your have a government to rule and some money with which to do so. However, now your leaders must make some important decisions for the future of your country and your people. How will you protect your people? How will you help them get around, stay healthy and be prepared for the future? Who will you trust to help you lead your people?

In this chapter you will flesh out your governmental structure and make some key decisions on important topics.

Words Worth Knowing

- Public Works

Public Works

Soon you will be mapping some of your country's public works. A country's **public works** involve all of the activities associated with building and maintaining things such as roads, schools and any structure or service required to maintain an acceptable quality of life for its citizens. While public works can cover a multitude of activities, for the purposes of this course we will focus on 3.

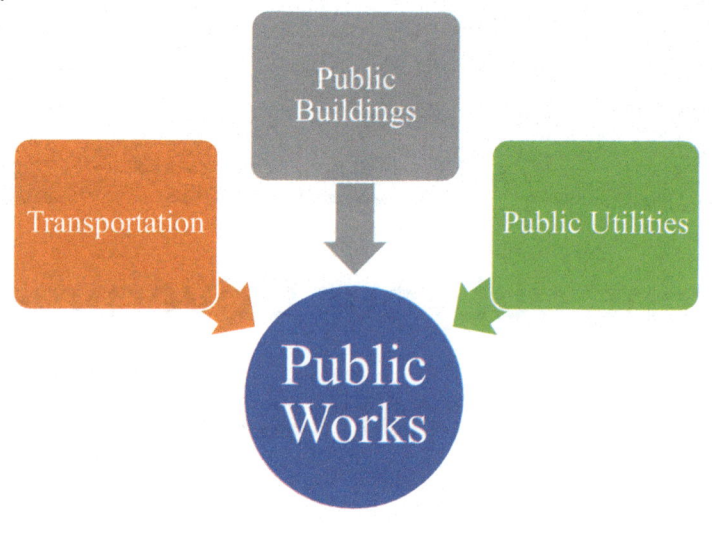

Transportation → Public Works ← Public Utilities
Public Buildings → Public Works

Transportation

From a public works perspective, Transportation needs include items such as roads, ports and train tracks. You will want to be able to get your raw goods from your resource collection areas or agriculture lands to your cities where your factories reside. You will also want to be able to get finished goods to the port for export as well as provide a means for your citizens to get around. Transportation solutions could include railway lines, waterways or train routes.

Public buildings

Public buildings include municipal buildings such as your capital buildings and courthouses, schools and hospitals. These buildings are constructed using public funds and often maintained by your government.

A **Civil engineer** designs, constructs and maintains infrastructure projects and systems.

There are nearly **4 million miles** of roads in the United State

Public Utilities

One of the key components to public works are public utilities. **Public utilities** are the entities that supply essential goods and services to the community such as water, gas, electricity, trash removal and communication systems. Your country won't thrive very well without reliable access to power and a way to deal with trash.

Words Worth Knowing
- Public Utilities

Websites and Articles Worth Exploring

- What is Public Works?
- Transportation and Public Works
- National Association of Regulatory Utility Commissioners
- What is Public Power?
- What Are Utilities in a Home, Apartment, or Business?

A <u>sanitary engineer</u> builds and operates hygienic projects such as waterworks, sewage, and trash disposal plants.

Videos Worth Watching

- What Is Public Works?
- Public Works 101
- Inside the Public Works Department
- Unseen, Unsung, Unnoticed | How do "Public Utilities" Work?
- utilities at a glance
- Empowered: The role of the Public Utilities Commission in Hawaii's 100% renewable energy future

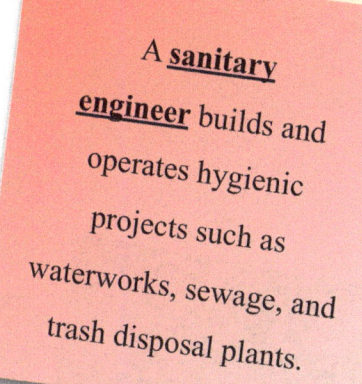

Considerations for Mapping Your Public Works

There are several maps that you have completed that will be useful as you begin to think about the location and types of public works.

Take a look at your Land Allocation Map. Remember you can only put major cities on land that you allocated for urban development. Likewise you would not want to put a highway through the middle of a natural reserve without considerable unrest from your people.

- **Take a look at your Physical Map.** You cannot drive a road through the middle of a lake, nor can you put a very successful airport on top of a mountain. Look at your fresh water sources? How will you ensure that your population has adequate access to water and power?

- **Take a look at your Population Density Map.** Where do your people live? What does that tell you about the types of transportation that will be needed? Will the majority of your population drive cars? Take a train? Travel by boat or plane?

- **Take a look at your Natural Resources Map.** How will you get your natural resources to either the manufacturing areas or to export locations?

There are more than 2.6 million miles of pipelines in the United States carrying water, sewage and different types of oil and fuels

Task #31: Mapping Your Public Works

Outlining your public works is a crucial part of understanding how your country operates. This tells you how your communicate, get around, and satisfy basic societal needs.

- Create a map of your **country**. Show the following on your map:

  - The Location and name of your capital city and any major cities. *Make sure to denote which city is your capital with a different symbol.*

  - The location of any major roads, train tracks, or other forms of transportation.

  - The location of any major train stations, ports and airports in your country.

  - The location of any major power stations/plants.

- Create a separate map of your **capital city** showing:

  - Any public buildings (capital building, other municipal buildings, schools, hospitals, libraries, etc.)

  - Any Major transportation (roads, railroads, ports, airports, etc.)

  - Any major public spaces (parks, beaches, etc.)

  - Any public utilities (water supply/treatment, sewage/trash treatment, etc.)

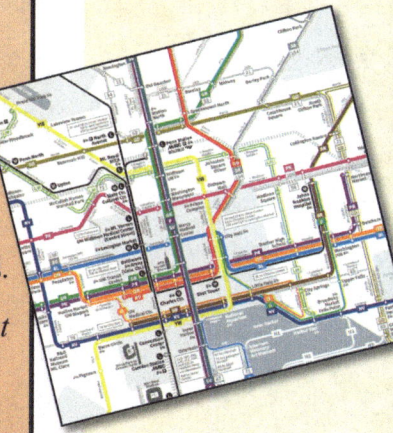

Words Worth Knowing

- National Defense
- Army
- Air Force
- Navy
- Marine Corps
- Coast Guard
- Space Force
- National Guard

Extension Activity #10: Building your Capital Building

Objective: Build a 3D representation of your capital building

❑ Construct a 3D model of your capital building.

- The building should represent the unique culture of your country
- Your capital should include a visitor area as well as several offices and a press room.
- You may construct your capital out of any physical material or virtually using a 3D modeling environment

National Defense

One of the responsibilities of a government is to provide for the safety of your people. A country's **National Defense** includes the agencies responsible for the security and defense of a country, its citizens, economy and institutions. The purpose of a national defense is threefold:

1. Protect your nation from those who wish it harm
2. Protect your citizens when they are abroad
3. Win any wars or conflicts you may be involved in

*The Department of Defense is the Federal Government's largest agency employing **over 1.3 million active duty service members and more than 1.5 million civilian, National Guard and Reserve service members***

Your national defense could be made of one or several individual branches. The United States Department of Defense is comprised of seven agencies: the **Army**, the **Air Force**, the **Navy**, the **Marine Corps**, the **Coast Guard**, the **Space Force** and the **National Guard**.

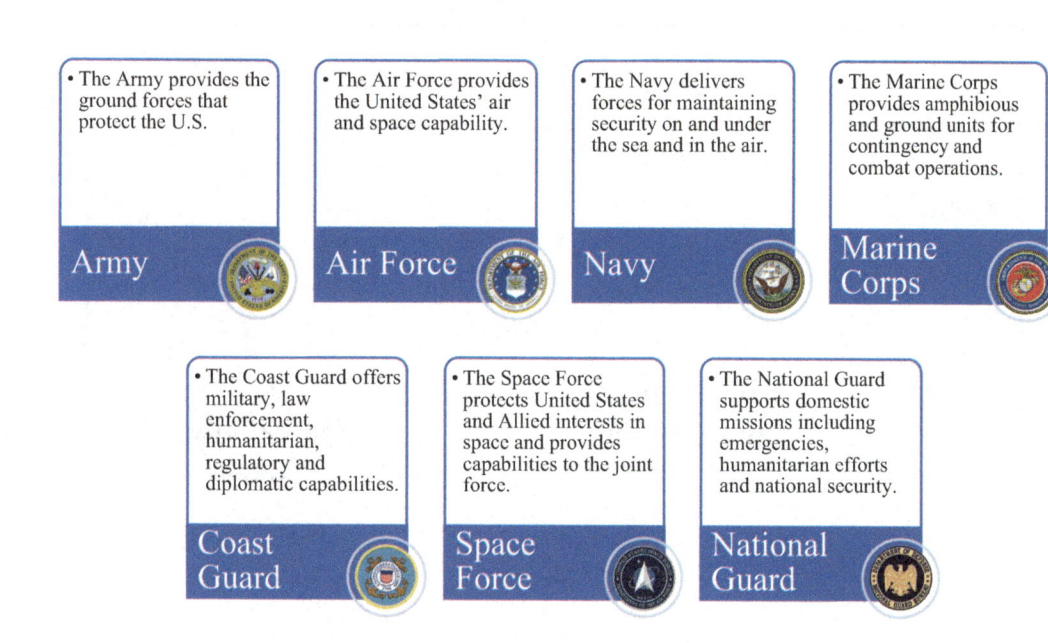

- The Army provides the ground forces that protect the U.S.

Army

- The Air Force provides the United States' air and space capability.

Air Force

- The Navy delivers forces for maintaining security on and under the sea and in the air.

Navy

- The Marine Corps provides amphibious and ground units for contingency and combat operations.

Marine Corps

- The Coast Guard offers military, law enforcement, humanitarian, regulatory and diplomatic capabilities.

Coast Guard

- The Space Force protects United States and Allied interests in space and provides capabilities to the joint force.

Space Force

- The National Guard supports domestic missions including emergencies, humanitarian efforts and national security.

National Guard

Words Worth Knowing

- Routine Peaceful Competition

Competition and Conflict

In unit 4 you will be mapping out your country's place on a global stage. Part of that work, however, begins here as you begin to think about your national defense in relation to your neighbors. Competition among countries is a healthy and fundamental part of international relations. All resources are, by nature, scarce and countries continually vie over access to them. This competition stimulates the global economy and helps all countries flourish. However, there are times when competition spills over into conflict. This is where your country's national defense will step in.

Conflict types exist on a continuum, from a stable, peaceful environment to war. The desired state of things is routine peaceful competition. **Routine Peaceful Competition** is the normal and desired end state where countries pursue their own interests with enough commonality of interests to avoid violence.

The **2020 National Defense Authorization Act**, signed by President Trump on December 20, 2019, created the United States Space Force (USSF) as the sixth branch of the U.S. military.

Each branch of the military also trains **Reservists**, military personnel who serve on a part-time basis.

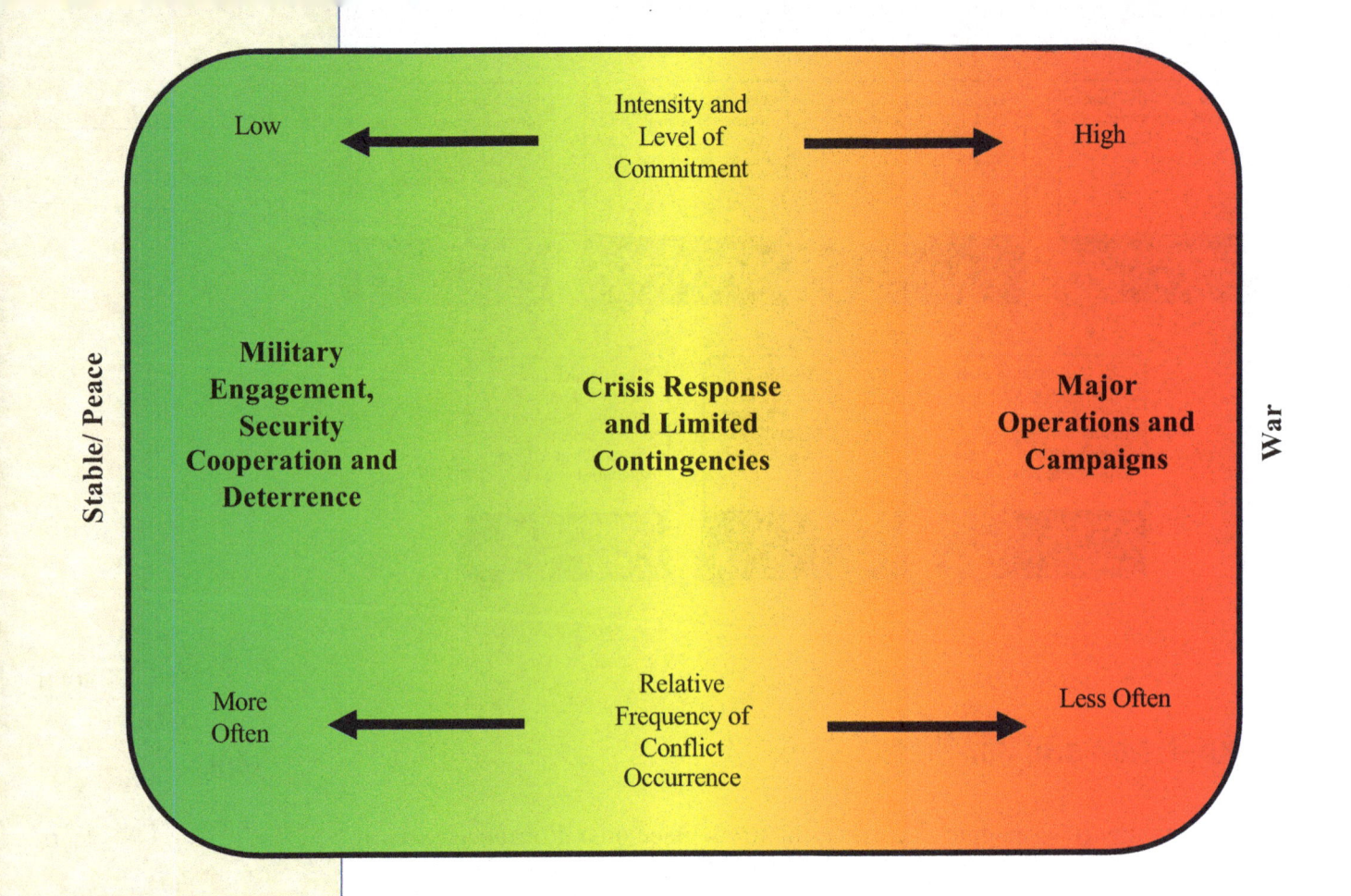

Stable/ Peace — War

Intensity and Level of Commitment: Low ← → High

- **Military Engagement, Security Cooperation and Deterrence**
- **Crisis Response and Limited Contingencies**
- **Major Operations and Campaigns**

Relative Frequency of Conflict Occurrence: More Often ← → Less Often

---

The **National Security Act of 1947** created the Central Intelligence Agency (CIA), the National Security Council and the Department of Defense (DoD)

Websites and Articles Worth Exploring

- National Defense Magazine

- U.S. Department of Defense

- What Are the Branches of the US Military?

- Our Forces

- In the beginning, there was competition: the old idea behind the new American way of war

Videos Worth Watching

- The National Defense Strategy of the United States | Learning Military

- 5 Things You Don't Know: Department of Defense

- US Armed Forces: Branches Explained

Considerations for Your National Defense

As you start to think about your national security consider:

- What is the physical terrain of your country and the surrounding area? Are you on an island? Landlocked? What implications does your physical terrain have in terms of providing for your national defense?

- Who are your neighbors? Are they countries with whom you anticipate friendly relations?

- Is your country more likely to be engaged in conflict on domestic (your) or foreign (other) lands?

- What types of peacetime missions will your military be responsible for?

A **Military recruiter** provides information regarding military service, training, and career opportunities to interested people.

Task #32: Your National Defense

Countries handle their militaries in different ways. Your country needs a military, but how will you create it? What will it look like?

Words Worth Knowing

- Formal Education

❑ Decide which types (branches) of militaries you will need to defend your country. Create an insignia for each branch.

❑ Create a pie chart showing the percentage of your total national defense capital you will use for each branch.

❑ Create a map showing the locations of any military bases in your country.
- You might want to use the map you made in the last task (#31) as a base template
- Be sure to note which of your branches use each base or if it is a joint base (Used by multiple branches).

❑ Decide if you will utilize a draft or not.
- If so – create an law outlining the rules for your draft
- If not – create a poster advertising for new recruits.

Types of Education

Throughout the world governments play varying roles in the education of their citizens. In the united states, for instance, the department of education establishes schools and colleges, develops curricula and curricula standards, and determines requirements for enrollment and graduation. However, not all aspects of education are, or need to be, regulated. There are three basic types of education.

In 1635 the **Boston Latin School** became the first public school in the American Colonies. It still exists today.

Formal education involves learning through schools or other institutions of learning. This type of education is usually hierarchical and results in a diploma, degree, or certification. This is the type most people think of when they hear the word education.

Non-formal education involves learning from experience or from home. Homeschools fall into this category as well as some types co-op groups, tutoring and travel-school.

Informal education involves practical learning or training. This type of education would include apprenticeship programs and on-the-job training activities.

> **Words Worth Knowing**
> - Non-formal Education
> - Informal Education
> - Education Policy

Formal Education
- School/institutions involved
- Hierarchical structure
- Uniform/ full time
- Certification/ Degrees/ Diplomas

Non-formal Education
- Learning from experience
- Learning from home
- Learning from environment
- Learning from work

Informal Education
- Practical Learning
- Training activities
- Built on learner participation
- Less organized

Education Policy

A country's **education policy** consists of the principles and government policies in the educational sphere as well as the collection of laws and rules that govern the operation of education systems.

Words Worth Knowing

- Healthcare Policy

In developing countries, each **additional year of education** can increase a person's future income by an average of 10%

Websites and Articles Worth Exploring

- What are the 3 Types of Education?
- THE DIFFERENT TYPES OF EDUCATION
- US Department of Education: Laws & Guidance
- Education policy in the United States

Videos Worth Watching

- Types of education : Formal , Non-formal , Informal education
- What is education policy?
- The art of policy making in education - Education Talks
- Globalisation and Educational Policy
- Saving Schools: History, Politics, and Policy in U.S. Education | HarvardX on edX | About Video
- The Basic Structure of Education Law: Module 1 of 4

Healthcare

A country's **healthcare policy** is a document that establishes guidelines to support the country's patients, hospitals and other healthcare organizations and healthcare system as a whole. According to the World Health Organization, an explicit health policy can perform three essential functions.

```
┌─────────────────────────────────────────┐
│      Define a vision for the future     │
└─────────────────────────────────────────┘
                    ↓
┌─────────────────────────────────────────┐
│ Outline priorities and the expected roles of different groups │
│   (patients, doctors, hospitals, insurances)  │
└─────────────────────────────────────────┘
                    ↓
┌─────────────────────────────────────────┐
│      Build consensus and inform people  │
└─────────────────────────────────────────┘
```

> **Words Worth Knowing**
> - Beveridge Model
> - Bismark Model

The type and scope of healthcare among different countries can vary widely. However most systems fall under 4 different models: the Beveridge Model, the Bismark Model, national health insurance, and the out-of-pocket model.

> An **L.P.N (Licensed Practical Nurse)** provides patients with primary and essential care, including monitoring vital signs.

The Beveridge Model

In the **Beveridge Model** the government provides for a single payer National Health Service. This service is funded exclusively through taxes and there are no out of pocket costs for the individual patient.

The Bismark Model

In the **Bismark Model** the responsibility for funding health insurance plans falls on employers and employees and funded through payroll deductions. There may be only a single insurer or multiple insurers however the government controls the pricing of both insurances and providers.

Words Worth Knowing

- National Health Insurance Model
- Out-of-Pocket Model

A **patient advocate** helps patients communicate with their healthcare providers to get the right information to make informed decisions about their health care.

National Health Insurance Model

In the **National Health Insurance Model** is a blend of the Beveridge and Bismark models of health systems. Medical providers are private, however the payments all come from one health insurance which is run by the government. Every citizen pays into this insurance and has access to the benefits.

Out-of-Pocket Model

In the **Out-of-Pocket Model** all providers are private and there is essentially no insurance. Patients pay for all medical procedures out of their own pockets. This model is generally only seen in areas where there aren't enough federal financial resources to create a more beneficial healthcare system.

Your Healthcare Policy

Regardless of which model that you use, a quality healthcare policy should address the following areas of healthcare operations:

Patient Care	Employee Health	Drug Policies	Security and Privacy
• Protocols for treatment procedures and how healthcare professionals should respond to different situations	• Rules governing treatment and wellness of employees	• Procedures around the handling and administering of pharmaceuticals, Security and Privacy	• Procedures regarding the safety and security of patients and medical professionals as well as the security of health related data and Personally Identifiable Information

Websites and Articles Worth Exploring

- Types of Health Systems

- The Formulation of Health Policy by the Three Branches of Government

- Six Components Necessary for Effective Public Health Program Implementation

- Healthcare Policy: What Is It and Why Is It Important?

Videos Worth Watching

- Health Systems

- Healthcare System Comparison: Canada v. UK v. Germany

- The Healthcare System of the United States

- (P002) Public Health Policy Making Process - Basic Concepts

- The Economics of Healthcare: Crash Course Econ #29

- The Structure & Cost of US Health Care: Crash Course Sociology #44

Considerations for Your Education and Healthcare Policies

As you begin to think about your Education and Healthcare policy creation in the next couple of tasks it may be helpful to refer to the following items from your National Library:

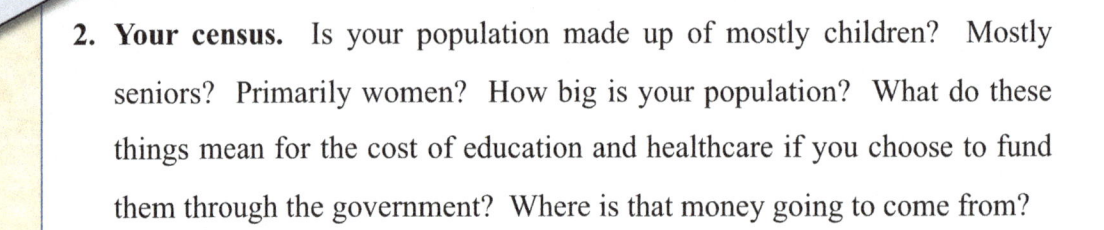

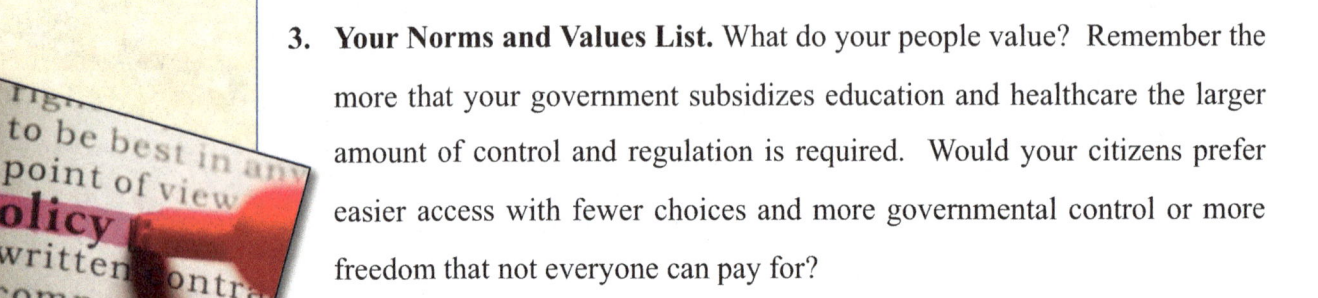

1. **Your physical map and your Population Density map.** How does your country's physical terrain and the dispersion of your population impact the access of your people to adequate healthcare and education? How might this effect the policy decisions that your government makes?

2. **Your census.** Is your population made up of mostly children? Mostly seniors? Primarily women? How big is your population? What do these things mean for the cost of education and healthcare if you choose to fund them through the government? Where is that money going to come from?

3. **Your Norms and Values List.** What do your people value? Remember the more that your government subsidizes education and healthcare the larger amount of control and regulation is required. Would your citizens prefer easier access with fewer choices and more governmental control or more freedom that not everyone can pay for?

4. **Your type of government.** The type of government that you have plays a large part in the drafting of education and healthcare policies. Think about whether your government is a monarchy, dictatorship, oligarchy or a democracy

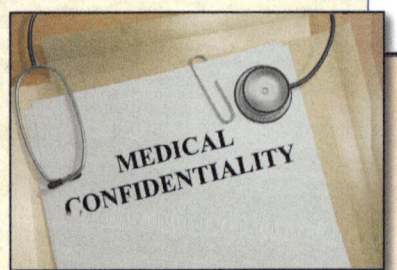

Task #33: Your Education and Healthcare Policies

❏ Complete **Worksheet 11.1: Your views on Education** in your Workbook

❏ Create an education policy for your country. Your policy must:
   1. State your country's major education viewpoints
   2. Outline the ages and guidelines for compulsory education

1. Describe how different types of educational institutions in your country are funded
2. Outline a method for evaluating the effectiveness of your educational system.

❑ Create a healthcare policy for your country. This policy should include

1. Your vision or goal statement for the heath care in your country
2. An outline of who has what kinds of access to healthcare
3. How your citizens will pay for healthcare (ie, public insurance, private insurance, self pay)
4. How your government will pay for healthcare (ie taxes, shared costs, exclusions)

Words Worth Knowing

- Cabinet
- Presidential Succession

Your Cabinet

A **cabinet** is a group of officials who's role is to advise your leader or leaders on issues relating to the running of your country. In some countries, like the United States, the cabinet also makes up the order of presidential succession. **Presidential succession** is the order in which the vice president and other members of a government assume the powers and duties of the president upon the elected official's death, resignation, removal from office or incapacity. In the United States the presidential succession begins with the Vice President who is followed by the Speaker of the House of Representatives, the President Pro Tempore of the Senate and the members of the presidential cabinet.

The **Presidential Succession Act**, Article II, Section 1, Clause 6 of the Constitution, establishes the official line of Presidential succession. First enacted in 1792, it was repealed and reenacted in 1886 and 1947 and revised again in 2006.

Words Worth Knowing

- Vice President
- Secretary of State
- Secretary of Agriculture
- Secretary of Commerce
- Secretary of Defense
- Secretary of Education
- Secretary of Energy

The United States currently has 16 official cabinet positions:

Vice President	Secretary of State	Secretary of Agriculture	Secretary of Commerce
Secretary of Defense	Secretary of Education	Secretary of Energy	Secretary of Health and Human Services
Secretary of Homeland Security	Secretary of Housing and Urban Development	Secretary of the Interior	Secretary of Labor
Secretary of Transportation	Secretary of Treasury	Secretary of Veterans' Affairs	Attorney General

- The **Vice President** presides over the Senate and acts as a tie-breaker. The Vice President is also the first in the line of Presidential Succession.

- The **Secretary of State** handles matters related to international relations and national foreign policy.

- The **Secretary of Agriculture** handles all matters related to farming, food, and rural economic development.

- The **Secretary of Commerce** handles matters related to economic growth, such as setting industrial standards and gathering data for policy-making.

- The **Secretary of Defense** handles matters related to national security and the United States Armed Forces.

- The **Secretary of Education** handles issues related to education, policy and schools as well as financial loans and grant management.

- The **Secretary of Energy** deals with issues related to energy production and supply, waste disposal, nuclear weapons, and the climate crisis.

- The **Secretary of Health and Human Services** oversees matters related to public health and family services.

- The **Secretary of Homeland Security** handles public security issues like terrorism, disaster prevention, cybersecurity, border security, and immigration.

- The **Secretary of Housing and Urban Development** manages programs that affect development and fair housing such as Housing and Community Planning and Development.

- The **Secretary of the Interior** deals with territorial affairs and manages all federal lands in regards to conservation and natural resources, such as dams, reservoirs, and wildlife.

- The **Secretary of Labor** handles regulations designed to help keep employees safe, as well as ensure their rights such as unemployment benefits, workplace safety, and wage standards.

- The **Secretary of Transportation** coordinates policy and action for ensuring the safety and modernity of the transportation system and services.

- The **Secretary of the Treasury** handles the production of currency and manages the public debt, finance and tax laws, and fiscal policy.

- The **Secretary of Veterans' Affairs** provides healthcare, benefits and support to veterans of the United States.

- The **Attorney General** serves as the chief lawyer to the United States Government and oversees all the areas of the Department of Justice.

Words Worth Knowing

- Secretary of Health and Human Services
- Secretary of Homeland Security
- Secretary of Housing and Urban Development
- Secretary of the Interior
- Secretary of Labor
- Secretary of Transportation
- Secretary of the Treasury
- Secretary of Veterans' Affairs
- Attorney General

On March 4, 1933, **Frances Perkins** was sworn in as Secretary of Labor becoming the 1st woman appointed to a presidential Cabinet when she.

There are also several other governmental positions that, while not official cabinet positions, have Cabinet Level Rank. These include:

- The White House Chief of Staff
- The US Ambassador to the United Nations
- The Director of National Intelligence
- The US Trade Representative
- The head of the Environmental Protection Agency
- The head of the Office of Management and Budget
- The head of the Council of Economic Advisers
- The head of the Office of Science and Technology Policy
- The head of the Small Business Administration

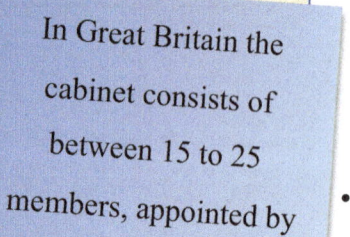

Websites and Articles Worth Exploring

- The Cabinet
- How the US Cabinet Works: 15 Offices of the Cabinet
- Order of Presidential Succession
- Presidential Succession Act
- Succession

> In Great Britain the cabinet consists of between 15 to 25 members, appointed by the Prime Minister, who in turn has been appointed by the monarch on the basis of ability to command a majority of votes in the Commons.

Videos Worth Watching

- America 101: What is the Cabinet? | History
- The Cabinet - A level Politics
- Inside the White House: The Cabinet
- Prime Minister vs. President: What's The Difference?
- The Origin of the President's Cabinet
- U.S. President, Presidential Line of Succession Explained
- The Presidential Line of Succession
- Royalty 101: The Rules of Succession

> James Madison first coined the term **"Presidents cabinet"** referring to the term "cabinet" which comes from the Italian word "cabinetto," meaning "a small, private room."

Considerations for your cabinet and other governmental departments

As you finish fleshing out your governmental infrastructure you may want to keep a few things in mind.

> In the United States, **pay for Cabinet-level officers** is set each year by Congress as part of its approval of the federal budget.

- **How big is your country in terms of land mass?** The bigger you country the more administrative support your leader will need to run it. You may want specific agencies to deal with transportation, rural or urban matters or environmental issues.

- **How big is your country in terms of population?** The more people you have the more administration is needed to accommodate them. If you have a large population you may want specific agencies to deal with social policies and public welfare.

- **How close and what kind of neighbors do you have?** Did you create a large national defense in task #32? Will that require a specific agency to oversee operations and advise your leader on those issues?

- **What kind of government do you have?** Is your leader the kind who will want to hear many voices and opinions or the kind that prefers to make all the decisions without outside input or interference?

- **What issues and values are specific to your people and culture?** Is the environment a big deal? What about specific issues or populations? Do you need a department to deal with any unique issues of your country.

Task #34: Other Governmental Departments and Your Cabinet members or Advisors

❑ Draft a new article for your constitution outlining the cabinet members or members of your leader's advisory team. Include what aspect of your country each position is responsible for. *Note: The number and types of advisors needed will depend on the type of government that you formed.*

❑ Complete **Worksheet 11.2: Qualities of a Cabinet Member** in your Workbook

❑ Create a Flow Chart outlining the line of succession for your country's leader. Include at least 6 levels of succession

Composition Activity #9: Your Cabinet Member's Resume

Create a resume for a fictional person that will serve as a cabinet member from one of the cabinet positions that you used in **Worksheet 11.2: Qualities of a Cabinet Member.**

- Your cabinet member's fictional resume must include objective, key skills and competencies, education and experience sections.

- Draft a cover letter for the resume highlighting why this person possesses the right combination of skills, traits and experience to be perfect for that position.

Chapter 11 Review

The following sections help you review and think about some of the concepts and activities that you performed in this chapter.

Words Worth Knowing Review

The following terms were very important throughout this chapter.

Public Works	Public Utilities	National Defense	Army
Air Force	Navy	Marine Corps	Coast Guard
Space Force	National Guard	Routine Peaceful Competition	Formal Education
Non-formal Education	Informal Education	Education Policy	Healthcare Policy
Beveridge Model	Bismark Model	National Health Insurance Model	Out-of-Pocket Model
Cabinet	Presidential Succession	Vice President	Secretary of State
Secretary of Agriculture	Secretary of Commerce	Secretary of Defense	Secretary of Education
Secretary of Energy	Secretary of Health and Human Services	Secretary of Homeland Security	Secretary of Housing and Urban Development
Secretary of the Interior	Secretary of Labor	Secretary of Transportation	Secretary of the Treasury
Secretary of Veterans' Affairs	Attorney General		

❏ Complete the **Chapter 11 Words Worth Knowing Exercises** in the Workbook

For Discussion

- How did the global placement of your country affect the decisions that you made when it came to your national defense?

- How did the knowledge you gained from exploring your land and getting to know your people factor in to the types of decisions you made about your governmental infrastructure and cabinet makeup?

You as a Citizen

- As a citizen, how will your country's healthcare and education policies affect your day to day life? How would this change if you were in the lower or higher economic classes?

CHAPTER 11 REVIEW

CHAPTER 11 REVIEW

Your National Library

The following Items from this chapter should be filed in your national library

- **Guidebook**
    - Military Insignias
    - Governmental Cabinet flow chart

- **Official Documents**
    - Map of your Public Works
    - Map of your Capital City
    - Map of Military Base Locations
    - Pie chart showing percentages of capital to each military branch
    - *Military Draft Law
    - Education Policy
    - Healthcare Policy

- **Promotional material / media**
    - Military Recruitment Poster

Chapter 12

Making Choices with your Priorities

Making Choices with your Priorities

Congratulations! Your government is in place and running and your new economy seems to be flourishing.

You have ended the year with an unexpected budget surplus of $200,000,000. But, what will you do with the money?

In this final chapter of this unit you will be making some key decisions about what to do with your budget surplus. You will also complete some unit wrap-up activities.

Words Worth Knowing

- Intuitive Decision Making
- Rational Decision Making

A **data analyst** reviews data to identify key insights that helps make decisions and solve problems

Research has continually found that the majority of people use emotions more than logic to make decisions

Decision Making

Regardless of whether you are the leader of a new country or a parent cooking dinner for your kids, you are faced with the need to make rational and viable decisions in nearly every thing you do. In simpler matters, you are likely to apply an **intuitive decision making** process. Intuitive decision making does not formal tools and procedures. Instead, the decision maker uses sensitivity, gut instinct, a sixth sense, or intuition. You do what sounds best to you. However, as the stakes get higher, the cost of your decision is greater, and the breadth of your decision's impact expands, gut feeling is not enough. This is when a more scientific or **rational decision making** process is needed. Rational decision making is a step-by-step model that helps you identify a problem, pick a solution between multiple alternatives, and find an answer. The decision maker identifies possible solutions, and uses logic and research to choose the best.

If you search the internet, you are likely to find dozens of different models for decision making. Some are very complex, using mathematical formulas and calculations. Others are as simple as a flowchart with a series of yes/no questions. Most of them involve a step-by-step process. You identify the problem to be solved, develop various alternatives for solving it, evaluate each of those alternatives, and select the best alternative. After you've implemented the alternative, you evaluate the results and determine if adjustments are needed. If so, you redefine your problem based on the results thus far and begin the cycle again.

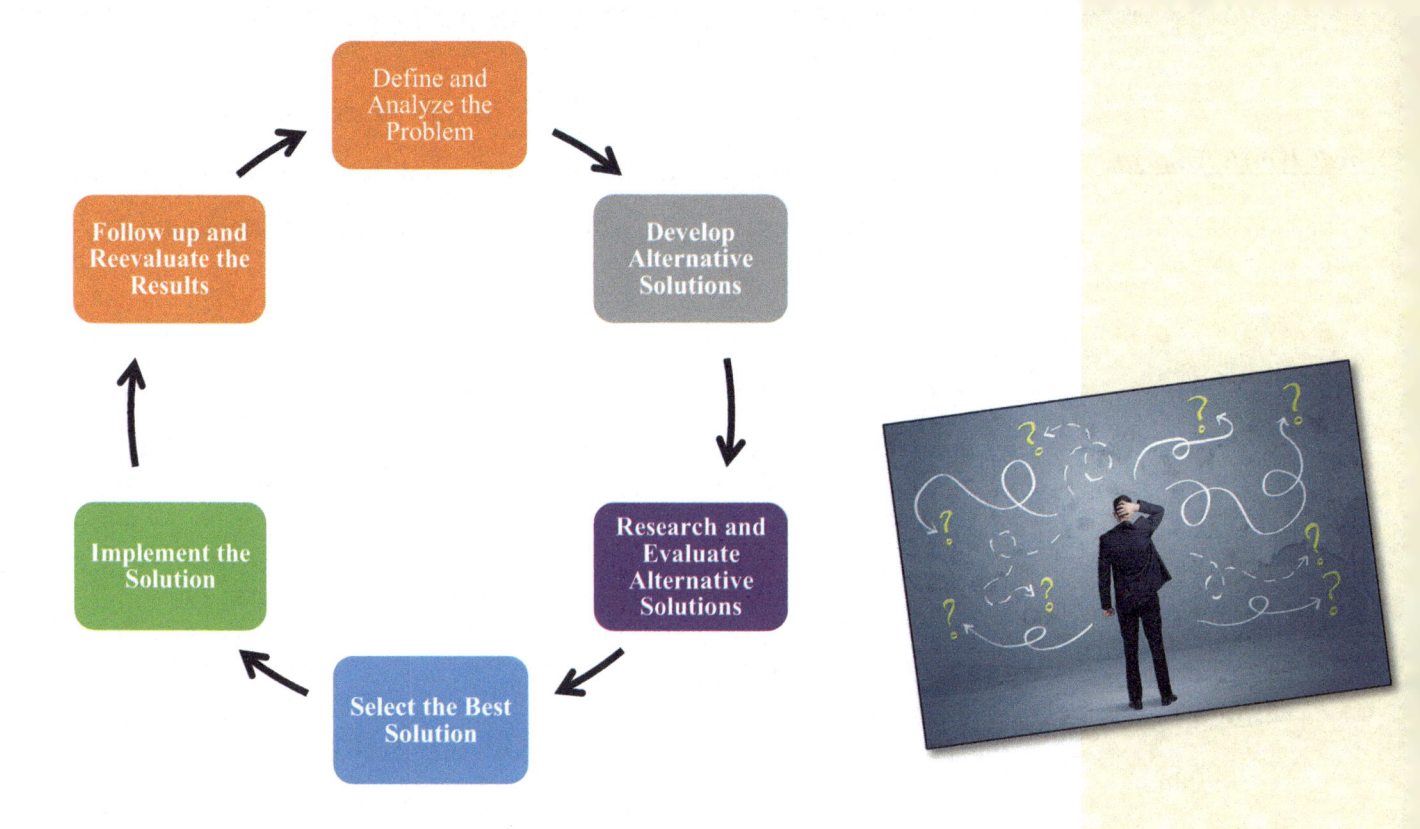

Define and Analyze the Problem → Develop Alternative Solutions → Research and Evaluate Alternative Solutions → Select the Best Solution → Implement the Solution → Follow up and Reevaluate the Results → (back to Define and Analyze the Problem)

Define and Analyze the Problem

This may seem perfectly obvious and simple. But in reality, it is the most important step in the process. To successfully solve the issue you have to have a realistic goal to focus on. If you define the problem too narrowly, you negate many viable and creative possibilities toward solving it. Likewise, if you define your problem too broadly, you are apt to solve world hunger rather than select something to take to a potluck dinner. Some things to think about when analyzing your problem are:

Information overload occurs when there are so many factors and choices that a person just can't process all the information to make the best decision.

- What happens if you don't make a decision? If this decision has little effect, you don't really have a problem. You have choices and can truly justify using intuitive decision making. Your gut instincts will likely be the best course to follow.

- Who will be affected by the decision you make? Does it have broad reaching implications? Who will benefit? Who might it harm? Who will you need support from to implement?

Words Worth Knowing

- Brainstorming

> A **consultant** provides expert opinions, analysis, and recommendations, based on their own expertise

> The more tired you get the less likely you are to make good or difficult decisions. This is called **decision fatigue**

- What are your time constraints? Is this a decision that needs to be implemented immediately? Do you need time for strategic planning, getting the necessary help, and actually complete the work required?

- How will you fund your decision? How much money will it take to implement your solution? How much is available? If not, what are your options for obtaining sufficient funding?

Develop Alternative Solutions:

First, don't ever think that you have to do step 2 AFTER step one. As you are analyzing and defining the problem you are trying to solve, you will be coming up with a number of ideas. Some you will discard as soon as they come to mind; others will move forward to step 2. If you only have a couple of possible solutions, you may want to involve others in this decision making process. The more minds involved, the more ideas develop. One popular method is brainstorming. **Brainstorming** is a method of generating ideas and sharing knowledge to solve a particular problem un which participants are encouraged to think without interruption.

Research and Evaluate Alternative Solutions:

In this step you take the ideas from step 2 and do some thorough analysis. Define the criteria to which you will weigh each alternative against (time, money, effects, social effects, size, color, etc.). Identify the "must-have" criteria and consider those as Go/No Go measurements. Any alternatives that don't meet the Go/No Go criteria should automatically be discarded. For example, if your problem MUST be completed by the end of the month, and you prefer it to be red, it should be discarded if it can't be completed in less than 6 weeks. Then weigh each alternative against the preference criteria. Research what you don't know so that you can be certain that you are making the most informed decision possible. Look at each alternative from as many angles as possible to ensure that you are basing your decision based on facts rather than personal biases.

Select the Best Solution:

Now you are ready to rank and select the best alternative that both meets the real goal identified in step 1 and the criteria established in step 3. Your thoroughness in steps 1 and 3 will play a huge part in the success or failure of your decision.

Implement the Solution::

Once the solution is selected you can begin the implementation process. Usually implementation begins with planning. What needs to be completed first, second and third. Plan, schedule, budget, and begin to put your decision into action.

Follow up and Reevaluate the Results:

Implementing your decision does not end the process. No matter how good your decision making was, you may run into unforeseen and unplanned circumstances. Sometimes something just didn't go the way it was supposed to. This is the very reason that the decision making process is a cycle rather than steps. Progress and performance needs to be monitored. As soon as you realize something is not working, you need to move on to step 1 again. It's not the same problem; you are not starting over. Rather, the new problem is what to do from this point to put you back on the path to the goal.

> Your brain needs **glucose** in order to make good decisions. When your glucose is low you willpower is reduced and your are more likely to yield to any kind of temptation

Websites and Articles worth Exploring

- Decision-making process
- Decision-Making
- The Effective Decision
- Decision making in the age of urgency

Videos Worth Watching

- Decision-Making Strategies
- Decision Making in Management
- Steps in Rational Decision Making
- The 7 step decision making process | Decision making model | Lauren Kress
- Government decision making in uncertainty

Task #35: Making Decisions Concerning your Budget Surplus

Remember that extra $200 million? It's to make some decisions on how to spend it. To get to the necessary decisions, worksheets are provided to walk through the decision making process just described. To make such a large decision for your country, you don't want to employ an intuitive decision making style. Gut feeling is not the best way to justify such a sum.

❑ **Use the decision making process to decide how to spend your new excess.**

- Criteria for your decision
    - You must choose at least 2 items, however they can be the same (i.e. you can build multiple theme parks if your wish)
    - You may choose as many of the options as you like as long as you don't go over your surplus amount.
    - For each option complete the associated activity or activities
    - You must spend at least 90% of the surplus.

❑ Complete **Worksheet 12.1: Define and Analyze your Problem** in your Workbook

❑ Complete **Worksheet 12.2a-b: Develop Alternatives** in your Workbook

- Your possible solutions are listed in **Appendix V** of this book. Review the appendix and choose at least 3 items. You may
- choose as many combinations of the options as you like as long as you don't go over your surplus amount.

❑ Complete **Worksheet 12.3: Evaluation Criteria** in your Workbook

❑ Complete **Worksheet 12.4a-b: Research and Evaluate Alternatives** in your Workbook

❑ Complete **Worksheet 12.5: Select the Best Alternative** in your Workbook

Note: For this task, we will not be doing the 6th and final step of the decision making process. Remember, though, that you will have to continually monitor the implementation process and make adjustments along the way.

> In April 2022, the U.S. government posted a record **$308 billion surplus**.

❏ **Implement your Solution by completing the required tasks for each option in the combination that you chose.**

  ❏ Remember these are listed on the page for each option in Appendix V

❏ **Prepare a 5 minute press conference to your people outlining and justifying your choice of expenditures.**

  1. Make sure to explain how your choices will promote economic growth?
  2. Make sure to explain your plans for any leftover amount of money.

Composition Activity #10: The Dissenting Opinion

Prepare a rebuttal by your critics outlining why the choices you made for the surplus are <u>NOT</u> the right choices for your country.

- Your rebuttal must speak to each of the points made in your presentation in task #35.

- You may present your rebuttal as wither a five minute speech or a 750 word essay

Extension Activity #11: Modeling Your Budget Surplus

Objective: Express one of your budget surplus expenditures in 3D

❏ Choose one of the following activities based on the choices you made in task #35

- A 3D model of your Apartment Complex or a single apartment layout
- A 3D model of your factory
- A 3D model of your renewable energy project
- A diorama depicting your defense invention in use
- A diorama of natural resource collection in progress
- A diorama of one of your farms/ranches
- A 3D model of your hospital
- A 3D model of your bus station or train station
- A diorama of your new port
- A Diorama of your theme park or a 3D model of your main theme park attraction
- A 3D model of your university's administration building
- A diorama of your leader enjoying his/her leadership perks

A **Budget analyst** helps public and private organizations make decisions regarding their budgets and finances.

Chapter 12 Review

The following sections help you review and think about some of the concepts and activities that you performed in this chapter.

Words Worth Knowing Review

The following terms were very important throughout this chapter.

Intuitive Decision Making	Rational Decision Making	Brainstorming	

❏ **There are no Vocabulary Exercises for this chapter.**

For Discussion

- How did utilizing the decision making process help you make a better decision when it came to using your budget surplus?

- How might the process be different as you increase the number of people involved in the decision making process?

You as a Citizen

- As a citizen, how can you apply the decision making process to major decisions in your own life?

Your National Library

The following Items from this chapter should be filed in your national library

- **Guidebook**
    - *Apartment Complex Design
    - *Factory Design
    - *Renewable Energy presentation
    - *Defense invention Design
    - *Additional natural resource presentation
    - *Agriculture presentation
    - *Hospital design
    - *Theme park design
    - *University design
    - *Rebate check social media campaign
    - *Leader Perk Social Media Campaign

- **Official Documents**
    - *Renewable Energy Map
    - *Additional Natural Resource collection map
    - *Additional Rural Land map

CHAPTER 12 REVIEW

- *Map showing hospital location
- *Map showing theme park location
- *Map showing university location
- *Apartment Complex Cost Estimate
- *Factory Cost Estimate
- *Defense invention description
- *Hospital cost estimate
- *University cost estimate
- *Intergovernmental Loan agreement
- *Rebate cost estimate
- *Leader Perks cost estimate

- **Promotional material / media**
    - Dissenting Opinion essay

Note: Items marked with an asterisk (*) may or may not be included based on your choices in task#35

Unit Review

Unit 2: Your Government

Your Government Words Worth Knowing Review

Choose **at least 20** Unit 2 Words Worth Knowing Review words from the tables below. Write a short essay, scene or story that uses each of the words in context. You may include labeled illustrations as well.

- You must include **at least 3 terms from each list**

Chapter 9 Words

Government	Sovereignty	Legitimacy	Jurisdiction
Anarchy	Communal Anarchy	Autocracy	Monarchy
Absolute Monarchy	Constitutional Monarchy	Dictatorship	Oligarchy
Theocracy	Plutocracy	Aristocracy	Democracy
Direct Democracy	Representative Democracy	Constituent	Principle
Goals	Constitution	Preamble	Right
Natural Right	Legal Right	Bill of Rights	Article

UNIT 3 REVIEW

Chapter 10 Words

Economy	Scarcity	Supply	Demand
Law of Supply and Demand	Externality	Unemployment	Inflation
Economic System	Traditional Economic System	Command Economic System	Market Economic System
Free Market	Mixed Economic System	Economic Ideology	Capitalism
Fascism	Socialism	Communism	Currency
Universal Design	Denomination	Exchange Rate	Tax
Tax Rate	Income Tax	Property Tax	Sales Tax
Allocation	National Budget		

Chapter 11 Words

Public Works	Public Utilities	National Defense	Army
Air Force	Navy	Marine Corps	Coast Guard
Space Force	National Guard	Routine Peaceful Competition	Formal Education
Non-formal Education	Informal Education	Education Policy	Healthcare Policy
Beveridge Model	Bismark Model	National Health Insurance Model	Out-of-Pocket Model
Cabinet	Presidential Succession	Vice President	Secretary of State
Secretary of Agriculture	Secretary of Commerce	Secretary of Defense	Secretary of Education
Secretary of Energy	Secretary of Health and Human Services	Secretary of Homeland Security	Secretary of Housing and Urban Development
Secretary of the Interior	Secretary of Labor	Secretary of Transportation	Secretary of the Treasury
Secretary of Veterans' Affairs	Attorney General		

Chapter 12 Words

Intuitive Decision Making	Rational Decision Making	Brainstorming	

For Discussion

1. Based on what you've learned and done in this unit, how would modern technology and the prevalence of social media affect the way your government operates? Do you think the ease and availability of information would make it easier or more difficult to govern effectively?

Check Your Understanding

Review Questions

1. Why is it important that your official choices are documented in your constitution?

2. How does the form of government that you chose and the laws that you created entice quality immigrants for continued growth of your country?

3. What role did the physical location of your country play in your creation of your national security and defense?

UNIT 3 REVIEW

UNIT 3 REVIEW

1. What are the trade-offs for government funded education and healthcare versus privatization of education and healthcare?

2. What are the steps in the decision making process and how could they this process applied when determining the need for additional governmental departments or cabinet positions?

Current Events in Your World: Governments in Transition

❑ Look up and find a country whose government that is currently undergoing a transition in the balance of power.

❑ Prepare a presentation on the country giving some background information about the country itself, and the situation which led to the upheaval or transition.

❑ Discuss what you think the outcome will be and what you believe the future holds for this country based on what you have learned in this course so far.

Unit 4: Your Global Position

Contents of Unit 4: Your Global Position

Chapter 13: Establishing Your Global Focus

Chapter 14: Forging Your Global Alliances

Chapter 15: Bringing Everything Together

Unit Overview

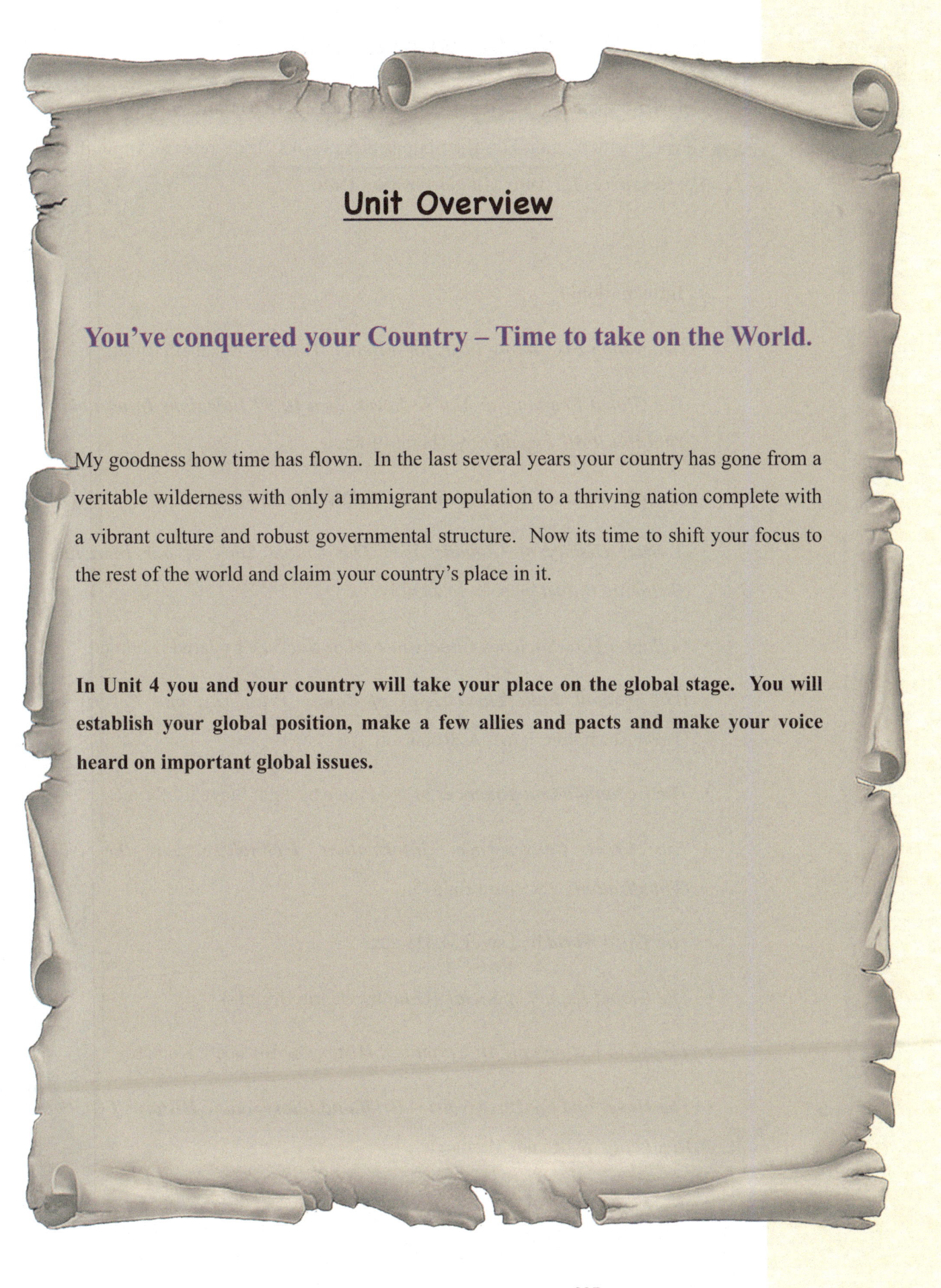

You've conquered your Country – Time to take on the World.

My goodness how time has flown. In the last several years your country has gone from a veritable wilderness with only a immigrant population to a thriving nation complete with a vibrant culture and robust governmental structure. Now its time to shift your focus to the rest of the world and claim your country's place in it.

In Unit 4 you and your country will take your place on the global stage. You will establish your global position, make a few allies and pacts and make your voice heard on important global issues.

Books Worth Reading with this Unit

Below are some suggested books that you can use to compliment the "Your Global Position" unit. For descriptions these books please refer to **Appendix IV: Resources for Your Global Position Unit.**

➢ **Informational**

- *Generation Fix: Young Ideas for a Better World* by Elizabeth Rusch.

- *The Global Economy as You've Never Seen It: 99 Ingenious Infographics That Put It All Together* by Thomas Ramge.

- *Global Issues: An Introduction, 5th Edition* by Kristen Hite.

- *A Brief History of Globalization: The Untold Story of our Incredible Shrinking Planet* by Alex MacGillivray.

- *Collapse: How Societies Choose to Fail or Succeed* by Jared Diamond

- *Why Nations Fail: The Origins of Power, Prosperity, and Poverty* by Daron Acemoğlu, James A. Robinson

- *The Economic Consequences of the Peace* by John Maynard Keynes

- *The Great Convergence: Information Technology and the New Globalization* by Richard Baldwin

- *The Third World* by David M. Haugen

- *The Global Impact of Social Media* by Dedria Bryfonski

- *The Sixth Extinction: An Unnatural History* by Elizabeth Kolbert

- *The Haves and the Have Nots: A Brief and Idiosyncratic History of Global Inequality* by Branko Milanovic

Literature

- *Around the World in 80 Days* by Jules Verne

- *Messy Roots: A Graphic Memoir of a Wuhanese American* by Laura Gao

- *The Upper World* by Femi Fadugba

- *Buried Beneath the Baobab Tree* by Adaobi Tricia Nwaubani

- *A Moveable Feast (Life Changing Food Adventures Around The World)" edited* by Don George

- *The Adventures of Tintin* by Hergé

Movie Selections for this Unit

Below are some suggested movies that you can use to compliment the "Your Global Position" unit. For descriptions of each of these movies as well as parental guidance ratings please refer to **Appendix IV: Resources for Your Global Position Unit.**

- Living on One Dollar
- Last Call at the Oasis
- Poverty, Inc.
- Girl Rising
- Superman IV: The Quest for Peace
- No Man's Land
- Sergio
- A Game of Thrones

- American Factory
- Pump!
- Life and Debt
- When Worlds Collide
- The Interpreter
- Hotel Rwanda
- Captain America: Civil War

Gameschooling selections for this Unit

Below are some suggested games that you can use to compliment the "Your Global Position" unit. For descriptions of each of these games please refer to **Appendix IV: Resources for Your Global Position Unit.**

- Risk
- Diplomacy
- A Game of Thrones
- United Nations: A Game of World Domination in our Time

- Axis and Allies
- Small World
- Trekking the World: Trivia
- Article 27: The United Nations Security Council Game

Unit 4 Science Exploration Project

Your Global Position Science Exploration: Fighting Against Global Poverty with Nutritional Aid

(To be completed while you work through Chapters 13-15)

Poverty exists when people live on less than $3.20 a day, while extreme poverty is less than $1.90 a day. As of 2015 over a quarter of the world's population were living below the poverty line. Your country has decided to send nutritional care packages to a country with a severe poverty issue and has allocated $1,000,000 to this effort. But what should you include in this package? What are some of the affects of malnutrition for the people who would receive your package? How do changes in nutrition affect a person's ability to perform?

Vocabulary

Your should understand the following terms for this project:

- Calorie (Cal) and Kilocalorie (kcal)

- Food group

- Dairy

- Proteins

- Fats

- Sugars

- Nutrition

- Portion size

- Carbohydrates

- Malnutrition

Background

Watch the following videos on global poverty, nutrition and nutritional aid

- Poverty
- Global poverty: Facts, FAQs, and how to help
- The evolution of global poverty, 1990-2030
- GLOBAL POVERTY AND HUNGER
- The World Bank and Nutrition
- Nutrition: World food programme

Then explore these websites

- Global Stratification & Poverty: Crash Course Sociology #27
- A Life in Extreme Poverty
- World's Poorest Country 'Burundi' (I can't forget the things I saw)
- Poverty & Our Response to It: Crash Course Philosophy #44
- Malnutrition and World Hunger: A Guide To Global Issues | Global Citizen
- Yemen: On the brink of starvation - BBC News
- Food, nutrition and poverty - An overview by Elizabeth Dowler

Fighting Against Global Poverty with Nutritional Aid Overview:

In this project you will be designing a nutritional aid package and comparing the energy of different foods.

Required Materials

Volunteers	Stop Watch	Scale	Tape measure	Food *according to nutritional plan

Instructions:

1. Research the following:

    - How many calories and what types of foods are recommended for a balanced diet?

    - What foods are considered both nutrient dense and also shelf stable?

    - How does a proper diet affect performance?

2. **Create a nutritional poverty aid proposal for your country's leaders.** This proposal must include

    - The country that you have chosen for your nutritional poverty aid packages and why

    - The contents of each care package. Each package should be designed to feed a family of 4 for one month.

- The cost of each care package and the number of families that your country will be able to help (remember the goal is to help as many people as possible, so choose the contents of your care packages well.)

3. Form a hypothesis regarding the impact proper nutrition will have on weight, measurements and performance.

4. Design your experiment.

    - Design a 2-4 week meal plan with similar nutritional content to your nutritional care package

    - Find some volunteers (can include yourself) to carry out your experiment. The volunteers should all be of a similar age and health. Create a consent form and have each volunteer sign.

    - Split the volunteer group in half and label one half as the control group

    - Design a series of tests to check both physical and mental abilities.
        - Physical ability tests could include:
            - sit-ups, pushups or jumping jacks in 1 minute
            - Time it takes to run a specific distance
            - Coordination tests such as standing on one leg or walking a straight line
        - Mental tests could include
            - How many simple math problems can be done in a certain amount of time
            - How many numbers or words can be remembered and given in a certain amount of time
            - How fast can a puzzle be assembled

5. Set up your lab notebook and take initial data measurements

    - Take initial weight and measurements of each participant
    - Conduct the physical and mental test on each participant and record the results

6. Perform the Experiment keeping a log of your observations

    - For 2 weeks have the control group eat normally, while the other group eats according to your meal plan.
        - Have each participant record their food intake in a food log.

7. At the end of your test period take final weight and measurements of each participant and conduct your physical and mental tests again. Record the results.

8. Make the following calculations based on your data

    - The change in weight, measurements and physical and mental performance of the participants over the time period

9. Prepare a final report and/or board on your nutrition. The report should not only include the results of your experiment, but also the application your results could have on the makeup of your nutritional aid kits and the impact on global poverty and nutrition

    - Refer to Appendix VI for information on how to construct a project report and board.

Note: For an **optional** extension activity –How would the results differ if the participants only consumed non-perishable food products?

CHAPTER 13

Establishing Your Global Focus

Establishing your Global Focus

Welcome to the Global Stage!

Now that your country is alive and strong, its time to turn your attention to your neighbors. These days its nearly impossible for countries to exist without some sort of interaction with other countries and yours is no exception. However, just how you interact with the world is not necessarily set in stone.

In this chapter your will make some initial determinations about how your country will interact on the global stage. You will begin to trade with the countries around you and open your first embassy. Finally you will apply for entrance into the United Nations.

Words Worth Knowing

- International Relations
- Globalization
- Isolationism
- National Interest

Note: For the purposes of this course, your country is choosing a stance of globalization.

Globalization and International Relations

International Relations involve how countries interact with each other. Nearly every country interacts in some way with the rest of the world. Most countries take a stance of globalization. **Globalization** refers to an interdependence on a global scale caused by cross-border trade in goods and services, technology, investment, people, and information. A country could, however, subscribe to a doctrine of isolation. **Isolationism** is a policy of remaining apart from the affairs of other countries. Basically isolationism is a "I'll leave you alone, you leave me alone" stance.

There are two key questions or issues when it comes to international relations:

1. How can a group (such as two or more nations) serve its collective interests when doing so may require its members to forego their individual interests?

2. How can you provide something that benefits all members of a group regardless of what each member contributes to it - especially without a central authority to enforce the necessary measures?

For those countries that choose a globalization stance there are several theories that could directly affect the nature of the country's international relations. The basis of these theories is the idea of national interest. **National interest** implies that each country will act in its own best interest, whether that interest involves national security, economic prosperity of global influence. There are three major theories of international relations:

340

```
        Realism
      Liberalism
    Constructivism
```

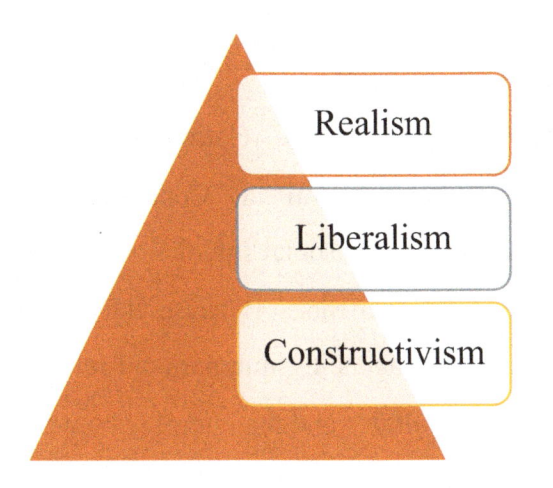

Words Worth Knowing
- Realism
- Liberalism

Realism

The **realism** theory of international relations proposes that the nature of relations is inherently anarchist because each nation or state is in it for themselves only. Realism is based on three principles:

1. Nations or states themselves are the main players in international relations.

2. There is no central authority. This means that there will always be a struggle between wholly self-interested parties.

3. No other nations or states can truly be counted on to ensure another state's survival.

The top 1% of Americans account for over 38% of the country's total income tax revenue.

Liberalism

The **liberalism** theory of international relations is in many ways, the antithesis of realism. This theory believes that cooperation is inevitable due to the necessity of international interdependence. Liberalism also contends that there are other players on the international stage besides just states/countries. Other players such as supranational authorities, non-government organizations, and multinational business organizations also help shape international relations.

Words Worth Knowing

- Constructivism

A **logistician** analyzes and coordinates an organization's supply chain—the system that moves a product from supplier to consumer.

Constructivism

The **constructivism** theory of international relations occupies a completely separate viewpoint than realism and liberalism. Constructivism believes that international relations is a product of social interaction between people and cultures, not just states and governments. Because the primary players in constructivism are people and not agencies, international relations react to the shifting and changing norms of cultures and the interplay between them.

Websites and Articles Worth Exploring

- Isolation Vs. Globalization
- Key Theories of International Relations
- Theories of International Relations
- Globalization – World 101
- What Is Globalization?

Videos Worth Watching

- Globalization explained
- Globalization II - Good or Bad?: Crash Course World History #42
- The untold story of American Isolationism | Christopher Nichols | TEDxPortland
- International Relations: An Introduction

- What is International Relations? (International Relations Defined)

- Realism vs. Liberalism - Global Politics Theories Compared

- Major Theories of International Relations

> **Words Worth Knowing**
> - International Trade
> - Exports
> - Imports
> - Balance of Trade

International Trade

International trade is the exchange of capital, goods, and services across international borders. Basically put, international trade involves **exports**, or the sale of goods and services to another country, and **imports**, or the purchase of goods and services from another country. International trade provides many key benefits for countries and the world in general.

- Allows for a greater variety of goods available for public consumption
- Allows for more efficient allocation and utilization of resources
- Promotes more efficiency in terms of production of goods
- Allows for greater consumption at a cheaper cost
- Generates more employment through increased demand and the establishment of newer industries
- Provides for better price stability
- Allows for the utilization of surplus products
- Fosters a sense of goodwill and peace through mutual understanding

*In 2021, the value of global trade reached a record level of **$28.5 trillion**.*

*A **stockbroker** is a financial professional who buys and sells stocks (goods traded on the global market) for clients.*

The Balance of Trade

The **balance of trade** is the difference between the total value of a country's exports and the total value of a country's imports. This balance can either result in a **trade surplus**, where a country exports more than it imports, or a **trade deficit**, where a country exports more than it imports. The issue of a trade surplus or deficit is not always straightforward. For example, in a **recession**, when the economy stops growing and starts shrinking, a country may prefer to export more and exist in a trade surplus to create jobs and demand in the economy. However, In times of economic expansion, a country may prefer to import more and exist in a trade deficit to promote price competition, which limits inflation.

Words Worth Knowing

- Trade Surplus
- Trade Deficit
- Recession

*In 2020, the United States represented **54.5%** of global market capitalization.*

*The United States generally operates in a **trade deficit**. In fact, in August of 2020, the US reported a deficit of over $67 billion.*

Websites and Articles Worth Exploring

- The Investor's Guide to Global Trade
- International Trade
- Trade – World 101
- Imports and Exports
- United States OEC
- Balance of Trade (BOT)
- Balance of Trade: Favorable Versus Unfavorable
- Balance of Trade
- United States Balance of Trade
- What Is the Current U.S. Trade Deficit?
- What Is A Recession?

Videos Worth Watching

- International Trade Explained | World101

- International Trade- Micro Topic 2.9

- How Global Trade Runs on U.S. Dollars | WSJ

- The Benefits Of International Trade: Econ-1 with John Taylor

- Imports, Exports, and Exchange Rates: Crash Course Economics #15

- How Imports and Exports Affect You | Economics

- International Trade: Imports and Exports

- Finance: What is Balance of Trade?

- The Balance of Trade

- What is a recession? | CNBC Explains

- What Is A Recession? In Context

Considerations for choosing your country's imports and exports

*In 2020, the United States exported **$1.4 trillion** worth of goods to the rest of the world.*

- Remember the natural resources and land allocation maps that you made before? Well, hopefully you have them handy, because they will be useful here. Based on the resources and distribution of your population what materials and goods will you have a surplus of that you can export? What materials and goods will you have a deficit of that you need to import?

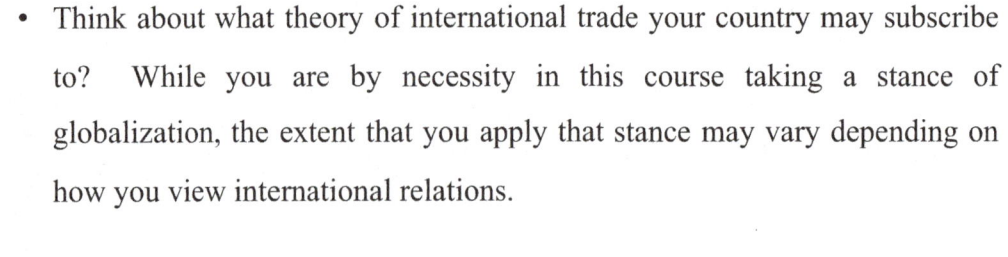

- Think about what theory of international trade your country may subscribe to? While you are by necessity in this course taking a stance of globalization, the extent that you apply that stance may vary depending on how you view international relations.

- Think about how you've allocated your land. Do you have more areas dedicated to resource collection and agriculture? Then you may be able to export food and raw materials but need to import finished goods and services. Did you allocate the majority of your land to urban areas? This would mean you have an abundance of factories and could export finished goods and services but may need to import raw materials or food products.

- Speaking of food, what is the physical geography of your land like? Are you able to grow plenty of corn, but need to import coffee? Is your land suited to rice production or orchards, but unsuited to large scale ranching? What would this mean in terms of imports and exports?

- Where is your land situated geographically? Who might be suitable trade partners? Which countries may need what you have to export and which countries could provide for your import needs?

*The top **importer** of goods in the United States in 2020 was **Walmart**, followed by Target in second.*

Task #36: Imports and Exports

❏ Complete **Worksheet 13.1: Suggested Exports** in your Workbook

❏ Complete **Worksheet 13.2: Suggested Imports** in your Workbook

❏ Prepare a presentation outlining your country's import and export strategy.

- Explain what you plan to import and export and why
- Include a list 2 countries for each item could be traded with and why each country is a suitable match for trade. (You may use the same country for multiple items as long as the country has a valid need for or excess of each item).

Words Worth Knowing

- Tariff
- Fixed Tariff
- Variable tariff

Composition Activity #11: Your Balance of Trade

Write an essay answering the following questions:

- Based on the market value of your imports and exports, do you think that your country will run a trade deficit? Why or why not?
- How does your country's leadership feel that the balance of trade will affect your country's future?

Tariffs

A **tariff** is a tax levied by the government on goods and services imported from other countries. Tariffs help increase the price of foreign goods and make imports less competitive compared to domestic goods and services. There are 2 types of tariffs:

*In 2018 and 2019, the United States imposed tariffs on more than **$300 billion** in imports from China.*

- **Fixed** – A **fixed tariff** is a constant sum per unit of imported goods or a percentage of the price
- **Variable** – A **variable tariff** is one in which the amount of tax varies according to the price of the item

Websites and Articles Worth Exploring

- Tariff
- Tariffs - WTO
- Tariff Schedules

*Tariffs on **non-agricultural goods** such as machinery, cars and transportation equipment, IT products, minerals and metals are called **industrial tariffs.***

Videos Worth Watching

- How do tariffs work? | CNBC Explains
- What is a Tariff? How do Tariffs Work?
- How to calculate the impact of import and export tariffs.

Task #37: Establishing Tariffs on Goods

❏ Choose 2 of your country's main imports on which to apply tariffs. **Create a fact sheet for each with a picture of the item and the particulars about the tariff that you are applying.**

- Decide if the tariff applies to a specific country or countries or across the board for that particular item.
- One import must be a fixed tariff and one import must be a variable tariff

Trade Agreements

A **trade agreement** is a treaty between two or more countries concerning taxes, tariff and trade. There are 3 types of trade agreements: **unilateral, bilateral** and **multilateral**.

Words Worth Knowing
- Trade Agreement
- Unilateral
- Bilateral
- Multilateral
- NAFTA

Multilateral
- Usually involves three or more countries, each with their own set of things that they need and or want

Bilateral
- An agreement between two countries or two groups of countries where both sides loosen their trade restrictions to help out businesses so that they can prosper better between the different countries

Unilateral
- When a country wants certain restrictions to be enforced but no other countries want them to be imposed

NAFTA

The North American Free Trade Agreement (**NAFTA**) went into effect on January 1, 1994. NAFTA is an agreement between the United States, Canada, and Mexico. The key components of NAFTA include:

- Eliminate tariff barriers to agricultural, manufacturing, and services;
- Remove investment restrictions;
- Protect intellectual property rights
- Address environmental and labor concerns

As of 2016 NAFTA's 3 partners represented **28%** of the world's gross domestic product (GDP)

The **United States-Mexico-Canada Agreement** went into effect On July 1, 2020, replacing NAFTA.

Words Worth Knowing

- OPEC

OPEC members control about **81.9%** of the world's total proven crude reserves.

OPEC

OPEC, or the Organization of the Petroleum Exporting Countries, went into effect on September 1960. The mission of the OPEC is to coordinate and unify the petroleum policies of its Member Countries and ensure the stabilization of oil markets in order to secure an efficient, economic and regular supply of petroleum to consumers, a steady income to producers and a fair return on capital for those investing in the petroleum industry. OPEC is a multilateral agreement between 14 countries:

Iran	Iraq	Kuwait	Saudi Arabia
Venezuela	Libya	The United Arab Emirates	Algeria
Nigeria	Ecuador	Gabon	Angola
	Equatorial Guinea	Congo	

Websites and Articles Worth Exploring

- Trade Agreements

- Trade Agreements – US Dept of State

- Free Trade Agreements: Their Impact, Types, and Examples

- International Trade Agreements

- Negotiations and agreements

- North American Free Trade Agreement (NAFTA)

- North American Free Trade Agreement (NAFTA) – International Trade Association

- OPEC in a Changing World

- OPEC

- Organization of the Petroleum Exporting Countries (OPEC)

Videos Worth Watching

- Trade Agreements

- Introduction to Free Trade Agreements (FTAs)

- Barriers and Benefits in Free Trade Agreements

- U S Free Trade Agreements for Importers & Exporters

- NAFTA explained by avocados. And shoes.

- Top 10 NAFTA Facts You Should Know

- What is OPEC? | CNBC Explains

- The History of OPEC | Casual Historian

- OPEC - The Organization of the Petroleum Exporting Countries

Task #38: Your Trade Pacts

❏ Complete **Worksheet 13.3: Trade Pact Countries** in your Workbook

❏ **Draft a trade agreement between your country and the other countries.** Make sure to outline what each side is giving and getting out of the deal.

Chapter 13 Review

The following sections help you review and think about some of the concepts and activities that you performed in this chapter.

Words Worth Knowing Review

The following terms were very important throughout this chapter.

International Relations	Globalization	Isolationism	National Interest
Realism	Liberalism	Constructivism	International Trade
Exports	Imports	Balance of Trade	Trade Surplus
Trade Deficit	Recession	Tariff	Fixed tariff
Variable tariff	Trade agreement	Unilateral	Bilateral
Multilateral	NAFTA	OPEC	

❏ Complete the **Chapter 13 Words Worth Knowing Exercises** in the Workbook

For Discussion

- How did the global placement of your country affect the decisions that you made when it came to your trade partners and pacts?

- How might your choices have been different if you prescribed to a different theory of international relations?

You as a Citizen

- As a citizen, how will your country's trade pacts and partners affect you in your day to day life?

- What types of individual buying choices would be more by an increase in tariffs on that good or service? Which of your choices would you still make regardless of the tariff level or lack thereof?

Your National Library

The following Items from this chapter should be filed in your national library

- **Guidebook**
    - Import and Export presentation

- **Official Documents**
    - Balance of Trade essay
    - Tariff fact sheets
    - Trade Agreements

CHAPTER 14

Forging your Global Alliances

Forging Your Global Alliances

If only your country provided everything that your people need or want. Unfortunately, unless you live in a veritable utopia (which you don't), this is seldom the case. To meet the varied needs of your people, your country and government will have to interact with your neighbors. You've already done some of this interaction through trade and trade pacts, but now its time to expand on those relationships a bit.

In this chapter you will learn about some multinational organizations, agreements and alliances and then make some decisions regarding your own country and and its relationship with the countries of the world.

Words Worth Knowing

- International Diplomacy

International Diplomacy

International diplomacy is a method that governments use to influence the actions of foreign governments through peaceful tactics. In 1961 the Vienna Convention on Diplomatic Relations outlined 5 key objectives of diplomacy and functions of diplomatic missions:

1. A representation of the sending state in the host state on multiple levels beyond merely ceremonial

2. The protection of the sending country and its citizens within the host country

3. The negotiation and signing of agreements between countries

4. Information gathering for the sending country on the conditions and developments in the host country

5. Promoting and furthering friendly economic, commercial, cultural, and scientific relations between the sending country and the host country

Cultural Diplomacy
- The exchange of arts and culture that aims to increase understanding between different countries

Economic Diplomacy
- Activities that help the economies thrive and the countries prosper. This is a huge part of international relations as it involves anything related to trade, investments and taxation, and foreign aid

Dollar Diplomacy
- The manipulation of foreign affairs for monetary gain

Gunboat Diplomacy
- The manipulation or backing up of foreign affairs and other diplomatic efforts through a show of military might

Public Diplomacy
- Communicating directly with foreign publics or citizens through press conferences and public statements

Global civics is the study of the rights and responsibilities of human beings toward each other in an increasingly interconnected and interdependent world.

Most of the activities of diplomacy are carried out through a county's diplomats. A **diplomat** is a person appointed by a national government to conduct official negotiations and maintain relations with another country or countries. The highest ranking diplomat in a country is called an **ambassador**. Diplomats usually work out of each country's embassy in other host countries. An **embassy** is the primary diplomatic representation of a country's government in a host country. Diplomats and other embassy staff work with representatives of the host government, local businesses, nongovernmental organizations, the media and educational institutions, to increase understanding of the sending country and promote shared interests.

Words Worth Knowing

- Diplomat
- Ambassador
- Embassy

Websites and Articles Worth Exploring

*An **Ambassador** is the highest ranking diplomat of a sending country in a host country.*

- Exploring international relations: What is diplomacy?
- Why You Should Study International Diplomacy
- What is diplomacy?
- What are the roles of a diplomat?
- How do you become a diplomat?
- Difference between Ambassador and Diplomat
- Vienna Convention On Diplomatic Relations And Optional Protocols
- Diplomatic immunity
- Websites of U.S. Embassies, Consulates, and Diplomatic Missions
- What is a U.S. Embassy?
- What Does an Embassy Do? What is the Purpose of Your Home Country's Embassy?
- What Is the Difference Between a Consulate and an Embassy?

*The first embassy was founded in **Northern Italy** in the thirteenth century.*

Videos Worth Watching

- What is International Relations? (International Relations Defined)
- International Relations 101 (#1): Introduction
- The Art of Diplomacy
- Diplomacy Crash Course
- International Relations: Diplomacy |History |Definition |Importance |Functions & Types of Diplomacy
- Diplomatic Tools of Foreign Policy
- What Is A Diplomat? | Who Is An Ambassador?
- What Diplomats Really Do | Alexander Karagiannis | TEDxIndianaUniversity
- What does it take to be a U.S. Diplomat?
- Why Diplomats Can't be Arrested
- How to Become an Ambassador | step-by-step guide
- Mini Countries Abroad: How Embassies Work
- How Do Embassies Work?
- 15 MOST SECURE Embassies
- Countries With The Most Embassies

China tops the list of the most embassies in the world with **276 embassies** and other representative offices globally.

Task #39: Your First Embassy

❏ **Decide what country will host your first embassy.** Think about the values and structure of your own country and government. What other country do you think would make the best ally?

❏ Draw a Map of your Host Country. Include any major physical features such as lakes, rivers or mountain ranges.
- Mark the location of the capital city
- Mark the location of your embassy

❏ Complete **Worksheet 14.1a-b: Host Country Information** in your Workbook

❏ **Design your Embassy building.** The architecture and design of your embassy should reflect both the culture of your country and the host country. This design can take the form of a drawing, painting or computer graphic.

> The bureau of diplomatic security (DS) is a part of the U.S. Department of State and is responsible for providing security at US embassies.

Extension Activity #12: Modeling Your Embassy

Objective: Build a 3D representation of your Embassy

❏ Construct a 3D model of your Embassy.
- The building should follow your design from task #37
- Your embassy should consist of main building is called the chancery, and at least one annex.

> The **Tanzanian and Kenyan embassies** are some of the most secure in the world.

Words Worth Knowing

- Defense Pact
- NATO

- Your embassy should have designated space to host formal dinners and receptions for visiting dignitaries as well as a visitor area, a press room and several offices.
- You may construct your embassy out of any physical material or virtually using a 3D modeling environment

Composition Activity #12: Your First Diplomat

Every embassy needs an ambassador to run it. **Write a fictional biography of the person that you choose to be your country's ambassador.**

- Be sure to include a description of this person's childhood, influences and qualifications to be ambassador.
- Include at least 2 anecdotes from this person's past.

Defense Pacts

A **defense pact** is a treaty or military alliance in which countries promise to support each other militarily and to defend each other. Defense pacts are often used to safeguard against known or unknown security threats. In a pact, the countries point out the threats each may face and how they can respond to it together.

*The **Warsaw Pact**, established in 1955, was created by the USSR. As a response to NATO.*

NATO

The North Atlantic Treaty Organization (**NATO**) was first established in 1949. Through its defense pact, NATO focuses on three key components:

- NATO strives to guarantee the freedom and security of its members through political and military means

- NATO promotes democratic values and enables members to consult and cooperate on defense and security-related issues to solve problems, build trust and, in the long run, prevent conflict.

- NATO is committed to the peaceful resolution of disputes. If diplomatic efforts fail, it has the military power to undertake crisis-management operations.

NATO has 2 official languages: English and French.

While there Were initially 12 founding members of NATO, it has now grown to 29 countries:

Albania	Belgium	Bulgaria	Canada	Croatia
Czech Republic	Denmark	Estonia	France	Germany
Greece	Hungary	Iceland	Italy	Latvia
Lithuania	Luxembourg	Montenegro	Netherlands	Norway
Poland	Portugal	Romania	Slovakia	Slovenia
	Spain	Turkey	United Kingdom	United States

363

Websites and Articles Worth Exploring

- U.S. Collective Defense Arrangements
- Mapped: America's Collective Defense Agreements
- What Is NATO?
- North Atlantic Treaty Organization

Videos Worth Watching

- What is NATO, why does it still exist, and how does it work? [2020 version]
- What is NATO? | CNBC Explains
- NATO Explained

The United Nations was founded following World War II to replace the League of Nations.

Task #40: Your Defense Pact

☐ Research a current situation that could pose a security risk for your country.
- This must be a real situation (even though your country is fictitious)

☐ Decide which country or countries would be most useful to have a pact with to protect your country against the threat of this situation.

❑ Draft a Defense Pact between your country and your "allies". This pact must include:
1. A description of the situation
2. A list of the country/countries involved and what each brings to the table
3. An outline of your shared response to the perceived threat

Words Worth Knowing
- United Nations

The United Nations

The **United Nations** (UN) is an international organization dedicated to promoting international cooperation. The duties of the UN center on five major areas of international concern.

- Maintain International Peace and Security
- Protect Human Rights
- Uphold International Law
- Deliver Humanitarian Aid
- Support Sustainable Development and Climate Action

The United Nations' **World Food Programme (WFP)** provides food and assistance to over 115 million people in 84 countries

Maintain International Peace and Security

The United Nations works, through the UN Security Council, the General Assembly and other bodies to prevent conflict, encourage peaceful resolutions to conflicts, and creating global conditions that would allow peace to endure. The UN accomplishes this through 5 major activities:

Words Worth Knowing

- Preventative Diplomacy
- Peacekeeping
- Peacebuilding
- Counterterrorism
- Disarmament
- Human Rights

*The **Paris Agreement** on climate change was signed at the UN headquarters in New York by the largest number of countries to ever sign in a single day*

- **Preventative Diplomacy** and Mediation – In an effort to prevent conflict in the first place, the UN employs many tools of diplomacy and mediation. These are actions taken to prevent disputes from escalating and to limit the spread of conflicts when they occur.

- **Peacekeeping** – The UN assists countries in navigating the complex and often difficult path from conflict to peace.

- **Peacebuilding** – Once peace is achieved, the UN employs peacebuilding which is helping to reduce the risk of relapsing into conflict by helping countries to lay the foundation for sustainable peace and development

- **Counterterrorism** – Counterterrorism includes all of the practices, tactics, techniques and strategies that go into preventing terrorists and terrorist organizations from thriving and acting. The UN is a major participant in coordinating the global fight against terrorism

- **Disarmament** – The UN actively pursues disarmament, which is the elimination of nuclear weapons and other weapons of mass destruction and the regulation of conventional arms.

Protect Human Rights

*The UN's **Universal Declaration of Human Rights** is the first document to detail the fundamental human rights that must be protected.*

The United nations works to protect human rights through both legal instruments and on-the-ground activities. **Human rights** are rights inherent to all human beings, regardless of race, sex, nationality, ethnicity, language, religion, or any other status. Through offices such as the Office of the High Commissioner for Human Rights, the Human Rights Council and the UNDG

Human Rights Working Group the UN upholds the principles of the Universal Declaration of Human Rights.

Deliver Humanitarian Aid

The United Nations coordinates **humanitarian aid** and relief to countries that are suffering from the effects of emergencies due to natural and man-made disasters. Humanitarian aid is material and logistic assistance to people in areas when the effects of a disaster are beyond the relief capacity of national authorities alone. Among other services, relief can come in the form of food, medical care and aid to refugees and children. Humanitarian aid is usually short-term help and lasts only until the long-term solutions by the government and other institutions replaces it.

Words Worth Knowing
- Humanitarian Aid
- Sustainable Development

Support Sustainable Development and Climate Action

Sustainable development is development that meets the needs of the present, without compromising the ability of future generations to meet their own needs. This principle involves balancing environmental protection with social progress and economic development in such a way that allows present populations to thrive without preventing future populations from being able to do so.

Climate change is a change in the composition of the global atmosphere that is attributed directly or indirectly to human activity.

Environmental Protection — Sustainable Development — Economic Development — Social Progress

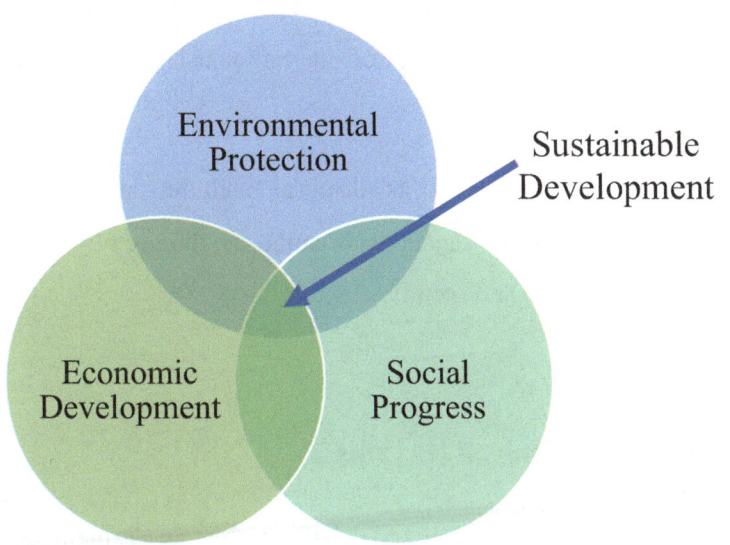

In 2016 many world leaders adopted the **UN's Sustainable Development Goals** to improve life, preserve the earth's resources and fight climate change.

The United Nations launched and champions a sustainable development agenda that aims to satisfy 17 development goals. These include

Words Worth Knowing

- International Law

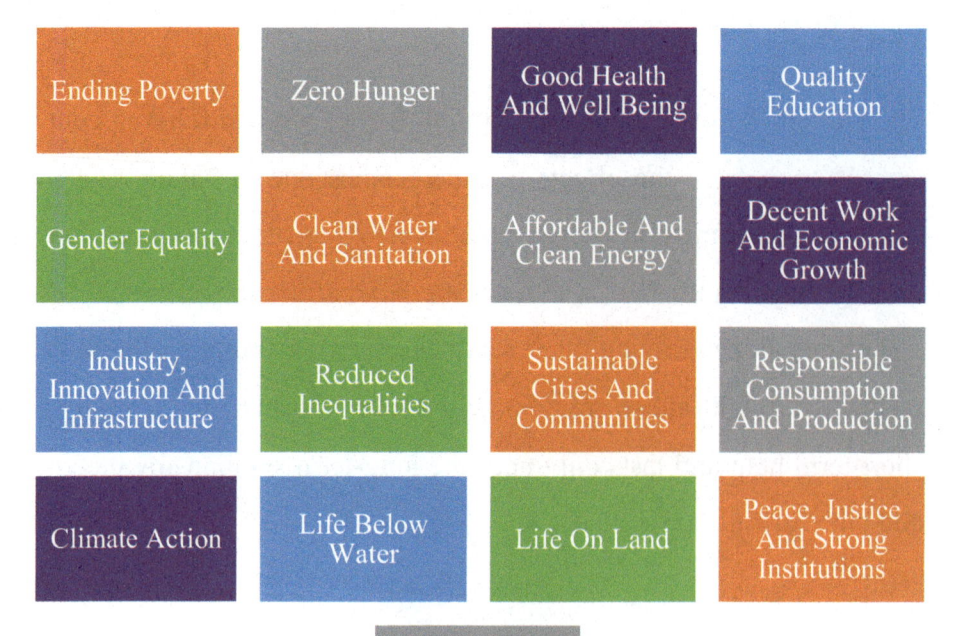

Ending Poverty	Zero Hunger	Good Health And Well Being	Quality Education
Gender Equality	Clean Water And Sanitation	Affordable And Clean Energy	Decent Work And Economic Growth
Industry, Innovation And Infrastructure	Reduced Inequalities	Sustainable Cities And Communities	Responsible Consumption And Production
Climate Action	Life Below Water	Life On Land	Peace, Justice And Strong Institutions

Partnerships For The Goals

Uphold International Law

International law is the collection of rules, norms, and standards generally recognized as binding between countries. The United Nations has as one of its main objectives "to establish conditions under which justice and respect for the obligations arising from treaties and other sources of international law can be maintained" (UN Charter Preamble).

The UN uses many avenues at its disposal including the ability to approve peacekeeping missions, impose sanctions, or authorize the use of force when there is a threat to international peace and security.

> International Law only applies to **countries who** consent to be bound by entering into a treaty with another country.

Steps to joining the United Nations

There are four steps for a new country or state to become a member of the United Nations

368

A country submits an application to the Secretary-General of the UN along with a letter formally stating that the country accepts the obligations under the UN Charter.

⬇

The Security Council considers the application. The application must receive positive votes from 9 of the 15 members of the Council, including all 5 permanent members

⬇

If the Security Council approves the application, it then goes to the General Assembly for consideration. A two-thirds majority vote is required in the Assembly for the application to be accepted

⬇

Once the resolution for admission is adopted by the General Assembly, membership is immediately effective..

The first session of the United Nations General Assembly met on January 10, 1946 with representatives from 51 countries in attendance.

In 2011 **South Sudan** became the most recent state to join is

Websites and Articles Worth Exploring

- What is the United Nations
- United Nations
- UN Global Issues

Videos Worth Watching

- The United Nations Explained
- How Does The UN Work?
- The United Nations Is Created | Flashback | History
- What Does the UN Do?
- Facts about the United Nations you should know in 2020
- The United Nations: It's Your World

Task #41: Entering the United Nations

❏ **Write a letter of application to the UN admissions committee.** In it be sure to state how your country will contribute to the five major areas of international concern.

❏ Take a look at some of the united nations highlighted global issues
   - UN Global Issues
     - https://www.un.org/en/global-issues/

❏ Choose 2 issues that will be a major focus for your country. **Create a poster highlighting each issue.**

Chapter 14 Review

The following sections help you review and think about some of the concepts and activities that you performed in this chapter.

Words Worth Knowing Review

The following terms were very important throughout this chapter.

International diplomacy	Diplomat	Ambassador	Embassy
Defense Pact	NATO	United Nations	Preventative diplomacy
Peacekeeping	Peacebuilding	Counterterrorism	Disarmament
Human rights	Humanitarian aid	Sustainable development	International Law

❑ Complete the **Chapter 14 Words Worth Knowing Exercises** in the Workbook

For Discussion

- How did your choice of global focus affect your decisions when it comes to creating trade and defense pacts?

- Why is it important that countries consent to be bound by international law? What do you think would happen if a country refused to consent?

CHAPTER 14 REVIEW

You as a Citizen

- As a citizen, which of the UN's 17 sustainable development goals would have the biggest and most direct impact on your day to day life?

Your National Library

The following Items from this chapter should be filed in your national library

- **Guidebook**
    - Design of your embassy

- **Official Documents**
    - Map of your host country including location of embassy
    - Defense Pact
    - United Nations Application

- **Promotional material / media**
    - Diplomat biography
    - UN Issue Focus

CHAPTER 15

Bringing Everything Together

Bringing Everything Together

It's Official! You Have a Country!

There you have it – your country is a thriving world player. You have a vibrant land filled with a diverse group of people all living and working together. Its about time for your country to step out on its own and continue the journey. There are just a few things left to do.

In this final chapter of the course your will draft your Emergency Preparedness and Continuity of Operations Plan . You will also begin to build up your tourism industry by creating your country's guidebook and preparing a final presentation for the world stage. Finally you will complete some course wrap-up activities.

Words Worth Knowing

- Continuity of Operations Plan

Continuity of Operations Plan

A **continuity of operations plan** is the internal effort of a country to make sure that critical functions and services are able to continue operating following an comprehensive array of potential emergencies or disasters. This is especially important in fledgling countries like yours. You wouldn't want an unexpected disaster to mean the end of your fragile economy and nation. A quality continuity of operations plan provides for seven key objectives:

1. Ensure the safety of government employees

2. Ensure the continuous performance of critical activities

3. Protect essential equipment, records and assets

4. Reduce disruptions to other operations

5. Minimize damage and losses

6. Provide for an orderly recovery and transition back to normal operations

7. Identify possible relocation sites and make sure that operational and managerial needs of those locations are available

The **National Emergencies Act (NEA)**, passed in 1976, formalizes the powers of a President during and following an emergency.

Phases of Continuity Implementation

Implementation of a Continuity plan generally follows a four phase process:

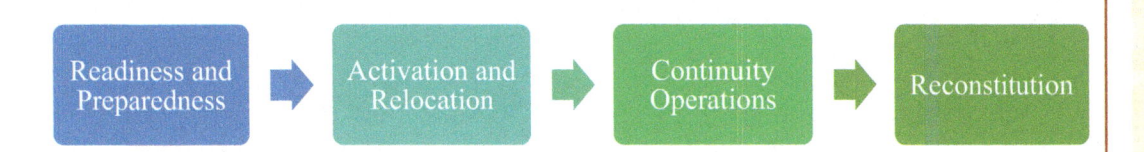

Readiness and Preparedness → Activation and Relocation → Continuity Operations → Reconstitution

> **Words Worth Knowing**
> - Readiness and Preparedness Phase
> - Activation and Relocation Phase
> - Continuity Operations Phase

Readiness and Preparedness

The **readiness and preparedness phase** includes all organization continuity readiness and preparedness activities including risk assessment and management and the development, review, and revision of plans.

Activation and Relocation

The **activation and relocation phase** includes the activation of all of the procedures necessary to support the continued performance of essential functions. This plan should include relocation procedures, if necessary, and all procedures necessary to attain operation of critical functions within 12 hours of plan activation.

> The **Continuity of Operations plan** was into effect for the first time following the **September 11 attacks by the** Bush administration

Continuity Operations

The **continuity operations phase** includes activities needed to continue essential functions. This could be maintaining communication lines or ensuring personnel requirements are met.

Reconstitution

The **reconstitution phase** begins after the emergency, or threat of emergency,

Words Worth Knowing

- Federal Continuity Directives (FCD)
- FEMA

A **disaster recovery specialist** develops response strategies disasters, both natural and manmade, and assists in managing relief efforts in the event of a disaster.

is over. This phase provides for the orderly transition back to normal operations.

Continuity of Operations in the United States

The **Federal Continuity Directives (FCD)** are documents that provide guidelines for implementing a continuity of operations plan in the United States. FCD-1 gives direction to the federal agencies for how to develop continuity plans and programs. FCD-2 provides specific guidance to the Executive Branch on how to identify Mission Essential Functions of the government. The Federal Emergency Management Agency **(FEMA)** also helps to provide continuity of operations guidance and assistance to citizens and the private sector.

Websites and Articles Worth Exploring

- Brief Overview: COOP (Continuity of Operations Plan) Plan
- What is Continuity of Operations?
- Continuity of Government
- Federal Continuity Directive 1 (FCD 1)
- Continuity Policy And Programs
- FEMA

Videos Worth Watching

- Resilient Operations: State and Local Government Continuity Strategies in the New Normal

- Speaker Series #2 - Government Responses and Continuity

- Infrastructure Resiliency and Continuity of Operations

- We're Here, Before, During and After Disasters

- FEMA's role in disaster relief

- What does FEMA actually do? - Interview with Pete Gaynor

Words Worth Knowing

- Cabinet
- Presidential Succession

Considerations for Your Continuity of Operations Plan

- Take a look at your physical map and your natural disaster risk assessment. How big is your country's risk for any natural disasters? What might those disasters do in terms of overall disruption of critical operations?

- Take a look at your country's political map and the stability of your neighboring countries. Is your country at risk for any sort of attack from a foreign entity or terrorist?

- Think about the type of government you have in place and how your government treats its people. Are you at risk for domestic terrorism or uprising? If you are at risk, how would you maintain order and control and keep you critical functions operating during a revolt?

Nearly half of all Americans lack emergency supplies for use in the event of a disaster.

Words Worth Knowing

- Healthcare Policy

- Think about the global state of affairs, politically and environmentally/climatologically. What catastrophic events are you most at risk for? How will your country adapt and survive those events?

Task #42: Your Continuity of Operations Plan

❏ Create an Emergency Preparedness and Continuity of Operations Plan for your country. This plan should:

- Provide a risk assessment for 5 possible emergency types

- Address each of the seven key objectives of a continuity of operations plan

- Provide protective actions for the life safety of your citizens

- Outline a 4 phase implementation process

Bringing Everything Together

This is it. Are you ready for your final task for the course? Don't worry though, this is just the beginning of the journey for your country. Going forward you can now begin to run your country through a myriad of real world scenarios and look at how your leaders and your people would react and adapt to the changing world around us. But for now, its time to end the way you started: by looking at and using your national library.

Task #43: Your Final Task

❑ Prepare a 15 minute presentation about your country. This presentation should entice future immigrants to settle in your country and future world leaders to want to trade and enter into agreements and partnerships with your country.

- Your presentation should include several of the pictures, maps, charts and statistics you have created throughout the course. You should be able to get these from your national library if you have been keeping up with it.

- You should cover the following topics:
    - Your land and the unique features of the land that make it special to your people. Be sure to mention your national symbols and any landmarks.
    - Your people and their unique cultural makeup. Where did they come from? Be sure to mention your national holidays and some of the cultural narratives that make your people unique.
    - Your government and its formation. Who are your leaders? Highlight a couple of your more important laws and why they are beneficial to your people. Discuss the steps your government takes to protect your people and ensure a quality infrastructure
    - Your global position and the space your country occupies on the world stage. Be sure to talk about your allies, any pacts your country may be a part of. Also discuss how global trade is affecting your people.

Chapter 15 Review

The following sections help you review and think about some of the concepts and activities that you performed in this chapter.

Words Worth Knowing Review

The following terms were very important throughout this chapter.

Continuity of Operations plan	Readiness and preparedness phase	Activation and relocation phase	Continuity operations phase
Reconstitution phase	Federal continuity directives	FEMA	

❑ Complete the **Chapter 15 Words Worth Knowing Exercises** in the Workbook

For Discussion

- What were the biggest risks and factors that you considered as you were planning your country's continuity of operations plan?

You as a Citizen

- How do you balance your responsibility as a citizen of your country with your responsibility as a citizen of the world?

Your National Library

The following Items from this chapter should be filed in your national library

- **Official Documents**
    - Continuity of Operations Plan

- **Promotional material / media**
    - Your Country Presentation

CHAPTER 15 REVIEW

Unit Review

Unit 4 Your Global Position

Your Global Position

Words Worth Knowing Review

Choose **at least 20** Unit 4 Words Worth Knowing Review words from the tables below. Write a short essay, scene or story that uses each of the words in context. You may include labeled illustrations as well.

- You must include **at least 3 terms from each list**

Chapter 13 Words

International Relations	Globalization	Isolationism	National Interest
Realism	Liberalism	Constructivism	International Trade
Exports	Imports	Balance of Trade	Trade Surplus
Trade Deficit	Recession	Tariff	Fixed tariff
Variable tariff	Trade agreement	Unilateral	Bilateral
Multilateral	NAFTA	OPEC	

Chapter 14 Words

International diplomacy	Diplomat	Ambassador	Embassy
Defense Pact	NATO	United Nations	Preventative diplomacy
Peacekeeping	Peacebuilding	Counterterrorism	Disarmament
Human rights	Humanitarian aid	Sustainable development	International Law

Chapter 15 Words

Continuity of Operations plan	Readiness and preparedness phase	Activation and relocation phase	Continuity operations phase
Reconstitution phase	Federal continuity directives	FEMA	

Final Discussion and Review

1. How did your initial decisions about the location of your country shape the rest of the decisions that you made throughout this course?

2. What role did your physical environment and ecosystem play in the success of your country?

3. How did the type of government that you chose affect your decision making process?

UNIT 4 REVIEW

UNIT 4 REVIEW

4. How did the mathematics and statistics you used help you to understand and make better decisions about your country?

5. What are the most important factors to consider when making social policy?

6. What is culture and how does the culture of your people help shape a government?

7. How does a country's environment, culture and government work together to respond to global events?

8. How do you balance your country's need for natural resources with the need to protect and preserve the environment? What responsibility does your country and government have when it comes to protecting the environment?

9. Based on what you have learned about your country, as a parent what are important laws and customs that your people should be teaching their children?

10. How would you as a leader work to establish patriotism for the next generation?

Current Events in Your World:

Famous Speech Research

❑ Research at least 2 current global events involving that country. How do these situations affect the lives of individual citizens? How would your country have reacted in this situation?

UNIT 4 REVIEW

Appendix I

Resources for

Unit 1: Your Land

Contents of Appendix I:
Your Land Resources

- ➢ **Books worth Reading with this Unit**
- ➢ **Movie Selections for this Unit**
- ➢ **Gameschooling Selections for this Unit**
- ➢ **Links for Websites and Articles Referenced in this Unit**
- ➢ **Links for Videos Referenced in this Unit**

Books Worth Reading with this Unit

- **On the Map: A mind-expanding exploration of the way the world looks by Simon Garfield**
  - Follow the history of maps from the maps of early explorers to Google Maps and the satellite renderings on our phones. Garfield explores the unique way that maps relate and realign our history—and reflects upon just what makes us human.

- **The Big ones: how natural disasters have shaped us by Dr. Lucy Jones**
  - Dr. Lucy Jones, a seismologist with the California Institute of Technology gives a fascinating history of natural disasters, their impact on our culture, and new ways to think about the ones in our future.

- **Nature Anatomy: The curious parts and pieces of the natural world by Julia Rothman**
  - Art and science combine in Julia Rothman's visual tour of the natural world. The book takes you on a trip to see how mountains are formed and examine the different types of feathers on a bird among others through Rothman's drawings, diagrams, and dissections. Her fascinating exploration of earth, water, flora, and fauna will open your eyes, mind, and heart to new views of the earth's natural wonders.

- **The weather book: an easy to understand guide to USA's weather by Jack Williams**
  - Featuring full-color weather graphics that star in America's favorite newspaper, Jack Williams presents a newly revised edition of the most readable guide to our nation's weather. It includes an updated guide to weather patterns and records on a state-by-state basis.

- **The Road to There: Mapmakers and their stories by Val Ross**
  - In this book are some of the most unexpected stories of history's great mapmakers. From fraud artists who deliberately distorted maps for political gain to the slaves on the run who found their way thanks to specially-pieced quilts and more. These are the people who helped us chart our way in the world, on land, on sea, and on to the stars.

- **Prisoners of Geography: Ten Maps That Explain Everything About the World by Tim Marshall**
  - Tim Marshall uses ten maps of crucial regions around the globe to explain the geo-political strategies of the world powers.

- **Cannibals and kings: Origins of cultures by Marvin Harris**
  - American anthropologist Marvin Harris shows how the many varieties of cultural behavior can simply be explained as adaptations to certain ecological conditions. Harris's aim is to account for the evolution of cultural forms: to show how cultures adopt their characteristic forms in response to ever changing ecological modes.

- **Tribe: On homecoming and belonging by Sebastian Junger**
  - Combining anthropology, history, and psychology, Tribe explores what we can learn from tribal societies about loyalty, and the eternal quest for meaning.

- **Journey to the Center of the Earth by Jules Verne**
  - A geology professor chances upon a manuscript where a 16th-century explorer claims they found a route to the earth's core. Professor Lidenbrock can't resist the chance to investigate, he sets off across Iceland with Hans Bjelke, a native guide, and his nephew Axel. The descend into an extinct volcano toward a sunless sea, and they encounter a subterranean world of luminous rocks, antediluvian forests, and fantastic marine life. A living past that holds the secrets to the origins of human existence

- **The Clan of The Cave Bear by Jean M Auel**
    - In the dawn of man, a natural disaster leaves a young girl wandering alone in an unfamiliar and dangerous land where she is found by a woman of the Clan, people very different from her own kind. To the Clan, blonde-haired, blue-eyed Ayla looks peculiar and ugly—she is one of the Others. However, Iza cannot leave the girl to die and takes her with them regardless of who she is.

- **Salvage the Bones by Jesmyn Ward**
    - A hurricane is building over the Gulf of Mexico, and threatens the coastal town of Bois Sauvage, Mississippi. Esch's father is growing concerned, a hard drinker, largely absent, he doesn't show concern for much else. Esch and her three brothers are stocking food, but there isn't much to save. Lately, Esch can't keep down what food she gets. Her brother Skeetah is sneaking scraps for his prized pitbull's new litter, and Randall and Junior try to stake their claim in a family low on child's play and parenting.

- **In the Beginning: Creation Stories from around the world by Virginia Hamilton**
    - A collection of 25 stories from different cultures that reflect upon the origins of the world and the people in it

- **The Story of World Mythologies by Terri-ann White**
    - A collection of myths, folktales and stories from throughout time and around the world Grouped together for easy comparison and enjoyment.

Movie Selections for this Unit

- *Planet Earth (2016) PG*
  - Vivid, breathtaking imagery highlights this fascinating documentary series featuring views of some of the world's most awe-inspiring natural wonders -- from oceans to mountains to the polar ice caps.

- *Planet Ocean (2012) NR*
  - Underwater cinematographers explore the link and bonds between humanity and the ocean.

- *Our Planet (2019) G*
  - Experience the planet's natural beauty through an examination of how climate change impacts all living beings on Earth in this documentary.

- *Into the Storm (2014) PG-13*
  - As a new day begins in the town of Silverton, the residents have no reason to believe it will be anything other than a regular day. Mother Nature, however, has other ideas. It only takes a few hours for an unprecedented onslaught of powerful tornadoes to ravage the town.

- *Oceans (2009) G*
  - 71% of the Earth's surface is covered by water. Using the best technology, filmmakers Jacques Perrin and Jacques Cluzaud explore the world that exists underwater.

- *A Beautiful Planet (2016) G*
  - Astronauts on the International Space Station capture stunning footage of the natural wonders of Earth.

- *Wings of Life (2011) G*
  - Filmmaker Louis Schwartzberg examines how the Earth's food chain is dependent on animals and insects like bees, hummingbirds, and bats.

- *Monkey Kingdom (2015) G*
  - In South Asia, Maya the monkey and her son Kip struggle to live in the competitive social hierarchy of the troop at Castle Rock.

- *Seasons (2015) PG*
  - Filmmakers Jacques Perrin and Jacques Cluzaud travel throughout Europe to film bears, wolves, and other animals in their natural habitat.

- *Earth (2007) G*
  - A journey around the world shows how animal mothers struggle to raise their children in an increasingly dangerous environment.

- *The Day after Tomorrow (2004) PG-13*
  - After climatologist Jack Hall is largely ignored by the U.N. when presenting his environmental concerns, his research proves correct when an enormous "superstorm" develops, setting off devastating natural disasters throughout the world.

- *San Andreas (2015) PG-13*
  - An ideal day turns disastrous when California's notorious San Andreas fault triggers a catastrophic, magnitude 9 earthquake, the largest in recorded history.

- *The Wave (2015) R*
  - A Norwegian geologist and his family fight for survival when a huge landslide causes a 250-foot tidal wave.

- *Pompeii (2014) PG-13*
  - In 79 A.D., Pompeii, a bustling port city, stands right under Mount Vesuvius. Milo, a former slave, is a gladiator who has caught the eye of Cassia, a wealthy merchant's daughter. Their difference in social status is not their only obstacle; Cassia has been promised to Corvus, a corrupt Roman senator. When Mount Vesuvius erupts and rains lava and ash down on the city, Milo races to save her before it's too late.

- *Twister (1996) PG-13*
  - Just before the most powerful storm in decades, university professor Dr. Jo Harding and a team of students prepare the prototype for Dorothy, a ground-breaking tornado data-gathering device devloped by her estranged husband, Bill.

- *10,000 BC (2008) PG-13*
  - In the prehistoric past, D'Leh is a mammoth hunter who bonds with the alluring Evolet. When warriors on horseback capture her and the tribesmen, D'Leh must embark on a journey to save his love.

- *The Clan of the Cave Bear (1996) R*
    - Based on the novel by Jean Auel, a young Cro-Magnon woman, Ayla, is raised by Neanderthals.

- *Alpha (2018) PG-13*
    - In the prehistoric past, a young man struggles to return home after being separated from his tribe during a hunt. He finds a similarly lost wolf and begins a friendship that would change humanity.

Gameschooling Selections for this Unit

- **Ecosystem**
    - Build your own ecological network in this biologically-derived card drafting game. Players choose, pass, and arrange 11 card types consisting of organisms and environments, among others. Earn points by aligning animals with the habitats where they flourish in.

- **Into the Forest: Nature's Food Chain Game**
    - Learn about natural food relationships, and the importance of plants in food energy. Each game card has a detailed illustration of a plant or animal commonly found in a forest, and lists what it eats and what it is eaten by. The cards can also be used independently to review knowledge about the food chain and life cycle of the forest.

- **Nature Fluxx**
    - Learn about the relationships between animals, their habitats and the food chain in this fast-paced game where the rules are constantly changing.

- **Planet**
    - In this unique game, each player's board is a 12-sided 3-dimensional planet core. Each player selects landscape tiles representing oceans, deserts, mountains or frozen lands, and arranges them on your board to create the best ecosystems. Win Animal Cards while fulfilling ''Natural Habitat'' objectives and create the most populated planet!

- **Wildcraft**
  - Wildcraft takes kids on quest through several ecosystems – while learning all about 25 edible and medicinal plants! With waterfalls to slide down and deer trails to wander down, wildcraft includes all the fun interactive elements that kids love.

- **Photosynthesis**
  - Plant and shape the ever-changing forest as you cultivate your seeds and strategy. Take your trees through their life-cycle and earn points as their leaves collect energy from the sun's rays. Carefully pick where you sow and when you grow in this fascinating game.

- **Discover: Lands Unknown**
  - When players find themselves stranded in the harsh wilderness, you must cooperate and compete] for water, food, and tools that will be essential to your survival.

-

- **Bios: Megafauna**
  - Start as a plant or animal making first landfall and evolve on drifting continents in the face of competition and huge ecological events: If you become the dominant herbivore or carnivore, you win.

- **Dominant Species**
  - Each player assumes the role of one of six major Animal groups and begins the game in a state of natural balance with regards to one another. But that won't last for it's "survival of the fittest."

- **Guess in 10: Animal Planet**
  - Ask up to 10 questions to guess the animal on the Game Card! Does it live in the forest? Is it a carnivore? Does it live in groups? Think hard, ask intelligent questions, use your clues wisely, and be the first player to win 7 Game Cards.

- **Guess in 10: Animal Planet**

  - Ask up to 10 questions to guess the animal on the Game Card! Does it live in the forest? Is it a carnivore? Does it live in groups? Think hard, ask intelligent questions, use your clues wisely, and be the first player to win 7 Game Cards.

- **Paleo**

  - Return to the stone age in a new adventure! Paleo is a strategy game that sends you back to the early days of humankind to undertake the ultimate paleolithic quest: completing your mammoth cave painting and cementing your legacy.

- **Prehistories**

  - You are the leader of a prehistoric tribe; you choose which members of your tribe go hunting and what prey they want to catch. To guide you, the Elders have created challenges that you can complete by painting on the cave wall. Each round, you and your fellow tribe leaders bid simultaneously and in secret to decide who hunts where.

Links for Websites and Articles Referenced in this Unit

Websites for Chapter 1: Introduction to Your Land

- The 5 Themes of Geography
    - https://www.thoughtco.com/five-themes-of-geography-1435624#:~:text=The%20five%20themes%20of%20geography,in%20the%20K%2D12%20classroom.

- The 5 Themes in Geography
    - https://www.worldatlas.com/the-five-themes-in-geography.html

- A Short Definition For Human Geography
    - https://researchguides.dartmouth.edu/human_geography

- Human geography
    - https://www.britannica.com/science/geography/Human-geography

- Overview of Political Geography
    - https://www.thoughtco.com/overview-of-political-geography-1435397

- Geopolitics
    - https://www.britannica.com/topic/geopolitics

- Geopolitics vs. Political Geography vs. International Relations
    - https://www.profolus.com/topics/geopolitics-vs-political-geography-vs-international-relations/

- National Libraries of the World
    - https://publiclibraries.com/world/
- United States Libraries and Archives
    - https://www.usa.gov/libraries

Websites for Chapter 2: Getting the Lay of the Land

- The Fundamentals of Cartography
    - https://gis.usc.edu/blog/the-fundamentals-of-cartography/
- Mapping Through the Ages: The History of Cartography
    - https://www.gislounge.com/mapping-through-the-ages/
- Cartographer Jobs: Are They Still Relevant In The 21st Century?
    - https://gisgeography.com/cartographer-job-salary/
- Types of Maps
    - https://geology.com/maps/types-of-maps/
- What are some Different Types of Maps and their Uses
    - https://mapgeeks.org/different-types-maps/
- Types of Maps: Topographic, Political, Climate, and More
    - https://www.thoughtco.com/types-of-maps-1435689
- Different types of maps - political and physical
    - https://www.youtube.com/watch?v=1Jp0n7L6DJM
- World Mapper
    - https://worldmapper.org/
- Latitude, Longitude and Coordinate System Grids
    - https://gisgeography.com/latitude-longitude-coordinates/

- The Quest for Longitude and the Rise of Greenwich – a Brief History
    - http://www.thegreenwichmeridian.org/tgm/articles.php?article=9
- Latitude/Longitude Distance Calculator
    - https://www.nhc.noaa.gov/gccalc.shtml
- The 17 Spheres of Earth
    - https://earthhow.com/spheres-of-earth/
- Earth's Systems
    - https://www.nationalgeographic.org/article/earths-systems/
- Earth's Spheres
    - https://gml.noaa.gov/education/info_activities/pdfs/TBI_earth_spheres.pdf
- What are the Earth's layers?
    - https://phys.org/news/2015-12-earth-layers.html
- Earth Structure
    - https://www.nationalgeographic.org/topics/resource-library-earth-structure/?q=&page=1&per_page=25
- Earth's Atmosphere: A Multi-layered Cake
    - https://climate.nasa.gov/news/2919/earths-atmosphere-a-multi-layered-cake/
- Atmosphere
    - https://www.nationalgeographic.org/encyclopedia/atmosphere/
- What is the Atmosphere?
    - https://scied.ucar.edu/learning-zone/atmosphere/what-is-atmosphere
- The Different Types of Landforms
    - https://sciencing.com/list-7644820-different-types-landforms.html
- Physical Maps
    - https://www.mapsofworld.com/physical-map/

- What are some Common Features Shown on Physical Maps?
    - https://www.youtube.com/watch?v=FnkrPMPi-68
- Introduction to natural resources (NR)
    - https://eschooltoday.com/learn/what-is-a-natural-resource/
- The economic significance of natural resources: key points for reformers in Eastern Europe, Caucasus and Central Asia
    - https://www.oecd.org/env/outreach/2011_AB_Economic%20significance%20of%20NR%20in%20EECCA_ENG.pdf
- Renewable and Non-renewable Energy Resources Explained
    - https://www.kqed.org/science/renewable-and-non-renewable-energy-resources-explained
- The House Committee on Natural Resources
    - https://naturalresources.house.gov/
- Natural Resource Maps of the World
    - https://www.mapsofworld.com/thematic-maps/natural-resources-maps/
- What's the Difference Between Weather and Climate?
    - https://www.ncei.noaa.gov/news/weather-vs-climate
- NASA - What's the Difference Between Weather and Climate?
    - https://www.nasa.gov/mission_pages/noaa-n/climate/climate_weather.html
- What is the difference between weather and climate?
    - https://www.americangeosciences.org/critical-issues/faq/difference-between-weather-and-climate
- All About Climate
    - https://www.nationalgeographic.org/article/all-about-climate/
- What Is a Climate Zone?
    - https://www.greenmatters.com/p/what-is-a-climate-zone

- Köppen Climate Classification System
    - https://www.nationalgeographic.org/encyclopedia/koppen-climate-classification-system/
- Guide to Determining Climate Regions by County
    - https://www.energy.gov/sites/default/files/2015/10/f27/ba_climate_region_guide_7.3.pdf
- Natural Disasters and severe Weather
    - https://www.cdc.gov/disasters/index.html
- Natural Disasters (National Geographic)
    - https://www.nationalgeographic.com/environment/topic/natural-disasters-weather
- Natural Disasters (Homeland Security)
    - https://www.dhs.gov/natural-disasters
- Risk Assessment
    - https://www.ready.gov/risk-assessment
- Disaster Risk Assessment
    - https://www1.undp.org/content/dam/undp/library/crisis%20prevention/disaster/2Disaster%20Risk%20Reduction%20-%20Risk%20Assessment.pdf
- Natural Hazards and Natural Disasters
    - https://www.tulane.edu/~sanelson/Natural_Disasters/introduction.htm

Websites for Chapter 3: Checking out the Ecosystem

- What is an ecosystem?
    - https://www.khanacademy.org/science/biology/ecology/intro-to-ecosystems/a/what-is-an-ecosystem
- Ecosystem: Definition, Examples, Importance – All About Ecosystems
    - https://youmatter.world/en/definition/ecosystem-definition-example/

- Levels of organization in an ecosystem
    - https://eschooltoday.com/learn/levels-of-organization-in-an-ecosystem/
- The Taxonomic Classification System
    - https://courses.lumenlearning.com/wm-biology1/chapter/reading-the-taxonomic-classification-system/
- Classification system
    - https://www.sciencelearn.org.nz/resources/1438-classification-system
- Know Scientific Classification for the ASVAB
    - https://www.dummies.com/test-prep/asvab-test/know-scientific-classification-for-the-asvab/
- Food Chain
    - https://www.nationalgeographic.org/encyclopedia/food-chain/
- Food Web: Concept and Applications
    - https://www.nature.com/scitable/knowledge/library/food-web-concept-and-applications-84077181/
- Food chains & food webs
    - https://www.khanacademy.org/science/ap-biology/ecology-ap/energy-flow-through-ecosystems/a/food-chains-food-webs
- Food Chains And Food Webs (Wwf)
    - https://wwf.panda.org/discover/knowledge_hub/teacher_resources/webfieldtrips/food_chains/

Websites for Chapter 4: Your Previous People

- About Archeology
    - https://www.saa.org/about-archaeology/what-is-archaeology

- 10 Archaeological Mysteries That Will Awe You
    - https://www.nationalgeographic.com/expeditions/get-inspired/top-ten/best-10-ancient-ruins-archaeological-sites/
- What is anthropology
    - https://www.americananthro.org/AdvanceYourCareer/Content.aspx?ItemNumber=2150
- What is Topography? The Definitive Guide
    - https://gisgeography.com/what-is-topography/
- Topographic maps: The basics
    - https://www.nrcan.gc.ca/sites/www.nrcan.gc.ca/files/earthsciences/pdf/topo101/pdf/mapping_basics_e.pdf
- Mapping the Site
    - https://digitalatlas.cose.isu.edu/arch/ArchDef/map.htm
- Establishing a Site Grid
    - http://www.archaeologydude.com/2011/12/hello-everyone-question-that-i-often.html
- The Power of Artifacts to Elevate the Story
    - https://www.historyassociates.com/the-power-of-artifacts-to-elevate-the-story/
- Looking at Artifacts, Thinking about History
    - https://objectofhistory.org/guide/index.html
- Archaeologists find vast network of Amazon villages laid out like the cosmos
    - https://www.livescience.com/clock-face-shaped-villages-amazon-rainforest.html
- Social Life
    - https://humanorigins.si.edu/human-characteristics/social-life
- Life In Ancient Cities
    - https://education.nationalgeographic.org/resource/life-ancient-cities

Websites for Chapter 5: Announcing Your Country

- This Enlightening Map Shows the Literal Meaning of Every Country's Name
    - https://theculturetrip.com/europe/articles/this-enlightening-map-shows-the-literal-meaning-of-every-countrys-name/

- The Four Things Almost Every Country in the World Is Named After
    - https://www.rd.com/article/every-country-named-four-things/

- The social and cultural value of place names
    - https://unstats.un.org/unsd/geoinfo/ungegn/docs/8th-uncsgn-docs/crp/8th_UNCSGN_econf.94_crp.106.pdf

- Good flag, Bad flag
    - https://nava.org/good-flag-bad-flag/

- Parts of a Flag
    - https://www.flagandbanner.com/customer_service/glossary-flag-terms.asp

- Country flags of the World
    - https://www.countries-ofthe-world.com/flags-of-the-world.html

- The (Brief) Stories Behind 15 National Mottos
    - https://www.babbel.com/en/magazine/stories-behind-national-mottos

- How to Make a Motto
    - https://bizfluent.com/how-10070083-make-motto.html

Links for Videos Referenced in this Unit

- Inside Biosphere 2: The World's Largest Earth Science Experiment
  - https://youtu.be/-yAcD3wuY2Q
- Jane Poynter: Life in Biosphere 2
  - https://youtu.be/a7B39MLVeIc

Videos for Chapter 1: Introduction to Your Land

- What Is A Country? | The MONTEVIDEO CONVENTION And The 4 Requirements Of A STATE
  - https://www.youtube.com/watch?v=VTX6gws9Nj8
- How are states born? Statehood and its elements | LexIcon
  - https://www.youtube.com/watch?v=xcLkkH14iVk
- Five Themes Of Geography (AP Human Geography)
  - https://www.youtube.com/watch?v=J1afrDnnyt4
- Five Themes of Geography Fortnite Edition
  - https://www.youtube.com/watch?v=BFDvrvp33EA
- Five Themes of Geography: Minecraft Edition
  - https://www.youtube.com/watch?v=A9Yszk57HoQ
- NGA Explains: What is Human Geography? (Episode 8)
  - https://www.youtube.com/watch?v=0azAnFmsNm4

- AP Human Geography Unit 1 Review [Thinking Geographically] *(In fact this whole series is fantastic)*
    - https://www.youtube.com/watch?v=wmDR2gCwgrg&t=11s

- Crash Course Unit 4- Political Organization of Space
    - https://www.youtube.com/watch?v=49zeYUVbL3A

- Introduction to Political Geography
    - https://www.youtube.com/watch?v=5E90dydJSfA&t=118s

- What is Political Geography? (1/2)
    - https://www.youtube.com/watch?v=P9SCUFo-LU0

- What is Political Geography? (2/2)
    - https://www.youtube.com/watch?v=BYMBci_vOnk

- What is Geopolitics | A Brief Introduction Geography Lecture
    - https://www.youtube.com/watch?v=SN5hXm1GsZs

- What is Geopolitics and Why Does It Matter?
    - https://www.youtube.com/watch?v=ECzi-bHA4jk

- The Library of Congress Is Your Library
    - https://www.youtube.com/watch?v=63Ze_bpATac

- The National Library (of Singapore)
    - https://www.youtube.com/watch?v=_cZ99pcytBQ

- An introduction to the National Library of Scotland
    - https://www.youtube.com/watch?v=SZRWFJQMXMI

- The bookworms of France's National Library
    - https://www.youtube.com/watch?v=ZPqx9Gl4x_0

Videos for Chapter 2: Getting the Lay of the Land

- A Brief History of Cartography and Maps
    - https://www.youtube.com/watch?v=fLdvInDrQ2c
- Lecture; Maps, Maps, Maps The Basics of Cartography
    - https://www.youtube.com/watch?v=pBAtrN0vOm0
- How to be a Modern Day Cartographer
    - https://www.youtube.com/watch?v=fqbRbMAPSXs
- Elements of a Map
    - https://www.youtube.com/watch?v=7Bt1UgwEUIQ
- The Map Features Song (Gentleman by PSY)
    - https://www.youtube.com/watch?v=A4GMno9p4g4
- 42 Amazing Maps
    - https://www.youtube.com/watch?v=dldHalRY-hY
- Using a Map Scale Song (Line it Up) Fall Out Boy Parody
    - https://www.youtube.com/watch?v=Xd8gJm5c4CY
- Map Skills: Geography, Latitude and Longitude
    - https://www.youtube.com/watch?v=0z9_t8DMk5k
- Introduction to latitude and longitude
    - https://www.youtube.com/watch?v=WPMZIJ-_a6w
- Latitude and Longitude - Sectional Charts
    - https://www.youtube.com/watch?v=upqmeiqr79c
    - This video has a great real world (and more advanced) application for latitude and longitude.

Videos for Chapter 2: Getting the Lay of the Land

- Earth's Interconnected Cycles
  - https://www.youtube.com/watch?v=6j5iHvYBIcg
- Introduction to the Spheres of Earth
  - https://www.youtube.com/watch?v=D78KvwWzRqs
- Working Together - Earth's Systems & Interactions
  - https://www.youtube.com/watch?v=8PnPt3rJQ2Q
- STRUCTURE Of The EARTH | 3D
  - https://www.youtube.com/watch?v=m0icjZLScaM
- Layers of the Geosphere (Interior of the Earth)
  - https://www.youtube.com/watch?v=thToqx5q23g
- 7 Ways We Know What's Inside the Earth
  - https://www.youtube.com/watch?v=tquABLc3Hhs
- The Atmosphere
  - https://www.youtube.com/watch?v=6LkmD6B2ncs&t=167s
- Reveal Earth's Atmosphere | National Geographic
  - https://www.youtube.com/watch?v=1YAOT92wuD8
- Landforms, Hey!: Crash Course Kids #17.1
  - https://www.youtube.com/watch?v=FN6QX43QB4g
- An Introduction to Landforms of the Earth
  - https://www.youtube.com/watch?v=NqVCrXrYSoU
- ESS3A - Natural Resources
  - https://www.youtube.com/watch?v=LxHdUd_Q12Y&t=33s
- Resources: Welcome to the Neighborhood - Crash Course Kids #2.1
  - https://www.youtube.com/watch?v=8LfD_EKze2M&t=42s

- Going, Going Gone: Natural Resource Depletion
    - https://www.youtube.com/watch?v=Y4Eiv16ZLtY
- Exploring Natural Resources
    - https://www.youtube.com/watch?v=Ogkb721UV1k
- How to use resource maps
    - https://www.youtube.com/watch?v=J8mvxq3I6xk
- Weather vs. Climate (Mike Sammartano)
    - https://www.youtube.com/watch?v=6Aigcv7UnTU
- Weather vs Climate (CoCoRaHS Educational Series)
    - https://www.youtube.com/watch?v=VHgyOa70Q7Y
- Climates for Kids | Learn about Different Weather and Climate Zones
    - https://www.youtube.com/watch?v=41Bt4eOg6HU
- Climate Zones of the Earth - The Dr. Binocs Show
    - https://www.youtube.com/watch?v=5tC8OOxOFEk
- The Koppen-Geiger Climate Classification System
    - https://www.youtube.com/watch?v=BsOL9Fafo2w
- Natural Disasters - Definition & Types
    - https://www.youtube.com/watch?v=Hfrp-gG7YcM&t=60s
- ESS3B - Natural Hazards
    - https://www.youtube.com/watch?v=1bmOmozR7ZQ
- Natural disasters
    - https://www.youtube.com/watch?v=zRwDc97Tc2A
- Integrated Approach to Disaster Risk Management:Prevent, Residual risk Prepare, Respond, Recover
    - https://www.youtube.com/watch?v=xjlPmSXj24Y

- Education for disaster preparedness
  - https://www.youtube.com/watch?v=USLHmwvpjX8
- United Nations Office for Disaster Risk Reduction - What we do
  - https://www.youtube.com/watch?v=_ELfN_fXpQk

Videos for Chapter 3: Checking out the Ecosystem

- Ecosystems for Kids
  - https://www.youtube.com/watch?v=SNF8b7KKJ2I
- Ecosystem Ecology: Links in the Chain - Crash Course Ecology #7
  - https://www.youtube.com/watch?v=v6ubvEJ3KGM
- ECOSYSTEM - The Dr. Binocs Show | Best Learning Videos For Kids | Peekaboo Kidz
  - https://www.youtube.com/watch?v=sKJoXdrOT70
- Taxonomy: Life's Filing System - Crash Course Biology #19
  - https://www.youtube.com/watch?v=F38BmgPcZ_I
- Classification of Life
  - https://www.youtube.com/watch?v=tYL_8gv7RiE
- Classification of Living Things
  - https://www.youtube.com/watch?v=sFMv7Gdryc0
- The Food Chain
  - https://www.youtube.com/watch?v=5Z8rKhXUYAg
- Food Chains & Food Webs
  - https://www.youtube.com/watch?v=mSeeWslTEkk
- Understanding Ecosystems for Kids: Producers, Consumers, Decomposers - FreeSchoo
  - https://www.youtube.com/watch?v=bJEToQ49Yjc

- Food chains, Food webs, & Energy pyramids
    - https://www.youtube.com/watch?v=H1EugAY97e8

Videos for Chapter 4: Your Previous People

- An introduction to the discipline of Anthropology
    - https://www.youtube.com/watch?v=J5aglbgTEig

- Anthropology 101 | The Science of the Human Species Explained (With Dogs!)
    - https://www.youtube.com/watch?v=9-gGpAttQmM

- Archeology – exploring the past with modern technology | DW History Documentary
    - https://www.youtube.com/watch?v=VpK8fpqPJT0

- Behind the Scenes of the First Excavation of Pompeii in 70 Years
    - https://www.youtube.com/watch?v=tlTqOmMSang

- What is a Contour (Topographic) Map?
    - https://www.youtube.com/watch?v=pvw5ZM1OKcY

- Understanding Topographic Maps
    - https://www.youtube.com/watch?v=L1AWNR-Y0pQ

- Archaeological Methods: Set up a 1m grid square
    - https://www.youtube.com/watch?v=xNdFDzQzqPk

- HOW TO DIG: Archaeological Excavation Methods
    - https://www.youtube.com/watch?v=ucQNhyHbQbw

- Field Mapping, GIS, and Continuity - Dig Deeper, Episode 28
    - https://www.youtube.com/watch?v=bj6_g70OSqM

- Archaeological Sites: Mapping Alpine Villages
    - https://youtu.be/eiDT7G3rObU
- What Archaeological Sites Used To Actually Look Like
    - https://youtu.be/5BJ6bsHuSZE
- The Birth of Civilisation - The First Farmers (20000 BC to 8800 BC)
    - https://youtu.be/g-bQx0ZtHUw
- Amazing Viking Age Village
    - https://youtu.be/dXp_C99yEMo

Videos for chapter 5: Announcing Your Country

- Country Names Explained
    - https://www.youtube.com/watch?v=mwzRKJPd9H4
- Learn Countries Of The World | All 195 Countries Of The World - World Geography With Pictures
    - https://www.youtube.com/watch?v=L_RgTDaAZY4
- Vexillology - Basic Principles of Flag Design
    - https://youtu.be/HPardMJdy1Y
- History of the U.S. Flag, in Paper
    - https://youtu.be/Qcviywh9Q_A
- Flag This!
    - https://www.youtube.com/channel/UCQnkPI_C0RQxrzZxcGBHH6A
- How Did "In God We Trust" Become the National Motto? | Billy Graham | American Experience | PBS
    - https://youtu.be/PeWUFJ6g40Q

- 30 Best NATIONAL MOTTOS from Around the World || Country Motto || national motto
  - https://youtu.be/MQEZlVDLFl8

Appendix II

Resources for Unit 2: Your People

Contents of Appendix II:
Your People Resources

- ➤ **Books worth Reading with this Unit**
- ➤ **Movie Selections for this Unit**
- ➤ **Gameschooling Selections for this Unit**
- ➤ **Links for Websites and Articles Referenced in this Unit**
- ➤ **Links for Videos Referenced in this Unit**

Books Worth Reading with this Unit

- **Open Borders: The Science and Ethics of Immigration** by Bryon Caplain
  - Bryan Caplan makes a bold case for unrestricted immigration in this fact and graphic filled nonfiction.

- *The Culture Code: An Ingenious Way to Understand Why People Around the World Live and Buy as They Do* by Clotaire Rapaille
  - Why are people so very different? What makes us live or love as we do? The answers are in the codes called The Culture Codes. They are what make us American, Chinese, or French, and they shape how we behave in our lives. What's more, we can learn to crack the codes that affect our actions and achieve an understanding of why we do certain things.

- *Counting Americans: How the US Census Classified the Nation* by Paul Schor
  - How could the one person be classified as black in 1900 and white in 1920 by the US census? The history of the categories used by the census represents a country whose and self-understanding is closely tied to the constant polling of the population.

- *The Sum of the People: How the Census Has Shaped Nations, from the Ancient World to the Modern Age* by Andrew Wilby
  - This captivating three-thousand-year history of the census follows the making of the modern-day survey and explores the political power it holds in the age of data and surveillance.

- ***The Usborne Encyclopedia of World Religions*** by Susam Meredith
    - Looks at the characteristics that religions have in common and presents the history, beliefs, and practices of the big world religions and of the earlier civilizations.

- ***This Land Is Our Land: A History of American Immigration*** by Linda Barrett Osborne
    - This book examines the way government policy and responses to immigrants evolved throughout U.S. history, particularly between 1800 and 1965. It concludes with a summary of events up to modern day, Aas immigration once again becomes a hot topic.

- ***Gulliver's Travels*** by Jonathan Swift
    - Swift tells the story of the four voyages of Lemuel Gulliver. First, he is shipwrecked in the land of Lilliput, where residents are only six inches tall. His second journey takes him to Brobdingnag, where the people are sixty feet tall. Further adventures bring Gulliver to an island in the sky, and to a land where horses hold the reason and beasts look like men.

- ***Census: a Novel*** by Jessie Ball
    - When a widower gets told by a doctor that he doesn't have long left to live, it begs the question of who will care for his adult son—a boy with Down Syndrome. With no answer in mind, and a desire to see the country one last time, the man signs up as a census taker for a strange governmental bureau and leaves town.

- ***The Jungle*** by Upton Sinclair
    - The Jungle follows Lithuanian immigrant Jurgis Rudkus, who came to the United States with his family to live the American dream. Instead, they are thrown into Packingtown where they constantly struggle in order to survive.

- ***Ink Knows No Borders: Poems Of The Immigrant And Refugee Experience*** by Patrice Vecchione
  - A sobering reflection of the trials experienced by first- and second- generation immigrants and refugees such as isolation, language difficulties, and difficult journeys.

Movie Selections for this Unit

- *Live and Become (2005) NR*
    - A Christian boy escapes to Israel from an Ethiopia plagued by famine by pretending to be Jewish.

- *Persepolis (2007) PG-13*
    - An outspoken Iranian girl grows up in the midst of the Islamic Revolution.

- *Gangs of New York (2002) R*
    - In 1862, Amsterdam Vallon returns to the Five Points area of New York City to seek revenge against Bill the Butcher, the man who killed his father.

- *A Day Without a Mexican (2004) R*
    - When a strange fog surrounds the border of California, there is a communication breakdown and all the Mexicans vanish, affecting the economy. The state stops working, as it misses the Mexican workers and dwellers.

- *The Joy Luck Club (1993) R*
    - The life histories of four East Asian women and their daughters reflect and guide each other.

- *My Big Fat Greek Wedding (2002) PG*
    - A Greek woman falls in love with a non-Greek man and struggles to get her family to accept him. At the same time, she comes to terms with her heritage.

- *Minari (2020) PG-13*
    - A Korean family starts a farm in Arkansas in the 1980s.

- *An American Tail (1986) G*
    - While emigrating to the U.S., a young mouse gets separated from his family and must find them while trying to survive in a new country.

- *The Godfather (1972) R*
    - The aging patriarch of an organized crime dynasty in New York City transfers control of his empire to his youngest son.

- *The Kite Runner (2007) PG-13*
    - After years in California, Amir goes back to his home country in Afghanistan to help his old friend Hassan, whose son is in trouble.

- *The Terminal (2004) PG-13*
    - An Eastern European tourist finds himself stranded in JFK airport and has to take up temporary residence there.

Gameschooling Selections for this Unit

- *Passport to Culture*
  - Travel the world with over 1,000 new and unique questions on every country in the world! Challenge your Cultural Intelligence and discover fascinating cultural facts.

- *Ticket to Ride*
  - Build your tracks across the United States in this strategic board game. Connect iconic cities across a map of the 20th-century USA and build your routes to earn points. It also comes in Europe, Asia and other fun varieties.

- *Where in the World is Carmen Sandiego*
  - Carmen is at it again, stealing artifacts from across the globe! Catch Carmen and recover the loot before the other Gumshoes. In a game of deduction and skill, this card game is packed full of twists and turns.

- *Culturetags*
  - The popular game that will test how well you know the culture. Grab a card, announce the category, and provide helpful hints to help the other person guess the Culture Tag before time runs out!

Links for Websites and Articles Referenced in this Unit

- What is agroecology?
    - https://www.soilassociation.org/causes-campaigns/a-ten-year-transition-to-agroecology/what-is-agroecology/#:~:text=Agroecology%20is%20the%20application%20of,and%20prioritising%20local%20supply%20chains.

- Agroecology Knowledge Hub
    - https://www.fao.org/agroecology/overview/en/

Websites for Chapter 6: Growing Your Population

- Ratios
    - https://www.mathsisfun.com/numbers/ratio.html

- Ratios and Fractions and How They Relate to Percentage
    - https://opentextbc.ca/mathfortrades1/chapter/ratios-fractions-and-percentage/

- Pie Chart
    - https://www.mathsisfun.com/data/pie-charts.html

- Immigration
    - https://www.britannica.com/topic/immigration

- How the United States Immigration System Works
    - https://www.americanimmigrationcouncil.org/research/how-united-states-immigration-system-works

- Conquest
    - https://www.britannica.com/topic/conquest-international-law

- Annexation
    - https://www.britannica.com/topic/annexation

- Refugees
    - https://www.unhcr.org/en-us/refugees.html

- Refugees
    - https://www.un.org/en/global-issues/refugees

- National Debt
    - https://www.investopedia.com/updates/usa-national-debt/

- The U.S. National Debt and How It Affects You
    - https://www.thebalance.com/what-is-the-national-debt-4031393

- Using and Handling Data
    - https://www.mathsisfun.com/data/index.html

- Which Type of Chart or Graph is Right for You?
    - https://www.tableau.com/learn/whitepapers/which-chart-or-graph-is-right-for-you

- Population Density
    - https://education.nationalgeographic.org/resource/population-density

- Understanding Population Density
    - https://www.census.gov/newsroom/blogs/random-samplings/2015/03/understanding-population-density.html

- Our World in Data: Population Density
    - https://ourworldindata.org/grapher/population-density?time=latest
- How to Create a Population Density Map
    - https://sciencing.com/create-population-density-map-8204638.html
- Census
    - https://education.nationalgeographic.org/resource/census
- What is a census and what kind of data is collected?
    - https://www.canr.msu.edu/news/what_is_a_census_and_what_kind_of_data_is_collected
- Census Records
    - https://www.archives.gov/research/census
- How to See the Bigger Picture with Data Sampling
    - https://www.g2.com/articles/data-sampling
- A Peek at Data Sampling Methods
    - https://towardsdatascience.com/a-peek-at-data-sampling-methods-5d7199c8aab8
- Population vs. Sample | Definitions, Differences & Examples
    - https://www.scribbr.com/methodology/population-vs-sample/

Websites for Chapter 7: Crafting Your Unique Culture

- Cultural Blending Case Study
    - https://www.sps186.org/downloads/basic/584765/ch18_2.pdf
- What Should Cultures Do To Benefit From Cultural Blending?
    - https://realonomics.net/what-should-cultures-do-to-benefit-from-cultural-blending/

- 12 examples of Cultural Diffusion
    - https://simplicable.com/new/cultural-diffusion
- The USA's 21 Most Popular Landmarks and Monuments
    - https://theculturetrip.com/north-america/usa/articles/the-usa-s-21-most-popular-landmarks-and-monuments/
- National Historic Landmarks Program
    - https://www.nps.gov/orgs/1582/index.htm
- National Natural Landmarks
    - http://npshistory.com/brochures/nnl-25.pdf
- American Culture: Traditions and Customs of the United States
    - https://www.livescience.com/28945-american-culture.html
- The Importance Customs in Society
    - https://www.thoughtco.com/custom-definition-3026171
- Difference Between Custom and Tradition
    - https://pediaa.com/difference-between-custom-and-tradition/
- Values and Norms of Society: Conformity, Conflict and Deviation in Norms
    - https://www.sociologydiscussion.com/society/values-and-norms-of-society-conformity-conflict-and-deviation-in-norms/2292
- What is the Difference Between Norms and Values
    - https://pediaa.com/what-is-the-difference-between-norms-and-values/
- Why do we follow the behavior of others?
    - https://thedecisionlab.com/biases/social-norms
- The 4 Types Of Norms (Folkways, Mores, Taboos & Laws)
    - https://helpfulprofessor.com/types-of-norms/

- Folkways, Mores, Taboos, and Laws

    - https://www.thoughtco.com/folkways-mores-taboos-and-laws-3026267

Websites for Chapter 8: Addressing Your People

- Federal Holidays: Evolution and Current Practices

    - https://sgp.fas.org/crs/misc/R41990.pdf

- The History and Timeline of Federal Holidays in the US

    - https://historyincharts.com/the-history-and-timeline-of-federal-holidays-in-the-us/

- How to Create Holidays and National Days

    - https://holidayinsights.com/create-national-holiday-days.htm

- Public Speaking

    - https://corporatefinanceinstitute.com/resources/careers/soft-skills/public-speaking/

- The 4 Types Of Public Speaking

    - https://soulcastmedia.com/the-4-types-of-public-speaking/

- The Top 10 Famous Speeches That Stand the Test of Time

    - https://www.themanual.com/culture/famous-speeches-from-history/

Links for Videos Referenced in this Unit

- Can we create the "perfect" farm? - Brent Loken
    - https://youtu.be/xFqecEtdGZ0
- The 10 Elements of Agroecology: Enabling transitions to sustainable agriculture and food systems
    - https://youtu.be/6Reh7c2-ewI
- Agroecology: farmer's perspectives
    - https://www.youtube.com/watch?v=GO7e5yrQuEI
- Regenerative Farming in Kenya | Circular food systems in East Africa 1/5
    - https://youtu.be/EVNSXB-3L1c

Videos for Chapter 6: Growing Your Population

- Land Use & Characteristics in Urban Areas (9:39)
    - https://youtu.be/bZPmxKqs9O4
- Video 14: Land Use - Agriculture
    - https://youtu.be/X7OnIT_rRCg
- The Top Agricultural Producing Countries 1960 to 2016
    - https://youtu.be/i0Uesek7KNI
- How Much to Plant Per Person for a Year's Worth of Food
    - https://youtu.be/e28Yhm1aY_s
- What is Mining - More Science on the Learning Videos Channel
    - https://youtu.be/K6FasptWdeU

- Sustainable Wood from Sustainable Forests
  - https://youtu.be/uNTPcJIdmPk
- Who owns the "wilderness"? - Elyse Cox
  - https://youtu.be/XJasV-itdoc
- What is a National Park?
  - https://youtu.be/55T6ZlSdgrY
- Every Type of US National Park, Explained
  - https://youtu.be/X3nxFnUCIO0
- Introduction to Ratios (What Are Ratios?) | Ratio Examples and Answers
  - https://youtu.be/xA435umOQuw
- Introduction to ratios | Ratios, proportions, units, and rates | Pre-Algebra | Khan Academy
  - https://youtu.be/HpdMJaKaXXc
- Math Antics - What Are Percentages?
  - https://youtu.be/JeVSmq1Nrpw
- Drawing Pie Charts by Hand
  - https://youtu.be/jND35xk1ktI
- How To Create A Pie Chart In Excel (With Percentages)
  - https://youtu.be/0WNJkBXywMU
- Why Do People Migrate?! (Push & Pull Factors: AP Human Geo)
  - https://youtu.be/4QrUegs-kUs
- U.S. Immigration | Let's Talk | NPR
  - https://youtu.be/m9zf8hkCqIg
- The Economics of Immigration: Crash Course Econ #33
  - https://youtu.be/4XQXiCLzyAw

- Annexation
    - https://youtu.be/B9m17AGxeWs
- What does it mean to be a refugee? - Benedetta Berti and Evelien Borgman
    - https://youtu.be/25bwiSikRsI
- Who is a Refugee?
    - https://youtu.be/GvzZGplGbL8
- Understand the Immigration System in 8 Minutes
    - https://youtu.be/oqAnzGNfxCY
- Understanding the National Debt and Budget Deficit
    - https://youtu.be/3ugDU2qNcyg
- Deficits & Debts: Crash Course Economics #9
    - https://youtu.be/3sUCSGVYzI0
- National debt
    - https://youtu.be/mT7xpWh3PgI
- Charts Are Like Pasta - Data Visualization Part 1: Crash Course Statistics #5
    - https://youtu.be/hEWY6kkBdpo
- Which is the best chart: Selecting among 14 types of charts Part I
    - https://youtu.be/C07k0euBpr8
- Which is the best chart: Selecting among 14 types of charts Part II
    - https://youtu.be/qGaIB-bRn-A
- Population Density
    - https://youtu.be/h5Tpy7MQcf0
- Population Densities (AP Human Geography)
    - https://youtu.be/xEb-7SfBGQI

- World Population
    - https://youtu.be/ZFe_UfL6EUE
- Population Density Map Introduction
    - https://youtu.be/egXFR1DwM-Y
- What's The U.S. CENSUS + Why's It SO IMPORTANT?
    - https://youtu.be/Vn4K3XoywlY
- Why have a Census?
    - https://youtu.be/3-O_bPHkt-o
- Introduction to sampling distributions | Sampling distributions | AP Statistics | Khan Academy
    - https://youtu.be/z0Ry_3_qhDw
- Population vs Sample
    - https://youtu.be/eIZD1BFfw8E
- Using a Sample to Make Predictions about a Population
    - https://youtu.be/lCN6m-Et1pY

Videos for Chapter 7: Crafting Your Unique Culture

- What is Cultural Diffusion?
    - https://youtu.be/rCFWqNwvyAE
- Cultural Diffusion Rap
    - https://youtu.be/QCt6zLE7uII
- Effects Of The Diffusion of Culture [AP Human Geography Unit 3 Topic 8] (3.8)
    - https://youtu.be/R3wX8bxD7r8

- A Blending of Cultures
    - https://youtu.be/biKDVSC_CBY
- America's Most Important Landmarks
    - https://youtu.be/6yZkXZXisNk
- National Natural Landmarks Program
    - https://youtu.be/QhQSeq-peBk
- Difference between customs and traditions
    - https://youtu.be/dvYBruOmf_E
- 10 Interesting Traditions Around The World That Are Still Practiced Today
    - https://youtu.be/j5da1f7NT4Q
- Preserving the Ways - Culture and Traditions
    - https://youtu.be/vge43MZTPU4
- Culture Norms and Values
    - https://youtu.be/OoBOXOLMmrg
- Symbols, Values & Norms: Crash Course Sociology #10
    - https://youtu.be/kGrVhM_Gi8k
- Norms, Mores, Folkways and Taboos
    - https://youtu.be/UNAQheU36ws
- What is normal? Exploring folkways, mores, and taboos | Behavior | MCAT | Khan Academy
    - https://youtu.be/tOEz6RC0aVo
- What are Social Norms? (Folkways, Mores, Taboos)
    - https://youtu.be/bxSolK-vVl4
- How Do Perceptions of Social Norms Affect Our Behavior? Featuring Dr. Margaret Tankard
    - https://youtu.be/65vp8c4alZc

Videos for Chapter 8: Addressing Your People

- The Importance of National Holidays.
    - https://youtu.be/hy2OFgOuUnY
- History of Holidays in the United States
    - https://youtu.be/G3Gm_4qGIl4
- My Own National Holiday
    - https://youtu.be/3ueqKZkUjkI
- Most Celebrated Holiday Comparison
    - https://youtu.be/FV49tvxQI3M
- What is Public Speaking?
    - https://youtu.be/mmx5ABUynQI
- What is Public Speaking? | Factors of Public Speaking
    - https://youtu.be/QO9qBCHqfmk
- Public Speaking 8: Types of Speeches
    - https://youtu.be/ppj3ejcu1hg
- 4 types of Audience for your Speech
    - https://youtu.be/3cL151iSRnU

Appendix III

Resources for

Unit 3: Your Government

Contents of Appendix III:
Your Government Resources

- ➢ Books worth Reading with this Unit
- ➢ Movie Selections for this Unit
- ➢ Gameschooling Selections for this Unit
- ➢ Links for Websites and Articles Referenced in this Unit
- ➢ Links for Videos Referenced in this Unit

Books Worth Reading with this Unit

- ***Words That Built a Nation: Voices of Democracy That Have Shaped America's History*** by Marilyn Miller
    - From the Constitution to the 2015 Supreme Court ruling on same-sex marriage, this updated collection introduces the landmark statements that impact our nation today.

- ***A Kid's Guide to America's Bill of Rights: Curfews, Censorship, and the 100-Pound Giant*** by Kathleen Krull
    - Find out what the Bill of Rights is and how it affects everyday life in this close up look at the history and significance of these laws that protect the individual freedoms of everyone.

- ***Constitution Translated for Kids*** by Cathy Travis
    - A simple translation of the entire U.S. Constitution, side-by-side with the original 1787 text.

- ***Understanding Politics & Government*** by Alex Frith
    - Learn about all types of government, how laws are decided on and applied, who gets to decide who rules a country, and more.

- ***This Is Our Constitution: What It Is and Why It Matters*** by Khizr Khan
    - This book shows why the Constitution matters to everyday life.

- ***The Cabinet: George Washington and the Creation of an American Institution*** by Lindsay Chervinsky
    - The US Constitution never established the presidential cabinet. So how did George Washington create one of the most powerful bodies in the government?

- *1984* by Orson Wells
    - Winston Smith longs only for truth and decency. But living in a social system where those with unorthodox ideas are brainwashed or put to death, he knows there is no hope for him. The year 1984 has passed, yet George Orwell's nightmare of the world we could have become is still a great modern classic portrait of a negative Utopia.

- *Animal Farm* by George Orwell
    - The transformation of Mr. Jones' Manor Farm into Animal Farm, a wholly democratic society built on the creed that All Animals Are Created Equal. The pigs Napoleon, Squealer, and Snowball emerge as leaders in the new community in an evolution that bears a certain familiarity.

- *Brave New World* by Aldous Huxley
    - A vision of an unequal future where humans are bred, indoctrinated, and anesthetized specifically to passively uphold an authoritarian ruling order–all at the cost of our freedom and full humanity.

- *Fahrenheit 451* by Ray Bradbury
  - Guy Montag is a fireman whose job it is to destroy the most illegal of commodities, the printed book and the houses in where they are hidden. He never questions the destruction his actions produce. But when he meets Clarisse, who introduces him to a past where people didn't live in fear and to a present where one sees the world through the ideas in books, Montag begins to question everything.

Movie Selections for this Unit

- *Bridge of Spies (2015) PG-13*
    - An American lawyer is recruited to defend an arrested Soviet spy in court, and then help the CIA exchange the spy for the Soviet captured American pilot, Francis Gary Powers.

- *All the President's Men (1976) PG*
    - Reporters Bob Woodward and Carl Bernstein uncover the details of the Watergate scandal that lead to President Richard Nixon's resignation.

- *Milk (2008) R*
    - The story of Harvey Milk and his struggles as a gay activist who fought for gay rights and became California's first openly gay elected official.

- *Lincoln (2012) PG-13*
    - As the American Civil War continues to rage, Lincoln struggles with continuing carnage on the battlefield as he fights with many inside his own cabinet on the decision to emancipate the slaves.

- *Wag the Dog (1997) R*
    - Before an election, a spin-doctor and a Producer join efforts to fake a war in order to cover up a Presidential sex scandal.

- *Mr. Smith Goes to Washington (1939) NR*
  - A naive youth leader is appointed to fill a vacancy in the U.S. Senate. His idealistic plans promptly collide with corruption at home and subterfuge from his hero in Washington, but he tries to forge ahead despite attacks on his character.

- *Thank you for Smoking (2005) R*
  - Satirical comedy follows the Big Tobacco's chief spokesman, Nick Naylor, who is lobbying on behalf of cigarettes while trying to be a role model for his 12-year old son.

- *Dave (1993) PG-13*
  - A Presidential lookalike named Dave is recruited by the Secret Service to become a stand-in for the President of the United States.

- *12 Angry Men (1957) NR*
  - The jury of a New York City murder trial is frustrated by a single member whose caution forces them to more carefully consider the evidence before jumping to a quick verdict.

- *Selma (2014) PG-13*
  - In 1965, an Alabama city became the battleground in the fight for suffrage. Despite violent opposition, Dr. Martin Luther King Jr. and his followers pressed forward on an epic march from Selma to Montgomery.

- *Vice (2018) R*
  - The story of Dick Cheney, an unassuming Washington insider, who wielded immense power as Vice President to George W. Bush, reshaping the country in ways that we feel today.

- *Lee Daniel's The Butler (2013) PG-13*
  - Cecil Gaines serves eight presidents during his time as a butler at the White House as the civil rights movement, Vietnam, and other major events affect his life, family, and society.

- *The Wolf of Wall Street (2013) R*
  - Based on the true story of Jordan Belfort, it documents his rise to a wealthy stockbroker to his fall involving crime and corruption.

- *Inside Job (2010) PG-13*
  - Inside Job takes a closer look at what brought about the 2008 financial crisis.

- *The Supreme court miniseries (2007) NR*
  - A documentary showing the evolution and major decisions of the Supreme Court from its creation through 2005

Gameschooling Selections for this Unit

- **Constitution Quest**
    - This is easy-to-play, educational roll-and-move trivia game tests your knowledge on Constitutional topics like the three branches of government, amendments, checks and balances, historical facts and dates, and more!

- **Campaign for President**
    - The game revolves around your political campaign's ability to woo voters before Election Day. Player candidates play cards to maintain political momentum by rallying support while diverting that momentum away from rivals Players can challenge each other to debates, directly appeal to the voters for support, and more in their bid to become President. When the Election Day card is drawn the candidate who gathered the most voters will win.

- **Diplomacy**
    - The Avalon Hill Diplomacy cooperative board game is a game of negotiation, cunning, and deceit. Through making deals and forming alliances, you'll expand your empire over pre-World War I Europe. You'll have to watch your back as you make and break deals, un-hatch traitorous plots, negotiate, and outwit others to gain dominance of the continent. It's a strategy game in which players must rely on their own cunning and cleverness, not the luck of the dice, to determine the outcome.

- **Chronology**
  - Think you know which came first? Test your knowledge with Chronology! Each player builds his or her own timeline of cards. On your turn, someone will read you a historical event from a card. You must decide where that event falls in your timeline. If you're correct, you keep it and your timeline grows. The first player to build a timeline of 10 cards wins.

- **Corinth**
  - In 4th Century BC Corinth, traders come from all corners of the Mediterranean Sea to sell their goods. Players have a few weeks to secure their place in Corinth as its most savvy trader! In each round, a few dice are rolled, and players choose groups of dice of the same value and deliver goods to the best shops in the Harbor, purchase herds of goats to help erect buildings, and more.

- **Election Night**
  - Two players or teams battle for critical electoral votes in a gripping race for the presidency. Use your dice pool to choose products or sums that could help you the most. Target key states with freezes and re-rolls to counter your opponent's progress, and be quick to adapt as conditions change. Strategize your way to gaining the 270 electoral votes you need to become President!

- **Professor Noggins Presidents of the United States**
  - Since the time of George Washington, important leaders have served from the Oval Office. Learn about the first 44 Presidents, the challenges they faced as leaders, and more! Each of the thirty game cards combines trivia, multiple-choice questions, and true or false. A special three-numbered die is included which adds an element of unpredictability.

- **Monopoly House Divided**
    - It's a Monopoly game in which players dream, and campaign, their way to the White House! Choose one of the Candidate tokens, get assigned to the blue or red party, and get ready for some political wheeling and dealing.

- **Mystic Market**
    - Mystic Market is a fast-paced card game where players buy and sell magical ingredients. The unique Value Track ensures that the values of the Ingredients are constantly shifting, so only the best traders will prevail.

Links for Websites and Articles Referenced in this Unit

- Fossil Fuels
    - https://education.nationalgeographic.org/resource/fossil-fuels
- Fossil
    - https://www.energy.gov/science-innovation/energy-sources/fossil
- Biofuel Basics
    - https://www.energy.gov/eere/bioenergy/biofuel-basics
- Biofuels explained
    - https://www.eia.gov/energyexplained/biofuels/
- Agrofuels
    - https://cban.ca/gmos/issues/agrofuels/

Websites for Chapter 9: Creating Your Government

- What is Government
    - https://world101.cfr.org/how-world-works-and-sometimes-doesnt/forms-government/what-government
- What is Government (2)
    - https://ceodelhi.gov.in/eLearningv2/admin/EnglishPDF/Chapter-3-What-is-Government.pdf

- Forms Of Government, 2018
    - https://education.nationalgeographic.org/resource/forms-government-2018
- Types of Government
    - https://www.ushistory.org/gov/1b.asp
- Understanding Types of Government
    - https://www.thoughtco.com/types-of-government-5179107
- Principles and Virtues
    - https://www.billofrightsinstitute.org/resources/principles-and-virtues
- Aims and values
    - https://european-union.europa.eu/principles-countries-history/principles-and-values/aims-and-values_en
- We the People
    - https://constitutioncenter.org/interactive-constitution/preamble
- Natural Rights
    - https://www.mtsu.edu/first-amendment/article/822/natural-rights
- Human rights and natural law
    - https://en.unesco.org/courier/2018-4/human-rights-and-natural-law
- What Are Natural Rights?
    - https://www.thoughtco.com/what-are-natural-rights-4108952
- The Bill of Rights: What Does it Say?
    - https://www.archives.gov/founding-docs/bill-of-rights/what-does-it-say#:~:text=The%20Bill%20of%20Rights%20is,speech%2C%20press%2C%20and%20religion.
- Bill of Rights Overview
    - https://constitutioncenter.org/interactive-constitution/learning-material/bill-of-rights-overview

- The Constitution: Articles
    - https://constitutioncenter.org/interactive-constitution/the-constitution
- U.S. Constitution
    - https://www.law.cornell.edu/constitution/index.html
- United States Constitution: How It's Organized
    - **https://guides.lib.uiowa.edu/c.php?g=132054&p=863932**

- How Laws Are Made and How to Research Them
    - https://www.usa.gov/how-laws-are-made
- How Our Laws Are Made
    - https://www.congress.gov/help/learn-about-the-legislative-process/how-our-laws-are-made
- Making Laws
    - https://www.visitthecapitol.gov/about-congress/making-laws

Websites for Chapter 10: Creating Your Economic Structures

- Economy
    - https://www.investopedia.com/terms/e/economy.asp
- Law of Supply and Demand
    - https://www.investopedia.com/terms/l/law-of-supply-demand.asp
- What is an Economic System?
    - https://corporatefinanceinstitute.com/resources/knowledge/economics/economic-system/
- Economic Systems
    - https://www.intelligenteconomist.com/economic-systems/

- 4 Types of Economic Systems
    - https://www.analyticssteps.com/blogs/4-types-economic-systems
- Capitalism, Socialism, or Fascism? A Guide to Economic Systems and Ideologies
    - https://home.heinonline.org/blog/2020/07/capitalism-socialism-or-fascism-a-guide-to-economic-systems-and-ideologies/
- Currency Design: Designing The Most Desirable Product
    - https://www.smashingmagazine.com/2016/01/learn-from-the-history-of-banknote-design-most-desirable-product/
- 20 examples of the world's best currency design
    - https://99designs.com/blog/creative-inspiration/20-examples-worlds-best-currency-design/
- What Money Should Look Like
    - https://econlife.com/2018/08/good-currency-design/
- The Seven Denominations
    - https://www.uscurrency.gov/denominations
- How Coins Are Made: The Design and Selection Process
    - https://www.usmint.gov/news/inside-the-mint/how-coins-are-made-design-and-selection-process
- Exchange Rate Definition
    - https://www.investopedia.com/terms/e/exchangerate.asp
- Read and Calculate Currency Exchange Rates
    - https://www.thebalance.com/how-to-read-and-calculate-exchange-rates-1978919
- Currency Converter
    - https://www.bankrate.com/investing/currency-calculator/
- Foreign Exchange Rates for U.S. Dollars
    - https://www.bankofamerica.com/foreign-exchange/exchange-rates/

- Taxes
    - https://www.annuity.org/personal-finance/taxes/
- What Are Taxes?
    - https://www.thebalance.com/what-are-taxes-5213316
- The Three Basic Tax Types
    - https://taxfoundation.org/the-three-basic-tax-types/
- Federal Spending: Where Does the Money Go
    - https://www.nationalpriorities.org/budget-basics/federal-budget-101/spending/
- Budget of the U.S. Government
    - https://www.usa.gov/budget
- Federal Budget
    - https://www.investopedia.com/terms/f/federal-budget.asp

Websites for Chapter 11: Fleshing out Your Governmental Infrastructure

- What is Public Works?
    - https://www.apwa.net/MYAPWA/About/What_is_Public_Works/MyApwa/Apwa_Public/About/What_Is_Public_Works.aspx
- Transportation and Public Works
    - https://www.statelocalgov.net/50states-public-works.cfm
- National Association of Regulatory Utility Commissioners
    - https://www.naruc.org/
- What is Public Power?
    - https://www.publicpower.org/system/files/documents/municipalization-what_is_public_power.pdf

- What Are Utilities in a Home, Apartment, or Business?
    - https://www.energybot.com/blog/what-are-utilities-in-a-home-or-business.html
- National Defense Magazine
    - https://www.nationaldefensemagazine.org/
- U.S. Department of Defense
    - https://www.defense.gov/
- What Are the Branches of the US Military?
    - https://www.military.com/join-armed-forces/us-military-branches-overview.html
- Our Forces
    - https://www.defense.gov/About/our-forces/
- In the beginning, there was competition: the old idea behind the new American way of war
    - https://mwi.usma.edu/beginning-competition-old-idea-behind-new-american-way-war/
- What are the 3 Types of Education?
    - https://www.cuemath.com/learn/3-types-of-education/
- THE DIFFERENT TYPES OF EDUCATION
    - https://www.througheducation.com/the-different-types-of-education/
- US Department of Education: Laws & Guidance
    - https://www2.ed.gov/policy/landing.jhtml?src=ft
- Education policy in the United States
    - https://ballotpedia.org/Education_policy_in_the_United_States
- Types of Health Systems
    - https://www.publichealth.columbia.edu/research/comparative-health-policy-library/types-health-systems-0
- The Formulation of Health Policy by the Three Branches of Government
    - https://www.ncbi.nlm.nih.gov/books/NBK231979/

- Six Components Necessary for Effective Public Health Program Implementation
    - https://www.ncbi.nlm.nih.gov/pmc/articles/PMC3910052/

- Healthcare Policy: What Is It and Why Is It Important?
    - https://www.usa.edu/blog/healthcare-policy/

- The Cabinet
    - https://www.whitehouse.gov/administration/cabinet/

- How the US Cabinet Works: 15 Offices of the Cabinet
    - https://www.masterclass.com/articles/us-cabinet-explained#what-is-the-us-cabinet

- Order of Presidential Succession
    - https://www.usa.gov/presidents#:~:text=If%20the%20President%20of%20the,Pro%20Tempore%20of%20the%20Senate

- Presidential Succession Act
    - https://www.senate.gov/about/officers-staff/president-pro-tempore/presidential-succession-act.htm

- Succession
    - https://www.royal.uk/succession

Websites for Chapter 12: Making Choices with Your Priorities

- Decision-making process
    - https://www.umassd.edu/fycm/decision-making/process/#:~:text=Decision%20making%20is%20the%20process,relevant%20information%20and%20defining%20alternatives.

- Decision-Making
    - https://www.psychologytoday.com/us/basics/decision-making
- The Effective Decision
    - https://hbr.org/1967/01/the-effective-decision
- Decision making in the age of urgency
    - https://www.mckinsey.com/business-functions/people-and-organizational-performance/our-insights/decision-making-in-the-age-of-urgency

Links for Videos Referenced in this Unit

- Fossil Fuels for Kids | Learn all about fossil fuels, what they are, and where they come from
    - https://youtu.be/JasIvS7oYw4
- Will Fossil Fuels Run Out? | Earth Lab
    - https://youtu.be/jjfs_7kwRks
- 300 Years of FOSSIL FUELS in 300 Seconds
    - https://youtu.be/cJ-J91SwP8w
- What are Biofuels and Where are They Going?
    - https://youtu.be/cp6lifuYXFw
- Biofuel instead of coal and oil - How promising are these renewable resources? | DW Documentary
    - https://youtu.be/I9arI2e5bkw
- Ethics of Biofuels-Corn as Agrofuel?
    - https://youtu.be/ggr4YbKKJNc
- How to make Biodiesel at Home in 5 Minutes..! | Biofuel From used Vegetable oil / Cooking Oil
    - https://youtu.be/8cZPP2at8HI

Videos for Chapter 9: Creating Your Government

- What is Government?
    - https://youtu.be/n6mqRreNLr4

- The Purpose of Government
    - https://youtu.be/IAnjKNUQERY
- What is a Government and Why Do We Need One?
    - https://youtu.be/eDxeBIcTAVU
- Every Type of Government Explained
    - https://youtu.be/YiLulvnHjWM
- POLITICAL SYSTEMS 101: Basic Forms of Government Explained
    - https://youtu.be/jJEuZrvNYg0
- Principles of the Constitutional American Government - Civics SOL
    - https://youtu.be/2iQcqjdYP_c
- Principles of the Constitution
    - https://youtu.be/iAYxkTBYMic
- American Fundamental Ideals, Values and Principles: The Basics of Constitutional Government, Part 13
    - https://youtu.be/F8Taa_4IPYU
- The Preamble of The Constitution Schoolhouse Rock
    - https://youtu.be/OqvLi7qZ_yU
- The Preamble to the Constitution | US Government and Politics | Khan Academy
    - https://youtu.be/V3tTnqznYwk
- What is the Difference Between Natural Rights and Legal Rights?
    - https://youtu.be/bPu1JnpaFGE
- John Locke, Natural Rights
    - https://youtu.be/T7-Abmn9lZY
- How are Natural Rights Related to Just Laws? [No. 86]
    - https://youtu.be/Ed8IDC0QoqQ

- Why wasn't the Bill of Rights originally in the US Constitution? - James Coll
    - https://youtu.be/aMCDikASE4o
- The Bill of Rights: Every Amendment, Why it's important, and How it limits the government
    - https://youtu.be/tBbELqqSyek
- The US Constitution - Breaking Down the Articles
    - https://youtu.be/UyUWDTruSAY
- The Articles and the Constitution (US History EOC Review - USHC 1.4)
    - https://youtu.be/wYInJTyk3Oc
- How a Bill Becomes a Law: Crash Course Government and Politics #9
    - https://youtu.be/66f4-NKEYz4
- Government Class: How Laws Are Made
    - https://youtu.be/kaVQtANo2A4
- A Few of the Most Interesting Parts of The US Constitution
    - https://youtu.be/BmdsE3sXcoU
- The U.S. Constitution, EXPLAINED [AP Government Required Documents]
    - https://youtu.be/1MW1eYICTzU

Videos for Chapter 10: Creating Your Economic Structures

- Economy Definition for Kids
    - https://youtu.be/CamHuVSm_IQ
- The economy explained, what is the economy
    - https://youtu.be/l1FLLax0ncg

- Supply and Demand: Crash Course Economics #4
    - https://youtu.be/g9aDizJpd_s
- Scarcity - Supply and Demand
    - https://youtu.be/vEhQiYghnV0
- Economic Systems and Macroeconomics: Crash Course Economics #3
    - https://youtu.be/B43YEW2FvDs
- Economics - Economic Systems
    - https://youtu.be/djPFUgUOujY
- Economic Schools of Thought: Crash Course Economics #14
    - https://youtu.be/tZvjh1dxz08
- CAPITALISM, SOCIALISM & COMMUNISM EXPLAINED SIMPLY
    - https://youtu.be/53vmQNVBm0w
- Capitalism, Communism, & Political Economies: Crash Course Geography #38
    - https://youtu.be/X2ZIDALAkXo
- Money Marvels - Design Your Own Banknote
    - https://youtu.be/59ZtA6bYIQY
- World's Coolest Banknotes 2021 - Voted By You!
    - https://youtu.be/srNI0g_4l_M
- How Money Is Made | How Stuff Is Made | Refinery29
    - https://youtu.be/kZ3xRQOhpQI
- Minting My Own Currency
    - https://youtu.be/FvKotETzOFg
- The United States Currency System
    - https://youtu.be/2XgDq7ELdcw

- Currency Exchange Introduction
    - https://youtu.be/itoNb1lb5hY
- How Exchange Rates Are Determined
    - https://youtu.be/-7ZSav8xvMU
- Currency Exchange Rates - How To Convert Currency
    - https://youtu.be/JRf7_RKF3uA
- Taxes: Crash Course Economics #31
    - https://youtu.be/7Qtr_vA3Prw
- Types of Taxes in the United States
    - https://youtu.be/rDWOpCJdtgQ
- What If People Stopped Paying Taxes?
    - https://youtu.be/s0SFNNu6RNw
- The 4 Main Types of Taxes We Pay
    - https://youtu.be/dD6gEVZxcSk
- How does the National Budget work?
    - https://youtu.be/cAw4CKynIGI
- Government Budgets and Fiscal Policy | IB Macroeconomics
    - https://youtu.be/PjgHplWoCJY
- Monetary and Fiscal Policy: Crash Course Government and Politics #48
    - https://youtu.be/_tULRch1PRQ
- U.S. Federal Budget Process 101
    - https://youtu.be/v67UoLRuH_c
- What If The US Budget Was Only $100 - How Would It Spend It?
    - https://youtu.be/65Vpyy43Fug

Videos for Chapter 11: Fleshing out Your Governmental Infrastructure

- What Is Public Works?
    - https://youtu.be/Pq9m4uUavrY

- Public Works 101
    - https://youtu.be/y5edoPGDiys

- Inside the Public Works Department
    - https://youtu.be/9uMOBD4FZcc

- Unseen, Unsung, Unnoticed | How do "Public Utilities" Work?
    - https://youtu.be/mHVEyUq6Dxg

- Utilities at a glance
    - https://youtu.be/0QWw7R-9upg

- Empowered: The role of the Public Utilities Commission in Hawaii's 100% renewable energy future
    - https://youtu.be/_F5vv77eMt4

- The National Defense Strategy of the United States | Learning Military
    - https://youtu.be/HT-OfN2bjlA

- 5 Things You Don't Know: Department of Defense
    - https://youtu.be/MT_tw4JKo_g

- US Armed Forces: Branches Explained
    - https://youtu.be/LYOCb9EYBiw

- Types of education : Formal , Non-formal , Informal education
    - https://youtu.be/IhD5uVlGHmM

- What is education policy?
    - https://youtu.be/PBn9T4hmdrs

- The art of policy making in education - Education Talks
  - https://youtu.be/SkKuHjTvrIc
- Globalisation and Educational Policy
  - https://youtu.be/a5x6CMpAYfc
- Saving Schools: History, Politics, and Policy in U.S. Education | HarvardX on edX | About Video
  - https://youtu.be/3JIuZr3GnEk
- The Basic Structure of Education Law: Module 1 of 4
  - https://youtu.be/mecjrCQzDqI
- Health Systems
  - https://youtu.be/ECkeJQd2IdY
- Healthcare System Comparison: Canada v. UK v. Germany
  - https://youtu.be/yKQxmoLTvy8
- The Healthcare System of the United States
  - https://youtu.be/yN-MkRcOJjY
- (P002) Public Health Policy Making Process - Basic Concepts
  - https://youtu.be/b0Qy2p1J5jk
- The Economics of Healthcare: Crash Course Econ #29
  - https://youtu.be/cbBKoyjFLUY
- The Structure & Cost of US Health Care: Crash Course Sociology #44
  - https://youtu.be/KriEIJ0ubh0
- America 101: What is the Cabinet? | History
  - https://youtu.be/8oier528TrE
- The Cabinet - A level Politics
  - https://youtu.be/EJhsuQop47g

- Inside the White House: The Cabinet
    - https://youtu.be/xxSvi6JCCfk
- Prime Minister vs. President: What's The Difference?
    - https://youtu.be/VOAYUwQTTdQ
- The Origin of the President's Cabinet
    - https://youtu.be/tnWZNyMyMig
- U.S. President, Presidential Line of Succession Explained
    - https://youtu.be/ugAL1L36fzo
- The Presidential Line of Succession
    - https://youtu.be/bn8e-WzKK9Y
- Royalty 101: The Rules of Succession
    - https://youtu.be/mNgyPWCTlMA

Videos for Chapter 12: Making Choices with Your Priorities

- Decision-Making Strategies
    - https://youtu.be/pPIhAm_WGbQ
- Decision Making in Management
    - https://youtu.be/Jg62oeEzMkU
- Steps in Rational Decision Making
    - https://youtu.be/GeA9ghb_WjM
- The 7 step decision making process | Decision making model | Lauren Kress
    - https://youtu.be/d53AFjxT5hQ
- Government decision making in uncertainty
    - https://youtu.be/QAzzTKTnQMw

Appendix IV

Resources for

Unit 4: Your Global Position

Contents of Appendix IV:
Your Global Position Resources

- ➢ **Books worth Reading with this Unit**
- ➢ **Movie Selections for this Unit**
- ➢ **Gameschooling Selections for this Unit**
- ➢ **Links for Websites and Articles Referenced in this Unit**
- ➢ **Links for Videos Referenced in this Unit**

Books Worth Reading with this Unit

- *Generation Fix: Young Ideas for a Better World* by Elizabeth Rusch
    - Features real life stories of kids doing incredible things to make the world a better place. Capturing kids' ideas on how to solve the problems that we face in this world - hunger, homelessness, violence, discrimination, and more– the book inspires them to act on their own ideas and resources.

- *The Global Economy as You've Never Seen It: 99 Ingenious Infographics That Put It All Together* by Thomas Ramge.
    - A conceived tour of the global economy and all its key components, illuminated in 99 large-scale, full-color graphics.

- *Global Issues: An Introduction, 5th Edition* by Kristen Hite.
    - A fundamental resource for students of global development, economics, politics, environmental science, and geography.

- *A Brief History of Globalization: The Untold Story of our Incredible Shrinking Planet* by Alex MacGillivray.
    - By identifying successive waves of globalization Alex MacGillivray tells the fascinating story of how a mysterious flat earth became a global village. Covering globalization from all angles, MacGillivray touches on the complex economics behind the controversies and gives equal play to technology and culture, politics and war.

- ***Collapse: How Societies Choose to Fail or Succeed* by** Jared Diamond
  - In Jared Diamond's follow-up to *Guns, Germs and Steel,* he explores how climate change, the population explosion and political discord can create the conditions for the collapse of civilization.

- ***Why Nations Fail: The Origins of Power, Prosperity, and Poverty* by** Daron Acemoğlu, James A. Robinson
  - Why Nations Fail dives into the reasons why economic inequality is so prevalent in the world today and debates whether poor decisions of those in political power are the main reason rather than culture, geography, climate, or any other factor.

- ***The Economic Consequences of the Peace* by** John Maynard Keynes
  - In *The Economic Consequences of the Peace,* Keynes predicts that stiff war reparations and other harsh terms imposed on Germany by the treaty after WW1 would lead to the financial collapse of the country, which would have serious repercussions on Europe and the world.

- ***The Great Convergence: Information Technology and the New Globalization* by** Richard Baldwin
  - This book covers 200,000 years of human trading practices, using insights from archaeology, anthropology, economic history, political science, and other disciplines as it goes. The author takes us on a journey from the ancient world to the 21st century, and from the global North to the developing South, in order to set the scene for globalization in the recent years.

- ***The Third World* by** David M. Haugen
  - This book presents arguments on both sides of issues on the Third World and the problems it faces, the effect of globalization, and more , and whether and how the United States should have provided assistance.

- *The Global Impact of Social Media* by Dedria Bryfonski
    - This book examines the political and personal effects of social media on global culture.

- *The Sixth Extinction: An Unnatural History* by Elizabeth Kolbert
    - A fascinating look at the evidence for the world currently being at the start of a sixth extinction event, and how this extinction is driven by human activity.

- *The Haves and the Have Nots: A Brief and Idiosyncratic History of Global Inequality* by Branko Milanovic
    - Who is the richest person in the world, ever? Does where you were born affect how much money you'll earn over a lifetime? How would we know? Why -- beyond the idle curiosity -- do these questions even matter? In *The Haves and the Have-Nots*, Branko Milanovic, explains these and other mysteries of how wealth is unevenly spread throughout our world. Milanovic uses history, literature and stories, to discuss one of the major divisions in our social lives: between the haves and the have-nots. He goes beyond mere entertainment to explain why inequality matters, and how it can threaten the foundations of the social order that we take for granted.

- *Around the World in 80 Days* by Jules Verne
    - In this classic adventure novel, Phileas Fogg of London and his newly employed French valet Passepartout attempt to circumnavigate the world in 80 days on a £20,000 wager (roughly £1.6 million today) set by his friends.

- *Messy Roots: A Graphic Memoir of a Wuhanese American* by Laura Gao
    - After spending her early years in Wuhan, China, Laura immigrates to Texas, where her hometown is as foreign as Mars, until COVID-19 makes Wuhan a household name. Laura illustrates her coming-of-age as the girl who simply wants to make the basketball team, escape Chinese school, and figure out why girls make her heart flutter.

- *The Upper World* by Femi Fadugba
  - Esso Adenon, is a high school student in South London. He is just trying to stay out of a rival gang war, figure out how to confess his feelings to his friend, and make sense of the journal belonging to his late father. After Esso is involved in a car accident, he is able to see a place his father referred to as "the Upper World." Meanwhile, 15-year-old footballer Rhia is searching for answers about her birth mother and her place in the world. When her mysterious new physics tutor, Dr. Esso, arrives carrying a photograph of her mother, Rhia may have found the answers she's been looking for, and Esso may have discovered the key to a deadly incident involving Rhia's mother years ago.

- *Buried Beneath the Baobab Tree* by Adaobi Tricia Nwaubani
  - Based on interviews with young women who were kidnapped by Boko Haram, this poignant novel tells the story of one girl who was taken from her home and her harrowing fight for survival

- *A Moveable Feast (Life Changing Food Adventures Around The World)" edited* by Don George
  - From bat on the island of Fais to from mutton in Mongolia - on the road, food nourishes us not only physically, but emotionally and spiritually too. It can be a gift that enables a traveler to survive and a doorway into the heart of a tribe. Celebrate the riches and revelations of food with this 38-course feast of true tales set around the world.

- *The Adventures of Tintin* by Hergé
  - Tintin, a young Belgian reporter and adventurer, who becomes involved in dangerous cases in which he takes actions to save the day. The Adventures feature Tintin at work in his investigative journalism, but seldom is he seen turning in a story.

Movie Selections for this Unit

- *Bridge of Spies (2015) PG-13*
  - During the Cold War, an American lawyer is recruited to defend an arrested Soviet spy in court, and then help the CIA facilitate an exchange of the spy for the Soviet captured American U2 spy plane pilot, Francis Gary Powers.

- *Living on One Dollar (2013) TV-14*
  - Four friends set out to live on just $1 a day for two months in rural Guatemala. Armed with only a video camera, they face hunger, parasites, and extreme financial stress as they attempt to survive.

- *American Factory (2019) TV-14*
  - In Ohio, a Chinese billionaire opens a factory, hiring two thousand Americans. Early days of hope and optimism give way to setbacks as China clashes with working-class America.

- *Last Call at the Oasis (2011) PG-13*
  - A documentary on the world's water crisis.

- *Pump! (2014) PG*
  - A documentary that tells the story of America's addiction to oil, from its corporate beginnings to its current monopoly, and explains clearly how we can end it - and finally win choice at the pump.

- *Poverty, Inc. (2014) NR*
    - From Toms Shoes to international adoptions and drawing from over 200 interviews filmed in 20 countries, Poverty, Inc. unearths a side of charity we can no longer ignore.

- *Life and Debt (2001) NR*
    - A look at the effects of globalization on Jamaican industry and agriculture.

- *Girl Rising (2013) PG-13*
    - This film follows 9 girls from across the globe on their journey to education.

- *When Worlds Collide (2010) PG*
    - When Worlds Collide chronicles the rise and fall of Spain's global empire. This documentary explores how the collision of the Old and New World completely transformed the nature of ethnicity and identity in the Americas.

- *Superman IV: The Quest for Peace (1987) PG*
    - The Man of Steel argues for nuclear disarmament and meets Lex Luthor's latest creation.

- *The Interpreter (2005) PG-13*
    - Political intrigue and deception unfold inside the UN, when a U.S. Secret Service agent is assigned to investigate an interpreter who overhears an assassination plot.

- *No Man's Land (2020) PG-13*
    - When a fight on the border turns fatal, a man flees on horseback to Mexico, seeking forgiveness from the victim's father.

- *Hotel Rwanda (2004) PG-13*
    - A hotel manager, houses over a thousand Tutsi refugees during their struggle against the Hutu militia in Rwanda, Africa.

- *Sergio (2020) R*
    - A drama set in the aftermath of the US invasion of Iraq, where the life of top UN diplomat Sergio Vieira de Mello hangs in the balance during the most dangerous mission of his career.

- *Captain America: Civil War (2016) PG-13*
    - The political involvement in the Avengers' affairs causes a rift between Captain America and Iron Man.

Gameschooling Selections for this Unit

- *Chronology*

    - Think you know which came first – the invention of mayonnaise or decaffeinated coffee? Lincoln's Gettysburg address or John Deere's first plow? Test your knowledge with Chronology by Buffalo Games – the game of all time! In Chronology, each player builds his or her own timeline of cards. On your turn, someone will read you a historical event from a card. You decide where that event falls in your timeline. If you are right, you keep the card and your timeline grows. The first player to build a timeline of 10 cards wins!

- *Corinth*

    - In 4th Century BC Corinth, traders come from all corners of the Mediterranean Sea to sell their goods. Players have a few weeks to secure their place in Corinth as its most savvy trader! In each round, a few dice are rolled, and players choose groups of dice of the same value and deliver goods to the best shops in the Harbor, purchase herds of goats to help erect buildings, and more.

- *Risk*

    - Take over the world in this game of strategy conquest. The goal is simple: conquer enemy territories by building an army, moving troops in, and engaging in battle.

- *Axis and Allies*

    - Take command of the forces from the UK, US, Soviet Union, Germany, or Japan, and plot their strategy for world domination

- *Axis and Allies*
    - A game of intrigue, and treachery, set in Europe, prior to WWI where players must rely on their own cunning and cleverness to determine the outcome.

- *Small World*
    - Small World is a light-hearted civilization game in which players vie for conquest and control of a board that is simply too small to accommodate them all. Pick the right combination from 14 different fantasy races and 20 unique special powers and rush to expand your empire.

- *A Game of Thrones*
    - Designed for ages 14 and up, A Game of Thrones: The Board Game is a classic game of warfare, diplomacy, and intrigue. Taking control of the well-known characters from the beloved fantasy series, players must fight for dominance of the realm. With opportunities for strategic planning, and clever card play, this game gives you a multitude of ways to spread your influence over Westeros.

- *Trekking the World: Trivia*
    - This trivia game will help you learn amazing facts and tidbits about cultures from all around the world with family-friendly questions that work for both kids and adults.

- *United Nations: A Game of World Domination in our Time*
    - Players vie for control of 40 global areas by using political or military strength. Using confrontation, negotiation, or the UN General Assembly and Security Council, areas are won or lost. Each area is worth a certain number of prestige points and the player with the most prestige at the end wins.

- *Article 27: The United Nations Security Council Game*
    - You assume the role of one of the permanent members of the Security Council, and you wield the power of the veto. No proposal can pass when a member uses their veto, so there had better be something in there for you. Each player takes a turn as the leader of the Security Council to try to get a proposal passed. Negotiations are encouraged, but once the gavel comes down it's time to vote, and the other players might not live up to their end of the deal. In the end, the player who has earned the most influence points is the winner.

Links for Websites and Articles Referenced in this Unit

- Poverty
    - https://www.worldbank.org/en/topic/poverty/overview

- Global poverty: Facts, FAQs, and how to help
    - https://www.worldvision.org/sponsorship-news-stories/global-poverty-facts

- The evolution of global poverty, 1990-2030
    - https://www.brookings.edu/research/the-evolution-of-global-poverty-1990-2030/

- GLOBAL POVERTY AND HUNGER
    - https://www.actionagainsthunger.org/global-poverty-hunger-facts

- The World Bank and Nutrition
    - https://www.worldbank.org/en/topic/nutrition

- Nutrition: World food programme
    - https://www.wfp.org/nutrition

Websites for Chapter 13: Establishing Your Global Focus

- Isolation Vs. Globalization
    - https://ivsg.weebly.com/

- Key Theories of International Relations
    - https://online.norwich.edu/academic-programs/resources/key-theories-of-international-relations
- Theories of International Relations
    - https://www.sparknotes.com/us-government-and-politics/political-science/international-politics/section2/
- Globalization – World 101
    - https://world101.cfr.org/global-era-issues/globalization?gclid=Cj0KCQjw8O-VBhCpARIsACMvVLOdwqR99QcPB6xEIh33ERAVEVFkenzOo1G1V2xptKulVMCZIzqZSQUaAnmLEALw_wcB
- What Is Globalization?
    - https://www.piie.com/microsites/globalization/what-is-globalization?gclid=Cj0KCQjw8O-VBhCpARIsACMvVLPOEpQ8TwYoCopI5WeVkMQUm_JJyFArpIIBOzejJMd_hzY0Lto914QaAuvgEALw_wcB
- The Investor's Guide to Global Trade
    - https://www.investopedia.com/insights/what-is-international-trade/
- International Trade
    - https://www.econlib.org/library/Enc/InternationalTrade.html
- Trade – World 101
    - https://world101.cfr.org/global-era-issues/trade?gclid=Cj0KCQjw8O-VBhCpARIsACMvVLMFci7qvZoo6AFmou5xHLRSCqUrgNig6_F2JXAfuP2adwBHjHd5uREaAqMGEALw_wcB
- Imports and Exports
    - https://corporatefinanceinstitute.com/resources/knowledge/economics/imports-and-exports/

- United States OEC
  - https://oec.world/en/profile/country/usa
- Balance of Trade (BOT)
  - https://www.investopedia.com/terms/b/bot.asp
- Balance of Trade: Favorable Versus Unfavorable
  - https://www.thebalance.com/balance-of-trade-definition-favorable-vs-unfavorable-3306261
- Balance of Trade
  - https://www.wallstreetmojo.com/balance-of-trade/
- United States Balance of Trade
  - https://tradingeconomics.com/united-states/balance-of-trade
- What Is the Current U.S. Trade Deficit?
  - https://www.thebalance.com/u-s-trade-deficit-causes-effects-trade-partners-3306276
- What Is A Recession?
  - https://www.forbes.com/advisor/investing/what-is-a-recession/
- Tariff
  - https://www.investopedia.com/terms/t/tariff.asp
- Tariffs - WTO
  - https://www.wto.org/english/tratop_e/tariffs_e/tariffs_e.htm
- Tariff Schedules
  - https://ustr.gov/issue-areas/industry-manufacturing/industrial-tariffs/tariff-schedules
- Trade Agreements
  - https://www.trade.gov/trade-agreements
- Trade Agreements – US Dept of State
  - https://www.state.gov/trade-agreements/

- Free Trade Agreements: Their Impact, Types, and Examples
    - https://www.thebalance.com/free-trade-agreement-types-and-examples-3305897
- International Trade Agreements
    - https://www.econlib.org/library/Enc/InternationalTradeAgreements.html
- Negotiations and agreements
    - https://policy.trade.ec.europa.eu/eu-trade-relationships-country-and-region/negotiations-and-agreements_en
- North American Free Trade Agreement (NAFTA)
    - https://www.investopedia.com/terms/n/nafta.asp#:~:text=The%20North%20American%20Free%20Trade%20Agreement%20(NAFTA)%20was%20implemented%20in,a%20huge%20free%2Dtrade%20zone.
- North American Free Trade Agreement (NAFTA) – International Trade Association
    - https://www.trade.gov/north-american-free-trade-agreement-nafta
- OPEC in a Changing World
    - https://www.cfr.org/backgrounder/opec-changing-world?gclid=Cj0KCQjw8O-VBhCpARIsACMvVLPh2mbsr_BLrhRx72r31aCegheEt72u__aNsgMFJzrYo7VC_YsqV_UaAg4mEALw_wcB
- OPEC
    - https://www.opec.org/opec_web/en/
- Organization of the Petroleum Exporting Countries (OPEC)
    - https://www.investopedia.com/terms/o/opec.asp

Websites for Chapter 14: Forging Your Global Alliances

- Exploring international relations: What is diplomacy?
    - https://www.futurelearn.com/info/blog/what-is-diplomacy#:~:text=Diplomacy%20is%20a%20method%20that,by%20the%20government%20they%20serve.

- Why You Should Study International Diplomacy
    - https://www.masterstudies.com/article/why-you-should-study-international-diplomacy/

- What is diplomacy?
    - https://www.diplomacy.edu/ufaq/what-is-diplomacy/

- What are the roles of a diplomat?
    - https://diplomacy.state.gov/diplomacy/what-are-the-roles-of-a-diplomat/

- How do you become a diplomat?
    - https://diplomacy.state.gov/diplomacy/how-do-you-become-a-diplomat/

- Difference between Ambassador and Diplomat
    - http://www.differencebetween.info/difference-between-ambassador-and-diplomat

- Vienna Convention On Diplomatic Relations And Optional Protocols
    - http://www.oas.org/legal/english/docs/viennaconvdiplomrelat..htm

- Diplomatic immunity
    - https://www.government.nl/topics/embassies-consulates-and-other-representations/diplomatic-immunity

- Websites of U.S. Embassies, Consulates, and Diplomatic Missions
    - https://www.usembassy.gov/

- What is a U.S. Embassy?
    - https://diplomacy.state.gov/diplomacy/what-is-a-u-s-embassy/

- What Does an Embassy Do? What is the Purpose of Your Home Country's Embassy?
    - https://www.clements.com/resources/living-abroad/embassy-purpose-what-does-embassy-do/

- What Is the Difference Between a Consulate and an Embassy?
    - https://www.onlinevisa.com/faq/what-is-the-difference-between-a-consulate-and-an-embassy/

- U.S. Collective Defense Arrangements
    - https://2009-2017.state.gov/s/l/treaty/collectivedefense/index.htm

- Mapped: America's Collective Defense Agreements
    - https://www.defenseone.com/ideas/2017/02/mapped-americas-collective-defense-agreements/135114/

- What Is NATO?
    - https://www.cfr.org/backgrounder/what-nato?gclid=Cj0KCQjw8O-VBhCpARIsACMvVLP47bMZ4L_1rUoQkOuN9wJF7R69sNJ7y-QgdiIIdWDqkrFA_YtSyL8aAnOyEALw_wcB

- North Atlantic Treaty Organization
    - https://www.nato.int/

- What is the United Nations
    - https://www.ecnmy.org/learn/your-world/international-organizations/what-is-the-un/?gclid=Cj0KCQjw8O-VBhCpARIsACMvVLPqBqniYCeVKl1g4ZWa4KeOhcTRYHtqS1OLqXTKmdkVYlCqGTx8q0YaAoPNEALw_wcB

- United Nations
    - https://www.un.org/en/

- UN Global Issues
    - https://www.un.org/en/global-issues/

Websites for Chapter 15: Bringing It All Together

- Brief Overview: COOP (Continuity of Operations Plan) Plan
    - https://www.k12.wa.us/sites/default/files/public/safetycenter/operationsplanning/pubdocs/briefoverview-continuityofoperationsplanning.pdf

- What is Continuity of Operations?
    - https://www.fema.gov/pdf/about/org/ncp/coop_brochure.pdf

- Continuity of Government
    - https://whitehouse.gov1.info/continuity-plan/

- Federal Continuity Directive 1 (FCD 1)
    - https://www.gsa.gov/cdnstatic/ELS_FederalContinuityDirective1and2_(1).pdf

- Continuity Policy And Programs
    - https://www.dhs.gov/sites/default/files/publications/mgmt/disaster-management/mgmt-dir_008-03-continuity-policy-and-programs_revision-01.pdf

- FEMA
    - https://www.fema.gov/

Links for Videos Referenced in this Unit

- Global Stratification & Poverty: Crash Course Sociology #27
    - https://youtu.be/6rts_PWIVTU

- A Life in Extreme Poverty
    - https://youtu.be/ElG5-nXD0B8

- World's Poorest Country 'Burundi' (I can't forget the things I saw)
    - https://youtu.be/n0gFsHf9cIw

- Poverty & Our Response to It: Crash Course Philosophy #44
    - https://youtu.be/D5sknLy7Smo

- Malnutrition and World Hunger: A Guide To Global Issues | Global Citizen
    - https://youtu.be/FWB7G7OzpZw

- Yemen: On the brink of starvation - BBC News
    - https://youtu.be/npk7tfKyXok

- Food, nutrition and poverty - An overview by Elizabeth Dowler
    - https://youtu.be/RwBFBQf1lVU

Videos for Chapter 13: Establishing Your Global Focus

- Globalization explained
    - https://youtu.be/JJ0nFD19eT8

- Globalization II - Good or Bad?: Crash Course World History #42
    - https://youtu.be/s_iwrt7D5OA

- The Untold Story of American Isolationism | Christopher Nichols | TEDxPortland
    - https://youtu.be/Ehlaox_bxi4
- International Relations: An Introduction
    - https://youtu.be/NVCDnUZqLzU
- What is International Relations? (International Relations Defined)
    - https://youtu.be/HQlyWnyVN7I
- Realism vs. Liberalism - Global Politics Theories Compared
    - https://youtu.be/Hl43BizGd5c
- Major Theories of International Relations
    - https://youtu.be/DGG2pJ3NyoY
- International Trade Explained | World101
    - https://youtu.be/HfN8BnRJryQ
- International Trade- Micro Topic 2.9
    - https://youtu.be/XGrKx2chuI4
- How Global Trade Runs on U.S. Dollars | WSJ
    - https://youtu.be/jsDwMGH5E8U
- The Benefits Of International Trade: Econ-1 with John Taylor
    - https://youtu.be/lFUG307RI4I
- Imports, Exports, and Exchange Rates: Crash Course Economics #15
    - https://youtu.be/geoe-6NBy10
- How Imports and Exports Affect You | Economics
    - https://youtu.be/2g7Wg0bemzM

- International Trade: Imports and Exports
  - https://youtu.be/P2qeaYS78Tk
- Finance: What is Balance of Trade?
  - https://youtu.be/YIHkUujsUpA
- The Balance of Trade
  - https://youtu.be/PmpN9e-d1cQ
- What is a recession? | CNBC Explains
  - https://youtu.be/sTUh-NQ7q3E
- What Is A Recession? In Context
  - https://youtu.be/3KcjXL2sbYk
- How do tariffs work? | CNBC Explains
  - https://youtu.be/LKCMnCZyxiQ
- What is a Tariff? How do Tariffs Work?
  - https://youtu.be/sCNVuaQuFcU
- How to calculate the impact of import and export tariffs.
  - https://youtu.be/zhD--UeRiOI
- Trade Agreements
  - https://youtu.be/DHIl_zmmhzg
- Introduction to Free Trade Agreements (FTAs)
  - https://youtu.be/L2oAkcNLnog
- Barriers and Benefits in Free Trade Agreements
  - https://youtu.be/PteICyQzbQ0

- U S Free Trade Agreements for Importers & Exporters
  - https://youtu.be/uMc7zmGmWcQ
- NAFTA explained by avocados. And shoes.
  - https://youtu.be/DwKR08t5BGA
- Top 10 NAFTA Facts You Should Know
  - https://youtu.be/_blj_fUQOI8
- What is OPEC? | CNBC Explains
  - https://youtu.be/mlWmJt8O8Kw
- The History of OPEC | Casual Historian
  - https://youtu.be/pl_u1cV7A6A
- OPEC - The Organization of the Petroleum Exporting Countries
  - https://youtu.be/XEgbLjBzrCc

Videos for Chapter 14: Forging Your Global Alliances

- What is International Relations? (International Relations Defined)
  - https://youtu.be/HQlyWnyVN7I
- International Relations 101 (#1): Introduction
  - https://youtu.be/y32cFdicW1U
- The Art of Diplomacy
  - https://youtu.be/ewc3ziZ8ReI
- Diplomacy Crash Course
  - https://youtu.be/Yssq2xtkf8U

- International Relations: Diplomacy |History |Definition |Importance |Functions & Types of Diplomacy
    - https://youtu.be/IFiDf6EJiGs
- Diplomatic Tools of Foreign Policy
    - https://youtu.be/xs434HAVePM
- What Is A Diplomat? | Who Is An Ambassador?
    - https://youtu.be/nCjnEvU5HNI
- What Diplomats Really Do | Alexander Karagiannis | TEDxIndianaUniversity
    - https://youtu.be/UQ8c0mGgsWI
- What does it take to be a U.S. Diplomat?
    - https://youtu.be/4wJgPhd7PKY
- Why Diplomats Can't be Arrested
    - https://youtu.be/5CesWbbsTTM
- How to Become an Ambassador | step-by-step guide
    - https://youtu.be/k7uPdqtTYm0
- Mini Countries Abroad: How Embassies Work
    - https://youtu.be/SUsqnD9-42g
- How Do Embassies Work?
    - https://youtu.be/U2LrCW_nXDI
- 15 MOST SECURE Embassies
    - https://youtu.be/t-Xi_hqbD40
- Countries With The Most Embassies
    - https://youtu.be/_eMs7UfxDIQ
- What is NATO, why does it still exist, and how does it work? [2020 version]
    - https://youtu.be/snXhtOpSXtI

- What is NATO? | CNBC Explains
    - https://youtu.be/JGc3v56_ZZY
- NATO Explained
    - https://youtu.be/6MidPEf30AE
- The United Nations Explained
    - https://youtu.be/WF6g23ydyuU
- How Does The UN Work?
    - https://youtu.be/tlmYtJiUK00
- The United Nations Is Created | Flashback | History
    - https://youtu.be/FnQESSTouNU
- What Does the UN Do?
    - https://youtu.be/XucDIQXMp2c
- Facts about the United Nations you should know in 2020
    - https://youtu.be/ScsechC-Eh0
- The United Nations: It's Your World
    - https://youtu.be/bHmXZXsABm0

Videos for Chapter 15: Bringing Everything Together

- Resilient Operations: State and Local Government Continuity Strategies in the New Normal
    - https://youtu.be/2496uI-TzQ8
- Speaker Series #2 - Government Responses and Continuity
    - https://youtu.be/Ro_ukHKyTR0

- Infrastructure Resiliency and Continuity of Operations
    - https://youtu.be/zFyHLqNflCk
- We're Here, Before, During and After Disasters
    - https://youtu.be/Gc1_e5Vzoeg
- FEMA's role in disaster relief
    - https://youtu.be/Ml-bLyLE-_A
- What does FEMA actually do? - Interview with Pete Gaynor
    - https://youtu.be/Vv-kXWJ3umg

Appendix V

Data Sets

Contents of Appendix V:

Data Sets

- ➢ **Artifacts: Data set for task #12**
- ➢ **Population Groups: Data set for task #16**
- ➢ **Census Results: Data set for task #17**
- ➢ **Choose Your Government Flow Chart: Data set for task #17**
- ➢ **Options for Your Budget Surplus: Data set for task #35**

Artifacts

Data Set for Task #12

Data Set for Task #12

List of artifacts found in main village site.

12A
- 8 small artifacts
- 3 medium artifacts
- 1 large mostly intact artifact/structure
- Remains of a second structure

12B
- 5 small artifacts
- 2 medium artifacts
- Remains of 1 structure

12C
- 3 small artifacts
- 1 medium artifacts
- Scattered remains of a single structure

12D
- 10 small artifacts
- 4 medium artifacts
- 2 large mostly intact artifacts/structures
- Remains of a third structure

12E
- 5 small artifacts
- 2 medium artifacts
- 1 large artifact/structure

12F
- 5 small artifacts
- 1 medium artifact
- Scattered remains of a single structure

12G
- 10 small artifacts
- 5 medium artifacts
- 2 large artifacts/structure
- Remains of 2 additional structures

12H
- 8 small artifacts
- 3 medium artifacts
- 1 large artifact/structure
- Remains of a second structure

12I
- 5 small artifacts
- 2 medium artifacts
- Scattered remains of a single structure

Population Groups

Data Set for Task #16

Your New Population: Group 1

Arriving From China	
Men with No Education	0
Men with <9th grade equivalent education	0
Men with high school/GED equivalent education	4,000
Men who are skilled tradespeople	3,000
Men who are college educated	9,000
Women with No Education	1,000
Women with <9th grade equivalent education	0
Women with high school/GED equivalent education	3,000
Women who are skilled tradespeople	2,000
Women who are college educated	6,000
Children	6,000

Arriving From Mexico	
Men with No Education	5,000
Men with <9th grade equivalent education	3,000
Men with high school/GED equivalent education	3,000
Men who are skilled tradespeople	8,000
Men who are college educated	2,000
Women with No Education	1,000
Women with <9th grade equivalent education	3,000
Women with high school/GED equivalent education	2,000
Women who are skilled tradespeople	0
Women who are college educated	3,000
Children	5,000

Arriving From El Salvador	
Men with No Education	2,000
Men with <9th grade equivalent education	5,000
Men with high school/GED equivalent education	2,000
Men who are skilled tradespeople	6,000
Men who are college educated	2,000
Women with No Education	3,000
Women with <9th grade equivalent education	1,000
Women with high school/GED equivalent education	2,000
Women who are skilled tradespeople	1,000
Women who are college educated	0
Children	7,000

YOUR NEW POPULATION: GROUP 2

Arriving From India	
Men with No Education	2,000
Men with <9th grade equivalent education	5,000
Men with high school/GED equivalent education	4,000
Men who are skilled tradespeople	5,000
Men who are college educated	4,000
Women with No Education	4,000
Women with <9th grade equivalent education	4,000
Women with high school/GED equivalent education	1,000
Women who are skilled tradespeople	1,000
Women who are college educated	4,000
Children	7,000

Arriving From the Dominican Republic	
Men with No Education	2,000
Men with <9th grade equivalent education	6,000
Men with high school/GED equivalent education	4,000
Men who are skilled tradespeople	2,000
Men who are college educated	1,000
Women with No Education	3,000
Women with <9th grade equivalent education	5,000
Women with high school/GED equivalent education	2,000
Women who are skilled tradespeople	2,000
Women who are college educated	0
Children	7,000

Arriving From South Africa	
Men with No Education	1,000
Men with <9th grade equivalent education	2,000
Men with high school/GED equivalent education	3,000
Men who are skilled tradespeople	3,000
Men who are college educated	3,000
Women with No Education	4,000
Women with <9th grade equivalent education	2,000
Women with high school/GED equivalent education	1,000
Women who are skilled tradespeople	0
Women who are college educated	3,000
Children	3,000

Your New Population: Group 3

Arriving From Kenya	
Men with No Education	5,000
Men with <9th grade equivalent education	3,000
Men with high school/GED equivalent education	3,000
Men who are skilled tradespeople	4,000
Men who are college educated	1,000
Women with No Education	1,000
Women with <9th grade equivalent education	2,000
Women with high school/GED equivalent education	1,000
Women who are skilled tradespeople	5,000
Women who are college educated	0
Children	6,000

Arriving From Vietnam	
Men with No Education	3,000
Men with <9th grade equivalent education	3,000
Men with high school/GED equivalent education	1,000
Men who are skilled tradespeople	3,000
Men who are college educated	4,000
Women with No Education	1,000
Women with <9th grade equivalent education	0
Women with high school/GED equivalent education	3,000
Women who are skilled tradespeople	3,000
Women who are college educated	2,000
Children	8,000

Arriving From Jamaica	
Men with No Education	5,000
Men with <9th grade equivalent education	5,000
Men with high school/GED equivalent education	3,000
Men who are skilled tradespeople	6,000
Men who are college educated	1,000
Women with No Education	1,000
Women with <9th grade equivalent education	2,000
Women with high school/GED equivalent education	2,000
Women who are skilled tradespeople	6,000
Women who are college educated	1,000
Children	6,000

Your New Population: Group 4

Arriving From Germany	
Men with No Education	3,000
Men with <9th grade equivalent education	3,000
Men with high school/GED equivalent education	4,000
Men who are skilled tradespeople	4,000
Men who are college educated	4,000
Women with No Education	2,000
Women with <9th grade equivalent education	1,000
Women with high school/GED equivalent education	0
Women who are skilled tradespeople	1,000
Women who are college educated	6,000
Children	4,000

Arriving From France	
Men with No Education	2,000
Men with <9th grade equivalent education	3,000
Men with high school/GED equivalent education	6,000
Men who are skilled tradespeople	4,000
Men who are college educated	3,000
Women with No Education	1,000
Women with <9th grade equivalent education	0
Women with high school/GED equivalent education	2,000
Women who are skilled tradespeople	2,000
Women who are college educated	2,000
Children	7,000

Arriving From Egypt	
Men with No Education	5,000
Men with <9th grade equivalent education	1,000
Men with high school/GED equivalent education	2,000
Men who are skilled tradespeople	5,000
Men who are college educated	1,000
Women with No Education	1,000
Women with <9th grade equivalent education	2,000
Women with high school/GED equivalent education	3,000
Women who are skilled tradespeople	1,000
Women who are college educated	6,000
Children	9,000

YOUR NEW POPULATION: GROUP 5

Arriving From Afghanistan	
Men with No Education	3,000
Men with <9th grade equivalent education	5,000
Men with high school/GED equivalent education	4,000
Men who are skilled tradespeople	3,000
Men who are college educated	4,000
Women with No Education	13,000
Women with <9th grade equivalent education	11,000
Women with high school/GED equivalent education	8,000
Women who are skilled tradespeople	2,000
Women who are college educated	4,000
Children	20,000

Arriving From Nigeria	
Men with No Education	6,000
Men with <9th grade equivalent education	3,000
Men with high school/GED equivalent education	5,000
Men who are skilled tradespeople	4,000
Men who are college educated	3,000
Women with No Education	7,000
Women with <9th grade equivalent education	6,000
Women with high school/GED equivalent education	8,000
Women who are skilled tradespeople	3,000
Women who are college educated	4,000
Children	24,000

YOUR NEW POPULATION: GROUP 6

Arriving From Venezuela	
Men with No Education	5,000
Men with <9th grade equivalent education	4,000
Men with high school/GED equivalent education	5,000
Men who are skilled tradespeople	5,000
Men who are college educated	3,000
Women with No Education	6,000
Women with <9th grade equivalent education	7,000
Women with high school/GED equivalent education	6,000
Women who are skilled tradespeople	4,000
Women who are college educated	4,000
Children	34,000

Arriving From Syria	
Men with No Education	4,000
Men with <9th grade equivalent education	5,000
Men with high school/GED equivalent education	4,000
Men who are skilled tradespeople	3,000
Men who are college educated	3,000
Women with No Education	10,000
Women with <9th grade equivalent education	10,000
Women with high school/GED equivalent education	7,000
Women who are skilled tradespeople	4,000
Women who are college educated	2,000
Children	15,000

YOUR NEW POPULATION: GROUP 7

Arriving From Yemen	
Men with No Education	6,000
Men with <9th grade equivalent education	3,000
Men with high school/GED equivalent education	4,000
Men who are skilled tradespeople	6,000
Men who are college educated	3,000
Women with No Education	9,000
Women with <9th grade equivalent education	10,000
Women with high school/GED equivalent education	8,000
Women who are skilled tradespeople	0
Women who are college educated	2,000
Children	23,000

Arriving From Burundi	
Men with No Education	6,000
Men with <9th grade equivalent education	3,000
Men with high school/GED equivalent education	4,000
Men who are skilled tradespeople	4,000
Men who are college educated	5,000
Women with No Education	12,000
Women with <9th grade equivalent education	8,000
Women with high school/GED equivalent education	7,000
Women who are skilled tradespeople	0
Women who are college educated	2,000
Children	25,000

Your New Population: Group 8

Arriving From Myanmar	
Men with No Education	6,000
Men with <9th grade equivalent education	3,000
Men with high school/GED equivalent education	3,000
Men who are skilled tradespeople	3,000
Men who are college educated	4,000
Women with No Education	15,000
Women with <9th grade equivalent education	7,000
Women with high school/GED equivalent education	5,000
Women who are skilled tradespeople	3,000
Women who are college educated	4,000
Children	17,000

Arriving From Iraq	
Men with No Education	8,000
Men with <9th grade equivalent education	4,000
Men with high school/GED equivalent education	4,000
Men who are skilled tradespeople	4,000
Men who are college educated	3,000
Women with No Education	9,000
Women with <9th grade equivalent education	8,000
Women with high school/GED equivalent education	6,000
Women who are skilled tradespeople	4,000
Women who are college educated	4,000
Children	26,000

Census Results

Data Set for Task #17

CENSUS DATA SET 1

	Record 1	Record 2	Record 3	Record 4	Record 5	Record 6	Record 7	Record 8	Record 9	Record 10
1. Number Of People In Household	2	2	6	7	3	3	1	5	2	3
2. # Of People With A Disability	0	0	0	1	0	0	0	0	0	0
3. Household Age										
0-3	0	0	1	2	1	0	0	1	0	0
4-18	0	0	2	1	1	1	0	2	0	1
19-65	2	2	2	2	1	2	1	2	2	2
>65	0	0	1	2	0	1	0	0	0	0
4. Work Status										
Work Full Time	2	2	2		1	2	1	2	1	2
Work Part Time	0	0	1	1	1	1	0	0	1	0
Farm/Ranch	0	0	0	2	0	0	0	0	0	0
Full Time Student	0	0	2	1	0	0	0	2	0	1
Does Not Work	0	0	1	3	1	0	0	1	0	0
5. Gender										
Male	1	2	2	3	2	2	1	2	1	2
Female	1	0	4	4	1	2	0	3	1	1
Prefer Not To Identify	0	0	0	0	0	0	0	0	0	0
6. Type Of Structure	A	H	H	H	A	M	A	H	O	H
7. Amount Of Land	<1	<1	>1	>10	<1	>1	<1	<1	<1	<1
8. Own Or Rent	R	O	O	O	R	R	R	R	O	R
9. Number Of Vehicles	2	2	3+	3+	2	2	1	2	0	2

A – Apartment	O – Own
H – House	R - Rent
M – Mobile Home	

CENSUS DATA SET 2

	Record 1	Record 2	Record 3	Record 4	Record 5	Record 6	Record 7	Record 8	Record 9	Record 10
1. Number Of People In Household	1	2	3	1	3	5	2	4	6	1
2. # Of People With A Disability	0	0	0	0	0	0	0	0	0	0
3. Household Age										
0-3	0	0	0	0	1	1	1	1	0	0
4-18	0	0	1	0	0	2	0	0	2	0
19-65	0	0	2	1	2	2	1	2	2	1
>65	1	2	0	0	0	0	0	1	2	0
4. Work Status										
Work Full Time	0	0	2	0	1	2	1	1	3	1
Work Part Time	0	1	0	0	1	2	0	1	1	0
Farm/Ranch	0	0	0	1	0	0	0	0	0	0
Full Time Student	0	0	1	0	0	0	0	0	2	0
Does Not Work	1	1	0	0	1	1	1	2	0	0
5. Gender										
Male	1	1	1	1	1	2	1	2	4	0
Female	0	1	2	0	2	3	1	2	2	1
Prefer Not To Identify	0	0	0	0	0	0	0	0	0	0
6. Type Of Structure	O	H	A	A	A	H	A	H	H	A
7. Amount Of Land	>1	<1	<1	<1	<1	<1	<1	<1	>1	<1
8. Own Or Rent	O	O	R	R	R	O	R	O	O	R
9. Number Of Vehicles	0	1	2	2	2	2	1	2	3+	1

```
A – Apartment      O – Own
H – House          R - Rent
M – Mobile Home
```

CENSUS DATA SET 3

	Record 1	Record 2	Record 3	Record 4	Record 5	Record 6	Record 7	Record 8	Record 9	Record 10
1. Number Of People In Household	6	1	2	3	1	5	3	7	4	4
2. # Of People With A Disability	0	0	0	0	0	0	1	0	0	0
3. Household Age										
0-3	1	0	0	0	0	2	0	2	1	1
4-18	1	0	0	1	0	1	0	2	1	2
19-65	2	1	0	1	0	2	2	2	2	1
>65	2	0	2	1	1	0	1	1	0	0
4. Work Status										
Work Full Time	0	0	1	1	0	0	1	0	2	0
Work Part Time	0	0	0	0	0	0	0	0	0	0
Farm/Ranch	2	1	0	0	0	1	0	3	0	1
Full Time Student	1	0	0	1	0	2	1	2	1	2
Does Not Work	3	0	1	1	1	2	1	2	1	1
5. Gender										
Male	3	1	1	1	0	3	2	2	2	3
Female	3	0	1	2	1	2	1	5	2	1
Prefer Not To Identify	0	0	0	0	0	0	0	0	0	0
6. Type Of Structure	H	H	A	A	A	H	H	H	M	M
7. Amount Of Land	>10	>10	<1	<1	<1	>10	>1	>10	<1	>10
8. Own Or Rent	O	O	R	R	R	O	O	O	R	O
9. Number Of Vehicles	3+	2	1	2	1	2	2	2	1	1

```
A – Apartment      O – Own
H – House          R - Rent
M – Mobile Home
```

CENSUS DATA SET 4

	Record 1	Record 2	Record 3	Record 4	Record 5	Record 6	Record 7	Record 8	Record 9	Record 10
1. Number Of People In Household	4	3	5	4	1	2	2	4	6	4
2. # Of People With A Disability	0	0	0	0	0	1	0	0	0	0
3. Household Age										
0-3	1	0	1	0	0	0	1	0	1	1
4-18	1	0	2	2	0	0	0	1	2	1
19-65	1	2	1	2	1	2	1	2	2	1
>65	1	1	1	0	0	0	0	1	0	1
4. Work Status										
Work Full Time	3	2	1	2	0	2	1	2	2	2
Work Part Time	1	1	1	1	0	0	0	0	2	0
Farm/Ranch	0	0	0	0	1	0	0	0	0	0
Full Time Student	0	0	2	1	0	0	0	1	1	0
Does Not Work	1	0	1	0	0	0	0	1	1	2
5. Gender										
Male	2	2	2	1	1	1	1	1	4	2
Female	2	1	3	3	0	1	0	3	2	2
Prefer Not To Identify	0	0	0	0	0	0	0	0	0	0
6. Type Of Structure	H	H	H	H	A	A	A	H	M	H
7. Amount Of Land	<1	<1	>1	<1	<1	<1	<1	<1	>10	>1
8. Own Or Rent	O	R	O	O	R	R	R	R	O	R
9. Number Of Vehicles	1	0	1	2	1	1	1	2	3	2

A – Apartment O – Own
H – House R - Rent
M – Mobile Home

CENSUS DATA SET 5

	Record 1	Record 2	Record 3	Record 4	Record 5	Record 6	Record 7	Record 8	Record 9	Record 10
1. Number Of People In Household	3	3	5	2	7	9	4	8	1	2
2. # Of People With A Disability	1	0	1	0	0	0	1	0	0	0
3. Household Age										
0-3	0	1	1	0	0	1	1	2	0	0
4-18	1	0	3	0	4	4	2	3	0	0
19-65	2	2	2	1	2	2	1	2	1	0
>65	0	0	0	1	1	2	0	1	0	2
4. Work Status										
Work Full Time	0	0	1	1	0	2	1	0	0	1
Work Part Time	0	0	0	1	0	1	0	0	0	0
Farm/Ranch	0	2	0	0	2	0	0	2	0	0
Full Time Student	1	0	3	0	4	5	2	3	0	0
Does Not Work	0	1	1	0	1	1	1	3	1	1
5. Gender										
Male	2	1	2	0	3	2	3	3	1	1
Female	1	2	3	2	4	7	1	5	0	1
Prefer Not To Identify	0	0	0	0	0	0	0	0	0	0
6. Type Of Structure	O	H	A	A	H	H	A	H	O	H
7. Amount Of Land	<1	>10	<1	<1	>10	>1	<1	>10	<1	<1
8. Own Or Rent	R	O	R	R	O	O	R	O	R	O
9. Number Of Vehicles	0	2	0	2	3+	3	1	3+	0	1

```
A – Apartment      O – Own
H – House          R - Rent
M – Mobile Home
```

CENSUS DATA SET 6

	Record 1	Record 2	Record 3	Record 4	Record 5	Record 6	Record 7	Record 8	Record 9	Record 10
1. Number Of People In Household	2	5	1	7	6	8	3	4	4	2
2. # Of People With A Disability	0	0	0	0	0	0	0	1	0	2
3. Household Age										
0-3	0	0	0	2	0	2	0	1	0	0
4-18	0	3	0	3	2	4	0	0	1	0
19-65	0	2	1	2	2	2	1	2	1	0
>65	2	0	0	0	2	0	2	1	2	2
4. Work Status										
Work Full Time	0	0	0	0	2	0	1	0	1	0
Work Part Time	0	0	0	0	0	0	1	0	2	1
Farm/Ranch	0	2	1	2	0	2	0	2	0	0
Full Time Student	0	3	0	3	2	4	0	0	1	0
Does Not Work	2	0	0	2	2	2	1	2	0	1
5. Gender										
Male	1	3	0	4	3	1	2	2	3	1
Female	1	2	1	3	3	7	1	2	1	1
Prefer Not To Identify	0	0	0	0	0	0	0	0	0	0
6. Type Of Structure	A	M	M	H	H	H	A	H	H	A
7. Amount Of Land	<1	>10	>10	>10	>1	>10	<1	>10	<1	<1
8. Own Or Rent	R	O	O	O	O	O	R	O	R	R
9. Number Of Vehicles	1	3+	1	2	2	2	0	3+	2	0

A – Apartment O – Own
H – House R - Rent
M – Mobile Home

CENSUS DATA SET 7

	Record 1	Record 2	Record 3	Record 4	Record 5	Record 6	Record 7	Record 8	Record 9	Record 10
1. Number Of People In Household	1	3	5	7	2	6	1	2	3	1
2. # Of People With A Disability	0	0	0	1	0	0	0	0	1	0
3. Household Age										
0-3	0	0	1	1	0	1	0	0	1	0
4-18	0	1	1	2	0	2	0	0	0	0
19-65	1	2	2	2	2	2	1	2	2	1
>65	0	0	1	2	0	1	0	0	0	0
4. Work Status										
Work Full Time	1	2	2	0	0	1	0	0	1	1
Work Part Time	0	0	1	0	0	2	0	1	0	0
Farm/Ranch	0	0	0	3	1	0	1	1	1	0
Full Time Student	0	1	1	2	1	1	0	0	0	0
Does Not Work	0	0	2	2	0	2	0	0	1	0
5. Gender										
Male	1	2	2	4	1	3	1	0	1	1
Female	0	1	3	3	1	3	0	2	2	0
Prefer Not To Identify	0	0	0	0	0	0	0	0	0	0
6. Type Of Structure	A	A	H	H	A	H	A	A	H	A
7. Amount Of Land	<1	<1	<1	>10	<1	>1	<1	<1	<1	<1
8. Own Or Rent	R	R	R	O	R	O	R	R	O	R
9. Number Of Vehicles	1	1	2	3+	1	2	1	2	2	1

```
A – Apartment      O – Own
H – House          R - Rent
M – Mobile Home
```

CENSUS DATA SET 8

	Record 1	Record 2	Record 3	Record 4	Record 5	Record 6	Record 7	Record 8	Record 9	Record 10
1. Number Of People In Household	3	5	7	2	4	7	5	6	2	1
2. # Of People With A Disability	0	0	1	0	0	0	1	0	0	0
3. Household Age										
0-3	0	1	1	1	1	1	0	1	0	0
4-18	1	1	3	0	1	3	3	2	0	0
19-65	2	2	2	1	1	3	2	1	1	1
>65	0	1	1	0	1	0	0	2	1	0
4. Work Status										
Work Full Time	1	2	0	1	1	3	2	3	0	1
Work Part Time	2	1	0	0	1	0	1	0	0	0
Farm/Ranch	0	0	3	0	0	0	0	0	0	0
Full Time Student	0	1	3	0	1	3	2	1	0	0
Does Not Work	0	1	1	1	1	1	0	2	2	0
5. Gender										
Male	2	3	3	0	1	3	4	3	1	1
Female	1	2	4	2	3	4	1	3	1	0
Prefer Not To Identify	0	0	0	0	0	0	0	0	0	0
6. Type Of Structure	A	O	H	A	M	H	M	H	A	A
7. Amount Of Land	<1	>10	<1	<1	>1	>10	>1	>1	<1	<1
8. Own Or Rent	R	O	O	R	O	O	R	O	R	R
9. Number Of Vehicles	2	2	2	1	1	2	1	2	1	1

```
A – Apartment      O – Own
H – House          R - Rent
M – Mobile Home
```

CENSUS DATA SET 9

	Record 1	Record 2	Record 3	Record 4	Record 5	Record 6	Record 7	Record 8	Record 9	Record 10
1. Number Of People In Household	3	3	5	4	3	7	4	2	6	3
2. # Of People With A Disability	0	0	1	0	0	0	0	0	2	0
3. Household Age										
0-3	2	0	0	0	0	1	0	0	0	0
4-18	0	0	1	1	1	2	3	0	3	0
19-65	1	2	2	1	2	2	1	2	2	2
>65	0	1	2	2	0	0	0	0	1	1
4. Work Status										
Work Full Time	1	0	2	1	2	0	1	1	0	1
Work Part Time	0	0	0	1	0	0	0	0	0	0
Farm/Ranch	0	2	0	0	0	2	0	0	2	0
Full Time Student	0	0	1	1	1	2	3	1	3	0
Does Not Work	2	1	2	1	0	1	0	0	1	2
5. Gender										
Male	2	2	2	2	1	4	3	1	4	1
Female	1	1	3	2	2	3	1	1	2	2
Prefer Not To Identify	0	0	0	0	0	0	0	0	0	0
6. Type Of Structure	A	M	H	A	H	H	H	A	H	H
7. Amount Of Land	<1	>10	<1	<1	>1	>10	<1	<1	>10	<1
8. Own Or Rent	R	O	R	R	O	O	R	R	O	O
9. Number Of Vehicles	1	2	2	1	1	2	1	0	3+	1

```
A – Apartment        O – Own
H – House            R - Rent
M – Mobile Home
```

CENSUS DATA SET 10

	Record 1	Record 2	Record 3	Record 4	Record 5	Record 6	Record 7	Record 8	Record 9	Record 10
1. Number Of People In Household	1	1	8	3	5	6	4	7	6	3
2. # Of People With A Disability	0	0	1	0	2	0	0	1	0	0
3. Household Age										
0-3	0	0	1	1	1	1	2	2	1	1
4-18	0	0	4	0	1	2	1	3	1	0
19-65	1	1	2	2	2	1	1	2	3	1
>65	0	0	1	0	1	2	0	0	1	1
4. Work Status										
Work Full Time	1	0	1	0	0	1	0	0	0	1
Work Part Time	0	0	0	0	0	1	1	0	0	0
Farm/Ranch	0	0	0	0	2	0	0	2	2	0
Full Time Student	0	0	4	1	1	2	1	3	2	0
Does Not Work	0	1	3	2	2	2	2	2	2	2
5. Gender										
Male	0	1	3	2	2	4	2	3	3	0
Female	1	0	5	1	3	2	2	4	3	3
Prefer Not To Identify	0	0	0	0	0	0	0	0	0	0
6. Type Of Structure	A	A	H	A	H	M	H	H	M	H
7. Amount Of Land	<1	<1	>10	<1	>10	>1	<1	>10	>10	>1
8. Own Or Rent	R	R	O	R	O	R	O	O	O	O
9. Number Of Vehicles	0	0	1	1	2	1	1	2	3+	1

A – Apartment
H – House
M – Mobile Home
O – Own
R - Rent

CENSUS DATA SET 11

	Record 1	Record 2	Record 3	Record 4	Record 5	Record 6	Record 7	Record 8	Record 9	Record 10
1. Number Of People In Household	1	5	3	7	2	2	6	5	3	4
2. # Of People With A Disability	0	0	0	0	1	0	1	0	0	0
3. Household Age										
0-3	0	1	0	0	0	0	1	0	0	0
4-18	0	2	1	3	1	0	2	2	1	2
19-65	1	1	2	2	1	2	2	2	0	2
>65	0	1	0	2	0	0	1	1	2	0
4. Work Status										
Work Full Time	1	1	2	1	1	0	0	2	1	0
Work Part Time	0	0	0	1	0	0	0	1	0	0
Farm/Ranch	0	0	0	0	0	2	2	0	0	2
Full Time Student	0	2	1	3	1	0	2	2	1	2
Does Not Work	0	2	0	2	0	0	2	0	1	0
5. Gender										
Male	1	2	1	5	2	1	3	4	1	1
Female	0	3	2	2	0	1	3	1	2	3
Prefer Not To Identify	0	0	0	0	0	0	0	0	0	0
6. Type Of Structure	A	H	A	H	M	H	H	H	A	M
7. Amount Of Land	<1	<1	<1	>1	<1	>10	>10	>1	<1	>10
8. Own Or Rent	R	R	R	O	O	O	O	O	R	O
9. Number Of Vehicles	1	1	0	2	1	1	3+	2	0	2

```
A – Apartment      O – Own
H – House          R - Rent
M – Mobile Home
```

CENSUS DATA SET 12

	Record 1	Record 2	Record 3	Record 4	Record 5	Record 6	Record 7	Record 8	Record 9	Record 10
1. Number Of People In Household	8	3	4	4	2	1	3	4	2	2
2. # Of People With A Disability	0	0	1	0	0	0	0	0	0	0
3. Household Age										
0-3	2	0	0	0	0	0	0	0	0	0
4-18	3	0	0	1	0	0	0	2	0	0
19-65	2	3	2	3	2	1	1	2	2	2
>65	1	0	2	0	0	0	2	0	0	0
4. Work Status										
Work Full Time	2	3	2	3	2	1	1	2	1	0
Work Part Time	1	0	1	0	0	0	2	0	0	0
Farm/Ranch	0	0	0	0	0	0	0	0	1	0
Full Time Student	3	0	0	1	0	0	0	2	0	0
Does Not Work	2	0	1	0	0	0	0	0	0	2
5. Gender										
Male	3	2	2	1	1	1	2	1	1	1
Female	5	1	2	3	1	0	1	3	1	1
Prefer Not To Identify	0	0	0	0	0	0	0	0	0	0
6. Type Of Structure	H	A	H	H	H	A	H	H	A	O
7. Amount Of Land	>10	>1	>1	<1	<1	>1	>1	>1	>10	>!
8. Own Or Rent	O	R	O	R	R	R	O	R	R	R
9. Number Of Vehicles	3+	3+	2	2	2	2	1	2	1	0

```
A – Apartment        O – Own
H – House            R - Rent
M – Mobile Home
```

Choose Your Government Flow Chart

Data Set for Task #17

Choose Your Own Government Flow Chart

Table 1. How many people do you want making decisions?

0	Anarchy	You cannot set up a government if you choose to have no government. **Start again** and choose another type.
1	Autocracy	Go to Table 2
Few	Aristocracy	Go to Table 3
Many	Democracy	Go to Table 4

Table 2 - Autocracy. How does your leader come into power?

Inherits power through Birthright	Monarchy	Go to Table 2.1
Seizes Power	Dictatorship	Complete Task using **Dictatorship** as the Government type

Table 2.1 - Monarchy. How much power does your monarch possess?

Absolute	Absolute Monarchy	Complete Task using **Absolute Monarchy** as the Government type
Limited/Defined	Constitutional Monarchy	Complete Task using **Constitutional Monarchy** as the Government type

Choose Your Own Government Flow Chart

Table 3 - Aristocracy. Which group do you want to have the power?

Church	Theocracy	Complete Task using **Theocracy** as the Government type
Wealthy	Plutocracy	Complete Task using **Plutocracy** as the Government type
Military	Junta	You don't have a military yet. **Go back** to table 1 and choose another government type
Other	Oligarchy	Complete Task using **Oligarchy** as the Government type

Table 4 - Democracy. Who do you want to vote and actually create laws?

All Citizens	Direct Democracy	Complete Task using **Direct Democracy** as the Government type
Elected Officials	Representative Democracy	Complete Task using **Representative Democracy** as the Government type

Options for Your Budget Surplus

Data Set for Task #35

PUT MONEY INTO URBAN DEVELOPMENT

Cost: Up to 30,000,000

You have decided to build an apartment complex in one of your cities. Your complex will be a mixture of 1, 2, and 3 bedroom homes. This project has the following deliverables:

1. **A description cost estimate of the project.** Include how many of what kinds of apartments you will have, how many people you will be able to house and which, if any, upgrades you are adding. Also include the total you are spending for this project. Your total estimate must be within 15% of your max budget but cannot go over. *Note: Each bedroom can hold a maximum of 2 people.*

2. **A design of your apartment complex.** This can take the form of a diagram, a painting, a model or a computer rendering.

Construction Cost Elements

BASE UNIT PRICES

$100 per square foot

1 bedroom – 800 square feet

2 bedroom – 1000 square feet

3 bedroom – 1200 square feet

APARTMENT UPGRADES

- Appliances - $1000 per apartment
- Kitchen - $1000 per apartment
- Flooring - $500 per apartment
- Storage – $500 per apartment
- Garage space - $1500 per apartment

COMPLEX UPGRADES

- Landscaping - $20,000
- Laundry center - $10,000 each
- Fitness center - $10,000 each
- Swimming pool - $15,000 each
- Playground - $8,000 each

PUT MONEY INTO MANUFACTURING

Cost: 150,000,000

You have decided to build an new factory in one of your cities. This project has the following deliverables:

1. **A description and cost estimate of the project.** Include what product you will be manufacturing and what kind of raw materials you will use and how many and what kind of jobs you will be creating. Also include the total you are spending to create and run the factory for 1 year. Your total estimate must be within 15% of your max budget but cannot go over. Your factory must include:
    1. A Factory floor
    2. Executive Space
    3. Lower level offices
    4. Loading Docks
    5. Restrooms Breakrooms

2. **A design of your factory.** This can take the form of a diagram, a painting, a model or a computer rendering. Be sure to include a legend, scale and compass rose.

BASE CONSTRUCTION COST

$50 per square foot

FACTORY COMPONENTS

- Executive Space – additional $25,000 per 500 sq feet office. Fits 1 executive at a salary of $100,000 per year
- Lower Level Offices - $35,00 per 1500 sq feet of cubicle space. Fits 25 administrative staff with a salary of $50,000 per year each.
- Machinery - $10 per square foot of factory floor space. You can fit 1 factory worker for every 200 square feet of factory floor space with a salary of $40,000 per year each.
- Loading Docks/Warehouse space – You can fit 2 warehouse/dock workers per 600 square feet of space with a salary of $20,000 per year each.

PUT MONEY INTO RENEWABLE ENERGY

Cost: 80,000,000

You have decided to invest in renewable energy. For your budget you can either:

a) Build a wind farm with 20 commercial grade wind turbines
b) Build a solar farm with 80 commercial grade panels
c) Build a hydroelectric plant.

This project has the following deliverables:

1. **A map of your country showing the location of your renewable energy project.** Keep on mind the terrain of your country. Wind farms need plenty of wind to be effective. Solar panels need abundant sunlight and hydroelectric plants require a river to dam. Also, none of these things can be created in a city.

2. **A presentation about your energy project either in a PowerPoint type software or using a display board. Your presentation must show:**
    1. What kind of renewable energy it is
    2. How it works and how much power it generates
    3. Pros and cons of this type of renewable energy over alternatives
    4. You must include pictures and/or diagrams

PUT MONEY INTO DEFENSE RESEARCH

Cost: 150,000,000

You have decided to invest in security and defense research. This culminated in a new invention that would give your country a competitive edge over its adversaries to either win in a conflict or keep the peace. This project has the following deliverables:

1. **A design of your invention.** This can take the form of a diagram, a painting, a model or a computer rendering

2. **A prototype of your invention.**

3. **A detailed description of the invention. This must include:**
    1. How it works
    2. What it is used for
    3. Which branch or branches of your military would get the most use out of it
    4. How it will give you an edge over your advisories during times of war or peace.

MINE ADDITIONAL NATURAL RESOURCES

Cost: 50,000,000

You have decided to invest in the collection of some more of your country's natural resources.

This project has the following deliverables:

1. **A map of your country showing the location the previously natural state or rural land that you are converting to resource collection.**

2. **A presentation about you're the type of resource that you are collecting either in a PowerPoint type software or using a display board. Your presentation must show:**
   1. What kind of resource it is
   2. A detailed description of how it is collected
   3. A list of uses for this resource and how it is prepared for transport and use
   4. Pros and cons of the reallocation of this land to resource collection
   5. You must include pictures and/or diagrams

PUT MONEY INTO AGRICULTURE

Cost: 75,000,000

You have decided to invest in the farming more of your country's land.

This project has the following deliverables:

1. **A map of your country showing the location the previously natural state land that you are converting to rural.**

2. **A presentation about you're the types of crops and/or livestock that you will grow on this land either in a PowerPoint type software or using a display board. Your presentation must show:**
    1. What kinds of crops and/or livestock you will have
    2. Why your country is particularly suited for the cultivation of those crops/livestock
    3. Pros and cons of the reallocation of this land to resource collection
    4. A detailed description of how to care for your crop/livestock
    5. You must include pictures and/or diagrams

3. **Create a food dish to share that honors your country's cultural heritage featuring the plant or animal that you will cultivate on this land.**

PUT MONEY INTO HEALTHCARE

Cost:
150,000,000

You have decided to build an new hospital for your citizens. This project has the following deliverables:

1. **A map of your country showing the location of your new hospital.**

2. **A description and cost estimate of the project.** Include what areas your hospital will specialize in and why those areas are of specific importance to your people. Keep in mind what you have learned about your citizens so far. Also include the total you are spending to create your hospital. Your total estimate must be within 15% of your max budget but cannot go over. Your hospital must include:

    1. An emergency room - $50,000,000
    2. An ICU – $20,000,000
    3. A Radiology Department - $10,000,000
    4. A Laboratory - $5,000,000
    5. Patient rooms - $100,000 per room
    6. Mediflight and Ambulance areas - $500,000
    7. **At least** 2 specialty areas
        1. Cancer research - $25,000,000
        2. Children's specialty ward - $10,000,000
        3. Dialysis center - $5,000,000
        4. Surgical suite - $30,000,000
        5. Neurology specialists - $8,000,000
        6. Neonatal and Pediatric ICU - $25,000,000
        7. A Maternity Ward - $10,000,000
        8. Primary care offices - $5,000,000
        9. Physical therapy center - $10,000,000
        10. Cardiac Specialists - $8,000,000

3. **A design of your hospital. You need to show both the outside design and the floorplan of your hospital.** These can take the form of diagrams, paintings, a model or a computer rendering.

PUT MONEY INTO TRANSPORTATION INFRASTRUCTURE - 1

Cost: 150,000,000

You have decided to invest in your transportation infrastructure. For your budget you can either:

a) Expand your highway system and build a bus terminal

b) Expand your railroad system and build a train station

c) Expand your cargo and passenger ship fleet and build a port

This project has the following deliverables:

1. **A description and cost estimate of your project.** Include what type of system you are improving and why this will have specific benefit to your people. You must purchase **at least** two items from the list below (although you may purchase more).

    Constructing new highways - $2 million per mile

    Constructing new railroad tracks - $1.5 million per mile

    Constructing a bus terminal - $1.875 million

    Constructing a train station – 3.75 million

    Constructing a port – $22 million per berth (spot for ship to dock)

    Cost of new bus - $550,000 per bus

    Cost of new Locomotive - $300,000

    Cost of train passenger cars - $55,000 each

    Cost of train freight cars - $22,000 each

    Cost of passenger ship - $100 million

    Cost of cargo ship - $15 million each

PUT MONEY INTO TRANSPORTATION INFRASTRUCTURE - 2

2. **A map of your country showing the location of your terminal, train station or port as well as the placement of any new roads or railroad lines.** Keep in mind the terrain of your country. How will your transportation adapt to the shape of the land? Will your system be running through urban areas, agriculture areas or natural state lands? What is the primary need that the new transportation solution will fulfil?

3. **A design of your terminal, train station or port.** This can take the form of diagrams, paintings, a model or a computer rendering.

DEVELOP A TOURIST ATTRACTION

Cost: 30,000,000

You have decided to build an new theme park for your citizens. This project has the following deliverables:

1. **A map of your country showing the location of your new theme park.**

2. **A design of your theme park.** This can take the form of a diagram, a painting, a model or a computer rendering.

3. **A 2 minute commercial spot advertising your theme park.** This should include:
    1. The name and location of your theme park
    2. The hours of operation
    3. A description of at least 5 rides or attractions
    4. A description of at least 1 show
    5. A list of prices for children, adults, senior and groups
    6. The announcement of the grand opening extravaganza and who will be performing.

PUT MONEY INTO EDUCATION

Cost: 150,000,000

You have decided to build an new University for your citizens. This project has the following deliverables:

1. **A map of your country showing the location of your new university.**

2. **A description and cost estimate of the project.** Include what areas your university will specialize in and why those areas are of specific importance to your people. Keep in mind what you have learned about your citizens so far. Also include the total you are spending to create the university. Your total estimate must be within 15% of your max budget but cannot go over. Your university must include:

    1. An administration building- $50,000,000
    2. Undergraduate Studies Classroom Building– $10,000,000 per building
    3. A Student Union and Bookstore- $5,000,000
    4. Residence Halls - $10,000,000 per building
    5. **At least** 2 specialty areas
        1. Graduate School- $25,000,000
        2. Sports Stadium- $10,000,000
        3. Fine Arts Academy- $8,000,000
        4. School of Medicine- $30,000,000
        5. Engineering School- $8,000,000
        6. Law School- $25,000,000
        7. Specific Science Department (physics, biology, etc)- $10,000,000
        8. Health Center- $5,000,000
        9. School of Agriculture - $10,000,000
        10. Recreation Facilities- $5,000,000

3. **A design of your university campus.** This can take the form of a diagram, a painting, a model or a computer rendering.

Issue a Rebate Check to your Citizens

Cost: Variable

You have decided to issue rebate checks to all adult and senior citizens of your country. Since your population has grown 12% while the ratio between the different age groups has remained the same. This project has the following deliverables:

1. **A cost estimate showing the amount of rebate for adults and seniors. This estimate must include:**
   1. The approximate number of adults now living in your country.
   2. The approximate number of seniors now living in your country.
   3. The amount of rebate check that each group (adults and seniors) will get if seniors only get 75% of the rebate amount of younger adults.
   4. The total amount of the your surplus budget that is being spent on rebates.

2. **A social media campaign to get the word out to your population about the rebate check. This campaign must include:**
   1. A Pinterest graphic
   2. A Facebook or Instagram post
   3. 2 Twitter posts
   4. All relevant hashtags

Spend Money on Leadership Perks

Cost: Variable

You have decided to improve the standard of living of your country's leader – yourself. This project has the following deliverables:

1. **A cost estimate showing how you plan to spend the money. This estimate must include:**
   1. A detailed description of each item you buy, build or do. This must include a picture, drawing or model.
   2. A cost estimate of each item that you buy or build
   3. The total cost of your Leader Perks

2. **A social media campaign to get the word out to the world your new lifestyle. This campaign must include:**
   1. A YouTube or TikTok video (or video script)
   2. A Pinterest graphic
   3. A Facebook or Instagram post
   4. 2 Twitter posts
   5. All relevant hashtags

Appendix VI

Science Project Report Sections and Display Board

Contents of Appendix VI:

Science Project Report Sections and Display Board

- ➢ **Science Project Report Sections**
- ➢ **Science Project Display Board**

Science Project Report Sections

Report Sections

1. Title Page

The title page contains the title of your project in the center of the page several inches from the top of the page. You should also list your name, school and grade (if applicable) in the lower right hand corner.

2. Table of Contents

List the sections of your paper and the page numbers where they begin.

3. Abstract

The abstract is a shortened version of your entire paper. The abstract should consist of three short paragraphs: the Purpose, the Procedure, and the Results.

4. Purpose, Question, Variables and Controls

Explain why you chose this project and state the question you are trying to answer with the project. Describe the control (the part of your experiment that you DO NOT CHANGE), your independent variables (what you DO CHANGE) and your dependent variables (the data you will record from conducting the experiment).

Note: Depending on your particular experiment your may not have variables and controls.

5. Hypothesis

Your hypothesis is an educated guess as to what you think will happen when you conduct your experiment. It should be written as an **if....then... because** statement.

6. Background research

Use at least 3-5 credible sources for your projects. This section is also where you should define any key terms that may be used in your project

7. Materials

As you build your biosphere and conduct your project you should keep track of **absolutely everything you used**. You should describe the items specifically and explain how they were used, and how much of each thing was used in your project.

8. Procedure

You procedure is the steps you used to construct and monitor your project. Be very specific. *Someone should be able to take your materials and procedure section of your report and replicate your project exactly.*

9. Data Observations

This is where you include the raw data that you collected. *This may be included as an appendix depending on your project.*

10. Results and Data Analysis

This is where you evaluate and interpret what happened in your project. This should include a detailed summary of what you observed. Make sure you explain your basis of measurements (units of size, time, etc.) Your data should be also be summarized and organized into tables and charts, as well as graphs if possible.

11. Conclusions

Your conclusion should be a comparison of what you actually observed and your hypothesis. This is where you state whether your hypothesis was right or wrong. Give an explanation as to why you were right or why you were wrong based on what you learned through your project and the results of your data.

12. Ideas for future research

List at least 3 ideas for how this project could be expanded upon.

13. Bibliography

List the sources you used in your research. This could be books, articles, websites, videos, or personal interviews. Use APA formatting style.

14. Acknowledgements

This is where you write a thank you to everyone who helped you with your project.

Science Project Display Board

A display board is a easy way to showcase your project and communicate your work to others. Most displays use a 3 panel project board of some type That unfolds to 36" tall by 48" wide. Display boards should be able to stand freely.

Your display board should include at least the following elements from your project:

- Title

- Question

- Variables and hypothesis

- Background research

- Materials list

- Procedure

- Results/Data analysis including any charts and graphs

- Conclusions

- Bibliography

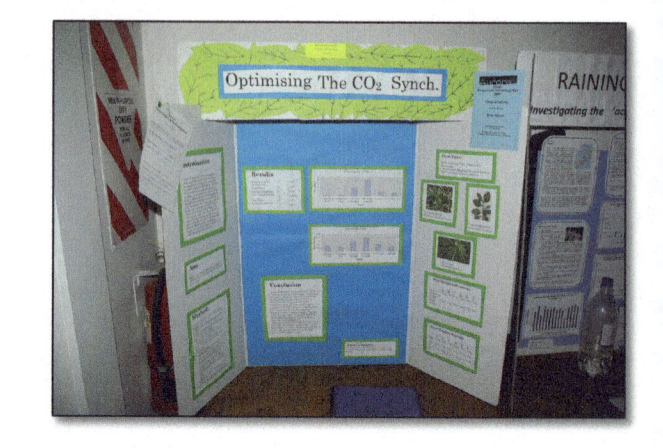

A good board is organized like a newspaper with a catchy title, easy-to-follow and easy-to-read text, and effective pictures and diagrams. Your board should be neat and eye-catching as well.

Appendix VII

Glossary

TERM	DEFINITION
5 Themes of Geography	Location- where places are Place- characteristics of places and the people who live there Human/Enviroment Interaction- relationships between people and their enviroments Movement- Movement of material, people, or ideas among places Regions- areas sharing several characteristics
Abiotic	Not derived from living organisms
Abiotic Factors	Factors of the earth that are not living such as ricks, minerals and soil
Absolute Monarchy	The monarch has unlimited power to rule his or her people and the right to rule comes directly from God and the dominant religious institution.
Activation and Relocation Phase	The activation of all of the procedures necessary to support the continued performance of essential functions
Agriculture	The science or practice of farming, including cultivation of the soil for the growing of crops and the rearing of animals to provide food, wool, and other products
Agroecology	The branch of science dealing withthe application of ecological principles to agricultural systems and practices
Air Force	Provides the United States' defense from the air
Allocation	The process by which a government decides how to use a parcel of land.
Allocation	The distribution of funds for a specific organizational unit or function
Ambassador	Highest ranking diplomat in a country
Anarchy	A system or group in which there is no governing authority
Annex	Absorbing another country's land and population
Anthropology	The study of human societies and cultures and their development

TERM	DEFINITION
Archaeology	The study of human history and prehistory through the excavation of sites and the analysis of artifacts and other physical remains.
Aristocracy	A government in which power is in the hands of a privileged few
Army	Provides the ground forces that protect the U.S.
Article	Parts of a constitution that describes how your government is set up
Artifact	An object made by a human being, typically an item of cultural or historical interest
Atmosphere	Blanket of gasses that cover the earth
Attorney General	Serves as the chief lawyer to the United States Government and oversees all the areas of the Department of Justice
Autocracy	A system of government where one person has all of the power
Autotrophs	An organism that is able to form nutritional organic substances from simple inorganic substances such as carbon dioxide- these are the producers, or plants
Balance of Trade	The difference between the total value of a country's exports and the total value of a country's imports
Bar Graph	Shows data using bars of different heights, also called a bar chart
Beveridge Model	The government provides for a single payer National Health Service. It's funded exclusively through taxes and has no out of pocket costs for the individual patient
Bilateral	An agreement between two countries or two groups of countries where both sides loosen trade restrictions to help out businesses in order to prosper better between the different countries

TERM	DEFINITION
Bill of Rights	Contained in the first 10 amendments of the U.S. constitution and spells out the rights of the country's citizens as they relate to the government
Binomial Nomenclature	The system of nomenclature in which two terms are used to denote a species of living organism, the first one indicating the genus and the second the specific epithet
Biodiversity	The variety of life in the world or in a particular habitat or ecosystem
Biome	A large naturally occurring community of flora and fauna occupying a major habitat
Biosphere	Part of the planet that can support life
Biotic	Relating to or resulting from living things, especially in their ecological relations
Bismark Model	The responsibility for funding health insurance plans falls on employers and employees and funded through payroll deductions. There may be one or multiple insurers and the government controls the pricing of both insurances and providers
Brainstorming	A method of generating ideas and sharing knowledge to solve a particular problem, in which participants are encouraged to think without interruption
Cabinet	A group of officials who's role is to advise your leader or leaders on issues relating to the running of your country
Cadastral Map	These maps show details of individual properties
Capitalism	An ideology the means of production, distribution and exchange should be regulated by private ownership and the law of supply and demand
Cartography	The science or practice of drawing maps
Census	A way of calculating, acquiring and recording information about the members of a given population.

TERM	DEFINITION
Ceremonial Speeches	Speeches given on a special occasion. These types of speeches are usually brief and focused on the occasion itself.
Climate	The average weather in a location over a long period of time.
Climate Zone	Areas with distinct climates that occur in an East-West direction around the Earth
Coast Guard	Offers military, law enforcement, humanitarian, regulatory, and diplomatic capabilities
Command Economic System	Based on strong governmental controls. The government sets the price on goods and services and there is very little freedom of choice
Communal Anarchy	The goal of Karl Marx in which citizens would have equal ownership in means of production and have no need to form government
Communism	An ideology which advocates communal means of production, distribution and exchange where the output is divided according to need
Communities	A group of people living in the same place or having a particular characteristic in common
Conquer	A country taking another country by force
Constituent	A voting member of the community which an elected official represents
Constitution	A document which outlines the principles, goals and laws that govern the land and people within its borders
Constitutional Monarchy	One where monarchs share governmental powers with elected legislatures and often serve as ceremonial executive leaders of their government.
Constitutive Theory of Statehood	Developed in the 19th century, it defines a state as a person of international law if, and only if, it is recognized as sovereign by at least one other state.
Constructivism	Believes that international relations is a product of social interaction between people and cultures, not just states and governments

TERM	DEFINITION
Consumers	Animals that eat the plants (herbivores), other animals (carnivores), or both (omnivores)
Continuity of Operations Plan	The internal effort of a country to make sure that critical functions and services are able to continue operating following a comprehensive array of potential emergencies or disasters
Continuity Operations Phase	Activities needed to continue essential functions
Counterterrorism	All of the practices, tactics, techniques and strategies that go into preventing terrorists and terrorist organizations from thriving and acting
Cryosphere	The part of the hydrosphere that is made up of frozen water
Cultural Blending	The cultural changes groups experience after interacting with other groups or cultures
Cultural Diffusion	The spread of cultural beliefs and social activities from one group of people to another
Cultural Narratives	Stories that help a community structure and assign meaning to its history and existence.
Cultural Transmission	The way of passing or learning knowledge, skils, attitudes, and values from person to person
Culture	1.) The arts and other manifestations of human intellectual achievement regarded collectively 2.) The customs, arts, social institutions, and achievements of a particular nation, people, or other social group
Currency	The medium of exchange used in a particular country. It is a country's money
Custom	A widely accepted way of behaving or doing something that is specific to a particular people, place, or time

TERM	DEFINITION
Declarative Theory of Statehood	The political existence of the state is independent of recognition by the other states. The theory defines a state as a person in international law if it has a permanent population, a governments, the ability to enter relations with other states and defined territory
Defense Pact	A treaty or military alliance in which countries promise to support each other militarily and to defend each other
Demand	The amount of something that your consumers are willing to by at given price
Democracy	A system of government where the power is held by the population itself.
Demonstrative Speeches	Speeches that explain how to do something.
Denomination	Is the the unit classification for the stated or face value of your currency bills or coins
Detritivores	An animal which feeds on dead organic material
Dictatorship	A government where one individual maintains executive authority via force
Diplomat	A person appointed by a national government to conduct official negotiations and maintain relations with another country or countries
Direct Democracy	A democracy where all citizens vote on everything
Disarmament	The elimination of nuclear weapons and other weapons of mass destruction and the regulation of conventional arms
Ecological Organization	The relationship of biological organisms to each other and their environments.
Economic Ideology	A set of views that form a basis about how an economy should function withing the relationship between the government and the people

TERM	DEFINITION
Economic System	The system by which money, industry, and trade are organized in a country
Economy	The wealth and resources of a country particularly when it comes to the production and consumption of goods and services
Ecosystem	1.) A biological community of interacting organisms and their physical environment 2.) A complex network or interconnected system
Education Policy	The principles and government policies in the educational sphere as well as the collection of laws and rules that govern the operation of education systems
Embassy	The primary diplomatic representation of a country's government in a host country
Equator	Imaginary line separating the northern and southern hemispheres.
Exchange Rate	The value of one nation's currency versus the currency of another nation or economic zone
Exports	The sale of goods and services to another country
Externality	Occurs when the costs or benefits of a transaction falls outside of the producer/consumer relationship
Fascism	An ideology which advocates that the nation and often race are placed above the individual. Characterized by severe economic and social regimentation, and forcible suppression of opposition
Fauna	The animals of a particular region, habitat, or geological period
Federal Continuity Directives	Documents that provide guidelines for implementing a continuity of operations plan in the United States

TERM	DEFINITION
Federal Holiday	A holiday that has been officially declared a public holiday by the government. Federal and many other workers get the day off in observance of these holidays
FEMA	Federal Emergency Management Agency- helps to provide continuity of operations guidance and assistance to citizens and the private sector
Fixed Tariff	A constant sum per unit of imported goods or a percentage of the price
Flora	The plants of a particular region, habitat, or geological period
Folkways	Organize the understanding of casual interactions between people
Food Chain	A hierarchical series of organisms each dependent on the next as a source of food.
FoodWeb	A system of interlocking and interdependent food chains.
Formal Education	Learning through schools or other institutions of learning. It's usually hierarchical and results in a diploma, degree, or certification
Free Market	A market in which prices are set by the law of supply and demand with no government interference
General Reference Map	Simple maps showing important physical (natural and man–made) features in an area. Their main purpose is to summarize the landscape to aid discovery of locations
Geopolitics	Politics, especially international relations, as influenced by geographical factors.
Geosphere	Makes up the interior and surface of the earth
Globalization	Interdependence on a global scale caused by cross-border trade in goods and services, technology, investment, people, and information

TERM	DEFINITION
Goals	Things that a country aims to achieve and are based on the country's guiding principles
Government	The system of rules and the people who make and administer them
Graphs	Helps us visualize information quickly and easily. They can reveal trends and comparisons as well as show the relationships between variables and groups of statistical information.
Grid	The series of lines on a map that match the index.
Grid Map	A map on which a network of horizontal and vertical lines are superimposed, for locating points
Healthcare Policy	A document that establishes guidelines to support the country's patients, hospitals and other healthcare organizations and healthcare system as a whole
Hemishpere	A half of the earth
Human Geography	The branch of geography dealing with how human activity affects or is influenced by the earth's surface
Human Rights	Rights inherent to all human beings, regardless of race, sex, nationality, ethnicity, language, religion, or any other status
Humanitarian Aid	Material and logistic assistance to people in areas when the effects of a disaster are beyond the relief capacity of national authorities alone
Hydrosphere	Made up of all of the water on the earth, no matter the state
Immigrant	A person who comes to live permanently in a foreign country.
Imports	The purchase of goods and services from another country
Income Tax	A type of tax that applies to personal and business revenue and interest income

TERM	DEFINITION
Individual	Once single living organism- lowest level of organization
Inflation	The increase in the price of goods and services relative to the value of your nation's currency
Informal Education	Practical learning or training. This include apprenticeship programs and on-the-job training activities
Informative Speeches	Speeches that are intended to merely give information about something
International Diplomacy	Method that governments use to influence the actions of foreign governments through peaceful tactics
International Law	The collection of rules, norms, and standards generally recognized as binding between countries
International Relations	How countries interact with each other
International Trade	The exchange of capital, goods, and services across international borders
Intuitive Decision Making	The decision maker uses sensitivity, gut instinct, a sixth sense, or intuition. You do what sounds best to you
Ionosphere	The magnetic field that surrounds the earth, also called the magnetosphere
Isolationism	A policy of remaining apart from the affairs of other countries
Jurisdiction	The ruling body has the right or power to exercise authority over a territory or people
Landforms	Natural physical features found on the surface of the earth.
Latitude Lines	Horizontal lines on a map that run east and west. They measure north and south of the equator.
Law of Supply and Demand	The relationship between what people want and what is available to them

TERM	DEFINITION
Laws	Social norms that are formally inscribed by state or federal governmen
Legal Right	An entitlement that is based on the norms of the society in which a person lives.
Legend	A description, explanation, or table of symbols printed on a map or chart to permit a better understanding or interpretation of it.
Legitimacy	A state of being where the people accept the government's power.
Liberalism	Cooperation is inevitable due to the necessity of international interdependence
Line Graph	Used to show changes in something over a period of time using several points connected by straight lines
Lithosphere	Also makes up the interior and surface of the earth, also known as the Geosphere
Longitude Lines	Vertical lines on a map that run north and south. They measure east and west of the Prime Meridian.
Map Projection	Method that is used to transfer the measurements of latitude and longitude from a spherical Earth onto a flat surface
Marine Corps	Provides amphibious and ground units for contigency and combat operations
Market Economic System	Based on the idea of a free market where prices are set by the law of supply and demand
Material Culture	Aspect of social reality grounded in the objects and architecture that surround people. It includes the usage, consumption, creation, and trade of objects as well as the behaviors, norms, and rituals that the objects create or take part in.
Mitigation	The effort to reduce the impact of a disaster, specifically in regards to the loss of life and property.

TERM	DEFINITION
Mixed Economic System	Combines aspects of both a market and a command system. It operates as a free market, with some governmental controls that keep prices from going too extreme in either direction
Monarchy	A type of autocracy where one individual maintains executive authority via divine right (king, queen, czar, emperor, etc.) Usually one has to be born into the ruling family to rise to power
Mores	Help structure moral and ethical behavior of a culture.
Multilateral	Involves 3 or more countries, each with their own set of things that they need and/or want
Multiplier	The number that you would multiply your sample data by to get to your total data figure.
NAFTA	The North American Free Trade Agreement- an agreement between the United States, Canada, and Mexico
National Budget	An outline of a government's priorities and allocations of the country's income; also called a federal budget
National Debt	The total amount of money that your country's government has borrowed.
National Defense	The agencies responsible for the security and defense of a country, its citizens, economy and institutions
National Guard	Supports domestic missions including emergencies, humanitarian efforts, and national security
National Health Insurance Model	Medical providers are private, however the payments all come from one health insurance which is run by the government. Every citizen pays into this insurance and has access to the benefits
National Holiday	A holiday celebrated throughout the country
National Interest	Implies that each country will act in its own best interest, whether that interest involves national security, economic prosperity of global influence

TERM	DEFINITION
National Landmark	A historic property that illustrates the heritage or cultural identity of a people.
National Library	A national library is a library established by a government as a country's preeminent repository of information. They include numerous rare, valuable, or significant works.
National Mottoes	Used to describe the intent or motivation of the nation in a short phrase.
National Symbols	Any object, sign, or emblem that carries additional meaning and represents a cultural or political nation.
NATO	North Atlantic Treaty Organization- its purpose is to guarantee the freedom and security of its members, promote democratic values, and strives for the peaceful resolution of disputes
Natural Disaster	An event that occurs naturally and has a negative effect on humans
Natural Hazard	A threat of an event that could occur naturally and usually has a negative effect on humans
Natural Right	An entitlement derived from human nature or God and are considered fundamental and universal
Naural Resources	Materials or substances such as minerals, forests, water, and fertile land that occur in nature and can be used for economic gain.
Navigation Charts	A graphic representation of a sea area and adjacent coastal regions
Navy	Delivers forces for maintaining security on and under the sea and in the air
Non-Formal Education	Learning from experience or from home. Homeschooling, co-ops, tutoring, and travel-school fall into this category
Non-Material Culture	Nonphysical ideas that people have about their culture, including beliefs, values, rules, norms, morals, and language

TERM	DEFINITION
Non-renewable Resources	A natural substance that is not replenished with the speed at which it is consumed. Its supply is finite.
Oligarchy	A system of government where the country is ruled by a very small group of people who make decisions for everybody
OPEC	The Organization of the Petroleum Exporting Countries- coordinate and unify the petroleum policies of its Member Countries
Opportunity Cost	Loss of potential gain from other alternatives when one option is chosen
Orientation	The relationship between the directions on the map and the corresponding compass directions in reality. Normally paired with an orientation symbol like the compass rose
Out-of-Pocket Model	All providers are private and there is essentially no insurance. Patients pay for all medical procedures out of their own pockets
Outline Map	A map which only provides very basic information so that more details can be added.
Peacebuilding	Reduce the risk of relapsing into conflict by helping countries to lay the foundation for sustainable peace and development
Peacekeeping	Assist countries in navigating the complex and often difficult path from conflict to peace
Percentage	A figure that shows the proportion of a part to a whole.
Persuasive Speeches	Speeches that are intended to change someone's mind.
pH	The measure of the acidity or basicity of liquids
Physical Map	A graphical representation of physical locations of landmarks or markers
Pictograph	Uses symbols and pictures to represent data.

TERM	DEFINITION
Pie Chart	Special type of graph that shows the relationship of several parts to the whole.
Plutocracy	A government ruled by the wealthy either directly or via monetary influence of representatives
Political Geography	A branch of geography that is concerned with how politics shape geography.
Political Map	They show state and national boundaries and capital and major cities.
Population	All members of the same type of organism.
Population Density	Refers to the number of people who live in a specific area.
Population Density Map	Can show the population density of an area
Preamble	Is the introductory part that states its purpose, aims, and justification in a constitution
Precipitation	Any water that falls to earth, whether in liquid or solid form.
Presidential Succession	The order in which the vice president and other members of a government assume the powers and duties of the president upon their death, resignation, removal from office or incapacity
Preventative Diplomacy	Diplomatic action taken to prevent disputes from escalating and to limit the spread of conflicts when they occur
Primary Effects	Occurs as an immediate result of the disaster itself
Prime Meridian	The line of longitude that is starting point for measuring distance of east and west at 0 degrees longitude.
Principle	A fundamental truth that serves as the foundation for a system of belief or behavior
Property Tax	A tax that is imposed on the value of real estate or other personal property

TERM	DEFINITION
Public Speaking	Is the art of presenting before a live audience, also called oration
Public Utilities	Entities that supply essential goods and services to the community such as water, gas, electricity, trash removal and communication systems
Public Works	The activities associated with building and maintaining things such as roads, schools and any structure or service required to maintain an acceptable quality of life for citizens
Ratio	Shows the relationship between two or more items written as a notation (2:5) or a fraction (2/5)
Rational Decision Making	Step-by-step model that helps you identify a problem, pick a solution between multiple alternatives, and find an answer
Readiness and Preparedness Phase	All organization continuity readiness and preparedness activities including risk assessment and management and the development, review, and revision of plans
Realism	Proposes that the nature of relations is inherently anarchist because each nation or state is in it for themselves only
Recession	The economy stops growing and starts shrinking
Reconstitution Phase	Begins after the emergency, or threat of emergency, is over. This phase provides for the orderly transition back to normal operations
Refugees	People who are in danger in their own country and flee to another
Regenerative Farming	The conservation and rehabilitation approach to food and farming systems. It focuses on topsoil regeneration, increasing biodiversity, improving the water cycle, enhancing ecosystem services, increasing resilience to climate change, and strengthening the health and vitality of farm soil
Renewable Resources	Grows again and comes back again after we use it.

TERM	DEFINITION
Representative Democracy	Citizens vote on representatives and the representatives vote on behalf of the citizens that elected them
Resource Map	Designed to show the locations of natural resources. They do not show every place that every little thing is located, rather they show the general area or most important places in which you might find the resources
Right	A legal or social entitlement afforded to people based on a predefined convention
Risk Information	Any information which can influence a decision.
Routine Peaceful Competition	The normal and desired end state where countries pursue their own interests with enough commonality of interests to avoid violence
Sales Tax	A tax on a percentage of the sales price of a particular item
Sample Data	A representative subset of your Total Data Set.
Scale	Tells what the distance a unit of measure represents in the area shown on the map
Scarcity	Refers to when the demand for a resource is greater than the supply of that resource.
Secondary Effects	Occurs as a result of a primary effect
Secretary of Agriculture	Handles all matters relating to farming, food, and rural economic development
Secretary of Commerce	Handles matters relating to economic growth, such as setting industrial standards and gathering data for policy-making
Secretary of Defense	Handles matters relating to national security and the United States Armed Forces

TERM	DEFINITION
Secretary of Education	Handles issues related to education, policy and schools as well as financial loans and grant management
Secretary of Energy	Deals with issues relating to energy production and supply, waste disposal, nuclear weapons, and the climate crisis
Secretary of Health and Human Services	Oversees matters relating to public health and family services
Secretary of Homeland Security	Handles public security issues like terrorism, disaster prevention, cybersecurity, border security, and immigration
Secretary of Housing and Urban Development	Manages programs that affect development, and fair housing such as Housing and Community Planning and Development
Secretary of Labor	Handles regulations designed to help keep employees safe, as well as ensure their rights such as unemployment benefits, workplace safety, and wage standards
Secretary of State	Handles matters related to international relations and national foreign policy
Secretary of the Interior	Deals with territorial affairs and manages all federal lands in regards to conservation and natural resources, such as dams, reservoirs, and wildlife
Secretary of the Treasury	Handles the production of currency and manages the public debt, finance and tax laws, and fiscal policy
Secretary of Transportation	Coordinates policy and action for ensuring the safety and modernity of the transportation system and services
Secretary of Veterans' Affairs	Provides healthcare, benefits and support to veterans of the United States
Social Norms	Unwritten rules, beliefs, attitudes, and behaviors considered acceptable in a particular group or culture
Social Role	The part that a person plays in a given social group

TERM	DEFINITION
Social Values	A set of principle that are generally accepted by a group.
Socialism	An ideology which advocates that the means of production, distribution, and exchange should be owned or regulated by the community as a whole
Sovereignty	The power that a country or group has to govern itself or another country or state
Space Force	Protects the U.S. and their allies in space and provides capabilities to the joint force
Statistics	The science that deals with the collecting, analyzing, interpreting and presenting of data.
Supply	The total amount that can be offered to consumers
Sustainable Agriculture	Farming in sustainable ways meeting society's present food and textile needs, without compromising the ability for current or future generations to meet their needs
Sustainable Development	Development that meets the needs of the present, without compromising the ability of future generations to meet their own needs
Taboos	Behaviors with strongly negative connotations within a culture
Tariff	A tax levied by the government on goods and services imported from other countries
Tax	A charge usually of money imposed by the government or other authority on persons or property for public purpose
Tax Rate	The level (usually a percentage) that a government taxes a person, business or item
Taxonomy	System of classifying living things.

TERM	DEFINITION
Tertiary Effects	Long-term effects that occur as a result of the primary disaster
Thematic Map	These maps highlight specific types of information about one topic like climate, or population density
Theocracy	A government ruled by a religious leader or leaders and use religious law to rule the people
Title	A label that describes what the map shows
Topographic Map	A type of map that shows physical features and elevation changes using contour lines
Topography	The arrangement of the physical features of a land, either by colors or as shaded relief
Toponymy	System of classifying living things.
Trade Agreement	A treaty between two or more countries concerning taxes, tariff and trade
Trade Deficit	A country exports more than it imports
Trade Surplus	A country exports more than it imports
Traditional Economic System	Based on goods, services and work that follow traditions or customs. Prices are set according to values established through barter or trade
Tradtion	The transmission of customs or beliefs from generation to generation, or the fact of being passed on in this way.
Unemployment	Occurs when there are not enough jobs for those of your citizens who are both able and wanting to work
Unilateral	A country wants certain restrictions to be enforced but no other countries want them imposed

TERM	DEFINITION
United Nations	An international organization dedicated to promoting international cooperation
Universal Design	The state of being accessible and usable as much as possible, in the easiest way possible, to the greatest possible number of people and in the broadest range of situations
Urban	A human settlement with a high population density and infrastructure of built environment
Variable Tariff	The amount of tax varies according to the price of the item
Vexillography	Art of flag-designing
Vexillologist	Person who studies flags
Vice President	Presides over the Senate and acts as a tie-breaker. They are also the first in the line of Presidential Succession
Weather	Different events that happen each day in our atmosphere, like rain or snow, hot or cold.

Appendix VIII

About Exploring Expression

Welcome to Exploring Expression

Brandy Champeau

Nancy Holt

Exploring Expression is a Leader in cross-curricular, project-based curriculum and unit studies for both children and adults.

At Exploring Expression, we focus on 4 specific offerings:

1. We build quality learning resources for K12 students
2. We create resources for parents and educators to help them become the best expressions of themselves and equip them to better facilitate learning opportunities for their children
3. We utilize public speaking platforms to spread the message of becoming the best expression of yourself through the cultivation of a learning lifestyle
4. We help people with a message and a passion for learning find their voice, publish their books and create curriculum or training to share with the world

As you can see, our passion is learning - learning about yourself and learning about the world. We focus on self-improvement and education. Because in the end it all comes down to learning. Learning doesn't have to be hard, and it doesn't have to be boring. At Exploring Expression, we want to help you put the engagement and excitement back into education and to put the education back into life.

Contact Us!

ExploringExpression@gmail.com

https://ExploringExpression.com

www.facebook.com/ExploringExpression

www.Instagram.com/ExploringExpression

https://bit.ly/2KZrSFG

Check out these other Books and Courses by Exploring Expression

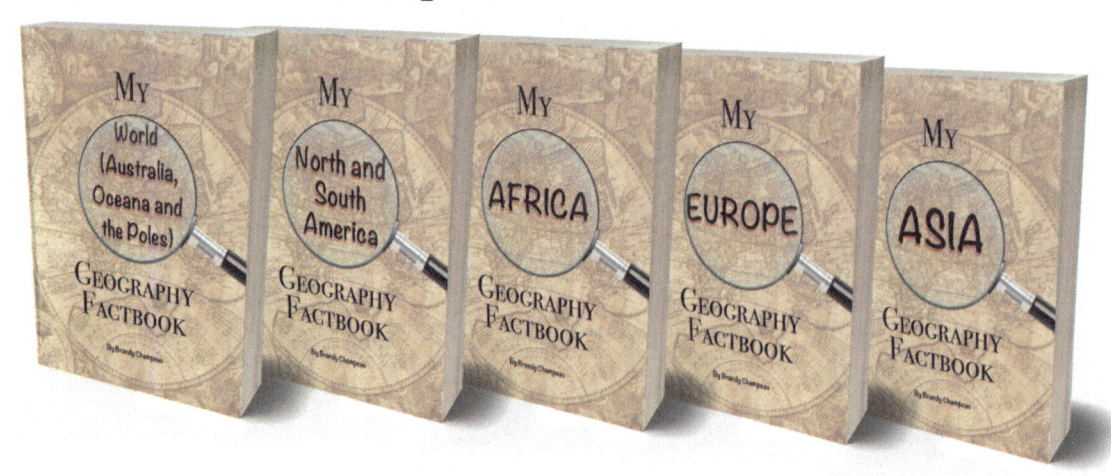

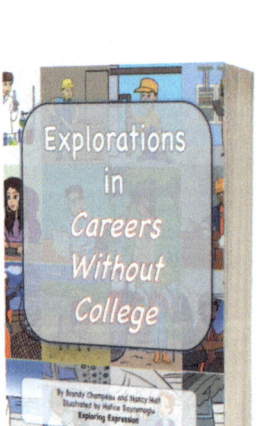

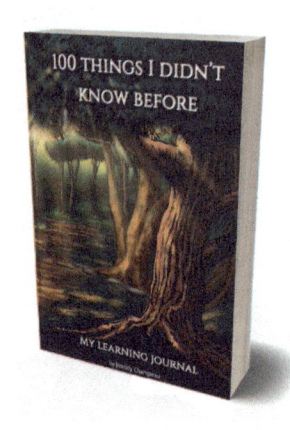

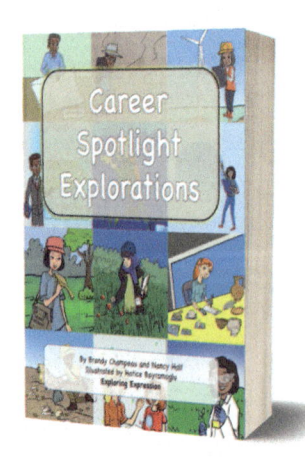

Order these and more at https://ExploringExpression.com

Made in the USA
Columbia, SC
03 August 2022

Copyright © 2020 by ACTA Research

All rights reserved. No part of this book may be reproduced or used in any manner without the copyright owner's written permission, except for the use of brief quotations in a book review.

FIRST EDITION

www.BoostYourBalance.com

BOOST YOUR BALANCE

THE AUTHORITATIVE GUIDE TO SENIOR EXERCISE FOR IMPROVING FITNESS, DEFYING AGING, AND PREVENTING FALLS

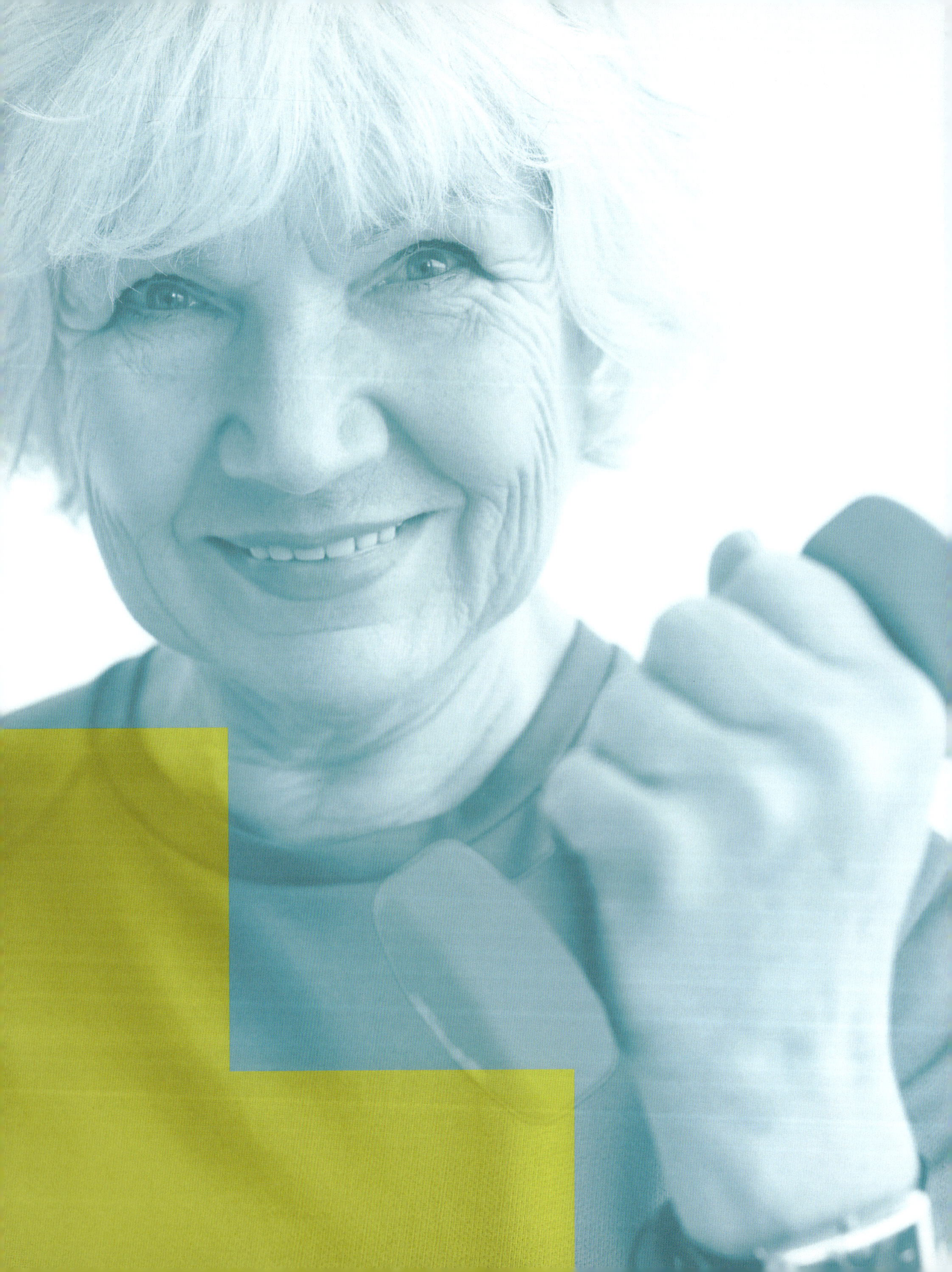

ACKNOWLEDGMENTS

I have wanted to write this book for some time – a practical guide to better balance, founded on research and written for a broad audience. This aspiration became possible through the support of my family, friends, and colleagues. Though many of them live and work in different countries and diverse fields, they were all willing to expand their circle of concern, offer authentic guidance, and selflessly work to make my vision a reality. To these incredible people, I extend my deepest gratitude.

To my parents for their love, encouragement, and unconditional support. Special thanks to my brother, Julius, for lending his artistic talent, good humor, and for somehow always making time despite the overwhelming demands on his schedule.

I am very grateful to my friend Abdallah for his invaluable input, thoughtful comments, and consistent support throughout this journey. He always is a source of inspiration and motivation, and without him, this book would have remained a work in progress for a long time.

My appreciation extends to Chris and Glenn for their wisdom, patience, and encouragement. To Mayra, for her contagious positivity and unwavering enthusiasm. Thank you for the support, especially during the final stretches of this book.

To my friend and colleague, Gesche, who applied her knowledge as a psychologist to help motivate the reader and improve their likelihood of success.

Finally, I owe a significant debt of gratitude to my fellow researchers and healthcare professionals, whose work positively impacts so many lives. Their outstanding contributions in the field of healthy aging inspired this book. Throughout the writing process, I have reached out to many experts in the field, and I am grateful for their kindness, insight, and advice.

"You can't help getting older, but **you don't have to get old.**"

—GEORGE BURNS

CONTENTS

Disclaimer 9
About this book 10
Why I wrote this book 11
How to use this book 13

PART I – THE BASICS OF STABILITY, AGING, AND BALANCE INTERVENTIONS 14

What is balance, and how do we do it? 16
The high cost of falls 18
Decreased balance and fall risk factors 20
Aging and muscle strength 23
Aging of the senses 24
Aging and brain function 27
Aging and preparing for balance challenges 28
Aging and reacting to balance challenges 29
Summary 30
Better Balance – what factors can we influence? 30
Training to improve balance - what really works 32

PART II – BOOST YOUR BALANCE: A UNIQUE WORKOUT PROGRAM TO PROMOTE HEALTHY AGING AND BETTER BALANCE 36

How should you exercise? Basics of a well-rounded training regimen 38
Safety and equipment 43
Track your progress 45

Warm-up and Cool-down 47
The Balance program 48
Week 1 50
Week 2 51
Week 3 53
Week 4 54
Some important notes on how to get going - and keep going! 56

THE EXERCISES 60

Posture, flexibility, and mobility exercises 60
Strength exercises 92
Balance focused exercises 112

Beyond this book – Keep Boosting Your Balance! 129
Epilogue 131
Bibliography 133

DISCLAIMER

You are encouraged to read *Boost Your Balance* in the context of your physical abilities. Before performing any of the exercises presented in this book, please consult with your healthcare provider. Your safety is paramount, and you must be healthy enough to perform the referenced activities without risk of injury.

Boost Your Balance is not to be used for diagnosis, treatment, or as a substitute for professional medical care and does not replace or supersede the medical advice of your physician. You should regularly consult a physician in matters relating to your health, particularly regarding any symptoms that may require deviation from the book's recommendations.

Boost Your Balance contains recommendations for healthy individuals who seek to improve their balance and promote general health through exercise. The included exercise regimen is not suitable for frail individuals, recurrent fallers, or individuals suffering from any injury or impairment that may put them at an increased risk of accident or injury.

The material in this book is meant to supplement, not replace, proper exercise habits. Like any activity involving movement, balance, equipment, and environmental factors, the exercises presented here pose some inherent risk. I advise you to take full responsibility for your safety and remain mindful of your physical limitations. Before practicing the skills described in *Boost Your Balance*, be sure that your equipment is well-maintained and your environment is safe. Do not take risks beyond your level of experience, aptitude, training, or comfort level. If you are unsure whether you can safely perform an exercise, you are advised to first consult with your physician.

ABOUT THIS BOOK

Boost Your Balance is for you if you are interested in the effects of aging and what can be done to prevent falls and improve wellbeing. This book is also for those interested in the fascinating ways the human body stands, walks, and performs complex movements.

You will gain insight into the importance of exercise for aging adults, and you will also receive an actionable workout plan specially designed to boost your health and balance. Don't be discouraged if you haven't participated in physical activities for a while. Boost Your Balance will serve as your guide, walking you through the best way to prepare for physical activity, safely perform exercises, and preserve the benefits of fitness for the long term. You will discover the 'do's and don'ts' of effective training and establish a firm foundation for a safe and challenging exercise routine. Finally, you will learn how to create and modify your exercise program as your fitness and balance improve over time.

Effective, consistent training improves balance and prevents falls and injuries. Additionally, fitness promotes better health, delays the aging process, and leads to an improved quality of life. The knowledge contained in this book will help unlock a fitter, more capable version of you, and I am excited to embark on this fitness journey together.

A note for fitness professionals:

If you are a fitness coach or someone who cares for older adults, you too may benefit from the information contained in this book. You will develop a deeper understanding of the aging process and its effects on balance. Further, you will find research-backed tools, such as our weekly fitness plan, designed to improve seniors' health and fitness. For additional resources, I invite you to visit our website at **www.BoostYourBalance.com**.

Why I wrote this book

Learning how to balance is a natural part of growing up. As toddlers and young children, we fall frequently. Gradually, our steps gain confidence, and by adolescence, we perfect our balance. For most adults, this mastery carries us through the next few decades of life. At later stages in life, we lose some of our balance skills due to the effects of aging and falls become more likely. Though falling in our youth helps us understand our capabilities and limitations, it can have disastrous consequences for older adults.

Imagine the following hypothetical scenario: Becky, a mother of two and grandmother of five, is in good health, active, and regarded as an independently-living senior citizen. Due to a combination of factors, including a more sedentary lifestyle, Becky's health begins to decline. Unbeknownst to Becky, a domino effect is slowly taking place. Becky's lack of physical activity results in additional health issues; she gains weight, her blood pressure increases, and her energy levels decrease, making activities increasingly difficult. In turn, Becky's physical activity continues to lessen, which further compounds the effects on her health.

Most significantly, Becky's balance and ability to multitask have become impaired. While walking, she can no longer hold a conversation, and friends and family note that she frequently "sways" while standing. To offset her reduced balance, Becky often holds a chair or uses a nearby wall for stability. After a series of falls, Becky gradually develops reluctance to going outside and doing the things she loves. She has become more hesitant to socialize with friends and family. As a result, Becky's mental and physical decline accelerates even further.

Regretfully, this scenario is all too common, but the outcome is entirely avoidable in many cases.

FACTS ABOUT FALLS

- Each year, about 30-60% of older adults experience a fall, and a significant number of those falls (10-20%) result in injury, hospitalization, and even death
- Many risk factors that are associated with falls can be addressed and ameliorated, e.g., by reducing fall-hazards around the home and committing to regular exercise programs

For decades, I have conducted and supported research related to human balance. This research has included studies involving healthy people, young and aged, and even individuals participating in voluntary bed rest to simulate the effects of spaceflight on the human body (and balance!). Many studies also involved patients suffering from illnesses (such as Parkinson's disease, diabetic neuropathy, and osteoarthritis) that affect balance and increase fall risk.

My professional experience has helped me gain a better understanding of how falls affect older individuals and their families, as well as how older individuals may most effectively prevent falls.

Decades of research have demonstrated what interventions serve to 'boost your balance,' and my hope is that the exercises suggestions that arose from such research will improve your life, as well as the lives of your loved ones. Finally, I wish to inspire you to stay active, not just in the short term, but for a lifetime of healthy aging.

How to use this book

Part I will teach you the basics of human postural control (which is a fancy way of saying "human balance"). These chapters cover the scientific foundations of balance and existing research on the effects of healthy (and unhealthy) aging. They will help you better understand the factors that influence your balance and why lifelong exercising is vital to healthy aging. This knowledge will enhance your use of the valuable tools shared later in this book.

If you prefer to skip that information, you may jump ahead to the exercise basics and the routine outlined in **Part II**.

In **Part II**, you will learn the fundamentals of exercise, the "Boost Your Balance" workout, and the many specific activities you can and should incorporate into your routine. We will combine the essential aspects of strength, balance, flexibility/mobility, and coordination to boost your general wellbeing and improve your balance. You will also find useful information for staying motivated and overcoming obstacles on your exercise journey.

PART
01

The basics of stability, aging, and balance interventions

What is balance, and how do we do it?

Balance is a broad term that plays a significant role in all our lives. Whether it's the importance of a 'balanced diet,' a healthy 'work-life balance,' or even a 'balanced checkbook,' we recognize the importance of living in harmony. In this book, we are keenly focused on balance related to standing, moving, and walking.

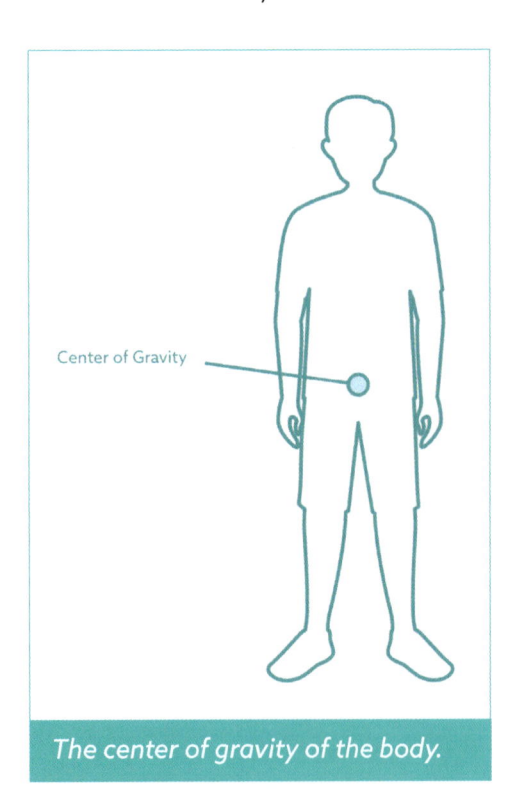

The center of gravity of the body.

We may generally define balance in standing humans as how an individual's mass is distributed so that he or she does not fall over. In more technical terms, balance is the "center of gravity" aligned over the "base of support." In the human body, the center of gravity is the point where all the forces acting on the body are equal to zero (the "balance point" or "equilibrium"). In a normal upright stance, that center is approximately in front of the sacrum bone (just above your lower back), and the base of support is found at the feet.

As you walk, bend over, or perform other movements, your center of gravity shifts. This shift occurs in concert with your orientation and the type of motion being performed. When your center of gravity moves beyond your base of support (as determined by your feet and stance), you become unbalanced.

> "Human stability is the ability to maintain, achieve. or restore a specific state of balance and not to fall."[1]

Fortunately, the human body is exceptional at maintaining composure. It will instinctively compensate to sustain an upright position. For example, imagine a person standing on one leg. They will activate numerous muscles in the legs, trunk, neck, and back. They may bend their upper body or naturally sway their arms to stay balanced. In more technical terms, this individual is counteracting shifts in their center of gravity by altering their position and orientation.

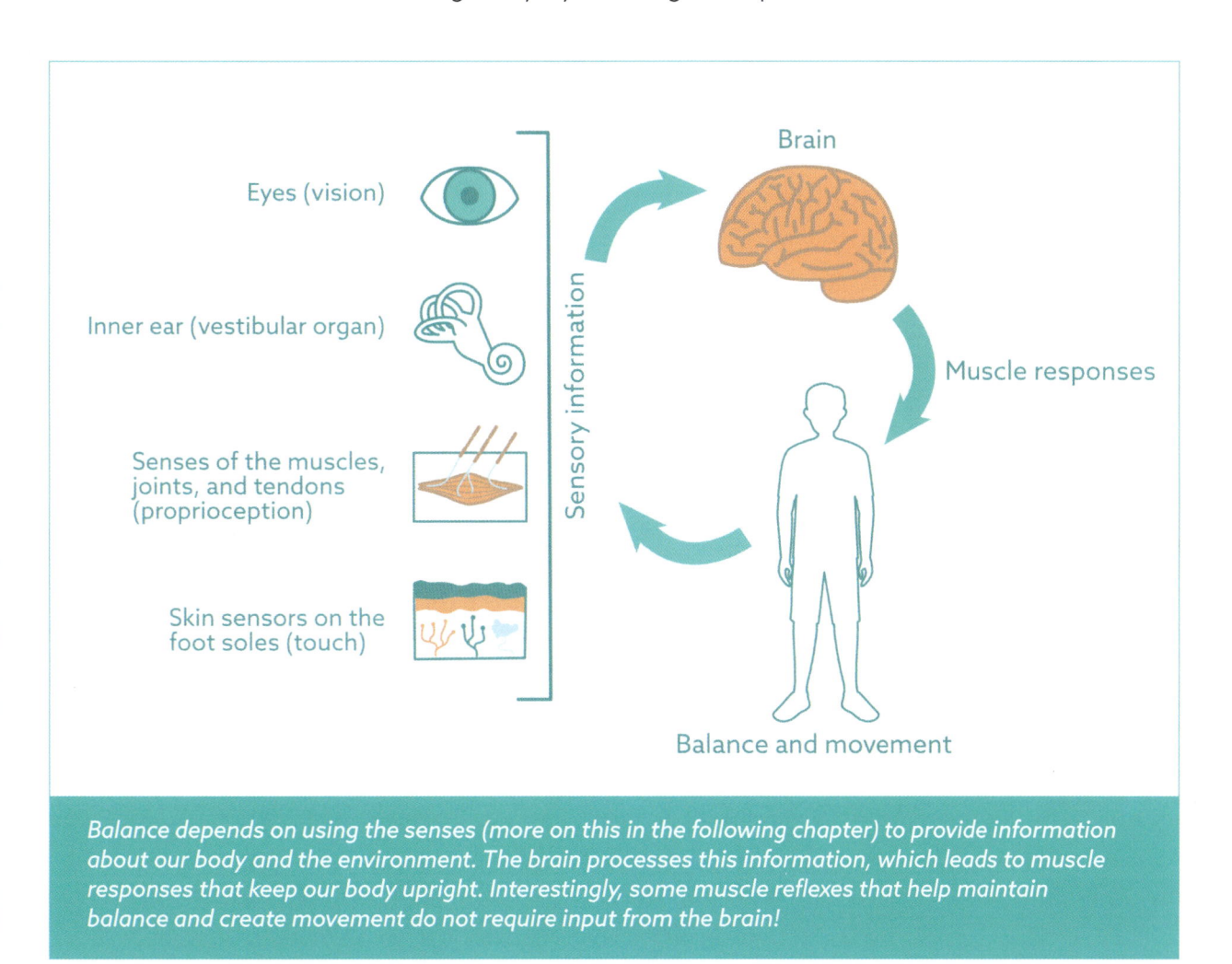

- Eyes (vision)
- Inner ear (vestibular organ)
- Senses of the muscles, joints, and tendons (proprioception)
- Skin sensors on the foot soles (touch)

Sensory information → Brain → Muscle responses → Balance and movement

Balance depends on using the senses (more on this in the following chapter) to provide information about our body and the environment. The brain processes this information, which leads to muscle responses that keep our body upright. Interestingly, some muscle reflexes that help maintain balance and create movement do not require input from the brain!

The process of balancing is essential for more static activities like standing, but also for dynamic activities, such as walking. Walking is one of our most common actions (for some more, some less) and is the basis for many other motions that challenge our ability to balance (e.g., direction changes and maneuvering around an obstacle).

THE BASICS OF STABILITY, AGING, AND BALANCE INTERVENTIONS

The many **individual** factors determining balance and balance performance include age, gender, and strength. Our balance also depends on the **environment** in which we perform a task[2] (e.g., an uneven terrain) and the challenges a balance **task** poses.

Tasks fall into one of three categories: steady-state, reactive, and proactive. Steady-state tasks involve static balancing (think standing in line while waiting at the grocery store) and dynamic balancing, such as in walking. Reactive tasks involve actively responding to a balance challenge, such as standing on a surface that suddenly shifts (e.g., walking on a rug that suddenly slips) or stepping onto a slippery surface. Finally, proactive tasks involve preemptive balance shifts made in anticipation of an action, such as adjusting the posture before reaching out to grasp a distant object. The interplay of all these factors and challenges determines balance and also the risk of falls. Why are falls and their prevention so important? Let's take a look at the significant individual and collective costs caused by falls.

The high cost of falls

Data collected by the National Council of Aging helps demonstrate the potentially severe consequences of falling:

- Falls are the leading cause of fatal injury and the most common cause of nonfatal trauma-related hospital admissions among older adults.

- Falls account for 2.8 million visits to the emergency room each year, including over 800,000 hospitalizations and over 27,000 deaths.

- The total cost of fall injuries was $50 billion in 2015, and this staggering expense is expected to exceed $67.7 billion in 2020.

When an older person falls, the consequences are often devastating. Hospitalization and subsequent health complications (e.g., infections, pneumonia) may lead to a loss of independence and sometimes death. Further, if an older adult has fallen more than once, they may start changing their behaviors out of fear, limiting their physical activity and social interactions. Unfortunately, this can exasperate the individual's recovery and lead to further physical decline, in addition to psychological and psychosocial issues, such as depression and social isolation.

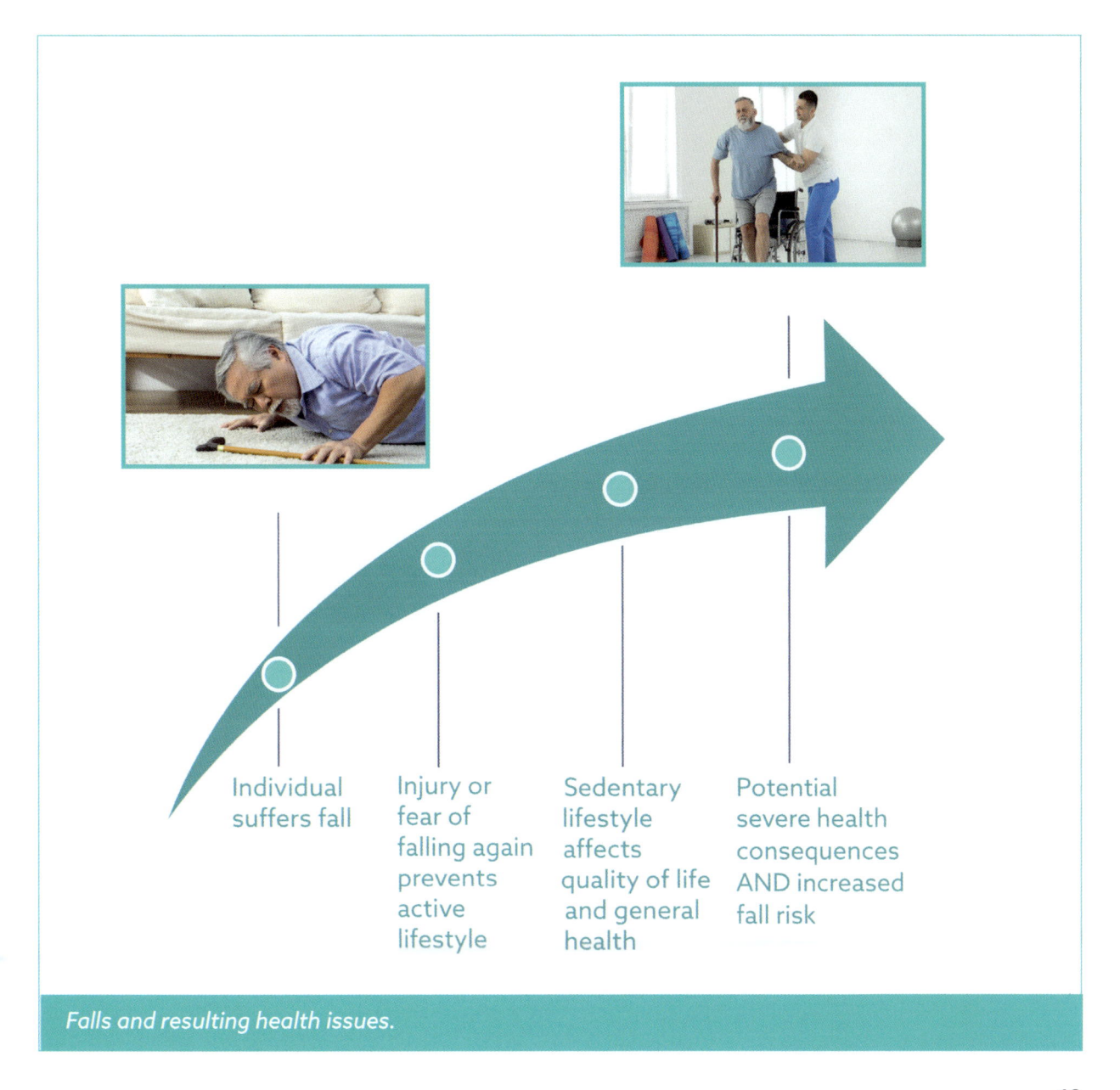

Individual suffers fall | Injury or fear of falling again prevents active lifestyle | Sedentary lifestyle affects quality of life and general health | Potential severe health consequences AND increased fall risk

Falls and resulting health issues.

THE BASICS OF STABILITY, AGING, AND BALANCE INTERVENTIONS

Unfortunately, falls among seniors represent the leading cause of traumatic death[3] and cause enormous costs for short and long-term patient care. These costs put a considerable burden on individuals and their families in the form of treatment costs and higher insurance premiums and on the healthcare system as a whole (e.g., Medicare). Older adults make up a growing percentage of the total population in the U.S. and most other Western countries. So the improvements of senior health, the maintenance of their independence, and prevention of falls have become major concerns of the U.S. health care system. Thanks to extended research efforts in the last decades, we better understand the risk factors associated with falls. In the following chapters, we will discuss the effects of aging on balance and fall risk over the lifespan.

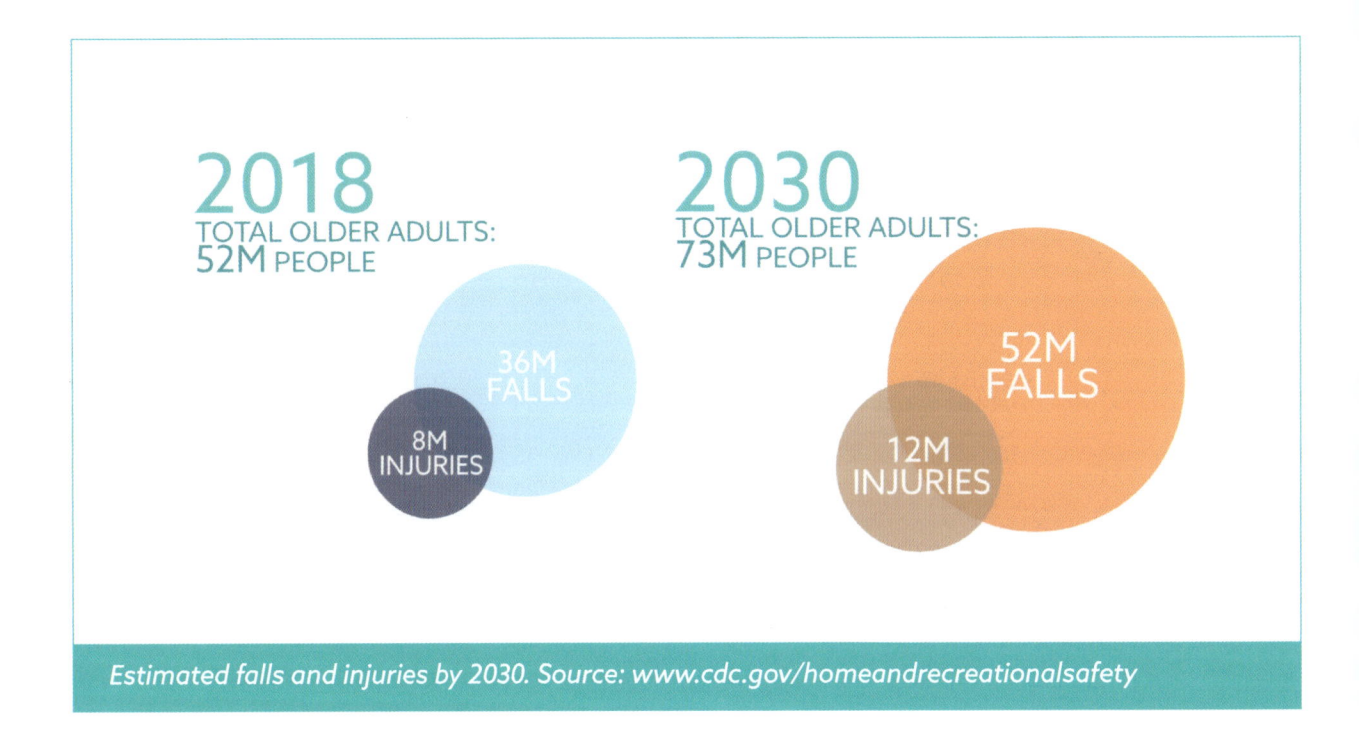

2018
TOTAL OLDER ADULTS: 52M PEOPLE
36M FALLS
8M INJURIES

2030
TOTAL OLDER ADULTS: 73M PEOPLE
52M FALLS
12M INJURIES

Estimated falls and injuries by 2030. Source: www.cdc.gov/homeandrecreationalsafety

Decreased balance and fall risk factors

As we age, our balance and control are naturally affected, and we experience multiple changes in the anatomy and physiology of the human body[4-6]. For example, at about forty years of age, the body's sensory and motor functions decline. These developments are accompanied by a loss of fine movement control, reaction time, and even muscle strength[7].

> **A fall is defined as "an unexpected event in which the participant comes to rest on the ground, floor, or lower level, as a result of a loss of balance)"[8]**

Aging affects us in many ways[9], and such factors are considered 'intrinsic' factors", as 'within' the individual. Examples of intrinsic factors that may pose problems for balance include (i) advanced age, (ii) an existing history of falls (being prone, to falls), (iii) gender (women are at a statistically higher risk of falls), (iv) use of certain medications, (v) loss of sensory function (touch, hearing, vision), and (vi) the existence of chronic illnesses. Many stroke patients, Parkinson's disease patients, and patients dealing with cognitive impairments are also at a higher risk of losing balance.

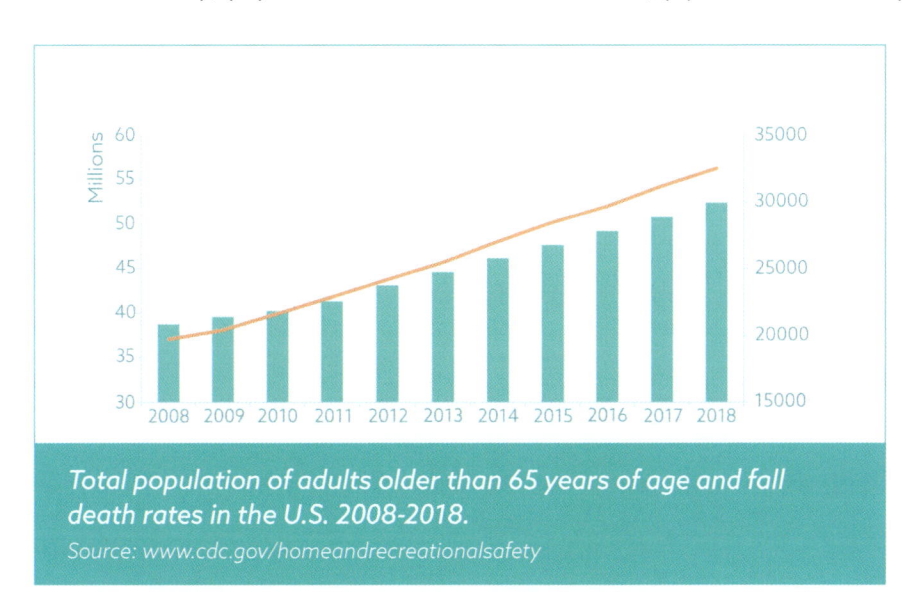

Total population of adults older than 65 years of age and fall death rates in the U.S. 2008-2018.
Source: www.cdc.gov/homeandrecreationalsafety

Ever stand up too quickly and feel lightheaded? That's another intrinsic factor to consider! A sudden drop in blood pressure and associated dizziness may also affect balance, such as when we stand up from a chair too quickly. This phenomenon is called "orthostatic hypotension," and it is especially prevalent in older adults.

BALANCE

- Maintaining vertical alignment when standing
- Maneuvering the environment safely when walking
- Preparing for or reacting to balance challenges adequately

Consider your intrinsic factors and how they may affect your daily life

Our environment may cause balance challenges and increase the risk of falls as well. Such environmental factors are referred to as 'extrinsic factors.' They include obstacles in our way (perhaps a rug that catches our step), a slippery floor, and poor lighting conditions.

In the following chapters, we will take a closer look at the intrinsic and extrinsic factors and what we can do to positively influence them.

> When do falls happen? Often during routine daily activities such as standing, walking, and transitioning, for example, when getting up from a chair too quickly.

We will discuss the negative effects of aging on the body's different systems and balance. But don't get discouraged! We also know effective ways of counteracting this decline. This book will teach you the many ways to improve balance effectively and to reverse aging effects.

Aging and muscle strength

Muscle strength describes your maximum strength and ability to create "explosive" power. It is a good predictor of mobility (the ability to actively move through the full range of motion of a joint) and function (how well you can perform movements) during daily activities.

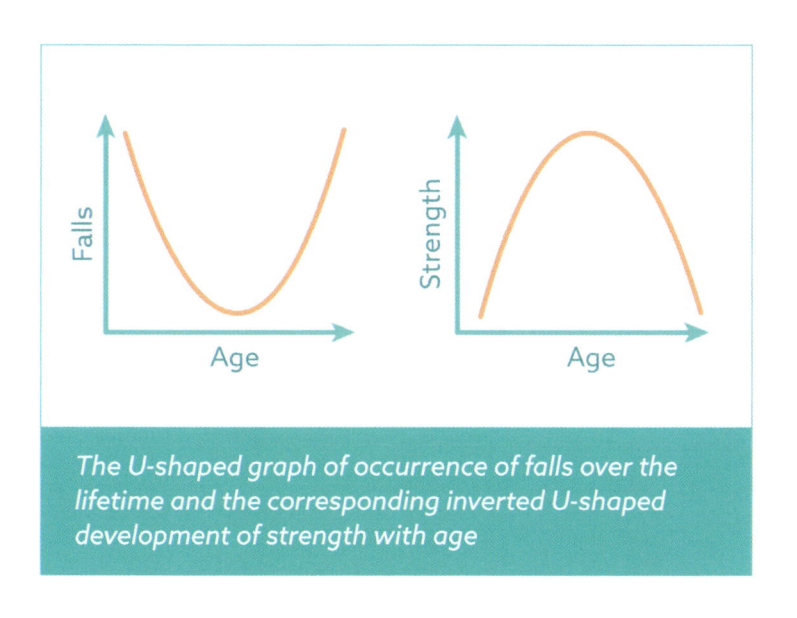

The U-shaped graph of occurrence of falls over the lifetime and the corresponding inverted U-shaped development of strength with age

Why do we lose strength as we get older? The most well-known aspect of strength loss is the reduction of muscle fiber size and quantity in older adults (called 'Sarcopenia'). Individuals suffering from Sarcopenia are more likely to have a diminished ability to balance, which results in an increased likelihood of falls and injury. If a balance threat occurs (e.g., tripping over an uneven pavement), such individuals may not be able to create a sufficiently quick and powerful muscle response to "catch" themselves and stay upright.

Sarcopenia is not the only reason for strength loss. The observed changes over a lifetime also depend on the complex interactions between the brain's planning systems and our muscles' ability to initiate activity. In other words, how well our brains can transmit signals to our muscles and, in turn, how ably our muscles respond[10].

THE BASICS OF STABILITY, AGING, AND BALANCE INTERVENTIONS

Aging of the senses

Sight, smell, hearing, touch, and taste - almost everyone is familiar with the five senses. Without them, we would lose our ability to perceive and understand the world. As you may have guessed, our balance is dependent on such vital systems as well.

As aging causes a decline in the sensory systems, slowing and even reversing this decline depends on understanding how our senses (and age) affect our balance performance.

Vision – Aging and our eyes

We primarily navigate our environment through vision. Our eyes perceive signals from our surroundings, and our visual cortex in the brain processes that information. Our visual performance declines through healthy aging or through illnesses that may affect eyesight (like hypertension and diabetes). This decline may impair our ability to assess our position in space accurately[7,11], and impairment often extends to balance performance, which is heavily influenced by vision[12].

The vestibular system – Aging and our inner ear sensors

Tiny sensory receptors in our inner ear as part of the vestibular system also play a significant role in our ability to maintain balance. In practical terms, when we look up, downwards, or sideways, fluid in our inner ear shifts within the different chambers and tracts of the organ. Small hair cell sensors detect such changes, and the brain uses that information to determine our orientation in space and even our motion. This information is critical to our body's ability to maintain balance and equilibrium. Patients with known vestibular issues often exhibit severe loss of postural balance control[13,14], as do many older adults.

> **QUICK FACTS**
>
> - **Vision:** our eyes provide information about us and our environment
>
> - **Vestibular System:** our inner ear indicates acceleration and orientation in space.
>
> - **Somatosensation:** sensory receptors of the skin, joints, muscles, and tendons provide information about position and movement of body parts in space and in relation to each other

However, some individuals with long-term vestibular impairments do not show significant balance loss. How can this be? Our bodies have a remarkable ability to adapt. The human body's central nervous system counteracts deficiencies in our senses by shifting reliance towards other sensory sources of the body - just as vision-impaired individuals often show elevated sensitivity to sound.

Senses of the muscles, the joints, the tendons, and the skin

If I ask you to touch your nose while your eyes are closed, you'd likely be successful on the first try. Sensors in our joints, muscles, and tendons help discern our extremities' position and how they move in relation to each other. The abilities of this remarkable sensory system are referred to as "Proprioception." Without it, we wouldn't be able to reach for an object without looking, eat without watching our hands, or even walk without staring at our feet. Proprioception is particularly important when other senses are not fully "available," for example when a dark environment diminishes vision.

Proprioception is part of the so-called somatosensory system that includes many sensors of the body that are vital for function. For balance, the foot's specific pressure sensors provide information about how we are swaying while standing. The foot sole sensors (called mechanoreceptors) are essential for good balance. A decline of the foot sole's sensitivity due to aging or chronic illness such as diabetes is a major predictor of falls in older adults[15,16].

Vision

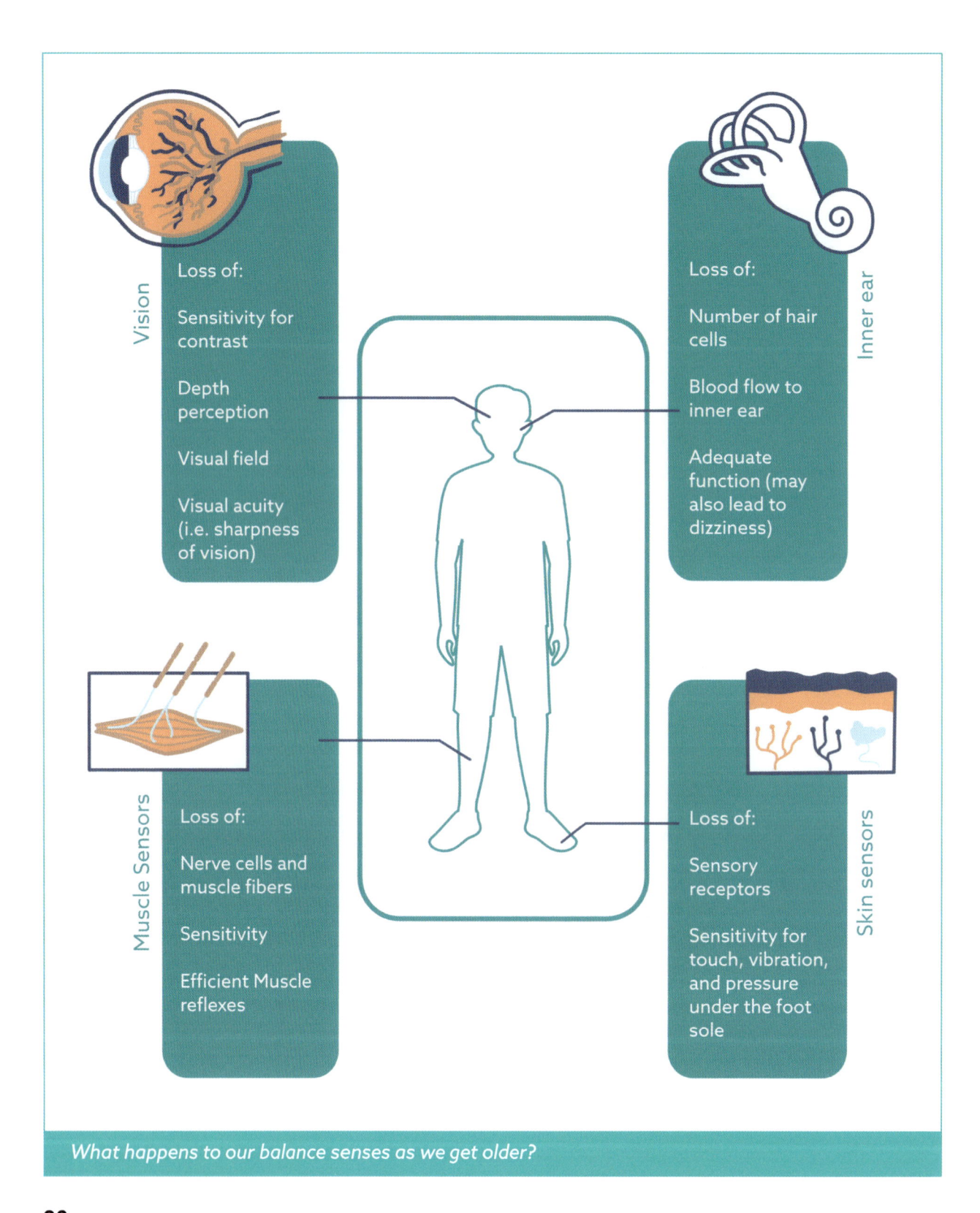

Loss of:

Sensitivity for contrast

Depth perception

Visual field

Visual acuity (i.e. sharpness of vision)

Inner ear

Loss of:

Number of hair cells

Blood flow to inner ear

Adequate function (may also lead to dizziness)

Muscle Sensors

Loss of:

Nerve cells and muscle fibers

Sensitivity

Efficient Muscle reflexes

Skin sensors

Loss of:

Sensory receptors

Sensitivity for touch, vibration, and pressure under the foot sole

What happens to our balance senses as we get older?

Aging and brain function

Balancing while standing and walking not only requires the muscles and sensors of the body to work in harmony - it also requires proper brain function. This scientific understanding is relatively novel. In the past, many people believed that walking was primarily an automatic task that you could always perform without conscious thought. Research has since indicated that our brain, as part of the central nervous system, is continuously working on planning, controlling, and modifying each step. This miraculous process is mostly done in the background, without conscious thought. However, some balance tasks need more "brainpower" and attention.

> People who have problems "walking and talking" often are more dependent in activities of daily living, and may be more prone to falls.

Multitasking

Doing two things simultaneously is commonly called "multitasking" (or "dual-tasking"), which may or may not be challenging, depending on the tasks involved. Think of a combination of a mental task, such as counting from one to ten, with a motor task, such as standing in place. That may sound easy to most individuals, but multitasking may present real challenges. Try multiplying 120 times 15, and now imagine performing that calculation while standing on one leg. Obviously, this task has become significantly more difficult! Even if an individual can independently perform either the mental or physical task with relative ease, combining these tasks often results in decreased performance in both.

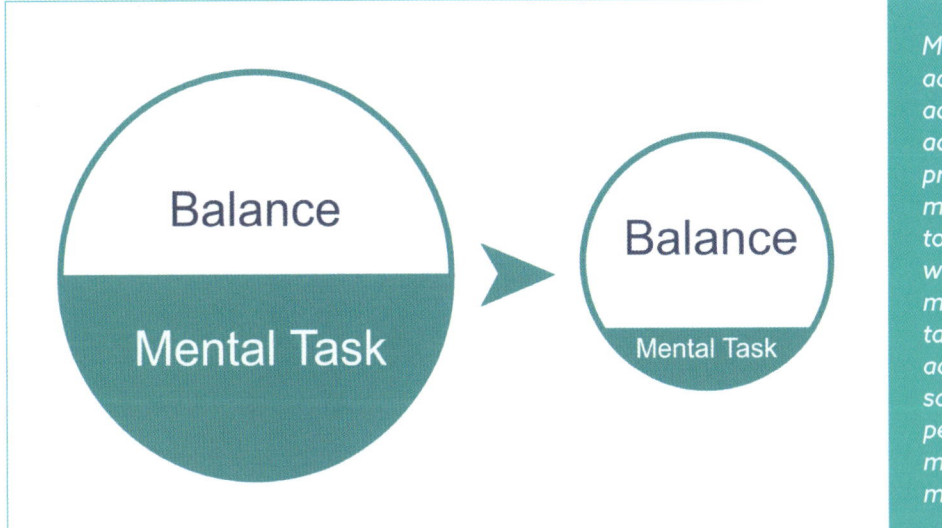

Multitasking in younger adults (left) and older adults (right): younger adults have more processing capacity and may be better equipped to concurrently balance while performing a mentally challenging task, whereas older adults may have to sacrifice cognitive performance to put more attention towards maintaining balance.

In the previous example, both tasks (balancing and calculating) compete for attention and "brainpower." When you put more attention on one task, less mental processing capacity is available for the other. Attention is a limited resource, and this resource is taxed when you have to process large amounts of information simultaneously.

Younger adults have fewer problems performing such tasks, as they have more "resources" in terms of cognition and movement control. Older adults often struggle more in such situations due to a decline in cognitive capacity and the increased effort balancing requires from seniors.

Aging and preparing for balance challenges

We instinctively employ strategies to maintain optimal balance while moving. Imagine standing still with your hands hanging by your side. If you suddenly raise your arm, your body shifts slightly, and you subconsciously flex your leg and trunk muscles - you are anticipating a slight disturbance in your balance. This preparation even happens before you actually raise your arm!

This preparation also occurs in response to external balance challenges. For example, you are bracing and adjusting before stepping on a floor expected to be slippery. Such active preparation responses help us maintain equilibrium through the range of our daily activities. With aging, preparatory adjustments to external stimuli and balance challenges become less efficient[17]. As a result, the risk of falling increases, and our muscles have to work even harder to maintain balance.

Aging and reacting to balance challenges

A balance challenge refers to an external or internal force that *challenges* our ability to remain balanced. We apply multiple strategies to address balance challenges.

We use an "ankle strategy" when we stand on firm ground or experience only a minor disruption in balance. While employing the ankle strategy, the human body acts like an inverted pendulum anchored by the feet – with sway occurring about the ankles. We control this by flexing muscles around the ankle, a process that relies on sensory feedback.

More considerable balance challenges may require a "hip strategy," in which we generate most muscle activity around the hip region and the trunk. In these instances, the ankles stay more rigid. This "stiffening" of the lower legs is produced by contracting various lower leg muscles.

If a balance challenge becomes too significant for either strategy, our body's last resort is to regain balance by taking a step in the direction of the potential fall. This response may work well for younger individuals, but the decline in reflexes, mobility, and leg strength associated with aging often makes this strategy ineffective for older adults.

We use an ankle strategy mostly for quiet stance under normal conditions. We employ a hip strategy when facing more difficult balance tasks (standing on an unstable surface). A stepping strategy becomes necessary when the other two strategies are not enough to maintain balance. To make a stepping strategy successful to prevent falls, muscle strength and adequate, quick responses are required.

SUMMARY

Decades of research have helped us understand how humans master balance and how aging may result in a decline of function. But humans have a remarkable capacity for "rewiring" the brain and physically adapting to training. This is where things become exciting: **in the next chapter, we will look at the methods known to improve balance and help prevent loss of balance in older adults**.

Better Balance – what factors can we influence?

Extrinsic factors – environment.

Earlier, we discussed the influence of both external and extrinsic factors on our balance. After identifying environmental risks, most notably in the home, you can take steps to reduce the potential hazards. While you should discuss home or office hazards with an occupational therapy practitioner, it is still an excellent idea to regularly evaluate your environment. Consider the following questions:

- Are there slippery floors?
- Are there secure hand railings?
- Do your chairs have armrests that you can use to get up safely?
- Is there appropriate lighting, especially at night?
- Are there uneven surfaces?
- Is there any clutter on the floor that could present a tripping hazard?
- Are there non-slip mats in the bathroom, shower, and bathtub?
- Are there shelves or cabinets that you need to get to sometimes and which are difficult to reach?
- Are there rugs that don't lie flat or have elevated/curled edges?
- Are there slip or trip hazards in the house's entrance area
- How does the ground around your home react when wet? Do certain steps or pathways become especially slippery?

Remember, the importance of ensuring a safe environment does not only apply to frail or less able adults. The American Geriatrics Society (AGS) clinical guidelines indicate that modifying the home environment is one of the most effective strategies to minimize risk.

> **Evaluating and changing your home environment helps prevent falls, and it is strongly recommended to improve health outcomes.**

Intrinsic factors – Factors within ourselves

Some intrinsic risk factors, such as age, gender, and history of previous falls, can't be directly changed. Nevertheless, it is crucial to identify and understand these risks. In this way, you can address proximate factors, such as your strength, which may help offset a persistent risk factor. The following section highlights the value of exercise to counteract intrinsic risk factors.

Training to improve balance - what really works

<u>Exercise is a great – if not the best – thing you can do for yourself</u>. A routine of effective exercises can help you move with confidence and prevent injuries and chronic diseases. Regular physical activity also improves energy levels and overall mood. Even if you haven't exercised recently, you too will benefit from incorporating such activities!

We've talked about the different balance components and how getting older affects the body's various systems required for balance. But what can we do to counteract the decline of our balance over the years? With exercise, we can delay or slow down some of the most common effects of aging, and in some instances, even reverse them. This includes counteracting a loss of balance due to a decline in senses, strength, and cognitive performance.

> "To date, physical exercise is the only intervention consistently demonstrated to attenuate functional decline among seniors"[18].

There is a vast amount of research related to the relationship between exercise and improved balance among older adults. A 2019 study found that a well-balanced exercise regimen, including functional exercises (exercises that resemble activities of daily living) and strength, can decrease the risk of falls by 34%[19]. In the next section, we will look at the specific exercise types beneficial for individuals seeking to boost their balance performance. Research suggests a combination of aerobic exercise (e.g., cycling, running, or swimming) with other exercise modes to maximize fall prevention[20]. The many positive health effects of aerobic exercise are well-known, and such exercise also helps lower your risk of falling[21].

The best intervention to boost your balance? Exercise!

Balance training

This type of exercise includes challenges to the body's balance. Balance training exercises aim to expose the senses and the body's neuromuscular system to challenges that resemble real-life situations. Extensive research has shown that balance training exercises are one of the best ways to improve performance. As a result, the number of falls may be significantly reduced by physical activity that combines balance and functional exercises[22].

Strength training

Strength training has many benefits for healthy aging, including managing weight, lowering the risk of osteoporosis, and decreasing osteoarthritis symptoms. Maintaining muscle strength is also a critical component of preventing motor function decline[23]. Strength training helps your balance as well, especially when combining it with other training types[24].

In addition to leg and hip exercises, core muscle (e.g., abdominal muscles) activities are especially beneficial. Improved spinal mobility and a more stable core allow for more efficient handling of forces and torque arising at the lower and upper extremities. In other words, it helps give you the strength to "stiffen" your core when needed, such as when bracing for expected balance challenges[25].

Power training

Improving power (the ability to generate quick and forceful contractions, such as in jumping) is essential for older adults[26]. Increased power benefits balance performance and plays a significant role in recovery from stumbles, trips, and other balance disruptions. Power training exercises such as quick squats are high-impact and intense. You should perform these activities under professional supervision and after discussing such training with your physician. The "Boost Your Balance" workout program does not contain this particular type of exercise.

MORE BENEFITS OF EXERCISE

- **Faster reaction time:** Improvement of neuromuscular function helps prevent falls

- **More muscle mass:** Stronger and larger muscles can buffer the impact of a fall, providing some protection to bones and joints

- **Stronger bones** that are more resistant to fractures

- **Better brain function** helps you avoid situations that increase fall risk and helps manage balance better

Complex '3D' exercises

Studies have shown the beneficial effects of complex exercises (sometimes called '3D exercises,' since they include movements in all three dimensions). Dancing, yoga, or tai-chi (an ancient, low-impact style of movement practice that focuses on weight transfer, relaxation, and body positioning) may reduce the risk of falls significantly[27-29]. Some motions practiced in these exercises mirror the actions we perform in our daily activities, thereby *transferring* to our real-life habits. These balance training activities also stimulate the sensors in our muscles responsible for indicating joint position and movement[10].

BETTER BALANCE MEANS:
- Better mobility
- Better function/performance
- Better coordination
- Better reactions
- Better agility
- Fewer injuries

Flexibility

While flexibility training alone may not promote better balance, it is worth incorporating into your exercise regimen. This is mainly due to the known health benefits and potential injury prevention associated with increasing flexibility, increasing mobility, and developing a better "feel" for your body's capabilities. Some experts have suggested that flexibility exercises (that are more static and don't include much movement) may be most valuable when combining them with more dynamic activities (that include more movement). Many flexibility exercises provided in this book involve dynamic balancing and strengthening components.

Multitask training

Multitasking exercises can be beneficial for balance[30]. Such activities combine different movements and cognitive challenges (e.g., walking while counting backward by 7s from 800) or multiple motor tasks (e.g., tossing and catching a ball while balancing on one leg). These exercises also simulate real-life situations, such as navigating through a crowd or walking while talking.

PART
02

Boost Your Balance – a unique workout program to promote healthy aging and better balance

In the following chapters, we will focus on exercise types, applying training principles, exercising safely, and measuring progress. We will also discuss common exercise terminology. After reading these next chapters, you'll be ready to get going and to boost your balance!

How should you exercise? Basics of a well-rounded training regimen

The exercises in this book are specifically designed to improve your overall balance, flexibility, strength, coordination, and efficiency in reacting to balance challenges. Improvement in these areas will not only enhance your balance but also boost your general fitness levels. As with any exercise program, you will achieve your goals if (i) the training is specific to your personal needs and (ii) if you adhere to certain exercise principles.

Challenge Yourself: The Progression Principle

When performing any exercise, it is critical that you feel challenged. You should continue to test and improve upon your capabilities. That said, there is no need to push yourself to the point of exhaustion. If the exercise becomes too easy, simply modify it!

This suggestion brings us to the Progression Principle: once you can perform an exercise with confidence and in a stable manner, <u>only then</u> should you increase difficulty and workload.

Different foot positions increase difficulty and help make balance exercises more challenging.

Normal Stance

Semi-Tandem Stance

Tandem Stance

As an example, you could increase the number of repetitions you perform during strength exercises over time. For balance exercises, this could mean performing a particular exercise with a varied stance, without using support for balance, or with the eyes closed. Use a yoga/exercise mat - you could perform balance exercises on that mat instead of "solid" ground once you are comfortable. The great thing about a mat is that you can also fold it over to make it twice as thick, which means a softer surface to stand on and more challenging conditions. How would that progression look in practice? Imagine feeling comfortable with standing on one leg on a stable floor. Next, you could take it a little further by trying the same exercise on an exercise mat. After practicing for a while and feeling safe to do so (always remember you should use support like holding on to a chair or desk if necessary), you could take it up a notch and balance on a thicker and softer mat.

> **KEY ELEMENTS FOR PROGRESSION IN BALANCE TRAINING**
>
> - Reduce assistance (e.g., not holding on to chair for balance)
> - Decrease support (e.g., standing on one leg or unstable surface like an exercise mat)

How long, how often, how many?

Exercise professionals use clear and concise descriptions of the exercise parameters that should unambiguously tell you *what* to do and *how* to perform the workout at hand. Let's dive into terminology:

> **The "FITT" Principle**
>
> Exercise prescriptions can be described by **F**requency, **I**ntensity, **T**ime, and **T**ype

- Exercise **Frequency**: *how many times* (usually per week) you should workout.

- Exercise **Intensity** describes *at what level of effort* you should train. This determination of effort level is an important factor regarding the goals you seek to achieve.

- Exercise **Time** describes either (i) the *volume* of your exercise session (e.g., how many exercises and repetitions in total) or (ii) how long your exercise session should last.

- Exercise **Type** describes *what kind of activity* you perform. Some examples include flexibility exercises, such as yoga, strength exercises, balance exercises, or even a combination of various exercises.

The workout program in this book combines elements of frequency, intensity, time, and type based on recommendations from multiple institutions and organizations, including The American College of Sports Medicine (ACSM)[21].

Exercise parameters for training

To optimize the Boost your Balance training benefits, you should strive to exercise three times per week for about 35-45 minutes per session (including warm-up and cool-down). For optimal recovery, you should rest for 48 hours between the Boost your Balance training sessions. In other words, try to avoid exercising on consecutive days, as this may not give you enough recovery time and work against your progress.

Exercises either include maintaining a position for a certain amount of time (e.g., "balance on one leg for 20 seconds") or repetitions (e.g., "perform ten squats"). One round of repetitions is called a "set," and individual sets are separated by a brief period of rest. The duration of rest or breaks between sets depends on the nature of the exercise and how hard it is; more challenging activities may require longer rests.

Suppose an exercise description says "10 repetitions of 3 sets, with 2-minute breaks." In that case, you should perform ten repetitions and take a break of two minutes. After that, perform another ten repetitions and take another break. Then, perform a third and last set of ten repetitions.

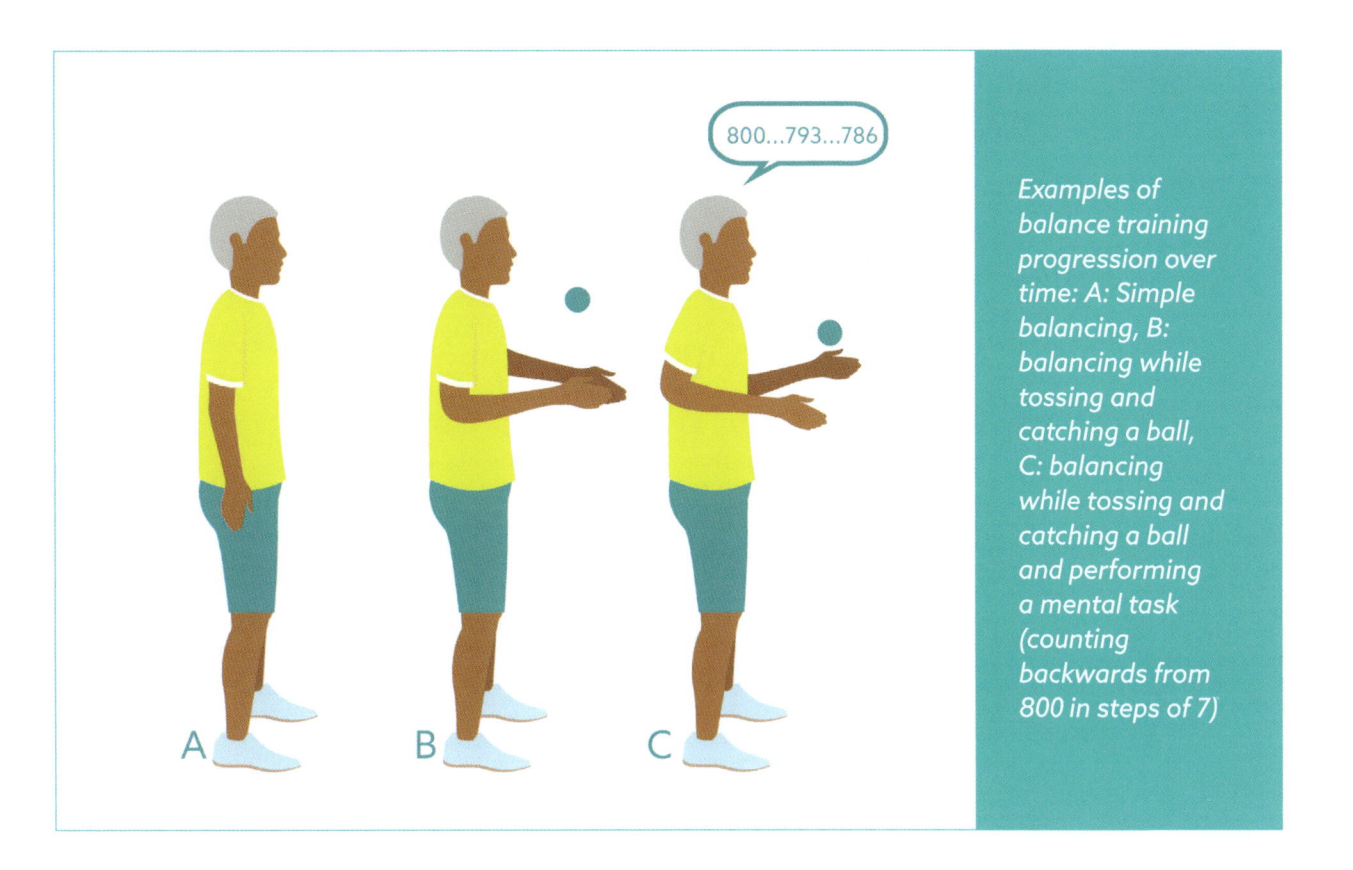

Examples of balance training progression over time: A: Simple balancing, B: balancing while tossing and catching a ball, C: balancing while tossing and catching a ball and performing a mental task (counting backwards from 800 in steps of 7)

To ensure safe, steady progress related to strength exercises, we will adhere to a "repetitions first, load later" approach. That means, if you feel comfortable performing an exercise for ten repetitions (e.g., have the feeling you could do more than ten repetitions without too much effort) and get the sense it becomes easy, do not rush to increasing weight (also referred to as load). Instead, first increase the number of repetitions, e.g., from 12 to 15 repetitions. Once you have successfully increased your number of repetitions, it should be safe to increase the load (for example, by adding light dumbbells to squat exercises).

GENERAL EXERCISE PRINCIPLES

Individuality

No two people are the same. Genetics, age, and prior exercise experience require that training routines be tailored to each person.

Specificity

Task-specific exercises that closely resemble activities of daily living are often best suited to improve the performance of such activities (e.g., walking under challenging conditions).

Progression

Over time, the exercise regimen should progress towards higher complexity, demand, and difficulty. This concept is crucial for continued success and motivation!

Overload

The human body is a master of adaptation, and your progress will likely surprise and excite you. In physical training, you accomplish adaptation by "overload." To achieve this, ensure that your training involves a higher than usual demand on your body.

Recovery

Recovery is essential; the human body can only improve when enough rest is provided. A common saying in the athletic world is "your muscles don't grow during the workout, but between workouts." Sufficient rest and sleep are just as important as the workout itself.

Consistency

The only way to preserve your progress and improvements is to make exercise a long-term habit. Strength, balance performance, and all other positive effects of physical activity are not "for keeps." **Consistency and lifelong physical activity are the keys to better health!**

Safety and equipment

As mentioned at the beginning of this book, it is important to consult with your doctor before performing any suggested exercises. Remember, if any health issues put you at an increased injury risk, the preventive activities presented in the following chapters may not be appropriate for you.

Tips for safe exercise:

TOOLS OF THE TRADE

- An exercise mat is excellent when performing exercises sitting or lying down. A mat is also beneficial for some balance exercises since its softness makes balancing more difficult

- Your footwear should provide stability. Shoes should be slip-proof and suitable for where you are performing your exercise. If you are comfortable with going barefoot (and without socks), that is also a great alternative. Remember, a major factor for preventing falls is what you have (or don't have) on your feet!

- Make sure there is a chair, counter, or desk nearby to hold onto for added stability. When appropriate, the exercise description will help you use these aids effectively. We will also cover when it may be beneficial to stand close to a wall so that you may lean on it for support.

PUT FORM FIRST

- Proper exercise form enhances the effectiveness and safety of the exercise. If you feel like you are getting too tired to finish an exercise using good form, take a break.

- Breathe normally during the exercises and never hold your breath.

FALL FACTS

- One in four Americans falls each year.

- Every 11 seconds, an older adult is treated in the emergency room for a fall.

- Many risk factors are identifiable (e.g., weakness, cognitive impairment, psychoactive medications).

- Detecting and managing risk factors can significantly reduce the rate of future falls.

- For flexibility exercises, use gentle, slow stretches – no ballistic stretching (bouncing into the stretch).

- Stop any time you feel shortness of breath, dizziness, or any other feeling of being unwell: challenging yourself does not mean overdoing it!

CLEAR THE WAY

- Prepare your exercise area before each session. Whether you are working out in the home, the backyard, or at your local gym, keep an eye out for potential hazards that may lead to injury. Pay special attention to items on the floor that may catch your foot while in motion. A good rule of thumb is to have a clear space of about six feet in every direction from where you are standing.

BOOST YOUR BALANCE

Track your progress

Just as tracking your spending is an important part of maintaining financial wellbeing, tracking your physical activity will ensure that each session moves you closer to your fitness goals. In practical terms, logging your exercises will help you visualize your progress and areas of improvement. This book suggests logging the following items after each workout session:

1. the date;

2. exercises performed;

3. number of repetitions or duration of the exercise; and

4. notes, for example, how it felt (e.g., stretch felt great in the lower back) or how you modified the activity (e.g., performed the exercise on a mat instead of on a hard surface).

Writing down what you did and how it felt will help to stay focused and motivated. Feel free to include personal goals that you can look back to, such as "I want to increase my number of squats from ten to twelve."

Use copies of the log on the next page or
the website's exercise log template:
www.BoostYourBalance.com/ExerciseLog

BOOST YOUR BALANCE EXERCISE LOG

Date:

Name of Exercise	Number of sets	Number of repetitions (or duration in seconds)	Notes (e.g., weight felt light, grasped chair, etc.)

Date:

Name of Exercise	Number of sets	Number of repetitions (or duration in seconds)	Notes (e.g., weight felt light, grasped chair, etc.)

Warm-up and Cool-down

Warming-up raises your body temperature, increases blood flow to your muscles, and primes the cardiovascular system for exercise. Warming up is also essential for joint health, quicker recovery, and injury prevention.

You should perform about five to ten minutes of warm-up before starting the main part of your exercise session. In the exercise section, you will find some exercises to add to your warm-up routine. If you are working out at home and do not have access to exercise equipment (such as a stationary bike), you can even warm-up by marching in place. While warming up, aim for an intensity/speed that allows you to speak without getting out of breath.

The workout plan includes a few exercises at the beginning of each session designed for specific additional warm-up, mainly mobility work and gentle stretches.

After finishing your workout, it is time to slow down the heart rate and prepare for rest: the "**cool-down**." When done properly, cooling down after a workout brings the heart rate and blood pressure back to pre-exercise levels. You should cool-down for about five to ten minutes after you exercise. Once again, you can do some light jogging, use an exercise device (e.g., a treadmill), or march in place.

The Balance program

The Boost your Balance program covers many types of physical activity that are beneficial for healthy aging. In this chapter, we will look at an initial four-week schedule for you to follow, a plan which you can modify based on your preferences and abilities. In a perfect world, you'll be doing the Boost your Balance workout three times a week for about 35-45 minutes. But there may be times when you have other commitments, or you can't get yourself to exercise. Please don't get frustrated by such days; it is essential to develop an exercise habit, but it is okay to skip a session from time to time. It is also okay to sometimes skip some exercises to save time.

In such situations, you may do a short session that doesn't require much warm-up and cool-down or even athletic apparel (you could choose some flexibility or balance exercises you enjoy from the library). Any activity is better than no activity – you should feel good about it. **It is better to do a little bit - but consistently - instead of starting at a high level and then stopping altogether shortly after**.

You may also incorporate some exercises into your daily habits and chores. For example, if you did not exercise according to plan, you can include some balancing on one leg while you brush your teeth or do the dishes.

You should enjoy the proposed activities. Otherwise, you will have a hard time staying motivated in the longer term. If there are any exercises you don't enjoy or feel intimidated by, don't get discouraged! You can choose a different activity that you like better. Just select some exercise(s) you prefer from the library whenever needed. You can do the same if there is an exercise you cannot perform, for example, due to not having appropriate space. Feel free to substitute a different activity from the library (preferably from the same section, such as strength or flexibility).

SOME MOTIVATIONAL TRICKS

- We can trick our brain a little by using rewards like "if I manage to work out today, I will reward myself with a fancy dinner."

- If you're too busy for exercise, maybe make your chores a physical activity on some days! If you feel like you don't have time during the day, try to exercise first thing in the morning.

- When you feel as if you don't have the energy to exercise, keep reminding yourself of the tremendous immediate effects of exercise: It will help you gain more energy and reduce tiredness

- You feel too stressed to exercise? Remind yourself that exercise is a great stress reliever!

The workout plan tables below show you which exercises you should perform on each workout day and where to find each activity in the exercise library.

WEEK 1

Day 1

Perform general warm-up before training

		Page
1	Back stretch	61
2	Active standing	63
3	Chin Tuck	64
4	Calf stretch	78
5	Low lunge	88
6	Heel raises	92
7	Toe raises	94
8	Lunges	98
9	Hip extensions	106
10	Tandem stance	112
11	Object following	120

Cool-down

Day 2

Perform general warm-up before training

		Page
1	Active sitting	65
2	Seated lower back stretch	72
3	Hip stretch seated	76
4	Neck mobility exercise	80
5	Chest and Shoulders opener	81
6	Seated abs exercise	100
7	Superman	107
8	Tandem walk	126
9	Planks	108
10	Star steps	122
11	Ball toss	117

Cool-down

Day 3

Perform general warm-up before training

		Page
1	High March	62
2	Side to side stretch	66
3	Mobility for shoulders	70
4	Frog stretch	71
5	Cobra pose	73
6	Dead Bug	102
7	Bridge with arm/leg extension	105
8	Calf raises w overhead extension	115
9	Tandem walk	126
10	Star steps	122

Cool-down

WEEK 2

Day 1

Perform general warm-up before training

		Page
1	Thigh stretch	86
2	Mobility for ankles, knees, hips	68
3	Active hamstring stretch	82
4	Extended puppy pose	84
5	Abdominal crunches	99
6	All around hip exercise	96
7	Step-ups	109
8	Multitask bouncing and catching	118
9	Sway exercise	121
10	Walking with head nods	123

Cool-down

Day 2

Perform general warm-up before training

		Page
1	Active standing	63
2	Tai Chi – Draw the bow	79
3	Cobbler's pose	87
4	Extended puppy pose	84
5	Cat cow stretch	74
6	Chair squat	111
7	Seated abs exercise	100
8	Sideways leg abduction	104
9	Gaze stabilization	114
10	Sidestepping	124

Cool-down

Day 3

Perform general warm-up before training

		Page
1	Hamstring stretch	85
2	Warrior II pose	91
3	Lumbar rotation	60
4	Downward dog	75
5	Seated push-ups	110
6	All around hip exercise	96
7	Conscious sit-to-stand	111
8	Tree pose	116
9	Ball toss	117
10	Backward stepping	125

Cool-down

WEEK 3

Day 1
Perform general warm-up before training   Page

1	Active standing	63
2	High march	62
3	Chin Tuck	64
4	Step-ups	109
5	Seated Push-ups	110
6	Heel raises	92
7	Chair squat	111
8	Wall Sit	97
9	Eyes-closed arm raises	113
10	Tandem stance	114
11	Tandem walk	126

Cool-down

Day 2
Perform general warm-up before training   Page

1	Active sitting	65
2	Side-to-side stretch	66
3	Mobility for shoulders	70
4	Neck mobility exercise	80
5	Step-ups	109
6	Sidestepping	124
7	Ball Toss	117
8	Planks	108
9	Seated abs exercise	100
10	Superman	107

Cool-down

Day 3

Perform general warm-up before training

		Page
1	Shoulder stretch	83
2	Chest and shoulder opener	81
3	Lumbar rotation	60
4	Downward dog	75
5	Gaze stabilization	114
6	Picking up objects while walking	127
7	Sidestepping	124
8	Backward stepping	125
9	Hip thrusts	103
10	Dead bug exercise	102

Cool-down

WEEK 4

Day 1

Perform general warm-up before training

		Page
1	Tai Chi Windmill	67
2	Thigh stretch	86
3	Hip Flexor stretch	77
4	Active sitting	65
5	Extended puppy pose	84
6	Multitask bouncing and catching	118
7	Calf raises w overhead extension	115
8	Bicycle	101
9	Lunges	98
10	Superman	107
11	Relaxation pose	90

Cool-down

Day 2
Perform general warm-up before training

		Page
1	Active standing	63
2	Leg lifts	93
3	Frog stretch	71
4	Cobra pose	73
5	Chair squat	111
6	Bridge with arm/leg extension	105
7	Heel raises	92
8	Toe raises	94
9	Multitask bouncing and catching	118
10	Tree pose	116
11	Eyes-closed arm raises	113

Cool-down

Day 3
Perform general warm-up before training

		Page
1	Active Hamstring stretch	82
2	Thigh stretch	86
3	Warrior II pose	91
4	Downward dog	75
5	Ball toss (partner exercise)	119
6	Backward stepping	125
7	Sidestepping	124
8	Chair squat	111
9	Hip extensions	106
10	Wall sit	97
11	Planks	108

Cool-down

Some important notes on how to get going - and keep going!

Create a mindset – a positive attitude towards exercise

After these last chapters, you know why and how you should exercise. But that is just one part of the whole story: For anyone who has not been engaging in regular physical activity, it isn't easy to get going and develop a habit of exercising. And that is despite all of us knowing about the health benefits of physical activity. Still, it seems as we get older, there are more and more good (?) reasons to postpone engagement in an exercise regimen or drop-out of a workout program after a short time. Why is that?

Like so many things in our life, it's psychology. Humans tend to prefer pleasurable experiences and try to avoid displeasure[31]. We try to avoid bad experiences and feelings, and that also applies to the topic of exercise:

Suppose we associate exercise with bad feelings and we don't enjoy it. In that case, we will most likely not adhere to a fitness plan and an active lifestyle.

This mechanism is crucial, especially if the alternative to exercise may "feel" better to us. If we are always very comfortable in our armchair watching TV, meanwhile the idea of exercising never sounds appealing, that's a problem – the armchair will almost always "win."

What helps is associating exercise with positive attributes like "enjoyable, good, pleasurable," and not with negative traits such as "painful, frustrating, dangerous." In other words, "learning to like exercise[32]" is crucial for motivation and long-term success! **If we feel well during physical activity (and afterward), we are more likely to do it again**[33] – and we start looking forward to exercising.

How do we do that? We have to make exercise safe but also an **exciting and enjoyable experience**. We need to make it **something we WANT to do, not only something we know we SHOULD do**.

Exercise is more enjoyable and connected with positive emotions when[34]:

- It is a novelty experience
- It challenges us, and we become more competent at it
- It involves socializing with others
- It includes comfortable physical exertion

Plan how to follow your plan

One remarkable finding from psychological research is that motivation may not be our main issue; we all are motivated to some extent. We need to follow through on that motivation. A great way to do that is to use three steps. 1) Create an action plan, 2) Think about potential obstacles, 3) Make an "if-then" plan.

Motivation has a short lifespan – Most of us need more than that to develop a habit!

The first step involves writing down where and when you plan to do a particular activity (like exercise). Research has shown that the act of putting a specific plan into writing already makes it much more likely for you to follow through with it. Be realistic about how much of a time commitment you are able and willing to make. Using this technique, you transform broad ideas like "I want to work out more" into a realistic, clear, and actionable plan to develop a habit and achieve your goals (this concept is called "implementation intentions").

> Making realistic and specific plans about how, where, and when you are going to perform activities helps to stick to the plan and achieve your goals – it's psychology!

Be specific and write down the activity, time, and location. Instead of saying, "I want to work out today," state, or better write down:

*I will **exercise** at **6 pm for one hour** at the **gym**.*

Instead of saying, "I want to finish this book," write down something specific like this:

*I will **read** the book on healthy diets for **thirty minutes at 10 pm** in my **bedroom**.*

The second step of the process involves thinking about potential obstacles that may interfere with the plan. We may be too busy on particular days to follow our exercise plan, which may lead to frustration. It is beneficial to think of such obstacles and then move on to the final step: preparing for such situations using "if-then" planning[35]. This technique helps you stay on track and overcome obstacles. The following shows how you could use the method in different settings:

Unfortunately, the neighbor came over to chat when you were ready to work out, so you missed a session. Plan ahead:

If I cannot work out at 7 pm on Monday, I will get up at 7 am on Tuesday to go running.

The plan to not eat any sweets on the weekend will probably fail because you will eat cake at your grandson's birthday party.

If I eat any sweets on the weekend, I will do "vegetables-only" days on Monday and Tuesday

- Enjoy physical activity – if you don't enjoy it, or feel anxious about it, modify your training, so you look forward to it!
- Create a specific plan for your workout goals – write down where and when you will work out.
- Plan for potential obstacles - use "if-then" planning to account for unforeseen events preventing you from following through with your exercise plan.

THE EXERCISES

Posture, flexibility, and mobility exercises

LUMBAR ROTATION

Lumbar rotations stretch muscles of the lower back and hips.

- Lie on your back on an exercise mat
- Spread your arms to the side at shoulder level
- Bend knees at about a 90-degree angle, and plant your feet next to each other on the floor
- Slowly rotate around your hips towards the right side until you feel a comfortable stretch or until your right knee touches the floor
- Your left shoulder blade and arm should not leave the floor, only rotate around the lower trunk and hips
- Keep breathing
- Hold the position for about 20-30 seconds
- Slowly move back up and rotate to the left
- After stretching to both sides, get back to the starting position, and rest for 30 seconds. Finally, perform another round of stretches on each side

BACK STRETCH

An exercise to both stretch and relax the lower back.

- Lie down on your back (preferably on an exercise mat) and put a box or pillows or a low chair under your lower legs, so your knees are at about a 90-degree angle

- Spread your arms out to the sides

- Relax your head

- Relax your whole body and take deep breaths

- Stay in this position for about 3 minutes

- Roll slightly to the left and right while rounding your lower back slightly for a gentle massage

- Turn your head to the left and right to add a gentle stretch to the neck

HIGH MARCH

A mobility exercise that also strengthens the legs.

- Position yourself close to a desk, wall, or a sturdy chair you can hold on to

- Position feet about shoulders width apart

- Lift one leg to about a 90-degree angle (lift higher if you can) between your trunk and thigh and hold the position for about 5 seconds

- Lower the leg slowly and do the same thing for the other leg

- Repeat for 10 repetitions on each side

- Take a break of about one minute and go again for 10 repetitions each leg

MAKE IT MORE CHALLENGING

1. During each repetition, hold the "leg-up" position for 10 seconds

2. Try balancing without holding on to support

CONSCIOUS, ACTIVE STANDING EXERCISE OR MOUNTAIN POSE

> **Good posture trains trunk muscles, prevents back problems and promotes better balance.**

MAKE IT MORE CHALLENGING

1. Perform this exercise by standing with the back to a wall – your heels, buttocks, shoulders, and back of your head should touch the wall

2. Try to stay in this position for 5 minutes, with a constant focus on posture and breathing, it is more difficult than you may think!

- Stand upright, feet shoulder-width apart, toes pointing forward

- Lift your head as if an invisible string is pulling it upwards

- Pull your shoulders back slightly, do not pull your shoulders up but let them move away from your ears

- Look straight ahead, try to squeeze your buttocks slightly and your abdominal muscles

- Arms hanging free on the side of the body

- Hold this active standing position for about two minutes while breathing in and out consciously

- Correct your position if you feel you are slouching again

THE EXERCISES **63**

CHIN TUCK

> Head-forward posture can lead to neck and back pain, this exercise also trains the muscles in your upper back and neck responsible for good posture and balance.

- Sit or stand upright

- Look at a wall in front of you and place either hand's index finger on your chin

- Gently push your head backward with your finger while keeping the head straight (look straight ahead)

- Tuck your chin as far as feels comfortable and hold for about 10 seconds

- Relax and go back to the starting position

- Perform 5 repetitions each time holding the "tuck" position for 10 seconds

- Take a break of one minute

- Perform two more rounds of 5 repetitions, with another one-minute break between

CONSCIOUS, ACTIVE SITTING EXERCISE

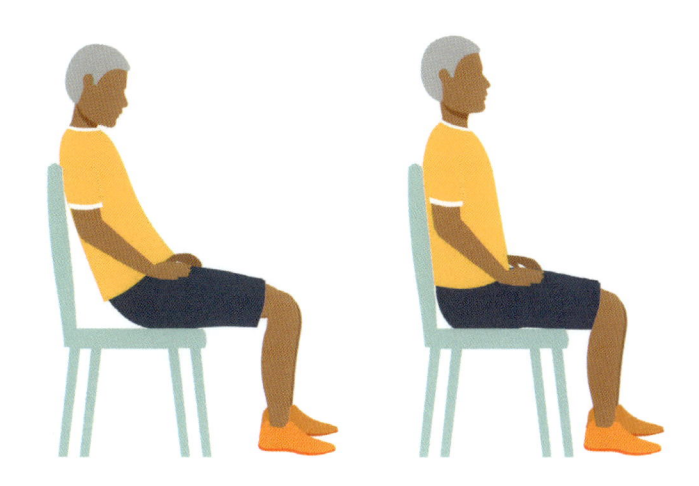

> Active sitting is an exercise for good posture and trains posture-relevant muscles of the trunk.

MAKE IT MORE CHALLENGING

Stay in the active position for 5 minutes

- It helps to start in a slightly slouched position to get a better feel of how sitting should NOT be
- Put your feet flat on the floor, shoulder-width apart
- Shift backward in your chair, so your lower and upper back are touching the backrest
- Pull your shoulders slightly back and down if they tend to "hang" forward
- Tuck your chin slightly, meanwhile pull your head up as if you were a puppet, and a string pulled it straight upwards
- Do not round your lower back; actively maintain the spine curvature
- Breathe slowly and maintain this active sitting position for at least 2-3 minutes
- Feel how your muscles are working to maintain this position

THE EXERCISES   **65**

SIDE TO SIDE STRETCH

> Trunk rotations improve mobility and help to strengthen core muscles.

MAKE IT MORE CHALLENGING

Hold a light dumbbell or a filled water bottle in your hands during the stretch to add a shoulder strength component to this exercise

- Stand upright with feet shoulder-width apart
- Raise your arms in front of you, fingers of both hands interlocked
- Inhale, then without lifting your feet, slowly rotate your trunk to the right until you feel a comfortable stretch in your back, trunk, and shoulders
- Hold the position for about 15 seconds, keep breathing (feel your abs working)
- Keep shoulders low and away from your ears
- Slowly come back to starting position
- Inhale, then without lifting your feet, slowly rotate your trunk to the left until you feel a comfortable stretch
- Hold the position for about 15 seconds, keep breathing (feel your abs working)
- Slowly come back to starting position
- Take a short break of 30 seconds
- Perform one more round of stretches to each side

BOOST YOUR BALANCE

TAI-CHI/CHI-GONG WINDMILL VARIATION

> Tai Chi exercises are known to promote mobility and balance, this windmill variation promotes core, hips, and shoulder strength and flexibility.

- Stand upright, feet shoulder-width apart, bend your knees slightly
- Arms hang down relaxed by the sides
- Stand "active" with head up high and chin slightly tucked back
- Raise arms above head with elbows slightly bent
- Slowly draw a big circle with your arms (like a windmill) down in clockwise direction, with your head and eyes following your hands
- As your hands reach sideways, bend slightly from your hips
- As you reach the 6 o'clock position, bend forward to facilitate the "windmill" circling
- Perform one full revolution, ending up in the starting position with your hands above your head
- Perform about 5 to 6 rotations clockwise, then 5 to 6 rotations counter-clockwise
- Return to a relaxed stance with hands hanging loosely by your side
- Keep breathing slowly and controlled throughout the exercise
- Don't force yourself into a stretch; just make the "windmill" as large as feels comfortable to you

THE EXERCISES

MOBILITY FOR ANKLES, KNEES, HIPS, AND WAIST

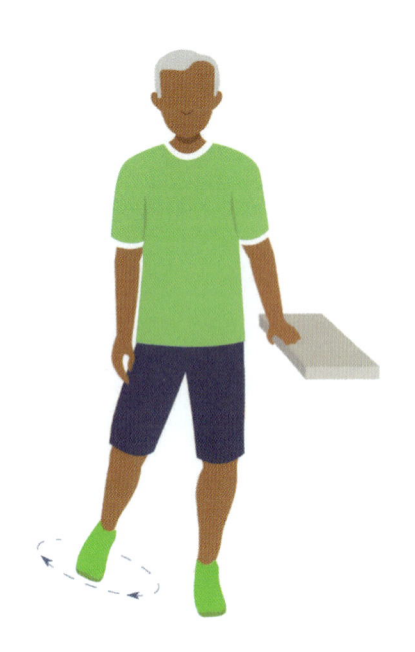

Mobility exercises help prepare joints for increased load and promote the flow of synovial fluid (the "grease" in the joints).

- Stand next to a chair, desk, or counter and hold on to it with your left hand

- Lift your right foot and rotate it clockwise ten times, then counter-clockwise 10 times

- Turn around and hold on with your right hand and perform ankle rolls with your right ankle

- Perform the same exercise, but this time rotate around your knee, both sides for 10 times clockwise and 10 times counter-clockwise each

- Perform the same exercise, but this time rotate around your hip, both sides for 10 times clockwise and 10 times counter-clockwise each leg

BOOST YOUR BALANCE

- Stand with your feet shoulders width apart

- Place your hands on your hips and rotate around the hips as if using a hula hoop

- Circle 10 times clockwise, 10 times counter-clockwise

- Perform one round of these exercises, take a break of about 1 minute, then do another round

THE EXERCISES

MOBILITY FOR SHOULDERS

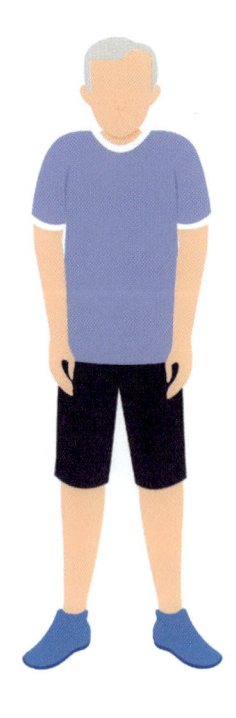

> This mobility exercise also prepares the body for exercises that put increased stress ("load") on the shoulders.

- Stand upright, feet shoulders width apart
- Rotate your shoulders in big circles forward (up, forward, down, backward)
- Perform 5 circles, then change direction to go backward for 5 circles
- Take a break of about 1 minute and perform another round of 5 forward and 5 backward rotations

FROG STRETCH

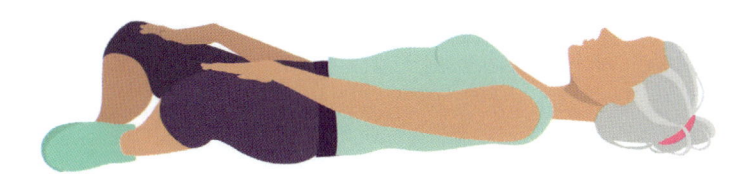

This exercise for hip mobility and flexibility is great for people sitting a lot during the day.

MAKE IT MORE CHALLENGING

Use your hands to actively push the knees to the floor for a deeper stretch

- Lie on your back on an exercise mat
- Place your hands on your thighs or knees
- Put the soles of your feet together while letting the knees sink to the side
- Stay in this position for about 1 minute
- Breathe slowly, relax and feel your knees sinking towards the ground slowly over time while you become more relaxed in your hips and thighs

THE EXERCISES

SEATED LOWER BACK STRETCH

This exercise promotes lower back flexibility and strength. It can help prevent back pain and improve posture.

- Sit in a chair upright and comfortably with feet planted on the floor (shoulder-width apart)

- Exhale and slowly and gently reach between your feet as if you are trying to pick something up

- Bend down as far as is comfortable until you feel a slight stretch in your lower back and your fingers or whole hands touch your ankles or the floor

- Stay in that position for about 15 seconds

- Keep breathing; with every inhale, straighten your back; with every exhale, go into the stretch a little further

- Come up slowly to an upright seated position again, using your hands on your knees to push yourself up if needed

- Take a break of 30 seconds and do one more round of this stretch

COBRA POSE / SPHINX POSE

Both variations stretch and lengthen the spine, the chest, abdomen, and shoulders.

- Lie on your belly on your exercise mat with legs straight, feet pointing out
- Put your hands on the floor next to or slightly below shoulders, bend your elbows (imagine you are about to do a push-up)
- Squeeze your back muscles and buttocks, and straighten your arms, lifting your chest off the floor,
- Raise your head
- Push your shoulders down and away from your ears
- Lift as high as feels comfortable for you
- Alternatively, perform the "sphinx" pose, where your elbows stay on the floor (great if you cannot extend your elbows fully yet)
- Hold for 15-20 seconds and slowly return to the starting position by bending your elbows
- Take a break of 30 seconds (lie flat down) and perform two more rounds of 15-20 seconds of stretches with 30-second breaks between

THE EXERCISES

CAT-COW STRETCH

> Flexing and extending the spine can help improve spinal disc circulation (for better back health) and relieve stress in combination with deep breathing.

- Get in an "on-all-fours" or "table" position on your exercise mat

- Slowly round your back up toward the ceiling like a stretching (or terrified) cat while tucking your chin (try to look towards your pelvis in this position) and exhaling

- Then arch your back while lifting your hips (knees stay on the floor) and head and inhaling ("the cow")

- Perform 10 reps of going "cat" and "cow" each

- Exhale during "cat," inhale during "cow"

- Relax, lie flat down, and take a break of 1 minute

- Perform one more round of 10 repetitions of cat and cow stretches

DOWNWARD DOG

This fundamental yoga pose promotes flexibility and strength of muscles of the back, the shoulders, and the legs.

- Start on hands and knees ("table" position)
- Tuck your toes under
- Lift your hips up and back until you get to a triangle position with the floor, upper body, and lower body as the sides of the triangle
- Shift your weight backward towards your feet to take the pressure off your wrists (if you still feel discomfort in your wrists, you can lower your elbows to distribute the weight over your forearms)
- Keep your back flat (and keep your legs straight or bent slightly)
- Look towards your feet
- Push your heels into the floor; if you cannot touch the floor with your heels, don't force them down
- You can also shift your weight from left to right foot alternating (like stepping)
- Keep breathing
- Hold for about 20- 30 seconds
- Slowly lower your knees down to the mat to get back into the starting position
- Relax and rest in the table position for 30 seconds, then perform two more rounds of stretching (20-30 seconds each) with 30-second breaks between

THE EXERCISES

HIP STRETCH SEATED

VARIATION

1. While stretching, use the hand on your knee to actively push the knee down gently for a deeper stretch

2. To add a lower back stretch, gently rotate your torso to the opposite side while you are stretching (imagine trying to look at something behind you). When stretching your left hip, look over your right shoulder, when stretching your right hip, look over your left shoulder

- Sit in a chair upright and comfortably with feet planted on the floor

- Place your left ankle on top of your right thigh and let the left knee slowly sink down

- Keep your right hand on the left ankle and the left hand on the left knee to stabilize

- Try to fully relax to let the left knee sink further until you feel a comfortable stretch in your hips

- Hold the position for about 30 seconds, then put the left foot back on the floor

- Change to other leg and perform the same stretch for the right hip

- After stretching both hips, take a one-minute break, then perform one more round of this stretch for each hip (for 30 seconds each leg)

HIP FLEXOR AND GLUTEUS STRETCH

- Lie on back on an exercise mat
- Extend your legs, plant your feet shoulders width apart
- Lift your left leg and interlock your left and right-hand fingers behind the thigh and slightly below the knee
- Pull your left leg towards your chest slowly while keeping your back flat (keep the other leg straight)
- You should feel a stretch in your left hip, buttocks, and front of your right hip (the hip flexors)
- Keep breathing
- Hold for about 30 seconds
- Slowly lower the leg and release your hands
- Repeat with the other leg
- Take a break of 1 minute and then perform one more stretch of 30 seconds on each side

THE EXERCISES   77

CALF STRETCH

> This pose stretches and strengthens the calves. Weak and tight calves may be the result of too much sitting. Other muscles may then be required to "take over" during activity, potentially leading to unwanted side effects like foot, knee, or back pain.

VARIATION

If you are practicing against a wall, slowly reach your hands up on the wall, as high as you can comfortably, while extending your back and shoulders

- Stand in front of a wall, table, or counter and place your hands in front of you

- Put your left foot close to the wall (or table, or counter) with your knee slightly bent and your right foot back

- Gently push your right foot heel down on the floor so you feel a gentle stretch in your calf

- If you don't feel a nice stretch, place your right foot a little further back

- Hold the stretch for about 30 seconds, then switch to the other foot (right foot closer to the wall and right foot towards the back)

- After stretching each side for 30 seconds, take a short break and then perform one more round of 30 seconds of stretching for each leg

TAI-CHI-DRAW THE BOW VARIATION

This is a simplified version of an exercise from the ancient Chinese practices of Tai chi and Qi gong (pronounced CHEE-gung, a combination of slow, deliberate movements coupled with breathing exercises and meditation). They have shown to be beneficial for promoting balance, mobility, and function during daily activities.

- Stand relaxed with feet about shoulder-width apart, arms hanging loosely by the sides
- Bend knees slightly and point toes slightly outwards
- Now increase the width of your stance by about one foot
- Put your hands together and raise them to about chin level
- Breathe in slowly and deeply
- Slowly rotate the waist to face to your left while extending your left arm in front of you at shoulder level; open your left fist and look towards your left hand
- Bend left elbow slightly
- At the same time, pull back (or "pull open") slightly with your right hand as if loading a bow
- Focus on "active" posture and keep breathing
- Go back to the starting position and repeat towards the other side (extending right arm and "pulling the bowstring" with your left hand
- Perform the exercise slowly and repeat 5 times on each side

THE EXERCISES   79

NECK MOBILITY EXERCISE

- Either stand upright or sit in a chair comfortably

- Gently tilt your head to the left until you feel a slight stretch on the right side of your neck (you may also actively push your right arm down as if trying to grab something on the floor to deepen the stretch)

- Hold for 10 seconds, then tilt to the other side and hold for 10 seconds

- Tilt your head back gently until you feel a comfortable stretch on the front of your neck

- Hold for 10 seconds

- Tilt your head forward until you feel a gentle stretch in the back of your neck

- Hold for 10 seconds

- From a straightforward position, turn your head to the left until you feel a comfortable stretch, hold for 10 seconds, then relax and turn your head to the other side, stretching for 10 seconds

- Relax and take a 30-seconds break, then perform one more round of stretches for each side

CHEST AND SHOULDERS OPENER

VARIATION

Stagger your feet further and push your back heel gently towards the floor to add a calf stretch

- Stand inside a door frame in a slightly staggered stance with bent knees and one leg in front

- Lift your arms and bend your elbows so you touch both sides of the door frame

- Keep your chest and head up high

- Lean forward until you feel a comfortable stretch in your shoulders and your chest

- Hold for 30 seconds

- Keep breathing

- Release and take a break of 30 seconds, then perform another round of stretching

THE EXERCISES

ACTIVE HAMSTRING STRETCH

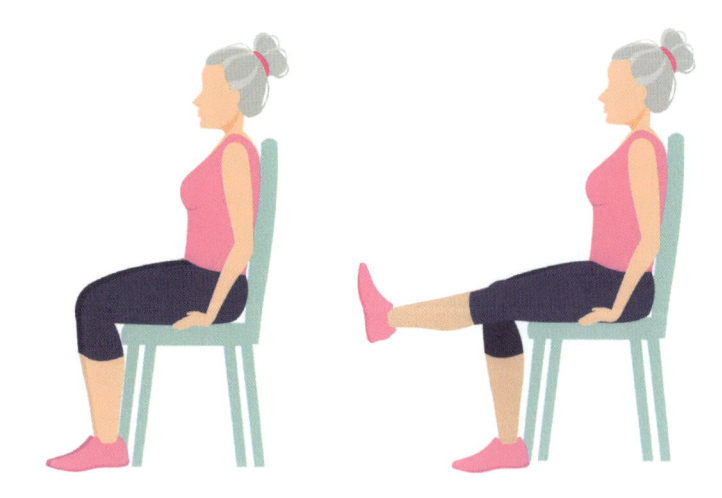

VARIATION

While extending your leg, alternate between extending your foot with your toes pointing away from you and pulling your toes towards you (for an added lower leg stretch)

- Sit upright in a chair, head high, feet planted on the floor

- Hold on to the sides of your chair to stabilize if necessary

- Extend your right leg in front of you, feel the muscles in front of your leg working while you feel a slight stretch in the back of your leg

- Hold for 10 to 15 seconds

- Release and then stretch the other leg

- After stretching both legs, take a break of 30 seconds and then perform one more round of stretches for each side

82 BOOST YOUR BALANCE

SHOULDER STRETCH

> Shoulder and neck stretches promote better posture, which is beneficial for overall musculoskeletal health.

VARIATION

Perform this as a "dynamic" stretch – while you press the elbows against the wall, extend your arms over your head without elbows and hands losing contact with the wall, then move the elbows back to the starting position. Perform 5 extensions

- Stand straight up with your back against a wall

- Lift your arms while pressing your shoulders against the wall (about 90-degree angle between arms and trunk; bend your elbows to 90-degree as well)

- Actively push your elbows and hands into the wall

- Hold for 30 seconds

- After 30 seconds, release and take a break of 30 seconds, then perform another stretch

EXTENDED PUPPY POSE

> This yoga pose is an excellent flexibility exercise for the lower back, spine, and shoulders.

- Get in an "on-all-four" or "table" position on your exercise mat
- Position hips over knees and shoulders over your hands
- Slowly walk your hands out towards the front while lowering your chest until it almost touches the floor
- Keep the hips over the knees.
- You should feel a stretch in your back and your shoulders, and your arms
- Keep breathing
- Hold the stretch for 20-30 seconds, then return slowly to the starting position
- Relax and take a break for about 30 seconds. Once complete, perform another round of 20-30 seconds of stretching

HAMSTRING STRETCH

> Inactivity and a lot of sitting lead to loss of flexibility and strength in the hamstrings.

VARIATION

Instead of bending the resting leg, try to keep it fully extended and on the floor to add a hip stretch

- This exercise requires the use of an exercise band, a towel, or a belt

- Sit on an exercise mat

- Wrap the towel or other band around your right foot (around the middle of the foot)

- Slowly lie down

- Now with your right leg fully extended (or as much as is comfortable), gently pull the foot towards your head until you feel a comfortable stretch on the back of your leg

- Hold the stretch for about 20-30 seconds

- Gently release the stretch and switch legs

- After stretching both legs, take a break of 30 seconds and then perform another round of stretches for each leg

THE EXERCISES

THIGH STRETCH

- Stand upright, hold on to a chair or counter for balance if necessary

- Bend your right leg and grab the foot with your right hand

- Keep balancing while pulling the foot gently back and up with your hand until you feel a stretch in the front part of your upper leg

- Gently push your hips forward to increase the stretch

- Hold the position for about 20-30 seconds, then release and perform the same stretch for your left leg

- Take a break of about 20-30 seconds, then perform one more round of stretching for each leg

COBBLER'S POSE

VARIATION

You can intensify the stretch by bending over from the hips with a straight back and using your elbows to push your knees a little further into the stretch

- Sit upright on your exercise mat
- Bring the soles of your feet together in front of you while keeping your back straight (look straight ahead and pull your shoulders back)
- Let your knees sink towards the floor slowly
- Keep breathing
- Hold the pose for about 20 to 30 seconds
- Get back to a normal sitting position slowly, relax, take a break of 30 seconds, and then perform one more round of stretching

LOW LUNGE

This pose is lower body flexibility and strengthening exercise that requires a lot of balancing work

- Stand upright with feet shoulders width apart; arms relaxed hanging by your side
- Step forward with the right foot and bend the knee until your knee is directly over your ankle.
- The left leg is straight behind you, with the shin touching the floor (toes pointing away from you)
- Keep breathing
- Your hands can be placed left and right from your hip on the floor to help you balance
- Keep your lower back straight
- If you feel comfortable balancing like this, raise both your arms over your head and back to feel a stretch in your core and shoulders
- Hold the position for 20 seconds, return to the starting position helping with your hands to push you up to an upright stance if necessary
- Repeat with left leg stepping forward and perform 20 seconds of stretching
- After stretching both sides, relax and take a 30-second break, then perform one more round of stretches for each side

This shoulders, trunk, and leg exercise for strength and flexibility also requires a lot of balance.

WALL STRETCH

This pose promotes lower back and hamstring flexibility and relaxation.

- Sit sideways next to a wall as close as you can
- Slowly lay down on your back, hands on the floor
- Slowly work your feet up the wall while rotating your body
- If this is too difficult, move slightly further away from the wall
- Try to fully extend your knees and keep your back straight and flat on the floor
- Keep breathing and stay in the position for about 1-2 minutes
- Slowly bring your legs down sideways on the wall

VARIATION

If you have problems getting into the position, you can also sit upright with your back pressed firmly against a wall with your legs fully extended in front of you

THE EXERCISES

RELAXATION POSE

This pose can help to relax, realign, or calm down after a workout

- Lie down on your exercise mat; hands placed palms up next to your hips
- Relax all muscles
- Keep breathing consciously with slow and deep inhales and exhales
- Stay in the position for 2-3 minutes

WARRIOR II POSE

This traditional yoga pose helps develop strength and flexibility around the hips. It also challenges balance.

- Begin with your feet shoulders width apart and your arms hanging relaxed by your sides
- Turn to the right and take a step to your right of about 3 to 4 feet
- Rotate your right foot out to a 90-degree angle (in relation to left foot)
- Raise your extended arms to shoulder level
- Exhale and bend the right leg until your thigh is approximately parallel with the floor while keeping your left leg straight and both feet firmly planted on the ground
- Keep your arms in a straight line with the elbows over your knees
- Hold the pose for 20 to 30 seconds
- Keep breathing
- Extend your right knee and get back to the starting position
- Take a break of about 30 seconds
- Perform the same exercise towards your left
- Relax and take a 1-minute break, then perform one more round of the stretch

THE EXERCISES

Strength exercises

HEEL RAISES

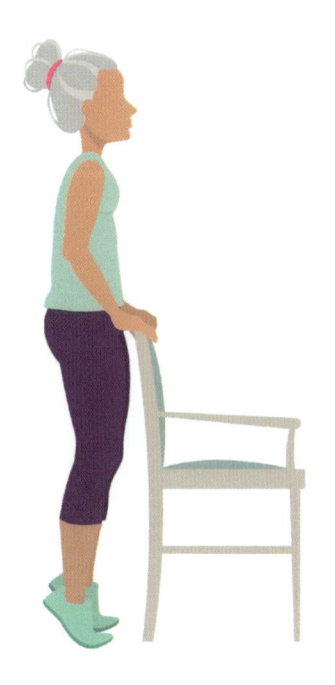

> This exercise strengthens the calf muscles that are important for standing, walking, and running.

- Hold on to a chair positioned in front of you (or stand close to a counter or table you can hold on to)
- Place your feet about shoulder-width apart, bend your knees slightly
- Lift your heels to stand on the balls of the feet
- Hold for 3-5 seconds
- Lower your heels to the ground and go up again
- Perform about 8-12 repetitions
- Take a break of about 2 minutes, then perform two more rounds of 8-12 heel raises, with breaks of about 2 minutes between rounds
- Lie down on your exercise mat

MAKE IT MORE CHALLENGING

1. Try the exercise on an unstable surface (e.g., folded exercise mat)
2. Perform single-leg heel raises

LEG LIFTS

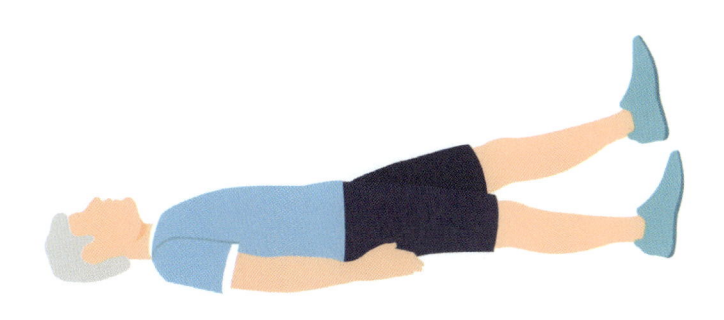

> Leg lifts strengthen your trunk, hip, and leg muscles.

MAKE IT MORE CHALLENGING

Lift our extended leg higher (12 to 15 inches)

- Place your hands next to your hips on the floor
- Extend your legs, plant feet next to each other on the floor
- While exhaling, lift your straight left leg off the floor slightly (about 7 to 10 inches)
- Hold the position for 15-20 seconds, keep breathing
- Lower left leg back to the floor
- Perform the same exercise for the right leg
- Take a break of about 30 seconds, then perform two more rounds of the exercise for each leg, with 30-second breaks between

THE EXERCISES

TOE RAISES

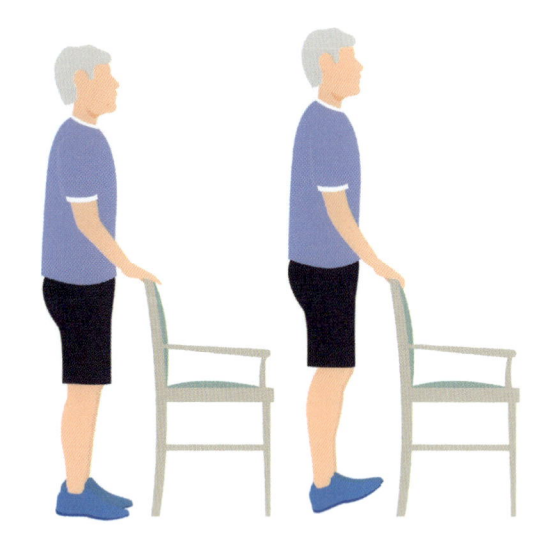

> Toe raises train the muscle located in the front part of your shin bone.

MAKE IT MORE CHALLENGING

Perform the exercise on an unstable surface (e.g., folded exercise mat) while using your hands as little as possible for support

- Hold on to a chair in front of you (or stand close to a counter or table you can hold on to)
- Place your feet shoulder-width apart
- Raise your toes and midsection of your feet (so you are standing on your heels only)
- Hold for about 5 seconds
- Lower your toes back down and perform 10 more repetitions
- Take a break of about 2 minutes, then perform another two rounds of toe raises, with 2 minutes breaks between

CHAIR / COUNTER / DESK SQUATS

> **Bodyweight squats are considered one of the most effective lower body strength exercises.**

- Hold on to the chair, counter, desk with both hands
- Place feet shoulders width apart feet facing slightly outwards, think of 11 and 1 position on a clock face
- Slowly "sit down" as if you were about to sit down in a chair
- Keep weight on your heels throughout the whole range of motion
- Keep your back straight
- Go as low as about a 90-degree angle in your knees or less, depending on what feels comfortable and safe
- Extend your knees and hips again until you are standing upright
- Keep breathing, inhale while going down, exhale while coming up and extending the legs
- Perform 10 repetitions
- Rest for about 2 minutes
- Perform two more sets of 10 repetitions, with 2-minute breaks between

MAKE IT MORE CHALLENGING

1. Perform the exercise on an unstable surface (e.g., folded exercise mat)
2. Hold the lower position for 5 seconds during each repetition

THE EXERCISES

ALL-AROUND HIP EXERCISE

This mobility and strength exercise trains muscles around the hip that are important for good balance while standing, walking, and running.

- Stand upright, feet shoulders width apart
- Hold on to counter, table, desk, or sturdy chair with the left hand
- Both knees should be slightly bent
- Lift your extended right leg in front of you as high as feels comfortable while maintaining a straight back, hold for about 2 to 4 seconds
- Move leg back down in a controlled manner
- Lift leg backward while squeezing your buttocks and without leaning forward much or bending your back, push your leg back as far as feels comfortable, hold for 2 to 4 seconds, and then move towards the starting position again
- Lift leg sideways as high as feels comfortable, keep back straight, hold for 2 to 4 seconds, move the leg back down
- Lift your leg across and hold for two to 2 to 4 seconds, keep back straight, move the leg back to the starting position
- Repeat sequence 3 times
- Turn around (with the right hand holding on to the chair or other object, perform the same sequence with left leg (3 rounds with the left leg)
- Keep your hips leveled throughout the whole exercise
- Relax, take a break of 2 minutes, then perform another round of the sequence for each leg

| MAKE IT MORE CHALLENGING | Hold each position for 10 seconds |

BOOST YOUR BALANCE

WALL SIT

MAKE IT MORE CHALLENGING

1. While in the wall sit position, fully extend your arms to the sides with the back of your hands and elbows touching the wall

2. Get into the wall sit position with a 90-degree angle in your knees

- Lean your back against a sturdy wall
- Now walk your feet out about one to two feet
- Slide your back down the wall so you have about a 120-degree angle in your knees
- Place your hands on your hips or on top of the thighs
- Hold this position for about 30 seconds or longer, depending on your strength
- Keep breathing
- You should feel this mostly in your buttocks or your thighs
- Slowly walk your feet back towards the wall while sliding your back up the wall
- Take a break of about 2 minutes, then perform two more rounds, with 2-minute breaks between

THE EXERCISES

LUNGES

- Stand left from a chair, counter, or desk, then take one step back

- Hold on to the support with your right hand

- Place feet next to each other, slightly less than shoulder-width apart

- Take a big step with your left leg and kneel as far down as feels comfortable (or until your back knee almost touches the floor)

- Make sure your left knee is not in front of your toes in the low-position

- Keep your head upright and your back straight throughout the movement

- Stay in the kneeling position for about 5 seconds, then push up and back to the starting position

- Perform 8-10 repetitions

- Turn around, so the support is to your left, and perform the 8-10 lunges with your right leg

- Perform two more rounds of lunges with 2-minute breaks in between

MAKE IT MORE CHALLENGING

1. Perform exercise on an unstable surface (e.g., folded exercise mat)

2. Hold the lower position for 5 seconds during each repetition

BOOST YOUR BALANCE

ABDOMINAL CRUNCHES

MAKE IT MORE CHALLENGING

1. Instead of your feet planted on the floor, extend your legs a little more and lift them off the floor

2. Hold the upper position for five seconds (keep breathing!)

- Lie down on your exercise mat

- Bend knees (about 90 degrees), plant feet next to each other on the floor

- While exhaling, lift your shoulders off the floor slightly (keep breathing)

- Either cross your hands on top of your chest or place them on the floor (to help push your shoulders up if needed)

- Keep your gaze straight up at the ceiling, so don't tuck your chin

- Return shoulders to the floor and lift them again for 12-15 repetitions

- Relax and take a break of 1 minute, then perform another two-rounds of 12-15 repetitions, with 1-minute breaks between

THE EXERCISES 99

SEATED ABS EXERCISE

MAKE IT MORE CHALLENGING

Hold the "legs extended" position for about 5 seconds each repetition

- Sit on a chair (sideways)or an exercise mat
- Place your hands next to your hips on the floor (or hold on to the chair)
- Bend your knees slightly
- Lift your feet to about hip level
- Extend your knees slowly while leaning back and balancing like a scale
- Pull your knees back towards your body
- Perform about 10 repetitions
- Take a break of about one minute
- Perform two more rounds of 10 repetitions with a 1-minute break between

BICYCLE

- Lie on your back on your exercise mat with your hands behind your head

- Lift your feet off the ground slightly

- Contract your abdominal muscles and bring your right knee and left elbow together as close as you can

- Keep breathing throughout the exercise

- Move back into the starting position and go the other way, bringing your right elbow and left knee together while contracting your abdominal muscles

- Go for 6-8 repetitions on each side, then lower your head, shoulders, and legs on the floor and relax

- Take a one-minute break, then perform another 2 rounds of 6-8 repetitions on each side, with 1-minute breaks between

- Do not use your hands to pull your head up; fingers should only slightly touch the head

MAKE IT MORE CHALLENGING

Hold the knee-to-elbow position for 3 seconds during each repetition

THE EXERCISES

DEAD BUG EXERCISE

- Lie on your back on an exercise mat
- Lift both legs to a 90-degree angle in your hips and knees
- Extend your arms towards the ceiling
- Move your extended right arm towards the floor behind your head
- Meanwhile, extend your left leg (do not let it touch the ground)
- Move back to the starting position and repeat with the left arm and right leg
- Keep alternating while engaging your core muscles and keeping a flat back
- Perform 8-10 repetitions on each side, then lower legs and arms to the floor and relax
- Take a one-minute break, then perform two more rounds, with 8-10 repetitions on each side and 1-minute breaks between

This core exercise that also challenges coordination between arms and legs

HIP THRUSTS

> This exercise challenges the muscles of your back, your buttocks, and the back of your legs. All together, these muscles are called the "posterior chain." Training of the posterior chain is vital for older adults and may improve function while preventing back problems.

MAKE IT MORE CHALLENGING

1. Hold the top position (hips elevated) for 10 seconds during each repetition

2. Perform the exercise while lifting one foot off the ground (alternate legs)

- Lie flat on your exercise mat, bend your knees slightly, plant your feet on the floor
- Put your hands on the floor, palms down
- Flex your core muscles and your buttocks and push your hips up as high as feels comfortable
- Hold the position for about 10-15 seconds
- Slowly lower your back on the floor and relax
- Take a break of about 30 seconds, then perform another 2 rounds of 10 seconds, each with 30-second breaks between

THE EXERCISES

SIDEWAYS LEG ABDUCTION

MAKE IT MORE CHALLENGING

Rotate your extended leg; Draw circles in the air with your toes

- Lie down on your exercise mat sideways (on your right side)
- Support your head with your right arm to keep a straight upper spine
- Stabilize by putting your left hand on the floor in front of your belly
- Bend your right leg to about 90-degree
- Extend your left leg
- While exhaling, lift your left leg as far as feels comfortable (if possible, about 8-10 inches)
- Hold the position for about 3 seconds, then lower the leg again
- Perform 8-10 repetitions
- Gently roll over to your left side and perform the same exercise with your right leg
- After 8-10 repetitions on each side, take a 2-minute break and then perform another round of 8 to 10 repetitions on each side

BRIDGE WITH ARM AND LEG EXTENSION

This exercise strengthens muscles of the shoulder, the back, and the leg.

MAKE IT MORE CHALLENGING

Hold the extended position for about 3-5 seconds during each repetition

- Get in an "on-all-fours" ("table") position on your exercise mat
- Look straight down to the floor
- Flex your core muscles and your buttocks
- Straighten your left arm in front of you while extending and lifting your right leg up
- Hold the position for about 2 seconds
- Relax and get back to the starting position
- Perform the same movement with the right arm and left leg
- Alternate for 8-10 repetitions on each side
- Take a break of 2 minutes, then perform one more round of 8-10 repetitions on each side

THE EXERCISES **105**

HIP EXTENSIONS

> This exercise strengthens muscles of the lower back, the buttock, and the thigh.

MAKE IT MORE CHALLENGING

1. Lift your shoulders and head off the floor (about one inch) while performing the exercise. Don't use your elbows or hands to lift the shoulders off the floor

2. Hold the extended position for about 3-5 seconds during each repetition

- Lie on your exercise mat belly down, point your toes away
- Hands positioned next to your head
- Lift your right leg off the floor slightly by squeezing your buttocks
- Hold for about 2 seconds
- Relax, lower leg back on the floor, and switch to the left leg
- Perform about 8 to 10 repetitions on each side
- Do not arch your lower back; try only to move the leg from the hip
- You can put either a rolled-up blanket or a pillow under your pelvis for more movement range
- Take a break of about 2 minutes, then perform another round of 8 to 10 repetitions on each side

BOOST YOUR BALANCE

SUPERMAN

An effective core strengthener that trains the muscles of the trunk, shoulders, and hips.

MAKE IT MORE CHALLENGING

Actively lift your left arm and right leg while lowering your right arm and left leg, then the other way around for a more dynamic exercise (keep alternating for about 20 seconds)

- Lie face down on the exercise mat with arms extended in front of you
- Raise your head, arms, and feet off the ground
- Hold the position for 3 to 5 seconds
- Lower arms, head, and feet back to the floor
- Repeat 8-10 times
- Take a break of one minute, then perform two more rounds of 8-10 repetitions, with 1-minute breaks between

PLANKS

Planks are a great exercise to train the muscles that stabilize the body during standing and moving. Planks are "anti-rotational" because we are trying to prevent rotation around the hip or other joints and remain "stiff."

MAKE IT MORE CHALLENGING

1. Lift one foot off the ground for 1-2 seconds (alternate feet) while you plank

2. Perform the exercise with your feet planted on an unstable surface (e.g., folded exercise mat)

- Lie face down on the exercise mat with the elbows placed next to your shoulders

- Tuck your toes and push your upper body up to rest on your forearms (with a 90-degree angle in your elbows)

- Flex your core muscles, lift your hips to create the plank, with only your forearms, hands, and your feet touching the ground

- Keep your back straight and keep breathing

- Try to keep a proper straight back position for as long as you can while flexing your belly muscle (try for about 20-30sec)

- Once you feel it is getting difficult to maintain good straight form, lower your hips back to the floor and relax

- Take a break of 2 minutes, then perform 1 or 2 more rounds of the exercise with 2-minute breaks between

STEP-UPS OR SIDEWAYS STEP-UPS

MAKE IT MORE CHALLENGING

1. Perform 15 repetitions per leg

2. Pull the non-stepping leg up towards the chest when stepping up

This exercise strengthens the hips and legs and challenges balance when transitioning between steps.

- Stand in front of a step or a step stool (or stand sideways next to it)
- Make sure there is a handrail or counter or chair you can hold on to when needed
- Step up on the stair with or stool using your right leg (keep back straight), fully extending your leg
- Slowly get back to starting position
- Perform step up with left leg
- Alternate for 8-10 repetitions on each side
- For a sideways version, perform all repetitions for one leg first
- Take a break of 2 minutes, then perform two more rounds of 8-10 repetitions for each leg with 2-minute breaks between

THE EXERCISES

SEATED PUSH-UPS

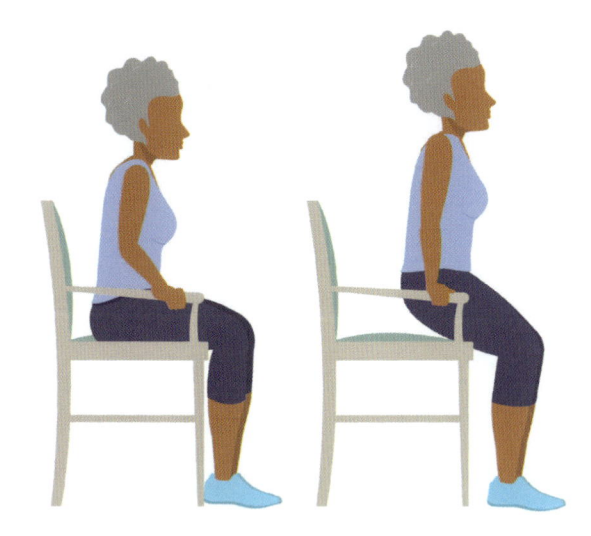

MAKE IT MORE CHALLENGING

Perform regular push-ups on the floor, either from a position on all fours or in a plank position

- Sit upright in a chair with sturdy armrests
- Push your shoulders down and away from your ears
- From this position, push yourself up and fully extend your elbows
- Try to use your legs as little as possible, focus on pushing with the arms
- Hold that extended position for 2-3 seconds
- Lower yourself back on the chair
- Perform 8-10 repetitions
- Take a break of 2 minutes
- Perform another two rounds of 8-10 repetitions with 2-minute breaks between

CONSCIOUS SIT-TO-STAND TRANSITION OR "CHAIR SQUAT"

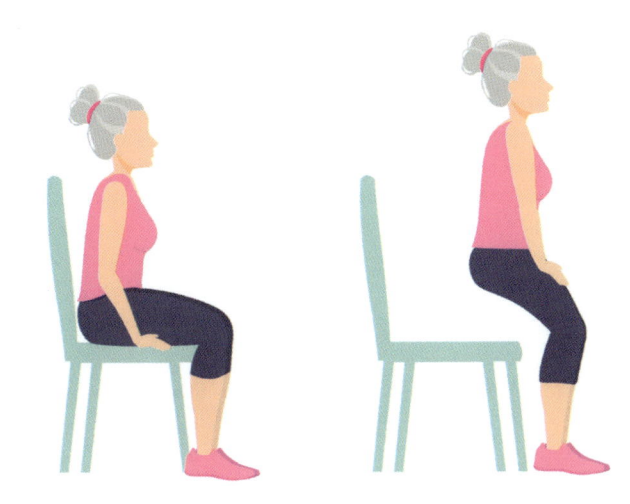

MAKE IT MORE CHALLENGING

Try to get up without using your hands to push; use exercise mat in front of your chair requiring you to balance "harder" while getting up

- Sit upright in a chair
- Bend knees to about 90-degree, plant feet shoulder-width apart
- Lean forward and actively extend your hips while squeezing your buttocks
- Extend your knees feeling the muscles in front of your legs working until you come to a fully upright position
- You can use your hands to help push yourself up
- Slowly sit back down and back with good posture
- Repeat about 8 to 10 times
- Take a break of 2 minutes
- Perform another round of 8 to 10 repetitions

Balance focused exercises

TANDEM (HEEL-TO-TOE) STANCE

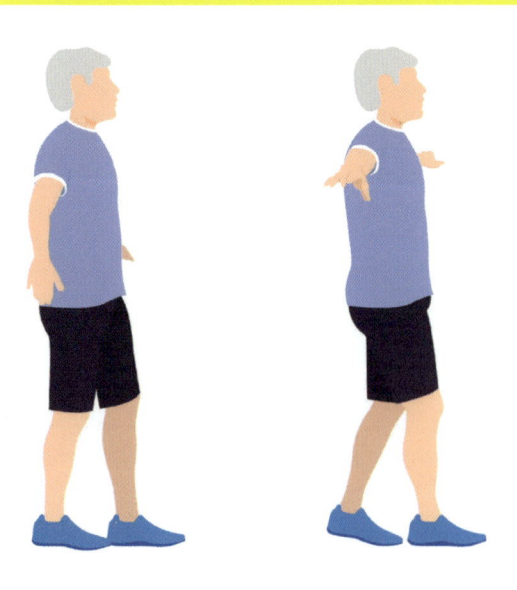

This balance exercise challenges the body by removing stable lateral support (like on a tightrope).

- Start with a relaxed upright stance; feet placed shoulder-width apart
- Put your hands on your hips or cross your arms in front of your chest
- Put your left foot in front of your right foot, toes pointing forward
- Get into a heel-to-toe position with both feet touching
- Stay in the position for 20-30 seconds
- Switch feet (right foot in front of left foot) and repeat for about 20-30s
- Take a break of 1 minute and balance again for 20-30 seconds with each foot in front once
- Whenever you must take a step to balance, do so and then get back into position

MAKE IT MORE CHALLENGING

1. Perform exercise on an unstable surface (e.g., folded exercise mat)

2. Close your eyes (make sure to have support like a counter or char you can hold on to if necessary

112 BOOST YOUR BALANCE

EYES-CLOSED ARM RAISES

> This practical exercise improves balance awareness and preparation. When you are about to perform a movement that will affect your balance, you automatically "brace" for that challenge. Practicing this ability helps improve balance.

MAKE IT MORE CHALLENGING

Perform exercise on an unstable surface (e.g., folded exercise mat)

- Stand upright, place feet shoulder-width apart, arms hanging relaxed by your side
- Close your eyes
- Rapidly lift one of your arms straight in front of you to about shoulder level
- Become aware of the sensation of weight shifting before and during the movement
- Slowly lower your arms to the starting position
- Perform 5 repetitions, then switch to rising the other arm for 5 repetitions
- Open your eyes, take a one-minute break, then close your eyes and perform another five repetitions on each side

THE EXERCISES

GAZE STABILIZATION AND BALANCING EXERCISE

This exercise combines coordinating head movements, focusing on an object, and balancing. This ability is essential for activities of daily living.

- Stand upright with feet shoulder-width apart and hold a small object like a ball or pen or your pair of glasses in front of you (arm fully extended and hand at shoulder level)

- Turn your head left and right will focusing on the object in your hand

- Try to stand as quiet as possible while you turn your head (try to go for one head turn per second, count "1" turn left, count "2" turn right, and so on)

- Perform 10 left and 10 right head turns

- Take a break of 1 minute, then perform two more rounds of 10 turns in each direction and 1-minute breaks between

MAKE IT MORE CHALLENGING

1. Perform the exercise while standing in tandem stance (like on a tightrope)

2. Add 10 and 10 down head movements to the exercise (i.e., nod your head)

3. Perform the exercise on an unstable surface (e.g., folded exercise mat)

CALF RAISES WITH OVERHEAD EXTENSION

MAKE IT MORE CHALLENGING

1. Perform the exercise on an unstable surface (e.g., folded exercise mat)

2. Raise your hands straight up over your head and follow with your gaze

- Stand relaxed, place feet shoulder-width apart (you can do this in front of a wall, about 2 feet distance to the wall)

- Raise your heels, get on your toes while lifting your extended arms above shoulder level, as if you are trying to reach a high cupboard

- Look at your hands while standing on your toes

- Stay in that position for about 3-5 seconds if possible (focus on balance)

- Lower your heels to the floor again and lower your arms

- Perform 8-10 repetitions

- Relax, take a break of about one minute, then perform another round of 8-10 repetitions

TREE POSE

- Start with an "active" upright stance, head high, flex your core muscles, place feet shoulder-width apart

- Place a chair close to you to hold on to if needed

- Put your hands on your hips or put your palms together in front of your chest

- Lift right leg off the floor slightly

- If you can, rest the lifted foot on the inside of the lower part of the leg you are balancing on, or you may be able to rest the foot slightly above the knee of the standing, opposite leg)

- If you need to put your foot down or hold on to the chair to regain balance, do so whenever necessary

- After 20-30 seconds, lower the leg down

- Switch over to the other leg and perform 20-30 seconds of balancing

- Take a break of 2 minutes and perform one more round of 20 to 30 seconds of balancing on each leg

MAKE IT MORE CHALLENGING

1. Perform exercise on an unstable surface (e.g., folded exercise mat)

2. Perform the exercise with eyes closed

This yoga pose is an excellent balance exercise. It also functions as a great strengthening exercise for the legs.

BOOST YOUR BALANCE

BALL TOSS

> Coordination of several independent tasks is important; practice this ability to improve your balance while performing other demanding movements.

MAKE IT MORE CHALLENGING

1. Perform this exercise standing in tandem stance, on one leg, or on an unstable surface (e.g., a folded exercise mat)

2. Perform the exercise while counting backward from 800 by 3s

3. Have a partner ask you trivia questions or simply try to hold a conversation with your partner during the exercise

- Stand relaxed and upright, and place your feet shoulder-width apart while holding a ball (e.g., golf ball, tennis ball, lacrosse ball) in your hand

- Toss the ball from your left to your right hand and back

- Try to stand as quiet as possible while tossing the ball back and forth between your hands

- Perform 10 tosses with each hand (20 total tosses)

- Take a one-minute break and perform two more rounds of the exercise (10 tosses each hand and 1-minute breaks between)

THE EXERCISES

MULTITASKING: BOUNCING AND CATCHING A BALL

> Combining a movement activity with a balance task is difficult but is often required in daily activities. Practicing this ability movement coordination and balance.

- Stand relaxed with your feet shoulder-width apart
- Hold a bouncy ball in your hand (in your right hand if you are right-handed, left hand if you are left-handed)
- Bounce the ball and catch it again
- While bouncing and catching, try to stand as quiet as possible
- Perform 10 repetitions, then take a one-minute break
- Perform two more rounds of 10 bounces, with 1-minute breaks between

MAKE IT MORE CHALLENGING

1. Try the same exercise with your non-dominant hand

2. Perform this exercise standing in tandem stance, on one leg, or an unstable surface (e.g., folded exercise mat)

BOOST YOUR BALANCE

MULTITASKING: BALL TOSS PARTNER EXERCISE

MAKE IT MORE CHALLENGING

1. Perform this exercise standing in tandem stance, on one leg, or an unstable surface (e.g., folded exercise mat)

2. Perform the exercise while counting backward from 800 by 3s

3. Have a partner ask you trivia questions or simply try to hold a conversation with your partner during the exercise

- Get together with an exercise partner, position yourselves facing each other at a distance of about 7-10 feet
- Your partner should have a dodge ball, tennis ball, or similar in their hand
- Stand relaxed with feet placed shoulder-width apart
- Give your partner a verbal "go" signal to toss you the ball
- Catch the ball while balancing on one leg (make sure your partner tosses a "catchable" ball)
- Toss the ball back while balancing
- If you don't have a partner to perform the exercise, toss the ball towards a wall (about 6ft distance) in front of you, catch the ball as it bounces off the wall
- Go back and forth for 10 tosses each
- Relax and get back on both feet
- Take a break of 2 minutes
- Perform the same exercise but while standing on the other leg
- Perform one more round of the exercise for each leg, with a 2-minute break between

THE EXERCISES 119

OBJECT FOLLOWING

MAKE IT MORE CHALLENGING

Perform the exercise while standing on an unstable surface (e.g., folded exercise mat

Moving the head stimulates the balance organ in our inner ear, making it harder to balance. This exercise challenges balance during head movements while focusing on a moving object. We use this ability during activities of daily living or recreational activities (e.g., playing ping pong).

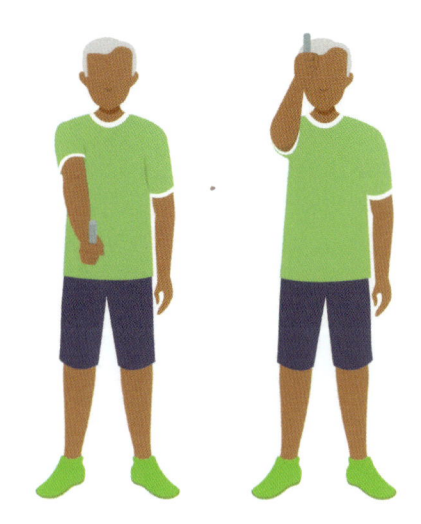

- Stand upright with feet placed shoulder-width apart
- Hold up an object like a pen in front of you at shoulder level (your arm should be fully extended). You can also perform this exercise with a partner holding the object
- Focus on the object while trying to stand as quiet as possible
- Move the object up and down and side to side in a mostly random manner
- Follow the object and keep focusing on it while moving your head (the head follows the item, not only the eyes)
- Keep going for about 20 seconds
- Take a break of about 30 seconds, then perform two more rounds with 30-second breaks between

BOOST YOUR BALANCE

"SWAY" EXERCISE

Stand upright with a sturdy chair in front of you (close enough to hold on to if needed) and a wall in your back (about a foot distance)

- Place feet shoulder-width apart
- Cross arms in front of your chest
- Slowly shift your weight forward as far as you can without having to take a step
- Feel your lower legs and toes working hard to maintain that position for about 10 seconds
- Sway back to a stable "neutral" middle position
- Now shift your weight towards your heels as far as you can without having to take a step back (hold for 10 seconds)
- Perform 5 shifts to the front, 5 shifts to the back
- Take a break of 1 minute, then perform another round of 5 forward and 5 backward shifts
- Perform the same exercise but shifting weight from left to right (position yourself between wall and chair sideways), bending your trunk slightly while keeping both feet on the floor

MAKE IT MORE CHALLENGING

1. Perform the exercise while standing on an unstable surface (e.g., folded exercise
2. Perform exercise with eyes closed

Exploring limits of stability challenges and improves balance and strengthens the trunk and leg muscles required for good balance performance.

THE EXERCISES 121

STAR STEPS

- Stand upright, place your feet shoulder-width apart

- Hold on to a desk, counter, or chair if necessary

- Imagine a star drawn on the floor with your left foot in the middle of it

- Keep your focus on an object in front of you (do not look down)

- While keeping your left foot planted, try to step/reach towards each point of the star with your right foot, as far as you feel comfortable

- Do not transfer your weight to your right foot; just touch the floor slightly with the toes or tip of the shoe and maintain weight on your left foot

- Perform one round with your right leg reaching, then switch and reach with the left leg while the right foot stays planted

This exercise trains coordination of "stepping" e.g., when balance is challenged. It also helps to explore limits of stability

BOOST YOUR BALANCE

WALKING WHILE NODDING HEAD

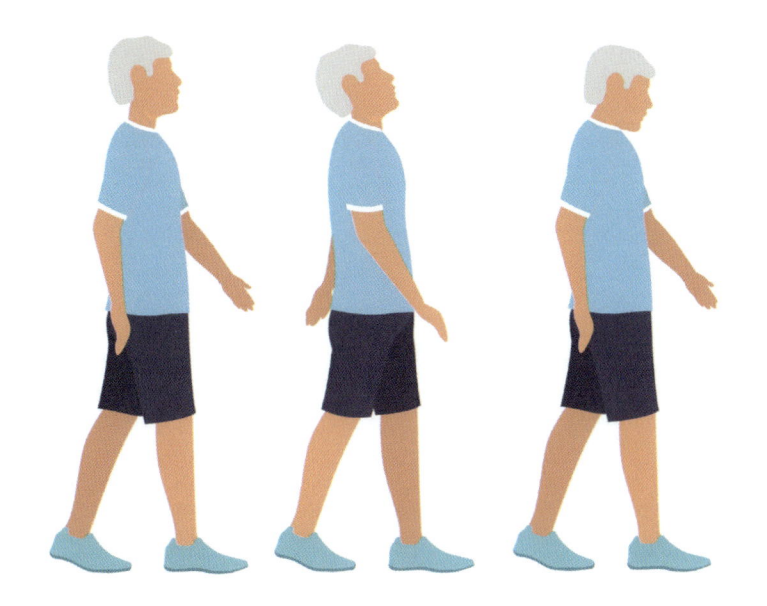

This exercise is designed to challenge walking balance by stimulating the inner ear "balance organ."

VARIATION

Walk while turning your head from left to right and back in the same manner

- Have a partner walk next to you or walk close and parallel to a wall if needed

- Make sure there are no obstacles/objects in your way (this exercise may also be performed on a treadmill)

- Start walking slowly while nodding your head up and down (tilt head up over three steps, then tilt the head down over the next three steps)

- Focus on maintaining a stable, straight walk

- Walk for about 15-30 steps (depending on how much space you have), then take a break of one minute and perform two more walks of 15-30 steps, with a 2-minute break between

THE EXERCISES

SIDESTEPPING

MAKE IT MORE CHALLENGING

1. Cross your feet over while stepping

2. Bend your knees about 45-degrees and stay in a low position while sidestepping

- Stand relaxed and upright, place your feet shoulder-width apart, put your hands on your hips

- Step sideways, do not cross your feet over

- Take 5 to 10 steps to the left, then 5 to 10 steps to the right to get back to the starting position (fewer steps if there is not enough space; just go back and forth more often)

- Focus on maintaining a straight line of progress, with emphasis on stability

- Take a break of 30 seconds and perform one more round of side steps in each direction

BACKWARD COMPENSATORY STEPPING

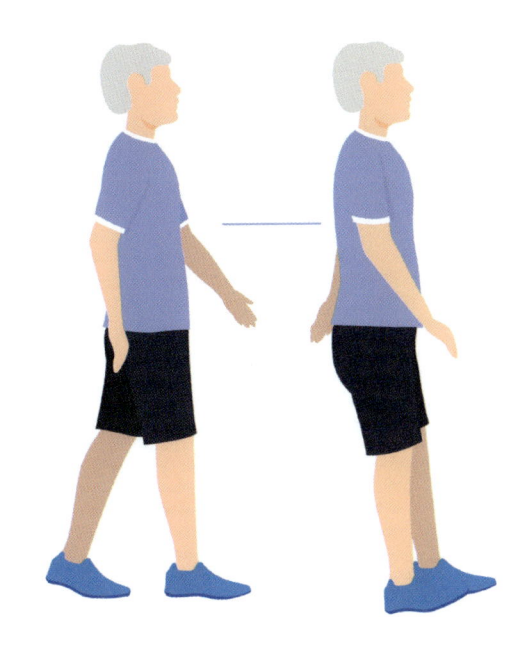

> Falls can happen when we lose balance and don't respond adequately with a quick and powerful step in the direction of the fall. This exercise teaches you to explore your limits of stability and to improve your response when losing balance.

- Start from a relaxed standing position, place your feet shoulder-width apart, arms hanging relaxed by your side

- Make sure to have a partner to support you or perform the exercise with a chair behind you if needed

- Shift your weight backward slowly towards your heels and beyond

- At some point, you have to take a step backward, perform that step with your right leg, stabilize and step back towards your starting position

- Perform 5 repetitions stepping with your right foot, then 5 repetitions stepping with your left leg

- Take a break of 1 minute, then perform one more round of 5 repetitions with each leg

TANDEM (HEEL-TO-TOE) WALK

This exercise specifically challenges lateral balance, like a walk on a tightrope. You can incorporate this exercise when you are walking outside (wherever it is safe), for example by alternating between 10 steps of normal walking and then 10 steps of tandem walking.

MAKE IT MORE CHALLENGING

1. Cross your arms in front of your chest so your arms cannot help you balancing

2. Perform 20 steps forward, then 20 steps backward

3. Perform tandem walking but use a "high-knee walk" lifting your knee extra high towards your chest during each step

- Place one foot directly in front of the other (heel of the left foot touches toes of the right foot)

- You can raise your arms sideways to help to balance or leave your arms hanging relaxed by your side if possible

- Start walking by placing one foot directly in front of the other in a straight line

- Perform 20 steps, then take a break of 1 minute

- Perform two more rounds of 20 steps, with a 1-minute break between

126   BOOST YOUR BALANCE

PICKING UP OBJECTS WHILE WALKING

> This complex exercise challenges your balance during movement in space (forward, sideways, and up-and-down) while performing additional movements.

MAKE IT MORE CHALLENGING

When approaching an object, lift one foot to pick it up while standing on one leg only.

- Place 5 crumbled sheets of paper or other small objects (keys, pens, tennis balls) in a line on the floor, with a distance of about 5-10 feet between items (depending on how much space is available)

- Walk up to each object and pick it up

- Bend from your knees and hips and maintain a fairly straight back when picking up the objects

- After picking all objects up, take a break of one minute, drop the objects in line again and perform another round of walking and picking up objects

THE EXERCISES

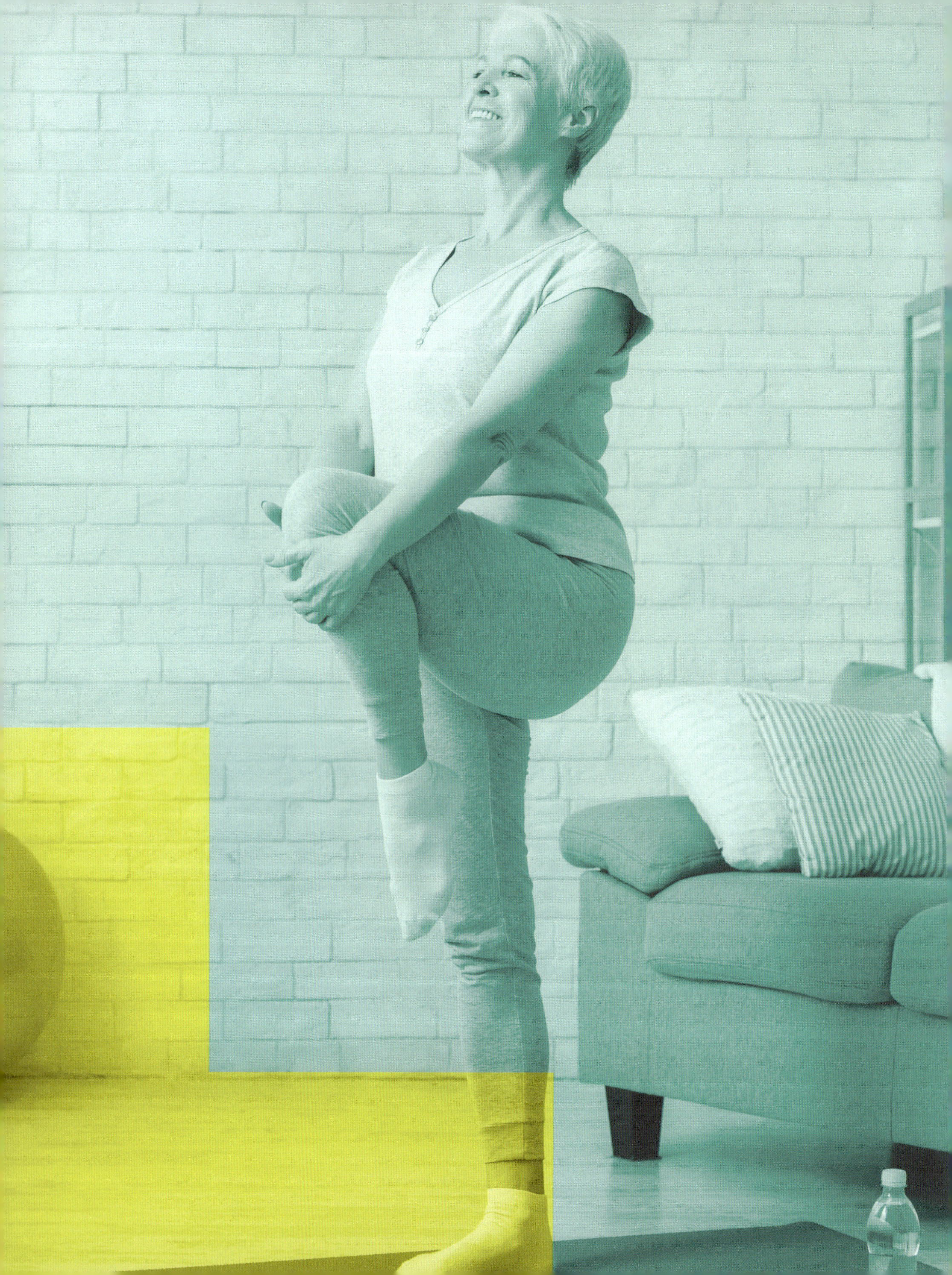

BEYOND THIS BOOK

KEEP BOOSTING YOUR BALANCE!

This book provides you with many exercise ideas that boost your balance and promote general health. Once you finish your one-month workout plan, feel free to combine exercises from the different library sections of this book according to your ability and preferences. Your chosen combination of activities should include components from each section: strength, flexibility, and balance.

To help you stay motivated, we invite you to sign up for our Boost Your Balance newsletter, which you can join at our website **www.BoostYourBalance.com**. Our newsletter will ensure that you receive the newest research on fall prevention, workout programs, and additional suggestions for improved balance training.

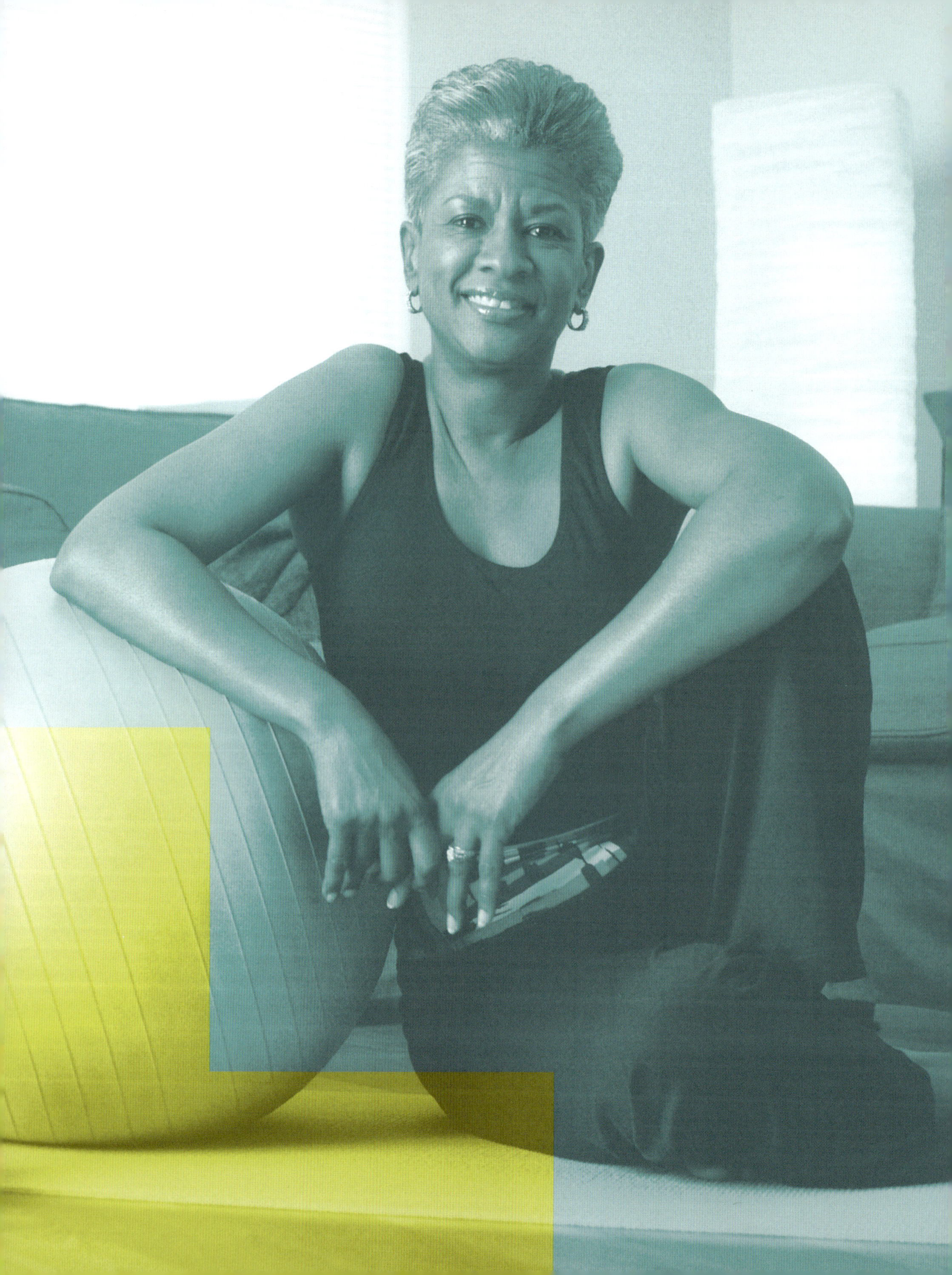

EPILOGUE

Congratulations on taking the first step towards Boosting Your Balance!

As discussed earlier in this book, falls are the most common cause of traumatic brain injury and accidental death in older adults. However, effective exercise offers the best method for improving your balance and boosting your general health. Remember, maintaining and improving your balance requires knowledge, dedication, and consistency for the longer-term: exercise for life!

Stay active, keep moving, and incorporate a diverse set of exercises into your routine.

I hope you enjoyed reading this book and continue to benefit from the tools presented in each chapter. Please contact me if you have any questions or if you would like to provide feedback. You can find contact information on our website: **www.BoostYourBalance.com**. Additionally, you will find helpful resources regarding balance training and fall prevention.

Sincerely,

Marius Dettmer, PhD

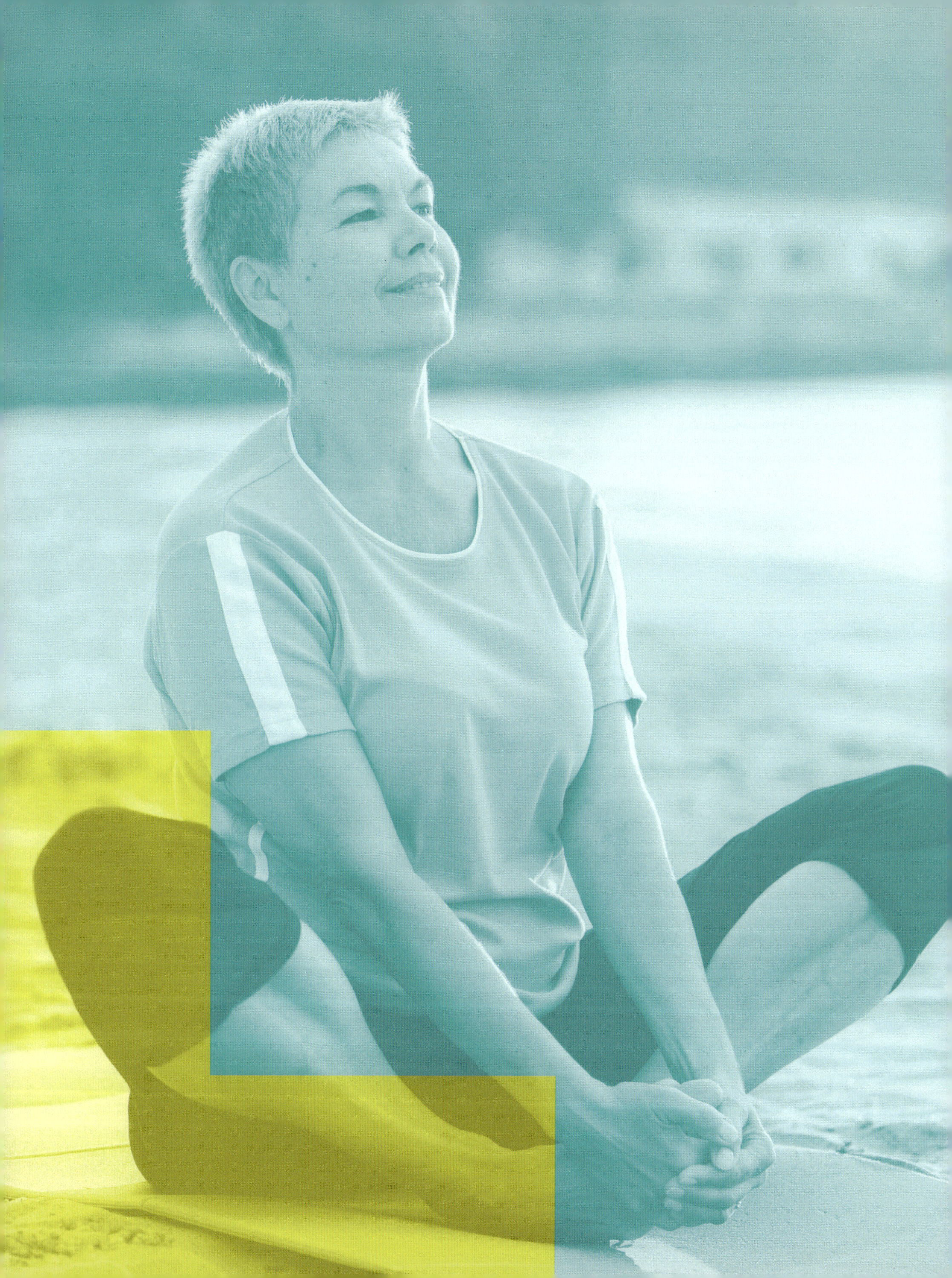